CONSTITUTIONALISING SOCIAL MEDIA

This book explores to what extent constitutional principles are put under strain in the social media environment, and how constitutional safeguards can be established for the actors and processes that govern this world: in other words, how to constitutionalise social media.

Millions of individuals around the world use social media to exercise a broad range of fundamental rights. However, the governance of online platforms may pose significant threats to our constitutional guarantees. The chapters in this book bring together a multi-disciplinary group of experts from law, political science, and communication studies to examine the challenges of constitutionalising what today can be considered the modern public square.

The book analyses the ways in which online platforms exercise a sovereign authority within their digital realms, and sheds light on the ambiguous relationship between social media platforms and state regulators. The chapters critically examine multiple methods of constitutionalising social media, arguing that the constitutional response to the global challenges generated by social media is necessarily plural and multilevel. All topics are presented in an accessible way, appealing to scholars and students in the fields of law, political science and communication studies.

The book is an essential guide to understanding how to preserve constitutional safeguards in the social media environment.

Hart Studies in Information Law and Regulation: Volume 1

Hart Studies in Information Law and Regulation

This series concerns the transformative effects of the digital technology revolution on information law and regulation. Information law embraces multiple areas of law that affect the control and reuse of information – intellectual property, data protection, privacy, freedom of information, state security, tort, contract and competition law. 'Regulation' is a similarly extensive concept in that it encompasses non-legal modes of control, including technological design and codes of practice. The series provides cross-cutting analysis and exploration of the complex and pressing issues that arise when massive quantities of digital information are shared globally. These include, but are not limited to, sharing, reuse and access to data; open source and public sector data; propertisation of data and digital tools; privacy and freedom of expression; and the role of the state and private entities in safeguarding the public interest in the uses of data. In the spirit of representing the diverse nature of its topics, the series embraces various methodologies: empirical, doctrinal, theoretical and socio-legal, and publishes both monographs and edited collections.

Constitutionalising Social Media

Edited by
Edoardo Celeste
Amélie Heldt
and
Clara Iglesias Keller

•HART•
OXFORD • LONDON • NEW YORK • NEW DELHI • SYDNEY

HART PUBLISHING

Bloomsbury Publishing Plc

Kemp House, Chawley Park, Cumnor Hill, Oxford, OX2 9PH, UK

1385 Broadway, New York, NY 10018, USA

29 Earlsfort Terrace, Dublin 2, Ireland

HART PUBLISHING, the Hart/Stag logo, BLOOMSBURY and the Diana logo are trademarks of Bloomsbury Publishing Plc

First published in Great Britain 2022

A catalogue record for this book is available from the British Library.

A catalogue record for this book is available from the Library of Congress.

Library of Congress Control Number: 2022939002

ISBN: HB: 978-1-50995-370-7
ePDF: 978-1-50995-372-1
ePub: 978-1-50995-371-4

Typeset by Compuscript Ltd, Shannon

ACKNOWLEDGEMENTS

We started planning this edited volume in 2019, to see it become, only a few months later, one of the many academic projects defied by the exceptional challenges of the COVID-19 pandemic. Our book conference eventually took place online in May 2021, but still allowed us to have insightful discussions, adding great value to the final version of the chapters in this volume.

First and foremost, we are grateful to all our contributors, who, even amid complex circumstances, found the time and energy to be part of this project and contribute to the academic conversation on the issues and opportunities for constitutionalisation that pervade the social media environment. This book has given us the possibility to work with many of you, whose work we have long followed and admired. We are very glad to have had the chance to realise this book with you.

We are very grateful to our host institutions – Dublin City University, the Leibniz Institute for Media Research | Hans-Bredow-Institute, and the Politics of Digitalization Research Group at the WZB Berlin Social Science Center – for providing us with plenty of support and the necessary safety to pursue this project amidst the complex times of the current pandemic.

We would like to thank the Series Editors, Professor Tanya Aplin and Perry Keller, for their constructive feedback, the whole team at Hart Publishing for their fantastic support and full flexibility in these uncertain times, as well as Sorcha Montgomery, Leonard Kamps, Julius Böke, Maximilian Piet and Max Gradulewski for their assistance in the conference organisation and the editorial process.

We would also like to thank each other for the hard work and company, as well as our partners and family members for all their patience and support while preparing this volume.

Dublin-Hamburg-Berlin
December 2021

CONTENTS

LIST OF CONTRIBUTORS

Luca Belli is a Professor of Internet Governance and Regulation at Fundação Getulio Vargas (FGV) Law School, Brazil.

Edoardo Celeste is an Assistant Professor of Law, Technology and Innovation at the School of Law and Government of Dublin City University (DCU), Ireland, and the coordinator of the DCU Law and Tech Research Cluster.

Veronica Corcodel is an Assistant Professor in European and International Law at NOVA University of Lisbon, Portugal, and the coordinator of the NOVA Refugee Clinic.

Alessio Cornia is an Assistant Professor at the School of Communications, Dublin City University, Ireland, and Research Associate at the Reuters Institute for the Study of Journalism, University of Oxford.

Niva Elkin-Koren is a Professor of Law at Tel-Aviv University Faculty of Law, Israel, and a Faculty Associate at the Berkman Klein Center for Internet & Society at Harvard University, United States.

Giancarlo Frosio is a Professor of Law and Technology at the School of Law of Queen's University Belfast, Ireland. He is also a Non-resident Fellow at Stanford Law School CIS, United States, and a Faculty Associate at Nexa Center, Polytechnic and University of Turin, Italy.

Amélie Heldt was a Researcher at the Leibniz Institute for Media Research | Hans-Bredow-Institute, Germany until the end of 2021. She is now an Advisor in Digital Policy to the German Federal Chancellery.

Moritz Hennemann is a Professor of European and International Information and Data Law, and the Director of the Research Centre for Law and Digitalisation at University of Passau's Faculty of Law, Germany.

Clara Iglesias Keller is a Postdoctoral Researcher at the WZB Berlin Social Science Center and at the Leibniz Institute for Media Research | Hans-Bredow-Institute, Germany.

Niamh Kirk is a Microsoft Newman Fellow at the School of Information and Communication Studies, University College Dublin, Ireland.

Tetyana Lokot is an Associate Professor in Digital Media and Society at the School of Communications, Dublin City University, Ireland.

Nicola Palladino is a Research Fellow under the Human+ Co-Fund Marie Skłodowska-Curie Programme at the Trinity Long Room Hub Arts and Humanities Research Institute, Trinity College Dublin, Ireland.

Dennis Redeker is a Postdoctoral Researcher at the Centre for Media, Communication and Information Research (ZeMKI) at the University of Bremen, Germany.

Amy Kristin Sanders is an Associate Professor of Journalism and Law at the Austin's Moody College of Communication, University of Texas, United States.

Wolfgang Schulz is a Professor of Media Law and Public Law at the University of Hamburg, Germany, and director of the Hans-Bredow-Institut for Media Research of Hamburg and co-director of the Alexander von Humboldt Institute for Internet and Society of Berlin.

Eugenia Siapera is a Professor of Information and Communication Studies, and Head of the School of Information and Communication Studies, University College Dublin, Ireland.

Mariana Valente is an Assistant Professor at the University of St. Gallen Law School, Switzerland, and the director of InternetLab, Brazil.

Kinfe Micheal Yilma is an Assistant Professor of Law at the School of Law of Addis Ababa University, Ethiopia.

Yuner Zhu is a Postdoctoral Fellow at the City University of Hong Kong, China.

1

Introduction

EDOARDO CELESTE, AMÉLIE HELDT AND
CLARA IGLESIAS KELLER

When we decided to organise a conference on social media platforms, focusing in particular on their ongoing process of constitutionalisation, we were convinced that our proposed theme would be topical (which is very unusual for academics!). However, our expectations were exceeded by a series of events that made 2021 a particularly important year in the history of social media and, more broadly, for the development of what the scholarship calls 'the platform society'.[1]

Firstly, the COVID-19 pandemic that began in 2020 continued to threaten public health systems, leading governments around the world to impose movement restrictions and limit physical social interactions. In this context, social media played a crucial role in keeping us close to our relatives and friends, allowing us to 'travel' around the world, exchange news, ideas and, in some cases, even carry out our work. This 'new normality' has exposed the constitutional relevance of social media platforms in a way that had not been seen before. Before the pandemic, social media platforms already played an essential role in the daily life of individuals and, broadly speaking, the public sphere. They have always offered tools for exercising a series of fundamental rights around the principle of freedom of expression. Communicating, searching for a job, professing our political or religious faith, and organising meetings or protests are all examples of activities that we can no longer imagine performing without social media. In 2017, the US Supreme Court affirmed:

> While in the past there may have been difficulty in identifying the most important places (in a spatial sense) for the exchange of views, today the answer is clear. It is cyberspace – the 'vast democratic forums of the Internet' in general, … and social media in particular.[2]

[1] J van Dijck and T Poell, 'Social Media and the Transformation of Public Space' (2015) 1 *Social Media + Society* 1.

[2] *Packingham v North Carolina* [2017] 582 US ___ 4.

Social media platforms have become such important communication tools that restricting access to them may have significant constitutional consequences.[3] 2021 has exemplified this with the banning of the then President of the United States, Donald Trump, from major social media platforms. In January 2021, just a few weeks before the inauguration of Joe Biden as the new US President, Mr Trump fomented his supporters through social media claiming that the election victory of the Democrats was not legitimate. Hundreds of Trump's supporters, assembled in Washington, followed the appeal of the president to march on the Capitol building, in a tragic episode that cost the lives of five individuals and left several others injured. The incident led to Mr Trump being banned from the major social media platforms that represented some of his main channels of communications. However, this sad episode fuelled even more reflections on the 'constitutional' rules that govern social media platforms, their mechanisms of online content moderation, the rights that their users should enjoy, and the proportionality of the sanctions social media may impose.

Trump's case was also a test for the newborn Facebook's Oversight Board, which was announced in 2019 and adopted its first decisions in 2021. The institution of this adjudication body by a corporation and the emergence of its 'case law' relying heavily on internationally shared fundamental rights principles is one of the expressions of what in this book we call the process of 'constitutionalisation' of social media. For better or worse, social media are nowadays one of the factors that affect the constitutional ecosystem. These platforms foster the exercise of fundamental rights but are, at the same time, a dangerous source of threats. Data protection issues, disinformation, hate speech and other societal conflicts that have long been under the state's sole competence now challenge both online platforms and governments with greater complexity and scale. Old and new problems emerge in a novel scenario, where the prominence of state power is no longer a given, but finds itself threatened (and often overridden) by the expansion of private powers. Guaranteeing constitutional rights and constitutional conditions for the exercise of individual and collective autonomy now requires governance solutions that go beyond states' capacities.[4]

In this context, constitutionalising social media presents itself as a gradual process of translation and rearticulation of constitutional principles, which is in great part defined by strengthening old ways and seeking new means to protect and promote constitutional rights online.[5] It also requires acknowledging these systems' affordances and how they shape power relationships among different actors, as well as how constitutional rights are particularly threatened, or enhanced,

[3] E Celeste, 'Digital Punishment: Social Media Exclusion and the Constitutionalising Role of National Courts' [2021] *International Review of Law, Computers & Technology* 1.

[4] A Heldt, 'Let's Meet Halfway: Sharing New Responsibilities in a Digital Age' (2019) 9 *Journal of Information Policy* 336.

[5] E Celeste, 'Digital Constitutionalism: A New Systematic Theorisation' (2019) 33 *International Review of Law, Computers & Technology* 76.

by the hybrid regulatory forces in place.[6] It is impossible to approach the social media environment from a constitutional perspective without taking into account the peculiarities of this ecosystem. Only by adapting existing constitutional principles in a way that addresses the challenges of this new context will one gradually improve this ecosystem from a fundamental rights perspective. Contemporary constitutionalism offers a broad range of values that can help regulate social media, but they need to be reshaped in this new context so that the scope of their protection can address the complexity and reach of the digital environment.

The purpose of this edited collection is to understand and define motivations, claims and proposals for the constitutionalisation of social media. Traditionally, the term 'constitution' refers to the fundamental rules that govern the power, duties and rights of individuals and institutions within a state setting. In Western countries, 'constitutionalism' has emerged as an ideology advocating the adoption of constitutions to promote and achieve democratic forms of government based on fundamental principles such equality and the rule of law. 'Constitutionalisation' denotes a process, which, absent an univocal definition, can acquire at least three meanings. Firstly, constitutionalisation can refer to a process of acquisition of constitutional relevance. Here is the idea that something that was once unrelated to the constitutional ecosystem gains such importance that one needs to consider applying a constitutional framework to it. Secondly, constitutionalisation can denote a process of constitutional codification. The newly acquired constitutional relevance of an aspect of society is such that the legislator or the judge enshrines it into constitutional law in an explicit way. Thirdly, constitutionalisation can be intended as a gradual process of incorporation of constitutional principles and guarantees into a societal subsystem formerly deprived of them. Here, the application of constitutional principles to traditional constitutional actors can be heuristically used to highlight the gaps in the constitutional safeguards provided in the social media environment, thus prompting a process of gradual incorporation of constitutional values and principles.

These three definitions are certainly not mutually exclusive and, rather, denote the various angles from which one can study a process of constitutionalisation. Together, they have influenced the structure of this collection. Social media platforms have de facto acquired constitutional relevance. The rules that govern how people can interact on social media shape the way one can enjoy basic freedoms online. And this has led to an explicit constitutionalisation, in the sense of codification at the constitutional law level, in various jurisdictions. Moreover, a diffused awareness has arisen in relation to the need to instil constitutional guarantees into the social media environment. The relevance of these tools from a constitutional perspective imposes a rethinking of their architectures and internal rules. Contemporary constitutionalism principles such as transparency and accountability, usually associated with the rule of law, can guide us in ensuring

[6] See ch 2 (Lokot) in this volume.

that constitutional rights are also preserved in the social media context. The example of Facebook's Oversight Board is certainly evidence of this ongoing process of constitutionalisation, which ultimately seeks to incorporate constitutional guarantees into the rules and practices of these private actors.

Of course, applying the concept of constitutionalisation to social media platforms, which are private multinational corporations operating in multiple countries simultaneously, presents a series of conceptual challenges. First of all, it implies translating a conceptual framework, such as that of state constitutionalism, into an environment where unaccountable private companies perform public functions on a cross-jurisdictional basis, generating an inherent deficit of democratic legitimacy.[7] Here, the theoretical question of how to handle this conundrum remains open. On the one hand, one can assume social media platforms perform an 'unique public role'[8] as communication infrastructures, and thus argue in favour of modifying their internal rules and architectures in a way that satisfies constitutional guarantees, only insofar as they play public functions. Following this approach, the concept of constitutionalisation remains anchored to its state-centred origin, and continues to denote the regulation of public power, even if it is ultimately exercised by private actors.[9] On the other hand, one can detach the notion of constitutionalisation from its traditional state-centred conceptualisation and functionally apply it more generally to the limitation of power and the preservation of fundamental rights, without distinguishing between the public or private nature of the actors at stake.[10] This necessarily implies a conceptual process of generalisation of existing constitutional theories and their subsequent respecification in the social media environment.[11]

The second significant challenge of applying the notion of constitutionalisation to the social media environment is to adopt a post-national approach which overrides state boundaries and respective jurisdictions. This book does not focus on any specific state, but analyses the trans- and pluri-national ecosystem in which social media companies operate. In this context, geographical boundaries are blurred: they may overlap; they could be not enforced; they may simply fade. As Tornhill put it, 'the borders of nation states are replaced by functional borders as points of reference for constitutional foundation and constitutional validity'.[12]

[7] B Haggart and C Iglesias Keller, 'Democratic legitimacy in global platform governance' (2021) 45 *Telecommunications Policy*, available at doi.org/10.1016/j.telpol.2021.102152.

[8] O Sylvain, 'Internet Governance and Democratic Legitimacy' (2010) 62 *Federal Communications Law Journal* 205.

[9] See M Loughlin, 'What Is Constitutionalisation?' in P Dobner and M Loughlin (eds), *The Twilight of Constitutionalism?* (Oxford University Press, 2010).

[10] Celeste, 'Digital Constitutionalism: A New Systematic Theorisation' (2019); E Celeste, 'The Constitutionalisation of the Digital Ecosystem: Lessons from International Law' (2021) Max Planck Institute for Comparative Public Law and International Law (MPIL) Research Paper No 2021-16, available at papers.ssrn.com/abstract=3872818.

[11] See Celeste (n 5); G Teubner, *Constitutional Fragments: Societal Constitutionalism and Globalization* (Oxford University Press, 2012).

[12] C Thornhill, *A Sociology of Constitutions: Constitutions and State Legitimacy in Historical-Sociological Perspective* (Cambridge University Press, 2013) 212.

Following theories of societal constitutionalism, the book approaches the social media environment as a societal subsystem where multiple processes of constitutionalisation are currently ongoing.[13] The constitutional response to the global challenges generated by social media is necessarily plural and fragmented. Not only are state actors intervening, but also social media companies themselves as well as the civil society at large. Social media platforms, therefore, are not merely the object of a process of constitutionalisation triggered by external forces, but they emerge at the same time as active promoters and developers of this trend. This book acknowledges this diversity and critically examines potential ways to find a unity out of this plurality, considering its advantages and disadvantages.

The book is divided into four parts, reflecting the different angles from which the process of constitutionalisation of social media can be analysed. Part 1, 'Social Media as the New Public Square', highlights the constitutional relevance that social media platforms have acquired in the past few years. It will explore the many facets of social media platforms as powerful instruments for exercising fundamental rights, where promises for democratic participation are woven into power struggles that involve users, platforms and governments. This Part offers insights on the Janus-faced role that social media platforms play, in parallel with other dominant societal actors, in shaping how constitutional rights are enjoyed in the digital society. In chapter two, Tetyana Lokot approaches these power struggles by looking at the role social media platforms play in affecting protest opportunities. Focusing on recent experiences in Russia, Ukraine and Belarus, Lokot unfolds the social media affordances that can either enhance or jeopardise protest opportunities. The digital exercise of a right to protest is also the departure point of chapter three, where Amy Sanders explores the ways governments in the Middle East and North Africa have approached online speech and privacy rights in the years following the Arab Spring. Beyond painting a broad yet diverse picture of the normative background in some countries in these regions, the author shows how cooperation and power struggles between governments and social media companies are affecting the protection of constitutional rights.

The role of platforms in shaping constitutional narratives in the context of migration is the subject of chapter four. Veronica Corcodel introduces the concept of 'legal framings' to show how the social media posts of civil society actors in the context of search and rescue activities have produced alternatives to dominant legal frameworks on migration. The author shows how civil society actors' social media presence favoured migrant-centred solidarity from which relevant political and legal projects emerged. Chapter five, by Alessio Cornia, closes Part 1 by focusing on the role of social media as a source of news as well the consequences of this function both for legacy news media and democracies as a whole. Beyond the transformations that the expansion of social media has imposed on the traditional media's business practices, Cornia explains how this new trend can jeopardise the

[13] cf Teubner, *Constitutional Fragments* (2012); see Celeste (n 5).

democratic function of media by steering attention fluxes based on opaque criteria, or exacerbating existing inequalities in information access.

Part 2, 'Fundamental Rights and Platform Governance', provides an overview of some of the main deficiencies of state law in protecting fundamental rights in the social media environment and the simultaneous inadequacy of platforms' governance in addressing these issues. The gap left by state law allows social media platforms to exercise a quasi-sovereign authority within their digital realms. In chapter six, Luca Belli introduces the concept of 'structural power' to denote social media companies' ability to shape their own private normative order where they exercise a quasi-normative, quasi-executive and quasi-judicial power interacting with a plurality of actors from states to users. Belli explains how state authorities have acknowledged the risks posed by digital technologies since the 1970s, but intentionally left a significant margin of manoeuvre in relation to private companies. This is what has eventually allowed platforms to act as quasi-sovereigns within their own private order and to evade the oversight of state regulators.

The chapters that follow provide examples of contexts in which state regulation shows deficiencies and platforms' rules are ultimately insufficient to tackle such issues. In chapter seven, Mariana Valente focuses on women's rights on social media platforms. Valente builds on her empirical analysis to offer a series of powerful examples of how women's rights in Brazil were open to easy violation on social media. Valente analyses the shortcomings and failures of existing platforms' governance frameworks and proposes the replacement of limited concepts such as hate speech with the notion of 'misogynist public communication' in order to highlight more effectively online violence directed at women. In chapter eight, Eugenia Siapera and Niamh Kirk analyse the question of regulation of online political advertising, comparing EU and Irish law with platform-specific governance rules. A picture of an outdated regulatory framework is presented, and the authors propose a more comprehensive regulatory approach to political advertising centred on a reconceptualisation and on developing new communication rights. This would lead to a constitutionalisation of this normative framework by translating the democratic principles of fairness and equity of elections, as well as freedom of expression and participation in politics, into the hybrid political communication context that characterises platforms' governance.

In chapter nine, Hennemann analyses to what extent EU data protection law, as applied by major platforms, efficiently regulates the processing of personal data on social media. The author combines a legal and economic perspective, providing insights from data protection and competition law. Starting from a recent decision of the German Federal Competition Authority involving Facebook, Hennemann argues that the GDPR has stabilised Big Tech's market power, which is one reason why social media companies are so prone to accepting the GDPR and push towards the adoption of similar rules in other jurisdictions. In this way, the Brussels effect would not only be synonymous with the export of EU constitutional values, but also a way to preserve market power of dominant actors.

Part 3, 'States and Social Media Regulation', acknowledges the failures of platform governance in protecting fundamental rights and analyses the recent reaction of nation states to this scenario. An ambiguous relationship between social media platforms and regulators emerges from this analysis. In chapter ten, Giancarlo Frosio investigates the notable shift in regulating intermediary liability. Social media platforms have been exempt from strict liability regimes for user-generated content for two decades, but states are now increasingly calling upon them to act against unlawful content and online harms. In recent years, lawmakers have been pushing for a firmer approach, making platforms the enforcers of statutory regulation (where it exists) and potential allies in the fight against hate speech and disinformation. This leads to more responsibility for platforms regarding user-generated content, but brings with it the risk of power concentration when platforms and governments cooperate in an opaque manner, as shown in chapter eleven by Niva Elkin-Koren. In her contribution, Elkin-Koren sheds light on the questionable practice of Israeli state authorities flagging unwanted content on social media platforms without a legal basis to do so. In most cases, this phenomenon leads to a removal of user-generated content, which happens without the knowledge of the user concerned. Elkin-Koren identifies a misuse of power in what she calls the 'synergy' between states and social media platforms.

This form of cooperation can also become the basis for surveillance practices by state authorities, as argued in chapter twelve by Yuner Zhu. This chapter provides an insightful overview of social media regulation in China and analyses the interplay between authorities, businesses and citizens. What role does social media play in a system where censorship is normal, and obedience expected? This perspective is crucial in understanding the pitfalls of social media regulation and the challenges ahead of us. Indeed, while early legislation focused on liability exemptions for content-hosting web services and a mostly self-regulatory framework, co-regulation has recently been praised as a viable solution. In chapter thirteen, Clara Iglesias-Keller takes a closer look at what is referred to as 'co-regulation' and demystifies the concept. After the failures of lasting self-regulation came to light, both lawmakers and scholars around the world are now turning to co-regulation as a standard for platform regulation. This development has overlooked relevant conceptual implications of co-regulation. Iglesias-Keller explains why the concept is helpful only to a limited extent and why recent proposals that rest on its promises end up bearing little potential to promote structural changes in current power imbalances: policy-makers and lawmakers tend to adopt any regulatory concept they believe will help them overcome the current dilemma of platform regulation: damned if you do; damned if you don't.

The first three parts of the book make it apparent that the social media environment – whether it is regarded as an essential space for exercising fundamental rights or a source of threat, and whether it is regulated by states or left in the hands of private platforms – is in any case a context in need of constitutionalisation. Part 4, entitled 'Constitutionalising Social Media', accordingly reflects on how constitutional guarantees can be instilled in the social media environment. In chapter fourteen, Wolfgang Schulz starts from the assumption that social media companies have established private normative orders of their own within the intricate galaxy of normative orders of the Internet. These private legal ecosystems have been further institutionalised by the recent creation of oversight boards, internal bodies adjudicating online content moderation disputes. For Schulz, constitutionalisation is a specific form of institutionalisation that leads to the creation and stabilisation of a social entity using constitutional principles as reference points. Chapter fifteen by Amélie Heldt considers whether internal adjudicating bodies are sufficient or whether state courts still play an indispensable complementary role. Heldt extends the concept of separation of powers beyond state institutions to also encompass private ordering. Through Heldt's perspective, judicial review of content moderation is not only a mechanism of compliance with national constitutional orders, but also one of the remedies against concentration of private power of digital platforms.

Finally, in chapter sixteen, Edoardo Celeste, Nicola Palladino, Dennis Redeker and Kinfe Micheal Yilma argue that the process of constitutionalisation of online platforms does not merely involve state institutions and private companies, but also encompasses civil society actors that are advocating for the introduction of new constitutional guarantees for the social media environment through the adoption of charters of digital rights. The analysis of the principles emerging from these documents may help soothe the dilemma social media platforms are currently facing in terms of which normative principles to abide by. One could think that it would be sufficient for online platforms to refer to existing human rights standards, but a more careful analysis shows that a single human rights standard does not exist. This is one of the reasons why, since their inception, major social media platforms have set their own rules, values and parameters, which has raised serious concerns about their legitimacy and ultimate purposes. The chapter will then argue that civil society declarations may be a valuable tool in understanding whether a consensus is emerging among global communities as to which constitutional principles should govern social media platforms. Ultimately, the authors posit that the process of constitutionalisation of the social media environment is necessarily plural, multilevel and multistakeholder. Only in this way will one fully appraise the extent and complexity of the digital constitutionalism movement that is gradually translating traditional constitutional guarantees in the novel context of the digital society, and particularly in the social media environment.

PART 1

Social Media as a Modern Public Square

2

Social Media and Protest: Contextualising the Affordances of Networked Publics

TETYANA LOKOT

I. Introduction

Social media platforms and practices are now tightly woven into the fabric of everyday politics. This chapter focuses on the role of social media as both a space and a tool for political and civic protest. It conceptualises social media as a constellation of networked publics[1] and argues that these networked publics circumscribe a number of affordances and limitations for protest actors. These affordances can enable or limit specific forms of protest organising and mobilisation, claims-making and information-sharing during the protests. They can also shape the consequences of the attention garnered by protesters' activities, and the overall risks and tensions encountered by protesters in their interactions with the state and law enforcement.

By critically examining these affordances and limitations in the context of the hybrid media system,[2] the chapter argues that the structure of protest opportunities is shaped in equal measure by the technologies of social media platforms; the protest actors, including individuals, institutions, and governments; and the political, spatial and social contexts in which socially mediated protests occur. This analytical complexity is illustrated by case studies of recent protests in Russia, Ukraine and Belarus, which demonstrate how protest affordances of social media can be contentious. A nuanced understanding of how social media augment or constrain protest action and of the context-dependent possibilities or limits for participation in discontent can inform our understanding of how relevant

[1] d boyd, 'Social Network Sites as Networked Publics: Affordances, Dynamics and Implications' in Z Papacharissi (ed), *A Networked Self: Identity, Community and Culture on Social Network Sites* (Routledge, 2011).

[2] A Chadwick, *The Hybrid Media System: Politics and Power*, 2nd edn (Oxford University Press, 2017).

stakeholders (states, platforms and citizens) make decisions about regulating and using networked technologies in the context of political and civic agency.

This chapter focuses on the key affordances of networked social media publics for protest, as part of a broader conversation about the relationship between Internet governance, digital media regulation and networked citizenship in the context of key constitutional rights. Importantly, it seeks to bridge the various disciplines examining these issues and to bring scholarship from media, communications and Internet studies into conversation with academic literature on constitutional rights, civil rights and digital rights and regulations. Drawing on case studies of augmented protest events to argue for a broader trend towards the convergence of digital rights and civil rights, the chapter concludes with a provocative call to also conceptualise the broader notions of citizenship and constitutionalised human rights as hybrid or augmented. Understanding how networked platforms and their publics intervene in the hybrid rights landscape and how their affordances shape power relations between states and their citizens is a key part of the debate around constitutionalising social media.

II. Networked Protest Publics

Much of the early research on social media platforms examined their use by individuals in everyday life.[3] Increasingly, these technologies have also come to permeate civic activism, political change and geopolitical transformations.[4,5,6] Social media users no longer limit their activities to posting about breakfast options, celebrity crushes, or lockdown life. They use social media daily to join social movements, to represent their political identities, or to intervene in political debates about global events and issues, from climate change to Brexit and the US elections. Specifically, protest movements and participants have also embraced social media repertoires: Twitter hashtags and livestreamed videos now go hand-in-hand with street rallies and sit-ins. How, then, should we approach understanding the role of social media in modern protest events?

In my research on social media and protest, I follow the concept of *networked publics*, proposed by danah boyd. As boyd argues, when publics are restructured by networked technologies, they become simultaneously the space constructed by those technologies and the imagined community that forms 'as a result of the intersection of people, technology, and practice'.[7] Protest publics, which are

[3] L Rainie and B Wellman, *Networked: The New Social Operating System* (MIT Press, 2014).

[4] J Earl and K Kimport, *Digitally Enabled Social Change: Activism in the Internet Age* (MIT Press, 2011).

[5] Z Tufekçi, *Twitter and Tear Gas: The Power and Fragility of Networked Protest* (Yale University Press, 2017).

[6] N Maréchal, 'Networked Authoritarianism and the Geopolitics of Information: Understanding Russian Internet Policy' (2017) 5 *Media and Communication* 29.

[7] boyd, 'Social Network Sites as Networked Publics' (2011).

often conceptualised as counterpublics as they emerge in opposition to the elites or other dominant powers, are reconfigured by social media into both spaces of debate and protest communities. These communities are made up of the people, the technologies they use and what they do with those technologies to achieve their protest aims. Importantly, networked protest publics do not exist in isolation, but interact with other social and political actors, including state powers and their supporters, as well as the social media corporations who manage the technologies underpinning the platforms.

Since these protest publics are structured by networked technologies in specific ways, they give rise to distinct new affordances, or opportunities for action, that shape the dynamics of how these publics engage in protest and the tactical and strategic choices they make. boyd herself identified persistence, replicability, scalability and searchability as the core affordances of networked publics.[8] As noted by earlier scholarship on the Internet and activism, examples of such affordances also include the reduced need for physical co-presence to share activism-related knowledge and replicate organisation tactics and action patterns.[9] However, more recent literature on communicative affordances of technology has called for a more nuanced approach that attends to the specificity of online platforms, the actors using them, and the context in which they do so. For instance, Bucher and Helmond propose to make a distinction between high-level and low-level platform affordances,[10] The former are akin to boyd's affordances of networked publics and deal with the dynamics of platforms and social media writ large, while the latter are more medium- or platform-specific and deal with the materiality of platform features, yet remain open to interpretive possibilities for action despite their specificity.

The concept of affordances, describing human interaction with the material environment through a focus on what objects or technologies allow people to do, was originally developed in the field of ecological psychology[11] and later adopted by scholars working in design studies.[12] In my own research, I've adopted the understanding of affordances as opportunities or constraints that emerge at the nexus of 'actor intentions and technology capabilities that provide the potential for a particular action'.[13] Unlike features of a particular object or technology, designed with a specific action or outcome in mind, affordances are instead more latent possibilities that require an actor to perceive or imagine them with regard to a specific technology or platform. In this regard, Nagy and Neff propose the concept of imagined affordances[14] to account for the gap between the perceptions and

[8] ibid.

[9] Earl and Kimport, *Digitally Enabled Social Change* (2011).

[10] T Bucher and A Helmond, 'The Affordances of Social Media Platforms', *The Sage Handbook of Social Media*, 1st edn (SAGE Publishing, 2017).

[11] JJ Gibson, *The Ecological Approach to Visual Perception* (Houghton Mifflin, 1979).

[12] D Norman, *The Design of Everyday Things* (Basic Books, 2013).

[13] A Majchrzak et al, 'The Contradictory Influence of Social Media Affordances on Online Communal Knowledge Sharing' (2013) 19 *Journal of Computer-Mediated Communication* 38.

[14] P Nagy and G Neff, 'Imagined Affordance: Reconstructing a Keyword for Communication Theory' (2015) 1 *Social Media + Society*.

expectations of users and the materiality and functionality of technologies. For example, the Facebook 'like' button is designed to enable users to display a positive reaction to a post, but it can also afford the possibility of 'liking' something to express moral support, sympathy, or sarcasm, depending on the users' perceptions of the content of the post and the range of possibilities they have to react to it. At the same time, it can provide advertisers on Facebook with a completely different affordance of measuring user engagement.[15]

I argue that affordances are highly contextual,[16] as actors and technologies come together in particular environments or contexts that themselves shape action possibilities and their perceptions. This means that the affordances of networked protest publics are conditioned by the very specific environment of protest, its claims and its aims, its cultural and affective elements. At the same time, these affordances are also circumscribed by the political and social context in which the protest occurs, including the regime type, the level of media freedom, and the norms and regulations that apply to both protest activity and Internet or social media use in a given setting.[17]

In the next section, I consider the affordances of networked protest publics for protest organising and mobilisation; for claims-making and information-sharing during the protests; and for drawing attention to the protest action and making it more visible. These context-specific affordances – namely persistence, scalability, simultaneity, flexibility, ephemerality and visibility – go on to shape protest dynamics in different, context-dependent ways. They also shape the consequences of the attention garnered by protesters' activities and the overall risks and tensions encountered by protesters in their interactions with the state and law enforcement powers. I illustrate the analytical complexity and contentious nature of the protest affordances of networked publics through a comparison of recent protest events in Ukraine (2013–14 Euromaidan protests), Russia (2017–21 anti-government protests), and Belarus (2020–21 protests against election manipulations).

III. Country Contexts

Belarus, Ukraine and Russia share a common Soviet past that to some extent has impacted national governance and key decisions in the geopolitical arenas. But over the 30 years since the fall of the USSR these countries have taken increasingly divergent paths in terms of shaping their political and media systems, as well as their social contracts. In Ukraine, recent political transformations in the wake of

[15] Bucher and Helmond, 'Affordances' (2017).

[16] T Lokot, *Beyond the Protest Square: Digital Media and Augmented Dissent* (Rowman & Littlefield, 2021).

[17] On the role of institutional backgrounds in shaping protest affordances, Amy Sanders analyses their influence on Middle East/North Africa countries post-Arab Spring in ch 3 of this volume.

the Euromaidan protest have allowed civil society and diverse media outlets to blossom, while increasing pressure on the corrupt, but functionally democratic, elites.[18] At the same time, in Russia and Belarus, civil society, independent journalists and political activists are facing increasing state repressions and the space for free expression has narrowed dramatically,[19] resulting in waves of protest activity.

The 2021 Nations in Transit report by Freedom House,[20] which evaluates the state of democracy in the region, labelled Ukraine a 'transitional or hybrid regime', whereas Russia and Belarus were both labelled 'consolidated authoritarian regimes'. These labels point to certain tensions (in the case of Ukraine) or, indeed, acute crises (in the case of Russia and Belarus) in the relationship between elected and non-elected state institutions and non-state institutions, such as the media and civil society.

These differences are further nuanced if we consider indices and rankings that focus on media freedom and free expression online in these countries. Reporters Without Borders' 2021 World Press Freedom Index[21] ranked Ukraine as 97th among 180 countries for journalistic freedom, with Russia ranked as 150th and Belarus ranked as 158th (higher scores indicate lower press freedom status). While the media freedom situation in Ukraine is characterised by Reporters Without Borders as 'problematic', in Russia and Belarus it is classed as 'difficult'. With regard to Internet freedom, Freedom House's 2020 Freedom on the Net ranking[22] classed Ukraine as 'partly free', while Russia and Belarus were both labelled as 'not free' with regard to online rights and freedoms, including Internet access, limits on content and user rights.

Given the divergence between democratic and authoritarian tendencies, as well as the different levels of political, civic, media and digital freedoms, it is not surprising that protest organisers and participants in the three countries might perceive the affordances of social media for protest action differently. In the next section, I outline some of the key affordances identified by networked protest publics and the contextual variations in how Ukrainians, Russians and Belarusians adopted networked technologies into their protest repertoires. I then discuss the implications of how context-dependent affordances of social media for protest perceived by protest participants and state officials can shape the broader state approaches to regulating and policing the networked public sphere and the civic efforts to protect digital and constitutional rights of citizens.

[18] K Pishchikova and O Ogryzko, 'Civic Awakening: The Impact of Euromaidan on Ukraine's Politics and Society' (Fundación para las Relaciones Internacionales y el Diálogo Exterior, 2014).

[19] MM Balmaceda et al, 'Russia and Belarus' [2020] *Russian Analytical Digest (RAD)* 1.

[20] 'Nations in Transit 2021: The Antidemocratic Turn' (Freedom House, 2021), available at freedomhouse.org/report/nations-transit/2021/antidemocratic-turn.

[21] '2021 World Press Freedom Index' (Reporters Without Borders, 2021), available at rsf.org/en/ranking.

[22] 'Freedom on the Net 2020' (Freedom House, 2020), available at freedomhouse.org/report/freedom-net/2020/pandemics-digital-shadow.

IV. Key Opportunities and Limitations

When considering how networked protest publics coalesce around protest movements or events as both spaces of protest and public debate and communities engaging in discontent, several distinct affordances of social media can be identified. These offer protesters a number of possibilities to augment protest dynamics, but also become potentially available to those policing and cracking down on protest, namely government institutions and law enforcement powers. This relational nature of social media affordances is especially salient in authoritarian settings, but even in democracies more concerned with upholding the rule of law and protecting basic human rights, it can significantly shape the opportunities and constraints around protest engagement. Building on existing theorising of social media affordances discussed earlier in this chapter and my own research on digitally mediated protest events in Ukraine, Russia and Belarus, I propose the following six affordances as key to networked protest publics, and evaluate how they may enable or constrain the protesters' agency in particular political contexts.

A. Persistence

Persistence refers to the extended presence of public social media messages, posts, images and videos created by protest participants that are automatically recorded and archived, and remain available online.

For protesters, persistence affords the existence of records of protest actions and experiences, as well as a somewhat reliable repository of information that can be used to aid organising efforts. We can see evidence of this across all three countries, where protest communities online were used in conjunction with on-the-ground organising to share information about protest logistics and resources (Ukraine),[23] protest march routes (Belarus),[24] and tips about protester rights and legal assistance (Russia).[25] However, in Russia and Belarus persistent content on social media is also used by the state and law enforcement to conduct surveillance,[26] collect information about protest plans, and to identify and prosecute protest organisers. In this sense, persistence is seen as a dual-use affordance that, depending on the context, can both enable and limit protest action and organising efforts.

[23] Lokot, *Beyond the Protest Square* (2021).

[24] A Herasimenka et al, 'There's More to Belarus's "Telegram Revolution" than a Cellphone App' *The Washington Post* (11 September 2020), available at www.washingtonpost.com/politics/2020/09/11/theres-more-belaruss-telegram-revolution-than-cellphone-app.

[25] D Shedov, N Smirnova and T Glushkova, 'Limitations on and Restrictions to the Right to the Freedom of Peaceful Assembly in the Digital Age' (OVD-Info, 2019), available at ovdinfo.org/reports/freedom-of-assembly-in-the-digital-age-en.

[26] T Lokot, 'Be Safe or Be Seen? How Russian Activists Negotiate Visibility and Security in Online Resistance Practices' (2018) 16 *Surveillance & Society* 332.

B. Scalability

Due to their scale, popular social media networks can distribute protest messages far and wide, offering protesters the possibility of greater dissemination and, potentially, greater impact.

Dissemination of protest claims and grievances is key to protest mobilisation efforts, and social media afford broad reach to various audiences, though resonance can sometimes be hard to control. Though in Ukraine and Belarus networked publics were secondary to mobilisation efforts on the ground, which mostly depended on personal ties and word-of-mouth,[27] they afforded broad reach to protest support networks further afield, including diasporas living abroad,[28] who have historically played a crucial role in supporting nation-building and civil society in their home countries.

In Russia, too, social media were used to bypass state-controlled national channels and raise awareness of protest messages and, along with the establishment of local protest hubs, aided mobilisation across its vast territory. Whereas traditionally large protest rallies usually took place only in Moscow or other large cities, the recent waves of protests in 2019–20 saw sizeable street rallies in over 100 locations,[29] and social media were key to sharing updates about protest activity across time zones.

C. Simultaneity

Simultaneity or the ability to exchange messages or content in real time or synchronously is a key affordance of many social media platforms, including instant messengers, live blogs and live video streaming.

The simultaneity afforded by social media is a central feature of many recent protest events across the region. In all three countries, protest live streams (textual and visual) were a central feature of the action, as they provide an uninterrupted stream of updates from the protest locations and allow for transparency in terms of protester numbers. Real-time protest visuals and messages also create a sense of co-presence, aiding mobilisation efforts and contributing to what Gerbaudo

[27] O Onuch, 'Social Networks and Social Media in Ukrainian "Euromaidan" Protests' *The Washington Post* (2 January 2014), available at www.washingtonpost.com/blogs/monkey-cage/wp/2014/01/02/social-networks-and-social-media-in-ukrainian-euromaidan-protests-2; Herasimenka et al, 'Belarus's "Telegram Revolution"' (2020).

[28] S Krasynska, 'Digital Civil Society: Euromaidan, the Ukrainian Diaspora, and Social Media' in DR Marples and FV Mills (eds), *Ukraine's Euromaidan: analyses of a civil revolution* (Columbia University Press, 2015).

[29] 'Сколько Людей Вышло На Акции 26 Марта и Чем Все Закончилось: Карта ОВД-Инфо и «Медузы» [How Many People Came out for March 26 Rallies and How It All Ended: A Map by OVD-Info and Meduza]' *OVD-Info* (7 June 2017), available at ovdinfo.org/articles/2017/06/07/skolko-lyudey-vyshlo-na-akcii-26-marta-i-chem-vse-zakonchilos-karta-ovd-info-i.

(after Durkheim) refers to as the 'collective effervescence' of protest enthusiasm.[30] In Ukraine, protest live streams and live blogs by citizen journalists were central to event coverage and consolidating the core of the protest movement,[31] while in Belarus and Russia they also afforded access to multiple sources of reporting and news updates,[32] and allowed protesters to react to police presence and change their tactics and movements in real time.[33] However, in all three countries, synchronous broadcasting of events as they unfolded inevitably resulted in false alarms and reporting errors,[34] and created a fertile ground for spreading misinformation. In Belarus and, to a lesser extent, Russia, the state authorities attempted to limit real-time connections and transmission by disrupting or shutting down mobile Internet networks or selectively blocking social media applications.

D. Flexibility

The always-on nature of social media and their diverse range of vernaculars allow users to participate in protest through a variety of ways and offer some adaptability with regards to the forms, modes and intensity of participation. Though social media demand constant connection, they nonetheless can afford multiple ways of engaging with the protest action, from on-the-ground reporting to curating resources, managing protest logistics, providing medical assistance, or translating protest updates. In Ukraine, the flexible temporalities of digital media connections afforded a variety of creative participatory scenarios for Euromaidan protesters,[35] including part-time participation and long-distance protest engagement.

More recently, in Russia this flexibility further extended the repertoires of protest participation in a repressive environment, allowing citizens to engage through using protest hashtags or creating satirical TikTok videos, or, if they feared retribution, through anonymous donations to fund legal support for those detained or arrested.[36] In Belarus, where the authorities brutally cracked down on the post-election street protests, citizens also availed of the flexible social media repertoires, changing their profile images to the colours of the Belarusian flag

[30] P Gerbaudo, 'Rousing the Facebook Crowd: Digital Enthusiasm and Emotional Contagion in the 2011 Protests in Egypt and Spain' (2016) 10 *International Journal of Communication* 254; É Durkheim and J Ward Swain, *The Elementary Forms of the Religious Life* (Dover Publications, Inc, 2008).

[31] Lokot (n 16).

[32] Shedov, Smirnova and Glushkova, 'Freedom of Peaceful Assembly in the Digital Age' (2019).

[33] M Edwards, 'How One Telegram Channel Became Central to Belarus' Protests' *Global Voices* (18 August 2020), available at globalvoices.org/2020/08/18/how-one-telegram-channel-became-central-to-belarus-protests.

[34] C Sevilla, 'The Ukrainian Medic Who Tweeted She Was Dying Is Actually Alive' *BuzzFeed* (21 February 2014), available at www.buzzfeednews.com/article/catesevilla/the-ukrainian-medic-that-tweeted-she-was-dying-is-actually-a.

[35] Lokot (n 16).

[36] D Kartsev, 'Russia's New Resistance "Meduza" Analyzes the Rise of a New Wave of Protest Movements' *Meduza* (7 August 2019), available at meduza.io/en/feature/2019/08/07/russia-s-new-resistance.

(white and red), crowdfunding financial support for protesters who were issued with fines or lost their jobs as a result of their political activity, or organising flash mob-like scattered protests in urban neighbourhoods[37] when mass rallies became increasingly dangerous.

E. Ephemerality

A number of social media platforms now allow for ephemeral connections, enabling disappearing or encrypted messaging, thereby helping to preserve user anonymity and privacy, and minimising the risk of state surveillance. Private messaging platforms and tools for sharing content with a finite shelf-life are becoming increasingly popular and are entering protest repertoires. Especially in authoritarian regimes, secure, encrypted messaging is seen as central to protest coordination and logistics.

In Ukraine, where Euromaidan protesters did not perceive much risk in their online exchanges, ephemeral connections afforded by social media were used to build networked communities of volunteers, but digital security was never a central concern. In contrast, protesters in Russia and Belarus relied on the private messaging apps such as Telegram,[38] which, while not fully encrypted, offers disappearing chats and encryption options, while providing for some degree of privacy. Activists also developed and promoted virtual private network (VPN) tools[39] to circumvent government filtering and restore access to banned content or websites.

F. Visibility

Visibility is often singled out as a root affordance of social media,[40] as digital platforms offer the potential to make protest activity and protest claims visible to the public. To an extent, social media may also provide the tools to manage how this visibility is maintained.

Socially mediated visibility exemplifies the complex relationship between the role of networked technologies in protest events, protesters' strategic decisions about how they manage the content and presence on social media platforms, and the resulting consequences stemming from their visible activity on these platforms.

[37] G Asmolov, 'The Path to the Square: The Role of Digital Technologies in Belarus' Protests' *openDemocracy* (1 September 2020), available at www.opendemocracy.net/en/odr/path-to-square-digital-technology-belarus-protest.

[38] Edwards, 'One Telegram Channel' (2020); Herasimenka et al (n 24).

[39] TgVPN, 'VPN в Telegram [VPN in Telegram]' (TgVPN, 31 May 2017), available at medium.com/@TgVPN/vpn-%D1%81%D0%B5%D1%80%D0%B2%D0%B8%D1%81-%D0%B2-telegram-b63f1d02a6b0.

[40] KE Pearce, J Vitak and K Barta, 'Socially Mediated Visibility: Friendship and Dissent in Authoritarian Azerbaijan' (2018) 12 *International Journal of Communication* 1310.

In the context of protest, such visibility also tends to be strategic, as making choices about what and how is visible online helps protesters achieve certain goals, such as greater attention and awareness of the protest. However, total control of visibility is impossible[41] as it also tends to expose individuals and groups engaging in dissent to risks,[42] such as state surveillance and physical or cyberattacks.

In Ukraine, protesters used visibility strategically to ensure the spectacular protest events reached a wide audience as well as to mitigate the risks of riot police attacks. In the process, pervasive visibility also contributed to a multimodal experience of protest witnessing,[43] combining participation and bearing witness to the events and enabling the preservation of multiple protest histories. In Russia, making protest rallies visible online served as both a mobilising tactic to drive up protester numbers and as a way to capture evidence of police brutality during detentions and physical attacks.[44] Protest organisers were keenly aware that by making themselves too visible, they risked state sanctions, so much of the organising was done behind the scenes. The same was true in Belarus: though there were some very visible protest leaders at national level, whose faces were all over social media, much of the organising on the ground went on in off-the-radar Telegram groups,[45] administered by anonymous users.

As protest visibility affords certain outcomes, it also comes with costs, since the state has also become aware of this affordance and has used it to limit protest action. In Ukraine, these attempts were not particularly sophisticated, with threatening mass text messages[46] geotargeted to citizens in the vicinity of the main protest site. In Belarus, police specifically targeted journalists and activists filming videos and taking photos of the protest rallies[47] to curtail visual evidence of the crackdown, alongside intermittent Internet shutdowns to prevent transmission of the events live. More recently in Russia, law enforcement deployed more sophisticated technologies such as facial recognition[48] on photos and videos captured during the rallies to identify and prosecute protest participants. At the same time, other social media users were detained or fined for simply sharing protest-related content online.

[41] E Edenborg, *Politics of Visibility and Belonging: From Russia's 'Homosexual Propaganda' Laws to the Ukraine War* (Routledge, 2017).

[42] J Uldam, 'Social Media Visibility: Challenges to Activism' (2018) 40 *Media, Culture & Society* 41.

[43] Lokot (n 16).

[44] Lokot, 'Be Safe or Be Seen?' (2018).

[45] Herasimenka et al (n 24).

[46] EuroMaydan, '"Шановний Абоненте, Ви Зареєстровані Як Учасник Масових Заворушень" ["Dear Subscriber, You Have Been Registered as a Participant of Mass Protest"]' (*Facebook*, 20 January 2014), available at www.facebook.com/EuroMaydan/posts/553098384786503.

[47] 'Belarus: Unprecedented Crackdown' (Human Rights Watch, 2021), available at www.hrw.org/news/2021/01/13/belarus-unprecedented-crackdown.

[48] M Krutov, M Chernova and R Coalson, 'Russia Unveils A New Tactic To Deter Dissent: CCTV And A "Knock On The Door," Days Later' *Radio Free Europe/Radio Liberty* (28 April 2021), available at www.rferl.org/a/russia-dissent-cctv-detentions-days-later-strategy/31227889.html.

The fact that the visibility afforded to protesters by social media is also available to anti-protest actors seeking to derail or control the discontent is illustrative of the multiple potentialities of networked publics and of how they are shaped by the political, social and spatial context of each protest event. In addition, social media platforms as private actors also shape such visibility through their use of algorithmic sorting of posts, the application of internal content reporting and moderation policies, and through either rejecting or abiding by state-mandated content removal requests. The key affordances and supporting examples outlined above also point to the hybrid nature of modern protest, where the offline and online elements of protest activity merge and must be construed as part of the same augmented reality of discontent. This hybridity has implications for how states, platforms and civil society groups should conceptualise the role of social media regulation and the standards on which it rests, both in the context of protest events and more broadly.

V. Augmented Protest, Digital Citizenship and Constitutional Rights

This chapter demonstrates that, while networked communication technologies themselves may be imbued with certain values by their creators, they can be used both for and against democratic or liberal aims, depending on existing structures of power, regime types and the levels of digital media literacy among citizens or adoption of certain technological innovations by governments. Though the key affordances of social media for protest, such as persistence, scalability, simultaneity, flexibility, ephemerality and visibility, can be identified and assessed with regard to how they empower or limit protest actors, the environments shaping these affordances are constantly changing. Ongoing conflicts, political strife or social cleavages in stable or transitional democracies and authoritarian states may see spaces for dissent and online freedoms come under further threat. Under these conditions, the principles of regulating content and expression on social media gain renewed importance, and therefore their alignment with fundamental constitutional rights demands even greater scrutiny.

In Ukraine, which has been embroiled in an ongoing war with Russia since 2014, concerns about threats posed by cyberwarfare and disinformation have resulted in tighter regulation of the Internet and the blocking of popular Russian social media platforms, with continued attempts to introduce further controls on digital platforms and online expression. Yet there remains a cautious sense of optimism about the constructive potential of digital technologies, as evidenced by state-led efforts to develop e-governance initiatives and ongoing advocacy efforts by digital rights groups to ensure Ukrainian Internet regulation adheres to best practices and international norms.

In Belarus, the embattled de facto government of President Lukashenka and the mostly exiled opposition leaders remain in a prolonged standoff, and repressions against protesters continue apace, along with tighter policing of independent media and online spaces. Belarusian activists, some of them now living abroad, continue to organise in more private online spaces and to contest the state's monopoly on political expression. In response, the state is adopting new legislation that prohibits independent journalists from live reporting on protest events and shutting down independent digital media websites.

In Russia, the Kremlin continues to consolidate control over the digital realm, introducing new draconian laws curtailing free expression online and the right to public assembly. These laws include provisions that outlaw online calls for unsanctioned protest rallies and require social media platforms to take such content down or face sanctions, from fines to outright blocking. More recently, the state has also made moves to take over the remaining privately owned digital communications infrastructure in the country as part of a comprehensive 'Internet sovereignty' strategy aimed at protecting the Russian segment of the Internet from 'external foes' in line with the updated national security doctrine. This has further delegitimised the action possibilities afforded to activists and protesters by digital media, making the tension between the visibility of their discontent and the ephemerality of their networks increasingly evident.

The context-dependent interpretation of protest affordances by networked publics and their adversaries across these cases is also having an impact on the digital public sphere as a whole. The tensions between how states seek to police expression and civic action in hybrid online-offline spaces and how citizens seek to practice their rights to free speech and discontent in the same environments extend the debate about social media regulation beyond the protest context. The interlinked digital and physical realities of protest come to inform the broader reality of citizenship and constitutionalised human rights, which we can also conceptualise as hybrid or augmented.

Both the state and the citizens in countries around the world are coming to understand the spheres of citizens' digital rights and their right to protest and participate in politics as closely connected. This is reflected in the states' efforts to regulate and control both civic freedoms and digital infrastructure, addressing these within the same legislative acts, and in the citizens' converging perceptions of free expression, security, privacy and individual agency in the context of routine digital media use. Globally, there is a growing chorus of voices arguing that Internet access should be construed as a human right, while at the same time fundamental constitutional rights, civil liberties and the right to dissent continue to be seen as key to democratic development. Such convergence demands that social media platforms – as public spheres inhabited by networked protest publics – be understood in this context as potentially enabling or limiting the fundamental rights of citizens, and that they must therefore reckon with how and by whom such immense power and responsibility should be wielded.

In this regard, this chapter contributes to the broader conversation about Internet governance and digital citizenship. Such citizenship is defined by Isin and Ruppert[49] as the ability of individuals to productively participate in society online and to 'make rights claims about how their digital lives are configured, regulated and organised'. Networked citizenship highlights the intricate power relations between states, citizens and the networked platforms mediating such relations.[50] It also raises key questions about how these relations and these platforms should be governed to maximise citizen agency and the fulfilment of fundamental rights. A number of these questions are addressed throughout this volume.

The central role of the affordances of networked publics for performing dissent also makes them a key element of the performance of networked citizenship and, I argue, imbues them with the potential to shape the power relations between states and their citizens. Social media platforms provide the technological infrastructure for today's networked publics and play an outsized role in structuring people's experiences of political activism, civic engagement, and networked citizenship. However, the jury is still out on how seriously the powerful technology actors take this incredibly important and responsible task.

VI. Conclusion

Focusing on the key affordances of networked publics on social media for protest, this chapter contributes to the growing scholarship examining the intersections of political participation, Internet governance, constitutional and digital rights. It captures a key moment in the emergence of theoretical and conceptual ideas about digital citizenship alongside practical considerations of how to reckon with the impact of datafication and digitalisation on citizens' lives.

While the chapter provides a conceptual contribution, it should also be seen as a call for informed, reasoned and inclusive debate about the approaches to constitutionalising social media, and the rights of networked publics at stake. Such a debate should draw on a diverse body of scholarship, including theoretical and empirical contributions from the legal and regulatory domain, human rights scholarship, and scholarship from communications and Internet studies, but also on practitioner input from civil society stakeholders and digital rights advocates. An interdisciplinary and cross-sectoral approach would be best positioned to synthesise ideas from research, policy-making and practice about how to address the challenges of constructing regime-agnostic and resilient governance frameworks for the networked public sphere in accordance with fundamental human rights principles.

[49] EF Isin and E Ruppert, *Being Digital Citizens* (Rowman & Littlefield, 2015).

[50] K Wahl-Jorgensen, L Bennett and G Taylor, 'The Normalization of Surveillance and the Invisibility of Digital Citizenship: Media Debates After the Snowden Revelations.' (2017) 11 *International Journal of Communication* 740.

3

The Rise of Social Media in the Middle East and North Africa: A Tool of Resistance or Repression?

AMY KRISTIN SANDERS

I. Introduction

It was a warm day in December 2010 when Tunisian street vendor Mohamed Bouazizi doused himself in gasoline and lit himself on fire in the sleepy streets of Sidi Bouzid, some 275 km from the country's capital city of Tunis.[1] The news spread quickly around the small town, with Salah Bouazizi calling his nephew Ali around noon. In an interview with *Al Jazeera*, Ali Bouazizi recalled Salah saying, 'Get your camera and come film. Someone has set himself on fire in front of the provincial building'.[2] When family members eventually learned the protestor was Mohamed, they were in shock. As Ali recounts: 'The last time I saw my friend was a week before. We had chatted a little about work. As so often in his last weeks, he complained that he was tired because he had to work day and night to earn enough for his family. He used to joke around a lot, but not much as of late.' Eventually, it would come out that police had seized Mohamed's scales after he refused to pay a bribe, making it impossible for him to work. His attempts to complain to government officials were rebuffed, and he was not allowed into the provincial offices. 'What he did was not right,' Ali told *Al Jazeera*, referencing Islam's prohibition on suicide, 'but I understand why he did it.'

The same day, protestors gathered, and Ali posted his video of the demonstrations, titled 'The Intifada of the People of Sidi Bouzid' on Facebook that night. Mohamed's actions that day resonated with Tunisians around the country and

[1] K Robinson, 'The Arab Spring at Ten Years: What's the Legacy of the Uprisings' (Council of Foreign Relations, 3 December 2020), available at www.cfr.org/article/arab-spring-ten-years-whats-legacy-uprisings.

[2] T Lageman, 'Mohamed Bouazizi: Was the Arab Spring worth dying for?' (Al Jazeera, 3 January 2016), available at www.aljazeera.com/news/2016/1/3/mohamed-bouazizi-was-the-arab-spring-worth-dying-for.

sparked a wave of demonstrations in the weeks that followed.[3] Mohamed, 26, had earned a university degree, but he could not find work. Instead, he earned money selling produce in the streets. The protests eventually made international headlines, not because of traditional news media, but instead because of the viral videos that were being posted on social media. The Tunisian government tightly controlled the news media, and the protests clearly represented an affront to Tunisian President Zine El Abidine Ben Ali.[4]

A decade later, scholars continue to debate the role social media played in cementing the wave of protests that become known as the Arab Spring as well as the responses of the region's leaders, who quickly came to view the platforms' potential power as a threat to their legitimacy.[5] A few things, however, are clear. The rise of social media in the Middle East and North Africa (MENA) has provided a platform on which dissenters can unite and mobilise larger groups of activists for public demonstrations and other protests.[6] At the same time, although nearly every country in the region has written protections for freedom of expression and privacy in their constitutions, governments tend not to honor those protections when the speech is critical of their actions. Civil discontent, fueled in part by the rise of social media, has increasingly led government leaders to further criminalise expressive activities that occur on the Internet, and technology companies are often willing participants in this repression.[7] As a result, the platforms play a key role in government surveillance of political opponents, civil rights activists and other outspoken critics.

Often held up as an example of social media's democratising potential and its ability to facilitate and shape political participation and even protests,[8] the Arab Spring offers a cautionary tale. Rather than supporting the notion of social media as a digital public sphere, many examples from the decade following the region's wave of protests and civil unrest suggest the opposite. Short-lived democratic gains have, in many instances, resulted in heightened assertions of control from authoritarian governments. Further, the willingness of social media platforms to participate alongside government in surveillance and monitoring suggests significant legal reforms would be required before citizens are able to fully realise social media's democratising power.

[3] B Whitaker, 'How a man setting fire to himself sparked an uprising in Tunisia' *The Guardian* (28 December 2010), available at www.theguardian.com/commentisfree/2010/dec/28/tunisia-ben-ali.

[4] F El-Issawi, 'Tunisian Media In Transition' (Carnegie Endowment for International Peace, 10 July 2012), available at carnegieendowment.org/2012/07/10/tunisian-media-in-transition-pub-48817.

[5] A Smidi and S Shahin, 'Social Media and Social Mobilisation in the Middle East: A Survey of Research on the Arab Spring' [2017] *India Q* 196.

[6] DM Faris, 'Beyond "Social Media Revolutions". The Arab Spring and the Networked Revolt' (2012) 1 *Politique Etrangere*, available at www.cairn-int.info/article-E_PE_121_0099--beyond-social-media-revolutions.htm.

[7] T Timm and JC York, 'Surveillance Inc: How Western Tech Firms Are Helping Arab Dictators' (The Atlantic, 6 March 2012), available at www.theatlantic.com/international/archive/2012/03/surveillance-inc-how-western-tech-firms-are-helping-arab-dictators/254008.

[8] As explored in ch 2 (Lokot) of this volume.

In this chapter, I outline the rise of social media in the Middle East and North Africa, discussing the popular platforms and their uses in the context of institutional protections for freedom of expression and privacy (section I). Then I review legal protections for freedom of speech as well as laws increasing punishments for expressive activities online (section II). This includes an overview of the region's legal systems as well as relevant constitutional and statutory provisions. To better illustrate the legal landscape, specific cases from the region are discussed (section III). Finally, I describe the ways in which governments have cracked down on dissent and other online speech, often working in concert with technology companies, in the years following the Arab Spring by providing an overview of laws and their applications (section IV). In addition, I examine government attempts to shut off access to the Internet entirely or to specific platforms (section V).

Although it would be much easier to allude to the Middle East and North Africa in sweeping generalisations, dividing it simply into the Francophone North Africa, the Levant and the Gulf, that approach fails to address the differences that exist from country to country. Although space constraints require painting with a broad brush, this chapter endeavours to shed light whenever possible on the region's similarities and differences by using specific examples from numerous countries. Recognising the enormous undertaking that would be necessary to catalogue each and every law pertaining to online expressive activity across 14 nations, this chapter instead lays out a comparative framework – highlighting the influences of the common law and civil law traditions on the legal framework throughout the Middle East and North Africa. It provides a high-level overview of legal protections for free speech as they exist throughout the region – making reference to Algeria, Bahrain, Egypt, Iran, Iraq, Israel, Jordan, Kuwait, Lebanon, Libya, Morocco, Oman, Qatar, Saudi Arabia, Syria, Tunisia, the United Arab Emirates and Yemen.

II. Social Media as MENA's New Public Sphere

In countries operating under authoritarian rule, alternative media often spring up to provide access to information and promote discussion, particularly in times of crisis.[9] This was, without a doubt, a key aspect of the Arab Spring. Particularly in Tunisia, where the state-controlled media failed to cover the protests, citizens lacked trustworthy official sources of information. Instead, they turned to satellite channel Al Jazeera, based in Qatar, and the Internet for updates and to discuss the situation. When the protests began, just over one-third of Tunisians had access to the Internet, but mobile phone penetration exceeded 100 per cent in 2011.[10]

[9] M Wojcieszak et al, 'What Drives Media Use in Authoritarian Regimes Extending Selective Exposure Theory to Iran' (2018) 24 *The International Journal of Press/Politics*, available at journals.sagepub.com/doi/full/10.1177/1940161218808372.

[10] International Bank for Reconstruction and Development, 'World Development Indicators), available at datacatalog.worldbank.org/dataset/world-development-indicators.

About one in six Tunisians had access to Facebook in 2011, with that number increasing rapidly to one in three by 2013.[11] Evidence of the importance of the Internet and social media to the pro-democracy movement can be found in the Tunisian Government's decision to block access to the Internet, preventing Tunisians from accessing Facebook, YouTube and other social platforms that showcased opposition views.[12]

But Tunisians' behaviour was not particularly unique. In many ways, adoption of social media and high levels of cell phone ownership had a catalysing effect for the Arab Spring, with protests spreading from Tunisia into Egypt, Libya, Bahrain, Yemen and Syria.[13] Citizens throughout the Middle East and North Africa used the Internet and social media sites as fora to learn about and discuss the region's geopolitical climate. A 2012 Pew survey found that 34 per cent of respondents in Lebanon, 30 per cent of respondents in Egypt and 29 per cent of respondents in Jordan reported using social media sites generally.[14] Interestingly, of those who used social networking, more than 60 per cent of the respondents in Lebanon, Tunisia, Egypt and Jordan reported sharing their views about politics – compared to a median of 34 per cent across the 20 nations surveyed.

Tunisians themselves have acknowledged the importance of the Internet and social media as a reliable source of information during the Arab Spring. More than three-quarters of Tunisians surveyed reported regularly sharing information and news about the demonstrations that they had found on the Internet.[15] When asked about how reliable information sources were during the uprising, Tunisians rated video-sharing sites, Facebook, Internet news and the Internet in general as being among the most reliable – in the same realm as face-to-face conversation – and far more reliable than newspapers or the Government.[16] Further, survey respondents confirmed the use of these platforms was occurring across all generations.[17]

Many MENA citizens perceive social media as a more reliable source of information than traditional media because of the lack of strong protection for free expression throughout the region. Despite written guarantees of free speech and press in nearly every country's constitution, most media outlets in the region do not operate free from government control. Further, the weak rule of law in MENA

[11] F Salem and R Mortada, 'Citizen Engagement and Public Services in the Arab World: The Potential of Social Media' (The Arab Social Media Report, April 2014), available at www.researchgate.net/publication/264899760_Citizen_Engagement_and_Public_Services_in_the_Arab_World_The_Potential_of_Social_Media_The_Arab_Social_Media_Report.

[12] A Kavanaugh et al, 'The Use and Impact of Social Media during the 2011 Tunisian Revolution' (2016) Proceedings of the 17th International Digital Government Research Conference, available at dl.acm.org/doi/pdf/10.1145/2912160.2912175.

[13] PN Howard and MM Hussain, 'The Role of Digital Media' (2011) 22 *Journal of Democracy* 35.

[14] Pew Research Center 'Egyptians Embrace Revolt Leaders, Religious Parties and Military As Well' (Pew Global Attitudes Survey, 25 April 2011), available at www.pewresearch.org/global/2011/04/25/egyptians-embrace-revolt-leaders-religious-parties-and-military-as-well.

[15] Kavanaugh et al, 'The Use and Impact of Social Media' (2016).

[16] ibid.

[17] ibid.

countries can be traced to governments who do not implement the free speech guarantees in ways that provide equal treatment for all parties under the law.[18]

III. MENA's Legal Landscape: Constitutional and Statutory Protections

The important role that Islam plays in the development of social and legal norms throughout much of the Middle East and North Africa cannot be overstated. This is particularly true in countries – like those on the Gulf – where the law governs behaviours that call into question a person's moral or ethical practice. Religious texts and verses, including the *Quran* and the Sunnah, heavily influence rule of law in the region's Muslim-majority countries. Sharia law remains a principal source of authority for the lawmaking and legal traditions throughout MENA, where many countries recognise Islam as the official religion.[19] The resulting socio-religious norms in many MENA countries create a more conservative approach to freedom of expression than in secular, Western-influenced legal systems.[20]

A. Constitutional Protections for Free Expression

Despite the influence of Sharia law, MENA citizens theoretically have a right to engage in free speech. Nearly all of the constitutions of the MENA countries make some reference to freedom of expression, but the scope of those protections varies greatly. At one end of the spectrum, constitutions like Algeria's 2020 version make the vast promise that 'Freedom of expression shall be protected' while Oman's 2011 constitution says 'The freedom of opinion and expression through speech, writing and other means of expression is guaranteed within the limits of law'. Constitutional guarantees that include caveat language such as Oman's hardly offer meaningful protection because the country's authoritarian leaders can unilaterally enact laws that limit free expression.

The Arab Spring initially led to significant political upheaval, and a number of the countries updated their constitutions in response. However, not all the updates

[18] The World Justice Project, which evaluates rule of law in countries around the world, did not specifically address Tunisia in 2011, but it made the following observation about the Middle East and North Africa in its report: 'these countries have serious weaknesses in the areas of accountability, checks and balances on the executive branch, openness, and respect for fundamental rights, especially discrimination, freedom of opinion, and freedom of belief and religion.' MD Argast et al, 'The World Justice Project Rule of Law Index' (World Justice Project, 2011), available at worldjusticeproject.org/sites/default/files/documents/WJP_Rule_of_Law_Index_2011_Report.pdf.

[19] A Rasheed, *Prioritizing Fair Information Practice Principles Based on Islamic Privacy Law*, (2020) 11 *Berkeley Journal of Middle Eastern & Islamic Law* 13–14 (quoting MUHAMMAD B'QIR AL-SADR (Roy Parviz Mottahedeh, trans., intro. by, 2003)), DURUS FI 'ILM AL-USUL [LESSONS IN ISLAMIC JURISPRUDENCE]).

[20] ibid 13–15.

were positive, with some amendments providing greater protections for free speech while others inserted caveat language similar to that found in the Omani constitution. The Bahraini constitution, updated in 2017, clearly reflects concerns raised by the uprisings. Its free expression provision reads:

> Freedom of opinion and scientific research is guaranteed. Everyone has the right to express his opinion and publish it by word of mouth, in writing or otherwise under the rules and conditions laid down by law, provided that the fundamental beliefs of Islamic doctrine are not infringed, the unity of the people is not prejudiced, and discord or sectarianism is not aroused.

In contrast, Yemen's 2015 draft constitution gives a nod to protecting dissent: 'Freedom of expression, freedom to access information or ideas and freedom of literary, artistic and cultural creativity, freedom of scientific research and freedom to criticize the performance of State institutions shall be guaranteed for every person'.

Several countries' constitutions contain specific provisions guaranteeing constitutional rights to telecommunication – key to being able to access social media through mobile telephone or Internet service – but the efficacy of those provisions is questionable, particularly when telecommunications companies are often state-controlled. Egypt's 2014 constitution, drafted on the heels of the ouster of Mohamed Morsi, and keenly aware of the country's 2011 Internet shutdown, specifically contains protections for 'all forms of public means of communications. Interrupting or disconnecting them, or depriving the citizens from using them, arbitrarily, is impermissible'.[21] Yet in 2018, the Atlantic Council reported that 'Egypt leads the pack in Internet censorship in the Middle East'.[22] The country's cybercrime law blocks websites believed to threaten national security and penalises those who visit them. Shortly after this report, a new law permitted social media accounts and blogs with more than 5,000 followers to be treated (and persecuted) as media outlets.

Many MENA countries include constitutional provisions that purport to protect the secrecy of communications, even though government surveillance of social media and other Internet communication is commonplace in much of the region. For example, Article 39 of the Kuwaiti constitution provides: 'Freedom of communication by post, telegraph, and telephone and the secrecy thereof is guaranteed; according censorship of communications and disclosure of their contents are not permitted except in the circumstances and manner specified by law'. Bahrain,[23] Egypt,[24]

[21] The Constitution of Egypt, Art 57 (2014).

[22] E Miller, 'Egypt Leads the Pack in Internet Censorship across the Middle East (Atlantic Council, 28 August 2019), available at www.atlanticcouncil.org/blogs/menasource/egypt-leads-the-pack-in-internet-censorship-across-the-middle-east.

[23] The Constitution of Bahrain, Art 26 (2002), available at www.wipo.int/wipolex/en/details.jsp?id=7264.

[24] The Constitution of Egypt, Art 57 provides 'Private life is inviolable, safeguarded and may not be infringed upon. Telegraph, postal, and electronic correspondence, telephone calls, and other forms of communication are inviolable, their confidentiality is guaranteed and they may only be confiscated,

Jordan,[25] Syria[26] and the UAE[27] have similar constitutional provisions as does Israel in its Basic Law.[28] However, human rights and civil society groups have recently criticised a number of countries in the region for perceived erosions in communication privacy, particularly as they bow to pressures from the Western world to monitor various forms of public and private communications in the name of terrorism prevention.[29]

Regardless of the written constitutional protections, freedom of expression in most countries in the region is largely subject to the whim of the ruling government and unpredictable given the low rule of law in many MENA countries. In the case of the Muslim-majority countries throughout much of the region, this means protection for free expression is largely in the hands of theocratic monarchs. Government structures in the Levant are less repressive than those in the Gulf, with citizens from Israel (save Palestinians), Lebanon and Jordan, for example, having marginally more control over, and representation in, their governments, and somewhat more pluralistic media industries. Nonetheless, respect for the rule of law in the region remains inconsistent, particularly throughout North Africa and the Gulf, making constitutional protections for free expression largely symbolic.

B. The Lack of Statutory Protection for Freedom of Expression

Throughout the Middle East, the influence of civil law traditions also colours the legal systems, elevating the necessity for clearly written statutory protections for free expression and privacy. Lebanon follows the civil law tradition most closely, which is not surprising given that France occupied the country until 1943.[30] Egypt, too, draws strong connections to civil law, dating back to its occupation by Napoleon. Other countries, despite their colonial legacies, rely heavily on civil law

examined or monitored by causal judicial order, for a limited period of time, and in cases specified by the law.'

[25] The Constitution of Jordan, Art 18 provides: 'All postal and telegraphic correspondence, telephonic communications, and the other communications means shall be regarded as secret and shall not be subject to censorship, viewing, suspension or confiscation except by a judicial order in accordance with the provisions of the law.'

[26] The Syrian Constitution, Art 32 provides 'The privacy of postal and telegraphic contacts is guaranteed'.

[27] Art 31 provides 'Freedom of communication by means of the posts, telegraph or other means of communication and their secrecy shall be guaranteed in accordance with the law'.

[28] Art 7(d) of Israel's Basic Law provides 'There shall be no violation of the confidentiality of conversation, or of the writings or records of a person.'

[29] The Committee to Protect Journalists documents in detail the way these vague laws are impacting citizens' and journalists' abilities to speak out. See CC Radsch, 'Treating the Internet as the Enemy' (Committee to Protect Journalists, 27 April 2015), available at cpj.org/2015/04/attacks-on-the-press-treating-internet-as-enemy-in-middle-east.php.

[30] F El Samad, 'The Lebanese Legal System and Research' (GlobalLex, November 2008), available at www.nyulawglobal.org/globalex/Lebanon.html#_2._Legal_system.

traditions, eschewing the British influence of common law and the importance of judicial opinions as precedent. This marks a significant difference between the influence of British colonialism in the Middle East versus elsewhere, where the adoption of an English common law approach was standard. In particular, many of the countries in the Gulf Cooperation Council[31] fuse together a combination of civil and Sharia law, further complicating the adjudication of legal disputes. As a result of the civil law legacy, the interpretation and application of statutory provisions play a significant role in the resolution of cases involving social media speech and other expressive activity – which is regularly subject to national penal codes.

Constitutional and statutory protections for free expression represent only one piece of the regulatory puzzle in the Middle East and North Africa. Many countries have recently enacted statutory protections for privacy that target social media speech; others are simply interpretating existing laws more broadly to target speech on Internet platforms. Many of these statutory protections are codified in the countries' penal codes – a markedly different approach than that taken in the United States, where most litigation involving speech is civil. As a result, speech offences in the MENA region often result in imprisonment, fines or both – creating a significant chilling effect on free expression. In the US, for example, the First Amendment dramatically limits lawsuits over speech, and those lawsuits result in money damages rather than imprisonment.[32] Although nearly all Middle East countries have constitutional protections for freedom of expression, these do not circumscribe criminal prosecutions in the same fashion as the American constitutional guarantees.

IV. Leaders Strike Back against Pro-Democracy Resistance

Since the Arab Spring, leadership changes have occurred in four Middle Eastern countries, and protests have taken place in 13 more. Yet few, if any, pro-democratic developments in freedom of expression have taken hold in the region. The climate surrounding free speech has only deteriorated: 'Most Arab journalists nowadays are imitating the proverbial three wise monkeys – see, hear and speak no evil – to ensure survival in a region that quickly regressed to dictatorship mode after a brief lull brought about by the 2011 Arab Spring upheavals.'[33]

[31] In the early 1980s, six countries bordering the Arabian Gulf formed a strategic alliance colloquially known as the Gulf Cooperation Council. The countries are Bahrain, Kuwait, Oman, Qatar, Saudi Arabia and the UAE.

[32] T Barton Carter et al, *The First Amendment and the Fourth Estate: The Law of Mass Media* (Foundation Press, 2021).

[33] R Sabbagh, 'There is a long road ahead for Arab journalists and free speech' (Al Jazeera, 15 March 2021), available at www.aljazeera.com/opinions/2021/3/15/the-long-road-ahead-for-arab-journalists-and-free-speech.

As the rise of Western social media platforms increased regional connectivity with the non-Muslim world, the region's authoritarian leaders have grown increasingly anxious about their effects. Authoritarian regimes tightened their grips on their countries generally, and they found ways to crack down on dissent appearing on social media:

> Since the Arab Spring, Arab regimes have worked to ensure that no social or political movements are to ever emerge again. Under the pretext of 'fighting terrorism' and safeguarding 'national security,' authoritarian governments in the region have engaged in fear mongering, silencing independent media, orchestrating disinformation and smear campaigns, harassing and arresting journalists, activists and citizens over their social media content and internet activities.[34]

As access to the Internet improved, fear of online dissent fuelled government campaigns to suppress digital speech in a region that has historically endured some of the most rigid restrictions on expression.[35] Before 2012, however, government leaders prosecuted disfavoured speech largely through a patchwork of criminal laws designed to protect reputation, privacy and telecommunication.[36] Since then, nations have enacted sweeping cybersecurity laws sold as privacy and security protections but broadly used them instead to punish 'offensive conduct' and 'fake news' or 'misinformation'.[37] Often, this amounts to attempts to quell speech that does not support government ideology or paints the leadership in a poor light.

In fact, social media has not been spared from leaders' desire to assert and regain control in other regions of the world. In the wake of the 2019 Christchurch mosque shooting, leaders from around the world, including democratically elected heads of Western governments, renewed calls to criminalise hate speech and other offensive content on social media and chat apps, which only further empowered authoritarian leaders to do the same. Unlike in the US, the law in many parts of the world often criminalises these types of objectionable expression in the name of protecting privacy, reputation or social control by labelling it as 'offensive' or 'insulting'. Governments in much of the developing world – including the Middle East and North Africa – have the ability to stifle freedom of expression on a whim by relying on laws crafted around sociocultural norms. As an example, emojis and insulting words sent through chat interfaces such as WhatsApp can also be punished under the law as an affront to dignity.

[34] M Fatafta, 'From Free Space to a Tool of Oppression: What Happened to the Internet Since the Arab Spring' (The Tahrir Institute for Middle East Policy, 17 December 2021), available at timep.org/commentary/analysis/from-free-space-to-a-tool-of-oppression-what-happened-to-the-internet-since-the-arab-spring.

[35] Sabbagh, 'Arab journalists and free speech' (2021).

[36] MN El-Guindy and F Hegazy, 'Cybercrime Legislation in the Middle East: The Road Not Traveled' (27 February 2012), available at www.researchgate.net/publication/259583247_Cybercrime_Legislation_in_the_Middle_East.

[37] A Mustafa, 'Cyber-crime Law to Fight Internet Abuse and Protect Privacy in the UAE' (The National, 13 November 2012), available at www.thenational.ae/news/uae-news/cyber-crime-law-to-fight-internet-abuse-and-protect-privacy-in-the-uae.

A wave of cases involving conflicts between freedom of expression on social media and purported invasions of privacy spread throughout the region after the Arab Spring, when countries began passing tough cybercrime laws.[38] Often, the crackdowns on freedom of expression in the Middle East and North Africa undertaken in the name of protecting privacy, modesty and reputation are justified on the basis of religious beliefs and cultural norms.[39] But, governments in the region often use the sociocultural construction of privacy – in conjunction with vaguely worded laws – as a means to limit freedom of expression that criticises the Government or has negative political or religious undertones. Before 2012, none of the Middle East countries had comprehensive laws addressing cybercrime.[40] Instead, many relied on a patchwork of criminal laws designed to protect reputation, privacy and telecommunications.[41]

The United Arab Emirates led the way, enacting a wide-ranging cybercrime law that took effect in 2012.[42] Since then, several nations in the region have enacted similar provisions, and these laws often provide little to no guidance about prohibited expression that is punishable through stiff criminal sanctions. A Human Rights Watch director said:

> The UAE's cybercrime decree reflects an attempt to ban even the most tempered criticism. The determination to police and punish online dissent, no matter how mild, is incompatible with the image UAE rulers are trying to promote of a progressive, tolerant nation.

In 2018, the UAE sentenced an activist to 10 years in jail under its cybercrime law for sharing 'false information' and 'defaming' his country on social media after he contacted several international human rights organisations.[43]

Some legal experts speculated that these vague and draconian laws would be strictly enforced to punish offensive speech – namely that which takes the form of dissent or criticism – under the guise of 'protecting privacy' at the expense of freedom of expression.[44] In February 2019, more than 160 Bahrainis were sentenced to prison time after a 2017 sit-in outside the home of the country's leading Shi'ite cleric.[45] Nearly one-third of those sentenced received 10-year prison terms under

[38] See, eg, Law No 14 of 2014 Promulgating the Cybercrime Prevention Law (Qatar); Law No 5 of 2012 On Combating Cybercrimes (UAE).

[39] 'Human Rights in the Middle East and North Africa – Review of 2018' (Amnesty International, 2019), available at www.amnesty.org/download/Documents/MDE0194332019ENGLISH.PDF.

[40] MN El-Guindy, 'Cybercrime Legislation in the Middle East' (February 2012), available at www.researchgate.net/publication/259583247_Cybercrime_Legislation_in_the_Middle_East.

[41] ibid.

[42] 'Defamation and Social Media in the UAE' (Clyde & Co, 3 April 2019), available at www.clydeco.com/en/insights/2019/04/defamation-and-social-media-in-the-uae.

[43] J Lemon, 'Prominent UAE Activist Jailed for 10 Years Over Social Media Activity' (Newsweek, 30 May 2018), available at www.newsweek.com/uae-activist-ahmed-mansoor-jailed-10-years-949167.

[44] Mustafa, 'Cyber-crime Law to Fight Internet Abuse' (2012).

[45] A El Yaakoubi and N Eltahir, 'Bahrain sentences 167 people to prison in crackdown on dissent' (Reuters, 14 March 2019), available at www.reuters.com/article/us-bahrain-security/bahrain-sentences-167-people-to-prison-in-crackdown-on-dissent-idUSKCN1QV25V.

the cybercrime law, and many had been detained for six months before being granted bail while awaiting trial.[46]

Criminal law and cybercrime provisions have been used to target social media influencers who express views that run contrary to region's conservative cultural norms, or paint a country or regime in a negative light. Egypt targeted and jailed a number of female TikTok influencers in 2020, claiming their content was immoral.[47] Another TikTok celebrity was arrested in July 2020 and sentenced to three years in jail for posting racy videos.[48] The prosecutors argued she was 'inciting debauchery, immorality and stirring up instincts' with videos of her dancing and lip-syncing to popular music. The UAE imprisoned an Emirati social media influencer and another person for three months, confiscated their phones and banned them from social media after they posted video of a dangerous driving stunt.[49] The court explained that authorities found the video while monitoring 'negative phenomena and violations on social media'. The region is known for its deadly driving conditions and authorities' lax enforcement of traffic laws.

Not surprisingly then, the legal framework surrounding the protection of privacy, reputation and social control is intricate – boasting a complexity that allows governments to misuse the law as a means of squelching critical speech both online and offline:

> The killing of Palestinians protestors by Israeli forces in Gaza and the murder of journalist Jamal Khashoggi in a Saudi Arabian consulate glaringly illustrated the unaccountability of Middle Eastern and North African states that resorted to lethal and other violence to repress dissent.[50]

Further, the interrelationship between governments and state-controlled telecommunication providers in much of the region creates an environment ripe for corruption, allowing governments to condition access to do business on social media platforms' willingness to participate in government-directed surveillance of political opponents and dissidents.

Furthermore, governments in the region have responded to dissent in other ways. From shutting down the Internet or banning particular social media

[46] ibid.

[47] 'Egypt sentences TikTok female influencers to 2 years in prison' (Middle East Monitor, 28 July 2020), available at www.middleeastmonitor.com/20200728-egypt-sentences-tiktok-female-influencers-to-2-years-in-prison.

[48] 'Egypt releases social media influencer jailed for "immoral videos"' (Middle East Monitor, 30 July 2020), available at www.middleeastmonitor.com/20200730-egypt-releases-social-media-influencer-jailed-for-immoral-videos.

[49] 'UAE influencer put in jail for reckless stunt in viral video' (Esquire Middle East, 1 May 2021), available at www.esquireme.com/content/52228-uae-influencer-put-in-jail-for-reckless-stunt-in-viral-video.

[50] 'Human Rights in the Middle East and North Africa – Review of 2018' (Amnesty International, 2019).

platforms to propagating their own misinformation, repressive regimes have sought to punish dissidents and maintain control:

> After outlawing protests and slowly dominating traditional media, the Egyptian state has embarked upon a multipronged strategy aimed at completely controlling and curtailing digital spaces, including censorship through website blocking, arrests based on social media posts, hacking attempts against activists, and the legalization of these practices through a myriad of new draconian laws.[51]

Research suggests the use of stiff criminal penalties and draconian cybercrime laws to jail journalists and online critics are popular tools of repression. As the Middle East Research and Information Project reports:

> A notable development since 2011 is that the region's authoritarian rulers have increasingly relied on harsh repression to maintain their power – whether in direct response to protest, or as part of a broad crackdown on free speech and dissent aimed at deterring challenges from below.[52]

In Lebanon, for example, prosecutors launched an investigation into social media posts they claimed insulted the president while members of the military prevented reporters from filming protests.[53]

Qatar's criminal laws serve as a representative example. In March 2017, Qatar's Emir Sheikh Tamim Hamad Al-Thani approved a draft law that doubled penalties for a variety of criminal violations, including opening the correspondence of another person, eavesdropping on telephone calls, recording private conversations and taking photos or video in public places.[54] Law No 4 of 2017 not only doubled penalties but also criminalised additional behaviours. New sections were added to address:

> Taking or transmitting photographs or video clips of accident victims using any kind of device – unless legally permitted – and taking or transmitting photographs or video clips of an individual or group of individuals in a public place through any device with the aim of using these for abuse or defamation.[55]

[51] J Shea, 'Egypt's Online Repression Thwarts Both Growth and Democracy' (The Tahrir Institute for Middle East Policy, 16 August 2019), available at timep.org/commentary/analysis/egypts-online-repression-thwarts-both-growth-and-democracy.

[52] A Lawrence, 'Trump's Enabling Role in Rising Regional Repression' (Middle East Research and Information Project, 2019), available at merip.org/2019/12/trumps-enabling-role-in-rising-regional-repression.

[53] 'Repression threatens free speech in Lebanon, warns rights groups' (Al Arabiya, 14 July 2020), available at english.alarabiya.net/News/middle-east/2020/07/14/-Repression-threatens-free-speech-in-Lebanon-warns-rights-groups-.

[54] Qatar Penal Code, Art 333.

[55] MAchkhanian, 'You Can Be Booked for Uploading Videos Showing Illegal Acts' (Gulf News, 26 October 2016), available at gulfnews.com/news/uae/courts/you-can-be-booked-for-uploading-videos-showing-illegal-acts-1.1919207. Egypt has similar provisions in place in its Criminal Code. However, Arts 113 and 309*bis* are limited in scope to private places, bringing it more into line with the American approach to privacy. See generally 'State of Privacy Egypt' (Privacy International, 26 January 2019), available at privacyinternational.org/state-privacy/1001/state-privacy-egypt.

Not surprisingly, these changes in the law target the very types of content that often go viral when shared on social media platforms.

Other provisions in Qatar's criminal law specifically targeted online expression, particularly if it paints the country, its ruling family or its citizens in a poor light. Article 331 prohibits 'spreading news, photographs, or comments related to the secrets of the private life of families or individuals, even if they are true'.[56] A similar provision, enacted in September 2015, criminalises the sharing of photographs of automobile accidents or other incidents in which people have been injured – limiting discussion about the country's high number of traffic deaths and the Government's reluctance to prosecute Qatari nationals when they cause them.[57] Many of these provisions have been routinely reported on in the country's news outlets, but little coverage of subsequent prosecutions under them has been published.

Although each country's cybercrime law operates differently, they share similar characteristics. Most typically, they increase criminal penalties for speech or other activities that occur on the Internet – making them an effective tool to target myriad types of speech on social media with the goal of chilling dissent. Throughout the COVID-19 pandemic, MENA governments increasingly turned to these laws to try to control the public health narrative. Human Rights Watch documented more than 80 governments, including some in the Middle East and North Africa, who used the pandemic as a means of repressing speech.[58] In Egypt, for example, a prominent female activist was sentenced to jail time for using social media to advocate for the release of prisoners during the pandemic.[59] Prosecutors argued she was misusing social media to spread false information that would cause panic.

But cybercrime laws are not the only way authoritarian governments are cracking down on social media speech. Many regional rulers have quickly realised their ability to control access through pressures on social media platforms

[56] Qatar Penal Code, Art 331. A similar provision is found in Bahrain's Penal Code, which states: 'A prison sentence for a period not exceeding 6 months and a fine not exceeding BD 50, or either penalty, shall be inflicted upon any person who published by any method of publication news, photographs or comments relating to individuals' private or family lives, even though they are true, should the publication thereof be offensive thereto.' Bahrain Penal Code, Art 370.

[57] Israel Protection of Privacy Law. Israel, too, criminally sanctions to publication of photographs of someone who is injured or deceased. Chapter One states 'Publication of a victims photograph, shot during the time of injury or immediately thereafter, in a manner where he is identifiable and under circumstances by which the publication thereof is likely to embarrass him, except for the immediate publication of a photograph, from the moment of photographing to the moment of actual transmission of broadcast, which is reasonable under the circumstances; for this purpose, victim – a person who suffered physical or mental injury due to a sudden event and the injury thereof is noticeable.' A subsequent section goes on to address corpse photographs.

[58] 'Covid-19 Triggers Wave of Free Speech Abuse' (Human Rights Watch, 11 February 2021), available to www.hrw.org/news/2021/02/11/covid-19-triggers-wave-free-speech-abuse#.

[59] 'Egypt jails activist who called to free prisoners amid pandemic' (Reuters, 17 March 2021), available at www.reuters.com/world/middle-east-africa/egypt-jails-activist-who-called-free-prisoners-amid-pandemic-2021-03-17.

and telecommunications providers. As a result, citizens are stopped from speaking because they cannot even access the Internet or social spaces.

V. The Tenuous Relationship between Platforms and Governments

Aside from the challenging legal environment, the regulatory framework associated with telecommunications in the Middle East and North Africa impedes free expression online. Very often, access to the Internet – largely using mobile devices – relies on networks provided by state-controlled, heavily regulated telecommunication providers. In addition, consumers in the region often lack meaningful choice when it comes to telecommunication providers. As a result, regional governments have significant power over how the companies operate as well as access to the Internet. The close relationship between governments and telecommunication providers creates perfect conditions for unauthorised surveillance.

The lack of significant competition for telecommunication services, including mobile phone service and Internet service, heavily disadvantages citizens who want to use those services to engage in online expression that might be critical of authoritarian governments. In particular, it provides governments with almost complete control over whether their citizens can even access the Internet. In 2016, the Brookings Institute released a white paper documenting 81 Internet shutdowns in 19 countries worldwide between1 July 2015, and 30 June 2016:[60]

> In order to keep political opponents from organizing, governments were shutting down mobile networks and/or the internet to impede public communications. They understood that technology can be a democratizing influence and a way to help critics find like-minded individuals. Occurring mainly in authoritarian regimes or illiberal democracies, public officials saw internet shutdowns as a way to limit the opposition and keep themselves in power.[61]

Although they were troubling, the shutdowns were often short-lived and occurred locally rather than on a national scale. Today's digital disruptions are far more troubling. In February 2021, Netblocks noted several days of regional blackouts in Iran during a series of deadly protests as well as previous shutdowns in the country in late 2020. In July 2020, Facebook livestreaming features were restricted in Jordan while teachers protested; simultaneously, the Government imposed a gag order on the local media and limited online speech.[62]

[60] DM West, 'Global economy loses billions from internet shutdowns' (Brookings Institute, 6 October 2016), available at www.brookings.edu/blog/techtank/2016/10/06/global-economy-loses-billions-from-internet-shutdowns.

[61] ibid.

[62] 'Reports' (Netblocks, 2021), available at netblocks.org/reports/facebook-live-streams-restricted-in-jordan-during-teachers-syndicate-protests-XB7K1xB7.

Governments' ability to control telecommunication providers is directly related to their ownership. In the MENA region, carriers that are privately owned in other parts of the world are often largely owned by government, quasi-government entities or the ruling family.[63] In Qatar, for example, Ooredoo is 68 per cent controlled by 'Qatar Government Related Entities' with another 10 per cent controlled by the Abu Dhabi Investment Authority, which is associated with the UAE Government.[64] Etisalat, which operates one of the largest Internet hubs in the Middle East, is majority owned by the Emirati Government. It operates throughout the region, providing service in Saudi Arabia, Morocco and Egypt as well as in the UAE.[65] Even when it appears consumers have choice in their providers, a close look at ownership reveals a different story. As a result, consumers are often beholden to telecommunication networks controlled by the region's authoritarian governments.

These market conditions are ripe for oppressive monitoring of critics. Social media platforms operate on a surveillance capitalism business model, where they provide free services in exchange for access to users' personal data. Because the platforms amass large amounts of information about users, including the location from which they are posting, they are prime targets for repressive regimes.[66]

Additionally, although the use of social media platforms to surveil dissidents is troubling, residents of the MENA region face a far more pervasive issue given the rise of social media. Government actors have become adept at using the platforms to manipulate public opinion and spread false information that reaffirms their power:

> A recent survey by the Oxford Internet Institute found that 48 countries have at least one government agency or political party engaging in shaping public opinion through social media. Authoritarian-minded leaders routinely lambaste 'fake news' while at the same time shamelessly pushing patent falsehoods.

The COVID pandemic laid clear the power of these regimes to control the narrative by relying on misinformation and disinformation tactics. A report from civil society group Omelas details how governments around the world, including Saudi Arabia, spread disinformation on social media touting their COVID response.[67] The Middle East Institute documented similar falsehoods, including a May 2020

[63] 'Major Shareholders' (Vodafone, 2021), available at www.vodafone.qa/en/investor-relations/shareholder-structure/major-shareholders.

[64] 'Share Information' (Ooredoo, 2021), available at www.ooredoo.com/en/investors/share_information.

[65] 'Global Footprint' (Etisalat, 2021), available at www.etisalat.com/en/index.jsp#.

[66] R Deibert, 'The Road to Digital Unfreedom: Three Painful Truths About Social Media' (2019) 30 *Journal of Democracy*, available at www.journalofdemocracy.org/articles/the-road-to-digital-unfreedom-three-painful-truths-about-social-media.

[67] 'Viral Overload: An Analysis of COVID-19 Information Operations' (Omelas, 2021), available at www.omelas.io/viral-overload.

report from the Syrian health ministry that only 44 confirmed cases of the virus had been reported.[68]

VI. Conclusion

Social media platforms continue to play a dominant role in the MENA region, but they are no longer safe spaces for discussions on political topics for myriad reasons. In the decade since Mohamed Bouazizi's death, adoption of the Internet and concomitant use of social media have soared in nearly every country in the region. The World Bank (2020) estimates that two-thirds of Tunisia's population was using the Internet by 2019, up from 34 per cent in 2010. This trend continues beyond North Africa; on the Gulf side of the region, Bahrain has seen significant increases as well. More than 99 per cent of Bahrain's population used the Internet in 2019, up from 55 per cent in 2010.[69] Similar adoption rates also can be seen for social media usage. Nevertheless, as described in this chapter, most MENA governments adapted quickly to the use of social media to organise dissent and civil rights activism.

Because of this, social media has not been fully realised as a public sphere for advancing democratic ideals. In reality, it has provided an excellent platform for government surveillance of dissidents and political opponents.

Strong religious and cultural norms combined with the instability of rule of law in much of the Middle East and North Africa result in weak overall protections for freedom of speech in the region – particularly when that speech targets government leaders. Additionally, the bevvy of criminal laws protecting privacy and prohibiting any speech likely to cause unrest has a significant chilling effect on freedom of expression on the Internet. Vaguely drafted cybercrime statutes and a lack of common law precedent contribute to the arbitrary enforcement of the law – often targeting dissenters who take to social media and other online platforms. Finally, the intertwined relationship between authoritarian regimes and state-controlled telecommunication providers creates a thorny space in which social media platforms must operate, often leaving them beholden to the governments seeking to silence critical online speech.

Throughout the Middle East, little is reported in the media about the legal system. This is particularly true about enforcement of criminal provisions that target critical speakers, when arrests make the news but further actions taken within the criminal system are rarely made public. On rare occasion, a criminal disposition will become public – typically because the Government wanted to

[68] S Kenney and C Bernadaux, 'New ways of fighting state-sponsored COVID disinformation' (Middle East Institute, 13 January 2021), available at www.mei.edu/publications/new-ways-fighting-state-sponsored-covid-disinformation#_ftn1.

[69] World Bank (2020), available at data.worldbank.org/indicator/IT.NET.USER.ZS?locations=BH.

make an example of a defendant who was not a national or because a dissident defendant sought international publicity in an effort to avoid imprisonment or other sanction.

Although the lack of transparency in the criminal justice system flies in the face of Western expectations, one could argue it falls in line with the religious and cultural norms of the region. However, adherence to rule of law requires, at a minimum, that all parties – those who speak in support of the Government and those who criticise it – be protected equally. Given the implementation and enforcement of many of these laws in the region, it becomes apparent that authoritarian regimes use criminal provisions and cybercrime laws to protect their reputations and maintain their power. In much of the Middle East and North Africa, these regimes, many of which have a history of disrespecting human rights, often co-opt privacy laws to protect themselves while implementing widespread Internet and social media surveillance to gather information about their critics, effectively preventing citizens from participating meaningfully in civic life.

4

Legal Framings in Networked Public Spheres: The Case of Search and Rescue in the Mediterranean

VERONICA CORCODEL

I. Introduction

This chapter approaches social media platforms of civil society actors as technologically mediated public spheres and potential repositories of legal framings. Taking more specifically the example of search and rescue in the Mediterranean, it foregrounds the legal dimension of social media posts published by some of the most relevant civil society actors. It also explores whether such an approach facilitates the visibility of possible alternatives to existing migration framings. Such alternatives can be understood as forms of democratic participation and dissent in modern governance structures. They are particularly important in the context of migration, which concerns people who are often deprived of citizenship rights.

Shipwrecks and deaths in the Mediterranean have attracted a lot of attention in the media, academic scholarship and civil society, especially since the height of the so-called 'migration crisis' in 2015. Legal and socio-legal scholars working on search and rescue (SAR) have mostly addressed the international and European Union (EU) legal frameworks of SAR operations, with a critical eye towards the securitisation of EU policies.[1] Social media is rarely examined in this scholarship. Yet this chapter argues that it can be approached as a site of participation in – and production of – digital public spheres, in which existing legal arrangements can be debated, criticised or condoned.

Outside legal and socio-legal scholarship on SAR, social media in the context of migration has been mostly analysed as a tool facilitating the reaching of

[1] D Ghezelbash et al, 'Securitization of Search and Rescue at Sea: The Response to Boat Migration in the Mediterranean and Offshore Australia' (2018) 67 *International and Comparative Law Quarterly* 315.

destination countries and thus consolidating migrants' agency,[2] but also as prone to being used by public authorities and smugglers for enhanced surveillance and exploitation.[3] While acknowledging these dimensions of social media, this chapter approaches it first and foremost as a set of ideas that can be related to existing legal framings of migration, be it because they reproduce them or because they advance alternative ones. In this sense, networked platforms can be understood as technologically mediated public spaces, in which civil society actors rely on the opportunities offered by social media to advance legally relevant ideas.

In the context of migration, social media is widely used for activist purposes, especially when compared to mainstream media.[4] In other words, civil society actors' posts are often contributions to wider legal-political debates on migration. This chapter approaches SAR humanitarianism as inescapably political and thus part of such legal-political debates. This approach should be distinguished from the mainstream understanding of humanitarianism as a neutral project of saving migrants' lives with little – if any – reflection on the conditions that led to their distress in the first place.[5] As Nyers puts it, 'humanitarianism is an inherently political concept, and one that is already implicated in a [politically meaningful] relation of violence'.[6] In this sense, taking the example of SAR, which is often debated *within* humanitarianism, is an opportunity of both showing the networked political-legal space produced in relation to it, and questioning its alleged neutrality.

This chapter explores the relationship between law and social media on SAR and examines whether social posts by civil society actors produce alternatives to the dominant legal frameworks on migration. This issue is understood as inseparable from constitutional questions of dissent and democratic participation in the public sphere. Social media is a means – among others – of practicing such rights and, if their practice is to be approached widely, it includes a variety of forms of activism that question dominant legal-political arrangements.[7] Thus, the chapter shares with the other contributions to Part I of this volume their interest in dissent and democratic development, while looking at the specific context of social media activism. The second section elaborates on the theoretical framework and argues for an approach that considers social media platforms as sites of legal framings.

[2] R Dekker and G Engbersen, 'How social media transform migrant networks and facilitate migration' (2014) 14 *Global Networks* 401; R Dekker et al, 'Smart Refugees: How Syrian Asylum Migrants Use Social Media Information in Migration Decision-Making' (2018) 4 *Social Media + Society*; M Latonero and P Kift, 'On Digital Passages and Borders: Refugees and the New Infrastructure for Movement and Control' (2018) 4 *Social Media + Society*.

[3] Latonero and Kift, 'On Digital Passages and Borders' (2018).

[4] A Nerghes and L Ju-Sung, 'Narratives of the Refugee Crisis: A Comparative Study of Mainstream-Media and Twitter' (2019) 7 *Media and Communication* 275.

[5] P Nyers, *Rethinking Refugees: Beyond States of Emergency* (Routledge, 2006) 42; D Fassin, *Humanitarian Reason* (University of California Press, 2011) 224.

[6] Nyers, *Rethinking Refugees* (2006) 42.

[7] For a similar argument, see B de Sousa Santos and J Arriscado Nunes (eds), *Reinventing Democracy: Grassroots Movements in Portugal* (Routledge, 2019).

The next two sections build on this approach to analyse the Twitter posts of some of the most active civil society actors in the context of SAR in the Mediterranean, published between March 2019 and December 2020. Methodologically speaking, this required a thorough reading of posts for a selection of critiques with similar themes and their analysis in terms of the kind of framings they challenge and the alternatives that emerge. The third section shows that the main critiques relate to three legal framings of migration control: securitisation, criminalisation and externalisation. The fourth section argues that solidarity-based alternatives emerge in different forms from the examined posts. Finally, the chapter concludes with some thoughts on the implications of these findings.

II. Social Media Platforms as Sites of Legal Framings

Framing is understood here as a device that generates specific interpretations that seek 'to contain, convey, and determine what is seen', thus delimiting 'the sphere of appearance itself'.[8] To simplify, it refers to (often implicit) ways of framing certain issues, inevitably delimiting how these are understood and seen. When it comes to migration, an obvious example would be the framing of migrants as a security threat or as a humanitarian concern. Such framings are inseparable from law, in the sense that they structure a variety of legal rules and arguments, producing and delimiting what is seen as (il)legitimate. The expression 'legal framings' refers here precisely to this entangled relationship between legal rules/arguments and framings. This perspective is particularly useful when looking for alternatives to dominant legal-political arrangements, as it seeks for ways to go beyond the ideas that structure them.

Approaching social media activism from a framing perspective is not a novelty in media and communication studies, including in the context of migration.[9] Some scholars have emphasised xenophobic and securitised discourses on migration in social media.[10] Siapera and others have argued that 'networked framings' of refugees[11] – understood as framings mediated through networked technologies – usually replicate the dominant polarisation between security concerns and humanitarianism.[12] Their study focused on Twitter posts during the peak of the

[8] J Butler, *Frames of War: When is Life Grievable?* (Verso, 2009) 1, 10.

[9] S Meraz, 'Hashtag wars and networked framing' in A Serrano Tellería (ed), *Between the public and private in mobile communication* (Routledge, 2017); S Meraz and Z Papacharissi, 'Networked Framing and Gatekeeping' in T Witschge et al (eds), *The SAGE Handbook of Digital Journalism* (SAGE Publications Ltd, 2016).

[10] E Siapera et al, 'Refugees and Network Publics on Twitter: Networked Framing, Affect and Capture' (2018) 4 *Social Media + Society*; C Rebollo and E Gualda, 'The refugee crisis on Twitter: A diversity of discourses at a European crossroads' (2016) 4 *Journal of Spatial and Organizational Dynamics* 199.

[11] Meraz and Papacharissi, 'Networked Framing and Gatekeeping' (2016).

[12] Siapera et al, 'Refugees and Network Publics on Twitter' (2018).

so-called migration crisis, whose most prominent authors were found to be elite politicians, media and established non-governmental organisations.

More recently, Siapera also stressed the importance of social media for searching for alternative framings, especially by examining the accounts of small, grassroot refugee support groups.[13] In this sense, the type of actors involved in social media seems to be an important consideration. Smaller groups would be more prone to countering *both* humanitarian discourses of large NGOs and security-centred narratives, producing alternative solidarity-based political projects.[14]

In this sense, social media platforms can be a repository of ideas of alternative understandings of migration that might help push forward existing debates. Such framings are inevitably related to legal arrangements, as they also challenge the ideas that structure lawmaking and enforcement. As explained in the introduction, this is also meaningful in terms of dissent and participation in the public sphere. Given the multiplicity of actors participating in social media, compared to traditional sites of lawmaking, networked framings carry the promise of leaving space to more 'voice', although such promise coexists with a 'networked' power dynamic that limits this very space.[15] Indeed, the activities on social media operate in a 'networked' power dynamic, in which the dominant actors from the more traditional public sphere are still present. However, because of social media's affordance of visibility, individuals' or smaller groups' positions are easier to locate, compared to the physical public sphere. At the same time, visibility might have a negative side, as it can trigger a response from other more powerful actors, including securitised attempts to criminalise actions of solidarity with migrants.[16] In this sense, social media can potentially both enhance and limit dissent and participation in the public sphere.

Existing works on law and social media generally privilege approaches that are different from the one advanced in this chapter. They look at the use of social media for law enforcement purposes[17] or conceive it as a space that is or should be subject to a set of regulations, including privacy and data protection, freedom of expression, intellectual property and defamation law.[18] In this sense, introducing

[13] E Siapera, 'Refugee Solidarity in Europe: Shifting the discourse' (2019) 22 *European Journal of Cultural Studies* 245.

[14] ibid.

[15] N Couldry, 'Why voice matters: Culture and politics after neoliberalism' (SAGE Publications Ltd, 2010).

[16] For further approaches of visibility as an affordance of social media, see Siapera et al (n 10) 17, as well as ch 2 (Lokot) and ch 3 (Sanders) of this volume.

[17] J Brunty and K Helenek, *Social Media Investigation for Law Enforcement* (Routledge, 2013); R Levinson-Waldman, 'Government Access to and Manipulation of Social Media: Legal and Policy Challenges' (2018) 61 *Howard Law Journal* 523.

[18] This is the case for both legal scholarship and media and communication studies. J Harris Lipschultz, *Social Media Communication. Concepts, Practices, Data, Law and Ethics*, 3rd edn (Routledge, 2020); E Celeste, 'Terms of Service and Bills of Rights: New Mechanisms of Constitutionalisation in the Social Media Environment?' (2019) 33 *International Review of Law, Computers & Technology* 122; A Packard, *Digital Media Law* (Wiley, 2010).

the idea of legal framing adds a new perspective to the relationship between law and social media that redirects the focus to how social media can produce alternatives to existing legal arrangements.

It is important to note, however, that critically approaching law as discourses or narratives that reproduce dominant framings is not a novelty in the legal and socio-legal fields. Indeed, a variety of such perspectives have been developed, ranging from constructions of women subjectivities in human rights discourses,[19] to efforts of exposing the neoliberal assumptions of law,[20] or its representations of the 'Other'.[21] Exploring the relationship between resistance and law's statist paradigm, some scholars have also argued that certain social movements moved away from 'nationalist framings' in their claims of justice.[22] In a similar vein, de Sousa Santos and Nunes have argued for an approach that brings forward popular movements and citizen initiatives that developed alternatives 'to hegemonic globalization' and its legal frameworks, mainly through 'solidaristic and democratic forms of action'.[23] According to the authors, taking into consideration grassroot movements and their demands would mean taking possibilities of broader participatory conceptions of democracy and citizenship more seriously.[24] Communication technologies often mediate grassroot action and might be even necessary for the development of *transnational* public spheres.

In the migration field, there have been some attempts to think about alternatives to specific issues, such as the system on the determination of the Member State responsible for the asylum application, but there is an overall sense of disillusionment with law and its potential to be 'alternative'. This makes the need for new approaches even more pressing. Bringing together the insights on framings from media and communication studies, and legal and socio-legal scholarship, this chapter shows that social media platforms can be a valuable source for research on alternatives to contemporary patterns of migration governance. Such an approach relies on a broad conception of the public sphere, in which civil society actors' networked framings occupy an important place. The following section gives the example of social media platforms on SAR in the Mediterranean.

[19] K Engle, 'Female Subjects of Public International Law: Human Rights and the Exotic Other Female' (1992) 26 *New England Law Review* 1509; R Kapur, 'Un-Veiling Equality: Disciplining the "Other" Woman Through Human Rights Discourse' in AM Emon, M Ellis, and B Glahn (eds), *Islamic Law and International Human Rights Law: Searching for Common Ground* (Oxford University Press, 2012).

[20] H Brabazon (ed), *Neoliberal Legality Understanding the Role of Law in the Neoliberal Project* (Routledge, 2017).

[21] F Mégret, 'From "Savages" to 2Unlawful Combatants2: A Postcolonial Look at International Humanitarian Law's "Other"' in A Orford (ed), *International Law and its Others* (Cambridge University Press, 2006) 265; V Corcodel, *Modern Law and Otherness: The Dynamics of Inclusion and Exclusion in Comparative Legal Thought* (Edward Elgar Publishing, 2019).

[22] B Rajagopal, *International Law from Below: Development, Social Movements and Third World Resistance* (Cambridge University Press, 2003).

[23] de Sousa Santos and Arriscado Nunes, *Reinventing Democracy* (2019).

[24] ibid.

III. Social Media on SAR: Criminalisation, Securitisation and Externalisation

This section examines the Twitter accounts of some of the most important and active civil society actors and networks operating in the Mediterranean: Sea Watch, Proactiva Open Arms (Open Arms), SOS Méditerranée, Médecins Sans Frontières (MSF) Sea and WatchTheMed Alarm Phone, between March 2019 and December 2020. Some of them, like Open Arms and MSF Sea, are more active on Twitter than on Facebook. This is the main reason why Twitter has been the chosen platform for the analysis, knowing that those who are equally active on Facebook generally publish very similar posts on both platforms. The starting point of this period corresponds with the publication of European Commission's 'Factsheet on Debunking Myths About Migration', which arguably marks a shift in the institutional narrative on migration.[25] In this document, the Commission declared that 'Europe is no longer in crisis mode', due to the low number of the arrivals as a 'result of joint EU efforts on all fronts'.[26] Implicitly responding to existing critiques, the Commission also stated that the EU is not preventing NGOs from pursuing SAR operations in the Mediterranean and that it is a misinterpretation to conceive EU's relations with 'third countries' as outsourcing its responsibility to protect European external borders. Examining civil society actors' Twitter posts since March 2019 allows for interrogation of the Commission's position on how EU migration policies unfolded in a period that allegedly broke away from the 'crisis' mode of governance.

As will become apparent, there is a general agreement running through the examined Twitter accounts that migrants' pushbacks, coupled with the continuing shipwrecks and deaths in the Mediterranean, are direct effects of EU and/or Member States' restrictive migration policies and legal arrangements. The term 'crisis' continued to be used on some Twitter accounts despite the Commission's official position that the EU was no longer operating in a crisis framework. The very notion of the 'crisis' is, however, understood differently in these posts: not in terms of numbers of migrants attempting to reach the EU, but as a humanitarian or policy crisis to which the EU and its Member States contributed.[27] Only SOS Méditerranée and Open Arms refrained from using the term 'crisis', at least in relation to Europe and prior to the COVID-19 pandemic. Nevertheless,

[25] European Commission, 'Facts Matter. Debunking Myths about Migration' (2019), available at ec.europa.eu/home-affairs/sites/default/files/what-we-do/policies/european-agenda-migration/20190306_managing-migration-factsheet-debunking-myths-about-migration_en.pdf.

[26] ibid.

[27] MSF Sea, 'Commission Urges Humanitarian Refocus on Mediterranean' (Twitter, 19 June 2019), available at twitter.com/MSF_Sea/status/1141266004313563136?s=20; Sea Watch International, 'Humanitarian Crisis in the Mediterranean' (Twitter, 20 September 2019), available at twitter.com/seawatch_intl/status/1175012725627510784?s=20; Alarm Phone, 'Many Stranded in Lesvos' (Twitter, 22 September 2019), available at twitter.com/alarm_phone/status/1175721664543449088?s=20.

they similarly point to the failure of the EU and its Member States to adequately respond to the continuing distress calls sent from the Mediterranean.[28]

There are three main interrelated themes in the Twitter posts of the actors examined here: criminalisation of SAR actors – securitisation; and externalisation of migration control – and these are approached in relation to EU and/or Member States' policies. These themes are common both to established humanitarian NGOs, such as MSF, and more recent organisations or networks created in the context of the 'migration crisis' rhetoric through the initiative of European citizens.[29] Alarm Phone has an additional peculiarity: it is a network that does not conduct its own SAR operations, but operates a 'hotline' for people in distress at sea. This probably explains why it does not present itself as a proper humanitarian NGO, although it does advocate for prompt SAR operations, at least as a short-term solution.[30]

Among these main common themes, securitisation is probably the widest, in the sense that it generally includes both criminalisation of civil society actors and externalisation of border controls. Indeed, securitisation refers to the framing of migrants as potential security threats, and of migration policies as encompassing security-based measures, including criminalisation and externalisation.[31] The three themes are thus interrelated and sometimes appear in the same post. An example is the following post published by Alarm Phone and retweeted by Open Arms:

> Fortress Europe tries to prevent migrants to reach European shores by any means: blocking #CivilFleet assets & disguising it as security measure, letting rescued people wait for days at sea & collaborating with Libyan head-hunters. Sea rescue is not a crime! Liberate #SeaWatch3![32]

The SAR vessel Sea Watch 3 was suspected of facilitating migrant smuggling, and blocked and prevented from leaving the port to conduct SAR operations. Its blocking is decried as a measure in which security plays out as a pretext rather than a well-founded justification. Europe's collaboration with Libya, through

[28] SOS Méditerranée, 'Primary Account of Experience in Libya' (Twitter, 25 December 2019), available at twitter.com/SOSMedIntl/status/1209892897929269248?s=20 and 'Brutality of Conditions in Libya' (Twitter, 29 June 2021), available at twitter.com/SOSMedIntl/status/1409828373015244804?s=20; Open Arms, 'Harassment by Libyan Coastguard' (Twitter, 27 February 2021), available at twitter.com/openarms_found/status/1365607113972670469?s=20.

[29] M Esperti, 'Rescuing Migrants in the Central Mediterranean: The Emergence of a New Civil Humanitarianism at the Maritime Border' (2019) 64 *American Behavioral Scientist* 436; Open Arms started conducting SAR operations in 2015, but it previously existed as a lifeguard.

[30] 'About: AlarmPhone': alarmphone.org/en/about.

[31] Ghezelbash et al, 'Securitization of Search and Rescue at Sea' (2018) 315; D Bigo, 'The (in)securitization Practices of the Three Universes of EU Border Control: Military/Navy – Border Guards/police – Database Analysts' (2014) 45 *Security Dialogue* 209; G Campesi, 'Seeking Asylum in Times of Crisis: Reception, Confinement, and Detention at Europe's Southern Border' (2018) 32 *Refugee Survey Quarterly* 44.

[32] Alarm Phone, 'Migrants Prevented from Entering Europe' (Twitter, 9 July 2020), available at twitter.com/alarm_phone/status/1281228157534834688?s=20.

which the security-migration nexus becomes externalised, is also criticised and used for exposing Europe's contradiction: on the one hand, it collaborates with 'Libyan head-hunters' and, on the other hand, it criminalises SAR NGOs.[33] A similar contradiction is emphasised by MSF Sea in relation to the use of an 'anti-smuggling' Italian ship for contraband purposes:

> As NGOs are criminalised in #Italy for saving lives at sea, an Italian warship – central to #EU efforts supposedly combating smuggling by stopping people escaping #Libya – is alleged to have 'conducted a criminal enterprise below decks.'[34]

Criminalisation of civil society actors is probably the most explicitly decried. This is usually understood as unfolding in a context in which the EU and/or its Member States create obstacles for pursuing SAR operations and deny their own responsibility of saving lives at sea. The effect of such policies is criticised for leading to more migrants' deaths in the Mediterranean. As Sea-Watch puts it, 'criminalization kills!'.[35]

The examined posts reported legal actions brought against authorities' practices, as well as NGO vessels being detained in ports or being stranded for long durations without being able to disembark. This has been the case for vessels such as Ocean Viking (SOS Méditerranée), Sea Watch 3 and 4 (Sea Watch) and Open Arms. Some reported legal actions show hope for justice and call for public authorities to put an end to criminalisation. Sea Watch, for instance, referred to the successfully challenged arrest of Carola Rackete, the captain of Sea Watch 3, for the alleged crime of violence to warships when forcefully disembarking in Lampedusa.[36] MSF also expressed its solidarity with the captain of Sea Watch 3, emphasising that saving lives at sea is not a crime but a duty. In a post worth quoting here, Sea Watch also declared that:

> Every single court case we have been forced to be a part of has been decided in our favour. It is about time to end criminalization of humanitarian aid and set it straight once and for all: saving lives is a duty, not a crime.[37]

Alarm Phone and Sea Watch expressed their solidarity with another case of criminalisation of the activities of the NGO Jugend Rettet three years after its vessel's confiscation, pointing to the still pending criminal investigations of its crew.[38]

[33] M Akkerman, 'Expanding the Fortress: The Policies, the Profiteers and the People Shaped by EU's Border Externalization Programme' (2018), available at www.tni.org/en/publication/expanding-the-fortress.

[34] MSF Sea, 'Criminalisation of NGOs' (Twitter, 1 October 2020), available at twitter.com/MSF_Sea/status/1311687483646791680?s=20.

[35] Sea Watch International, 'Criminalization and Blockade of NGOs' (Twitter, 8 October 2020), available at twitter.com/seawatch_intl/status/1314204554536206336?s=20.

[36] Sea Watch International, 'Court Rejects Captain Rackete's Arrest' (Twitter, 2 July 2019), available at twitter.com/seawatch_intl/status/1146178020664889345?s=20.

[37] Sea Watch International, 'End Criminalisation of Humanitarian Aid' (Twitter, 29 January 2020), available at twitter.com/seawatch_intl/status/1222563821727965184?s=20.

[38] Alarm Phone, 'Solidarity with IUVENTA1' (Twitter, 2 August 2020), available at twitter.com/alarm_phone/status/1289948548465864704?s=20.

A member of Alarm Phone was himself accused, and later acquitted, for 'inciting criminal acts' pursuant to a call sent to the public at large to protect migrants who face the risk of deportation.[39]

MSF reported Italian authorities' practices of fining captains of SAR vessels, comparing them to hypothetical scenarios in which the ambulance driver would be fined for taking patients to the hospital.[40] As for SOS Méditerranée and Open Arms, they both refer to criminalisation in more general but still politically laden terms, by pointing to prosecutors who 'threaten us, … fine us and … leave us out of the ports for days',[41] or to the need to end both criminalisation and administrative measures taken against NGO vessels.[42]

Member States, however, were not always in ostensible opposition to SAR NGOs, having previously privileged a collaborative approach. Indeed, Italian authorities, for instance, used to coordinate NGO operations at sea.[43] In this sense, civil society actors inevitably contributed to public authorities' (securitised) practices of border control correlated with SAR activities, such as collecting personal information about migrants and assigning them bracelets depending on the SAR event or their medical status.[44] The relationship between states and SAR civil society actors changed in important ways in 2017, when criminalisation campaigns emerged against SAR NGOs, undermining their cooperation with states.[45] In parallel, an increased emphasis was put at the EU level on the need to consolidate cooperation with the Libyan coast guard and to privilege security concerns, such as combatting migrant smuggling networks.[46] In this sense, the examined period in this chapter shows a polarisation that has its roots in earlier developments of criminalisation, securitisation and externalisation. It also shows that, from civil society actors' perspective, such developments continued even after European Commission's statement that 'Europe is no longer in crisis mode', pointing to continuity with 'crisis' measures rather than rupture.

[39] Alarm Phone, 'Acquittal of Alarm Phone Member' (Twitter, 17 July 2020), available at twitter.com/alarm_phone/status/1284112768036155393?s=20.

[40] MSF Sea, 'Fining Captains of SAR Vessels' (Twitter, 12 June 2019), available at twitter.com/MSF_Sea/status/1138795737238691840?s=20.

[41] Open Arms, 'Criminalisation of SAR' (Twitter, 6 July 2019), available at twitter.com/openarms_found/status/1147480836884836352?s=20.

[42] SOS Mediterranee, 'Proposed Actions' (Twitter, 24 September 2020), available at twitter.com/SOSMedIntl/status/1309177749974773760?s=20.

[43] Esperti, 'Rescuing Migrants in the Central Mediterranean' (2019); M Stierl, 'Reimagining EUrope through the Governance of Migration' (2020) 14 *International Political Sociology* 252; M Stierl, 'The Mediterranean as a carceral seascape' (2021) 88 *Political Geography*, available at www.sciencedirect.com/science/article/abs/pii/S0962629821000779.

[44] ibid.

[45] Esperti (n 29).

[46] Council of the European Union, 'Malta Declaration by the members of the European Council on the external aspects of migration: addressing the Central Mediterranean route' (2017), available at www.refworld.org/docid/58a1ce514.html.

The three main themes identified in civil society's actors' critiques cannot be separated from the legal frameworks associated with them, which are also inevitably criticised. In this sense, the critiques produce and are part of a networked public space in which legal arrangements are disputed through forms of digital dissent and participation. Civil society actors use the visibility offered by social media – through retweets, likes and comments – to disseminate such critiques, at the same time participating in and producing a transnational online public sphere.

Analysing the way in which securitisation emerges in the examined tweets, it is important to note that this is first and foremost a legal framing in which migration and SAR become linked to security concerns. The 2014 EU Maritime Surveillance Regulation, for instance, refers in its first recital to the importance of border surveillance for countering cross-border criminality and illegal border crossings, including by intercepting suspect vessels.[47] Border-crossing, in this sense, is conceived as a threat that justifies surveillance measures like intercepting vessels. Saving lives at sea is not altogether absent from the Regulation but is understood as incidental to surveillance operations and, thus, not a priority.[48] Criticising securitisation in a networked public sphere is, thus, also about challenging legal framings that associate migration with security concerns and that subordinate processes of saving lives at sea to such concerns.

As for the criminalisation of SAR civil society actors, national legal provisions on the facilitation of illegal immigration are generally the main instruments used by Member States, though not the only ones.[49] In Italy, for instance, such activities have been criminalised since 1998, with the adoption of the legislative decree 286/98.[50] Subsequent amendments have widened the scope of such criminal acts and strengthened the sanctions attached to them.[51] EU law also has specific provisions on the facilitation of illegal immigration, contained in a Directive 'defining the facilitation of unauthorised entry, transit and residence' adopted in 2002.[52] This Directive does not require proof of financial or other material benefit for considering the actions facilitating entry and transit (as opposed to residence) as a crime.[53] In this sense, EU law authorises Member States to criminalise such behaviour without necessarily requiring proof of criminal intent.[54] Moreover, in

[47] Ghezelbash et al (n 1).
[48] ibid.
[49] Carola Rackete's accusation of violence to warships is an example of a different type of criminalisation.
[50] Legislative Decree No 286 of 1998 Testo Unico sull'Immigrazione 25 July 1998, available at www.refworld.org/docid/54a2c23a4.html.
[51] Legge 30 luglio 2002, n 189.
[52] Council Directive (EC) 2002/90/EC defining the facilitation of unauthorised entry, transit and residence [2002] OJ L 328.
[53] ibid; S Carrera et al, 'Fit for purpose? The Facilitation Directive and the criminalisation of humanitarian assistance to irregular migrants: 2018 update' (Technical Report, European Parliament), available at cadmus.eui.eu/handle/1814/60998.
[54] Carrera et al, 'Fit for purpose?' (2018).

its Article 1(2), the Directive specifically provides that it is up to Member States to choose whether to impose or not sanctions when 'the aim of the behaviour is to provide humanitarian assistance', thus leaving the possibility to criminalise humanitarian actions in the open.[55] Civil society actors' critiques of criminalisation in the networked public space are thus also about challenging legal framings that associate migration humanitarian assistance to criminal law.

In addition to these criminal legal frameworks, civil society actors' Twitter posts also refer to administrative measures taken against them, such as detention of vessels. These measures are not always justified in terms of investigations for suspicion of 'criminal' activities, but are also sometimes justified in terms of unauthorised disembarking, as well as concerns of safety compliance and suspected registration irregularities. Given the overall hostile context of 'policing humanitarianism',[56] however, these measures are often perceived as a form of punishment rather than as being purely administrative. In this sense, decrying the detention of the SAR vessel Eleonore, Alarm Phone emphasises that 'sea rescue is not a crime!'.[57] In a somewhat similar vein, Sea Watch reported that the detention of its ships by the Italian Coast Guard was not really about ship safety, but about obstructing SAR operations.[58]

As for externalisation, this is first and foremost about outsourcing a legally constructed understanding of border control and, in this sense, it cannot be dissociated from such legal construction. Perhaps one of the most relevant EU provisions here is Article 3(2) of the Treaty on EU, which offers EU citizens an 'area of freedom, security and justice', associating it with the (securitised) need to protect external borders. It is this external border control that is outsourced. This is complemented by national legal frameworks of border control and international agreements. Challenging externalisation might be merely about contesting the competence of a specific actor in 'protecting' EU external borders, but when coupled with critiques of securitisation and criminalisation, it becomes clear that civil society actors' posts cannot be reduced to such an interpretation. Indeed, their critiques disseminated in the online public sphere are both about the way in which border control is conceived and about its outsourcing to a third state.

Externalisation might be achieved through formal treaties, such as readmission agreements, but is mostly carried out through arguably informal agreements, such as Memoranda of Understanding.[59] The agreement most relevant to the examined civil society actors' posts is the infamous Italy-Libya Memorandum

[55] See n 52.

[56] Carrera et al (n 53).

[57] Alarm Phone, 'Seizure of vessel' (Twitter, 2 September 2019), available at twitter.com/alarm_phone/status/1168486689368621057?s=20.

[58] Sea Watch International, 'Port State Control Imposed' (Twitter, 19 September 2020), available at twitter.com/seawatch_intl/status/1307250490665840643?s=20.

[59] Its understanding as non-binding informal agreement is disputed in public international law. See J Klabbers, *International Law* (Cambridge University Press, 2013) 45.

of Understanding signed in 2017 and renewed in 2020.[60] Under the agreement, Italy offers investments for economic development and stability, as well as border security instruments and equipment, while Libya undertakes to intercept boats in distress and prevent migrants from reaching Europe. This Memorandum of Understanding is complemented by the cooperation between the EU and Libya, allowing Libya to receive funding under the EU Emergency Trust Fund for Africa to strengthen its capacity in border management, mainly through equipment and training. The EU also provides assistance to the Libyan Coast Guard through civil and military missions under its Common Security and Defence Policy.[61] These various arrangements are legally enabled in different ways, including through the concept of sovereignty in public international law, the EU provisions on common foreign and security policy and the EU Financial Regulation allowing the Commission to create and administer trust funds in relation to external action.[62]

The examined Twitter posts consistently denounce pushbacks to Libya, emphasising that Libya is not a safe place to disembark nor a safe country to return migrants to. In this sense, they implicitly – and sometimes explicitly – rely on the international law of the sea, as well as European and international human rights or refugee law for criticising the actions supported by a framework of collaboration between Italy, the EU and Libya.[63] MSF, for instance, reported that an Italian captain faced a legal action for sending rescued migrants back to Libya, stressing that 'Libya is not considered a place of safety under international law'.[64]

In conclusion, civil society actors' posts on securitisation, criminalisation and externalisation offer powerful critiques of the way in which migration is managed by the EU and its Member States, exposing continuities with previous restrictive policies of the 'crisis' mode of governance. These critiques produce and are part of a transnational networked public sphere and cannot be dissociated from the legal arrangements that structure EU migration governance. These are also politically meaningful forms of participating in the public sphere that are not usually associated with traditional humanitarianism. The latter is generally defined as based on

[60] 'Memorandum of understanding on cooperation in the fields of development, the fight against illegal immigration, human trafficking and fuel smuggling and on reinforcing the security of borders between the State of Libya and the Italian Republic' (2017), available at eumigrationlawblog.eu/wp-content/uploads/2017/10/MEMORANDUM_translation_finalversion.doc.pdf.

[61] These missions include EUBAM Libya and EUNAVFOR MED IRINI.

[62] Council Regulation (EU, Euratom) 2018/1046 of 18 July 2018 on the financial rules applicable to the general budget of the Union [2018] OJ L193/1.

[63] International Convention on Maritime Search and Rescue (adopted 27 April 1979, entered into force 22 June 1985) 1405 UNTS 119 (SAR Convention); Convention for the Protection of Human Rights and Fundamental Freedoms (European Convention on Human Rights, as amended) (ECHR) Art 3; Charter of Fundamental Rights of the European Union (EU Charter of Fundamental Rights, as amended) Arts 4, 18.

[64] MSF Sea, 'Pushbacks to Libya' (Twitter, 20 July 2020), available at twitter.com/MSF_Sea/status/1285195287489851392?s=20.

'apolitical' critiques of lacking commitments to provide sufficient SAR capacities.[65] The following section will elaborate further on these actors' politics and explore whether and to what extent alternative framings emerge from their posts.

IV. Towards a Solidarity-Based Humanitarianism?

The critiques posted by civil society actors herein examined go beyond traditional allegedly apolitical humanitarian concerns of insufficient commitments to ensure the saving of lives at sea. Indeed, they openly expose the relationship between migrants' deaths in the Mediterranean and EU and/or Member States' policies of securitisation, externalisation and criminalisation. This stands in contrast with official institutional narratives – to which one of the first NGOs operating in the Mediterranean, Migrant Offshore Aid Station (MOAS), openly adhered – that smugglers are the main evil-doers.[66]

The shift in the discourses of some of the examined civil society actors here has been already emphasised by Stierl and Esperti.[67] The emphasis on the 'political' is less surprising for the Alarm Phone network, created explicitly with a political project of open borders embedded in critiques of forms of global injustice.[68] However, concerning the other examined actors, who identify themselves as actors dealing with humanitarian action, this shows the possibility of developing a networked political space from within humanitarianism.[69] It is also worth noting that such discourses – though with some variations – can be identified both in the posts of MSF, an established large NGO, and more recent citizen-centred initiatives.

These findings bring some nuances to Siapera's argument that grassroot initiatives are more prone to produce networked alternatives to both humanitarianism and security-centred narratives. Indeed, when it comes to SAR activities, as this section will show, some important variations are produced both by citizen-based initiatives and an established NGO *within* humanitarianism, modifying its traditional meaning. It is no longer understood as a pity-based apolitical project of saving 'bare lives' and it is no longer deprived of concerns about the conditions that created migrants' suffering.[70] In this sense, Siapera's findings are best approached

[65] M Stierl, 'A Fleet of Mediterranean Border Humanitarians' and W Walters, 'Foucault and Frontiers: Notes on the Birth of the Humanitarian Border' in U Bröckling, S Krasmann and T Lemke (eds) *Governmentality: Current Issues and Future Challenges* (Routledge, 2011).

[66] ibid. MOAS interrupted its operations in the Mediterranean in October 2017, which is the main reason why it was not included in the actors examined here.

[67] Stierl, 'A Fleet' (2011); Esperti (n 29).

[68] M Stierl, 'A sea of struggle: Activist border interventions in the Mediterranean Sea' (2016) 20 *Citizenship Studies* 561.

[69] Stierl (n 65).

[70] Siapera (n 13); G Agamben, *Homo Sacer: Sovereign Power and Bare Life* (D Heller-Roazen tr, Stanford University Press, 1998).

as limited to a certain type of humanitarianism to be situated in a 'wide humanitarian spectrum', in which there might be space for alternative solidarity-based approaches.[71] Also, while the type of actor matters, the failure or success to move away from dominant framings cannot depend entirely on whether it is an established large NGO or a grassroot initiative.

Not all the actors examined here develop explicit arguments on solidarity with migrants, but the posts published by each of them show indeed the seeds of such emerging alternative approaches. The actors with the strongest explicit commitments to migrant solidarity are Alarm Phone, Sea Watch and Open Arms. When the New Pact on Migration and Asylum was first published on the European Commission's website, Alarm Phone openly defined its understanding of solidarity in opposition to the way in which it is conceptualised on the EU institutional level:

> Europe defines solidarity as a 'return sponsorship' that will strengthen European collaborations on deporting people who seek to live in Europe in peace. We define solidarity as standing with those who Europe wants to deter, deport, or drown out.[72]

In this sense, Alarm Phone stresses the importance of defining solidarity in relation to migrants, instead of confining it to an expanded version of 'burden sharing' among Member States that complements relocation measures with return sponsorships. Similar framings appear in the posts of Sea Watch and Open Arms. Indeed, both organisations seem to approach rescue as an act of solidarity with migrants, while acknowledging that mere rescue is not a sufficient solution. Reporting a successful operation at sea, for instance, Open Arms stresses that the rescue boat is first and foremost a group of citizens and that solidarity should also accompany migrants after disembarking in a safe port.[73] As for Sea Watch, quoting Captain Carola Rackete, it approaches the court decision in favour of the captain as a 'big win for #solidarity with all people on the move, and against the criminalisation of helpers'.[74] In this sense, decriminalisation of SAR activities is conceived as part of a broader politics of solidarity with migrants.

Both Alarm Phone and Sea Watch have also criticised the criminalisation of migrants in addition to that of SAR civil society actors. They denounced the terrorism charges brought by Maltese authorities against three teenagers who protested against rescued migrants' return to Libya by a commercial vessel that performed the rescue operations.[75] Their protest eventually led to the disembarking of

[71] Stierl (n 65).

[72] Alarm Phone, 'NGO Solidarity' (Twitter, 23 September 2020), available at twitter.com/alarm_phone/status/1308766906053259264?s=20.

[73] Open Arms, 'Solidarity Assurance for Migrants' (Twitter, 15 January 2020), available at twitter.com/openarms_found/status/1217494322515447809?s=20.

[74] Sea Watch International (Twitter, n 36).

[75] Sea Watch International, 'Migrants Enforce Rights' (Twitter, 14 May 2019), available at twitter.com/seawatch_intl/status/1128372164531503110?s=20; Alarm Phone, 'Distress Call' (Twitter, 21 November 2019), available at twitter.com/alarm_phone/status/1196720346780581888?s=20.

105 migrants in Malta, where they faced criminal charges. The posts related to this event show an approach based on solidarity and empathy, in which similar experiences of criminalisation bring migrants and civil society actors closer to one another.

The two organisations, together with Sea Watch, have also expressed their solidarity with the Black Lives Matter movement shortly after the murder of George Floyd, denouncing 'the systemic forms of racist violence' both in the Mediterranean and in the US.[76] Alarm Phone stressed that an additional form of violence of the European border regime lies in the difficulty of verifying the identities of missing migrants, making 'black lives ungrievable'.[77]

Discourses of solidarity with migrants are less intense in the Twitter posts of MSF and SOS Méditerranée, but the seeds of it are present nevertheless. Quite surprisingly, such solidarity is stronger in MSF's posts, despite its established status and its previous explicit adherence to a more traditional allegedly apolitical conception of humanitarianism.[78] However, in contrast to Alarm Phone, Sea Watch and Open Arms, neither actor has expressed its solidarity with criminalised migrants or with the Black Lives Matter movement.

On the humanitarian spectrum, MSF is closer than SOS Méditerranée to solidarity framings, but it is further away than Alarm Phone, Sea Watch and Open Arms. Some of its posts show an explicit association between solidarity and the need for governments to offer places of safety for migrants' disembarkations instead of orchestrating their return to Libya.[79] Moreover, somewhat similarly to Alarm Phone, it expressed its critical positioning in relation to the contradiction between European Commission's statements of solidarity and the deaths in the Mediterranean produced by EU migration governance.[80]

This marks an important difference with the way in which SOS Méditerranée uses the concept of solidarity. Indeed, its posts show an approach concerned with the insufficient capacities of frontline Member States to deal with boat migration, requiring the EU to step up its SAR efforts.[81] In this sense, it seems to demand

[76] Alarm Phone, 'All Black Lives Matter' (Twitter, 28 May 2020), available at twitter.com/alarm_phone/status/1266056451358961665?s=20; Sea Watch, 'Black Lives Matter' (Twitter, 2 June 2020), available at twitter.com/seawatch_intl/status/1267789745540739073?s=20; Open Arms, 'Black Lives Matter Solidarity' (Twitter, 1, and 7 June 2020), available at twitter.com/openarms_found/status/1267560800178311170?s=20 and and twitter.com/openarms_found/status/1269740255319597056?s=20.

[77] Alarm Phone, 'Violence of the Border Regime' (Twitter, 27 August 2020), available at twitter.com/alarm_phone/status/1299007141882327040?s=20.

[78] Stierl (n 65).

[79] MSF Sea, 'Hopes for EU Solidarity' (Twitter, 7 August and 23 October 2019), available at twitter.com/MSF_Sea/status/1159115863292874753?s=20 and twitter.com/MSF_Sea/status/1187083119993720832?s=20.

[80] MSF Sea, 'Questioning EU Solidarity' (Twitter, 5 March 2020), available at twitter.com/MSF_Sea/status/1235522947932205056?s=20.

[81] SOS Méditerranée, 'Call for EU Solidarity' (Twitter, 15 April 2020), available at twitter.com/SOSMedIntl/status/1250504582863691779?s=20.

solidarity of the EU towards its Member States rather than towards migrants.[82] However, it would be wrong to deny the presence of any migrant-oriented approach, at least because SOS Méditerranée has consistently stressed the need for the EU to ensure disembarkations in a place of safety instead of funding the Libyan coastguard.[83] In other words, it is concerned with migrants' treatment after disembarkation and not merely their rescue, but without using an explicit language of migrant-centred solidarity. Its cautious approach, despite it being a recently created citizen-based organisation, might be explained in part through its emphasis on 'professionalism' and its partnerships with more established NGOs, such as Médicins du Monde and the Dutch Operational Centre of MSF.[84] Paradoxically, however, MSF has adopted a stronger solidarity-based approach than SOS Méditerranée.

From a legal perspective, the migrant-centred solidarity framing has important implications on the ways in which legal alternatives to dominant narratives of European migration governance can be imagined. Alarm Phone is the only one among the examined actors to base its framings on critiques of global injustices without defining itself as a humanitarian actor and, in this sense, one would expect for its proposed alternative to be most radical. However, a great similarity exists between Sea Watch and Alarm Phone, both advocating for migrants' freedom of movement and the creation of safe legal routes to reach the EU, in addition to decriminalisation and the need to respect already existing provisions of the international law of the sea and European human rights law. Open Arms, though producing a discourse of solidarity similar to that of Sea Watch and Alarm Phone, refrains from advocating for freedom of movement and safe legal passage. Its migrant-centred conception of solidarity, however, calls for a development of its politics in such direction.

MSF goes further than Open Arms and stresses the importance of providing safe legal routes for migrants to reach the EU, without advocating for freedom of movement.[85] As for SOS Méditerranée, it limits itself mainly to the need to comply with the existing provisions of the international law of the sea and human rights law, without proposing radical changes to the current EU legal system. The only change would concern the decriminalisation of SAR activities, which would presumably take place on the level of domestic criminal legislation.

Despite their differences, all the actors examined here develop a networked political space in which the legal framings of securitisation, criminalisation

[82] SOS Méditerranée, 'State Solidarity' (Twitter, 8 April 2020), available at twitter.com/SOSMedIntl/status/1247963768195293184?s=20.

[83] SOS Méditerranée, 'Demands for EU Actions' (Twitter, 1 November 2019 and 24 September 2020), available at twitter.com/sosmedintl/status/1190339488922423297?s=21 and twitter.com/SOSMedIntl/status/1309177749974773760?s=20.

[84] Esperti (n 29) 442.

[85] MSF Sea, 'New Approach to Migrant Safety' (Twitter, 4 January and 24 September 2020), available at twitter.com/MSF_Sea/status/1213404073652899840?s=20 and twitter.com/MSF_Sea/status/1309108690784485382?s=20.

and externalisation are destabilised. The most radical alternatives appear in the posts of Alarm Phone and Sea Watch, followed by MSF and Open Arms. SOS Méditerranée is the most cautious, but its concern of migrants' treatment after disembarkation calls for the development of a politics of solidarity with migrants. In this sense, a legal-oriented analysis of 'networked framings' on migration is a promising avenue for identifying possible alternatives to dominant migration legal frameworks.

V. Conclusion

This chapter has stressed that civil society actors' social media platforms can be approached as constituting networked public spheres in which legal framings are (re)produced and potentially transformed. This chapter is an invitation to pursue such future research from a legal perspective informed by the concept of networked framings developed in media and communication studies. From a constitutional standpoint, it means highlighting the 'networked' ways of practicing rights to dissent and democratic participation, broadly understood. The visibility and plurality of forms of practicing such rights are particularly important in the context of migration, as migrants are often deprived of citizenship rights.

Taking the example of actors operating in the context of SAR in the Mediterranean, it has been argued that such an approach facilitates the visibility of alternatives to dominant legal framings on migration. This has been shown to be the case even for actors who define themselves as humanitarian, traditionally understood as neutral but ultimately inescapably political. Visibility is often seen as a crucial opportunity offered by social media.[86] Reaching a wide audience through the following function, but also through likes, retweets and comments, Twitter accounts make institutional practices and ideologies visible, as well as migrants' stories and experiences. While such visibility produces a networked public sphere, it cannot be entirely controlled and might also be used for surveillance purposes by public authorities. Social media remains, however, a fruitful site for exploring alternatives to dominant legal framings.

An analysis of the posts published by some of the most active civil society actors in the context of SAR shows that both established NGOs and more recent citizen-based initiatives elaborate similar critiques of dominant framings of migration. It is unclear whether grassroot initiatives related to SAR created in the context of the so-called migration crisis have had a determining influence on more established actors like MSF. However, considering the varying degrees of development of migrant-centred solidarity by the two types of actors, their failure or success to move away from dominant framings cannot be said to depend

[86] KE Pearce, J Vitak and K Barta, 'Socially Mediated Visibility: Friendship and Dissent in Authoritarian Azerbaijan' (2018) 12 *International Journal of Communication* 1310.

exclusively on its established or grassroots character. This is not to say, however, that such character is not important; it might indeed be significant in terms of shaping larger NGOs.

Securitisation of migration policies, criminalisation of NGOs and externalisation of border controls are all overlapping common themes in the examined critiques. They are also the main features of the EU 'migration crisis' governance, denounced by civil society actors even after the European Commission declared that 'Europe is no longer in crisis mode'.[87] Securitisation is the widest among the three, in the sense that it includes criminalisation and externalisation. In other words, what is being challenged is the security framing of migration, as well as its ramifications. Such critiques often explicitly link the actions of the EU or its Member States to migrants' deaths in the Mediterranean, as well as their mistreatment in disembarking or return processes. They are formulations of political dissent and ways of democratic participation which can take place even within humanitarianism.

Finally, this chapter has also shown that SAR civil society actors' social media posts produce some version of migrant-centred solidarity from which political and legal projects emerge with some variations. The most radical projects advocate for freedom of movement and the creation of safe legal routes to reach the EU, in addition to decriminalisation and the need to respect existing international and European legal frameworks. In this sense, researching social media platforms of civil society actors can be a promising way of identifying alternatives to dominant legal framings of migration.

[87] See n 25.

5

Social Media and the News Industry

ALESSIO CORNIA

I. Introduction

Social media platforms such as Facebook, Twitter and Instagram are now key actors in our news ecosystem and play a central role in connecting audiences with the institutional, political and social actors involved in the production of public and political communication. Because of this increased centrality, platforms are now able to establish asymmetric power relationships with a variety of institutions and organisations, including news media, and thus are strongly contributing to the transformation of the communicative space wherein the interactions among these actors, and between them and the public, take place.

Based on the most recent research on news consumption, news industry developments, and algorithmic selection, this chapter addresses, first, the major changes in the media environment associated with the rise of social media platforms and, second, the implications of these changes in terms of information inequality, fragmentation and polarisation. We argue that, although social media platforms can clearly favour the exercise of constitutional rights such as freedom of expression, access to information and citizens' ability to participate in the public debate, they also pose challenges for democratic institutions. In particular, we will discuss how social media are overtaking legacy news media in their gatekeeping role, as today the selection of the information that circulates in our society is increasingly operated by algorithms and social media platforms, and how this might endanger our democracy's ability to rely on professional journalism. Furthermore, we will discuss how social media affects fundamental rights such as universal access to information, and we will consider hypotheses which postulate that social media reduces the diversity of information citizens are exposed to (possibly leading users towards extreme viewpoints). We will finally see how empirical research on these issues is still inconclusive and does not fully support these concerns.

The term 'social media' is used here to refer to 'web-based services that allow individuals, communities, and organizations to collaborate, connect, interact, and build community by enabling them to create, co-create, modify, share, and engage with user-generated content that is easily accessible'.[1] This definition emphasises, first, the fact that social media allows for the creation and exchange of user-generated content (UGC), rather than content produced by professionals and distributed by the organisations they work for. Second, the definition stresses the participatory culture that is enabled by social media, ie the fact that these platforms enable people to connect with others who share similar interests and facilitate collaboration.[2] The terms 'digital platforms' and 'digital intermediaries' are used in a broader way and refer to both social networking sites (like Facebook) and search engines (like Google).

In section II of this chapter we will address two major changes in our news environment: the rise of social media platforms, which now represent an important source of news for many people; and the simultaneous decline of legacy news organisations, which – especially in the case of newspapers – are less effective than in the past in reaching audiences and generating revenues. We will also see how the decline of traditional news organisations represents a risk for the very survival of professional journalism, as newspapers and broadcasters still employ the large majority of existing journalists and therefore still play a major role in funding professional journalism. In section III, we will focus on three major implications of these changes. First, we will discuss how the reliance of news organisations upon social media for news distribution contributes to increasing the power that platforms exert on journalism and the news industry. Second, we will see how platforms are increasingly able to affect the public debate and to select the events that are worth of public attention. Finally, we will discuss some perspectives, such as the filter bubbles and echo chamber theses, which postulate that social media might exacerbate existing inequalities in information access and contribute to the increased fragmentation and polarisation of our society.

II. Major Changes Associated with the Rise of Social Media

A. Social Media Increasingly Used as Source of News

The first change in the media environment that we address here is the fact that people increasingly find the news through social networking services

[1] L McCay-Peet and A Quan-Haase, 'What is Social Media and What Questions Can Social Media Research Help Us Answer?' in Luke Sloan and Annabel Quan-Haase (eds), *The SAGE Handbook of Social Media Research Methods* (SAGE, 2017) 17.

[2] H Jenkins, *Fans, Bloggers, and Gamers: Exploring Participatory Culture* (New York University Press, 2006).

like Facebook and other digital intermediaries like Google. News organisations across the world report that a significant part of their online traffic does not come direct to their websites or apps, but rather from search engines and social media that refer audiences to them. This applies to both legacy players (such as newspapers and broadcasters) and digital-born outlets (which have started their operations in the digital age and offer online-only news services).[3] In other words, both well-established players like, for example, *The Daily Telegraph*, and comparatively newer outlets like BuzzFeed News and the HuffPost, have to increasingly interact with digital platforms, as using these platforms in a strategic and effective manner has a substantial impact on their online traffic. The Italian newspaper *La Repubblica*, for instance, reported that, in 2018, approximately 15 per cent of their website's traffic arrived from social networks (mainly Facebook), 20–25 per cent from search engines (mainly Google), and only the remaining 60–65 per cent was direct traffic or internal circulation (ie users who directly went to the news outlet website/app or internal referrals).[4]

Figure 5.1 Sources of news 2013–2021 in the US and the UK

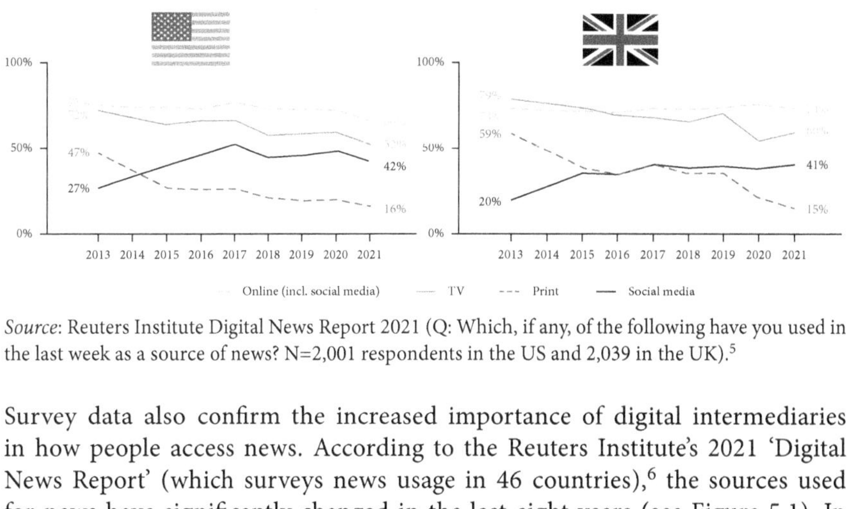

Source: Reuters Institute Digital News Report 2021 (Q: Which, if any, of the following have you used in the last week as a source of news? N=2,001 respondents in the US and 2,039 in the UK).[5]

Survey data also confirm the increased importance of digital intermediaries in how people access news. According to the Reuters Institute's 2021 'Digital News Report' (which surveys news usage in 46 countries),[6] the sources used for news have significantly changed in the last eight years (see Figure 5.1). In both the US and the UK (selected as examples of Western countries marked by high levels of technological development), social media use for news has significantly grown (especially between 2013 and 2017), while newspaper readership

[3] RK Nielsen and SA Ganter, 'Dealing with Digital Intermediaries: A Case Study of the Relations between Publishers and Platforms' (2018) 20 *New Media & Society* 1600.

[4] A Cornia et al, *Private Sector News, Social Media Distribution, and Algorithm Change* (Reuters Institute, 2018).

[5] N Newman et al, *Reuters Institute Digital News Report 2021* (Reuters Institute, 2021).

[6] ibid.

has declined, to the extent that, today, social media platforms are used for news more frequently than printed newspapers. In the UK, for example, 41 per cent of survey respondents use social media for news on a weekly basis, while only 15 per cent use printed newspapers. The same trend is observed in all the European countries and in most of the other countries included in the Reuters study: even in countries traditionally marked by high newspaper circulation, such as Germany and Finland, or in countries marked by a more vibrant and recent growth of the newspaper industry, such as India, social media is used for news more frequently than newspapers. One of the few outliers is Japan, where – according to the same survey – printed newspapers are used for news by 27 per cent of the respondents, while social media only by 24 per cent. The survey also shows that people use social media for news either because they consider them good places to find, for example, breaking news, local news or alternative perspectives that are not offered by mainstream media, or just because they are incidentally exposed to the news while navigating social media for other reasons.

Although Facebook's use as a news source is slightly declining, probably because of fears associated with the spread of disinformation and divisive content, this platform remains the most popular one: 44 per cent of the respondents across all the 46 countries surveyed in 2021 used it weekly for finding, sharing or discussing news. Other social media platforms used for news include YouTube (29 per cent), Twitter (13 per cent), Instagram (13 per cent) and TikTok (four per cent among all ages, but 31 per cent among those aged 18–24).[7]

How digital platforms have changed the way people discover and find the news is also shown in Figure 5.2. Across all 46 countries, just 25 per cent of the respondents get their news by directly going to the website or app of a news outlet. At the same time, 73 per cent find news through social networking sites, search engines, news aggregators, mobile notifications or via email. These patterns are even more evident when looking at younger people's news consumption patterns (see under-35s in Figure 5.2).

Therefore, direct access to news outlets' homepages or apps, which used to be the main gateways to news, is now overtaken by side-door access, and news is predominantly encountered when using the services provided by digital intermediaries. Compared to what most news outlets can currently offer, digital intermediaries are able to present more personalised services, such as news shared by friends or selected by algorithms on the basis of people's interests and connections. As Nielsen and Fletcher put it,

> this is an epochal shift on how news is distributed and curated. … [Our current] digital media environment is increasingly defined by algorithmically based forms of personalization, as people rely on products and services like search engines and social media that do not create content but help users discover content.[8]

[7] ibid.

[8] RK Nielsen and R Fletcher, 'Democratic Creative Destruction? The Effect of a Changing Media Landscape on Democracy' in N Persily and JA Tucker (eds), *Social Media and Democracy: The State of the Field and Prospects for Reform* (Cambridge University Press, 2020) 150.

Figure 5.2 Main gateways to news by age

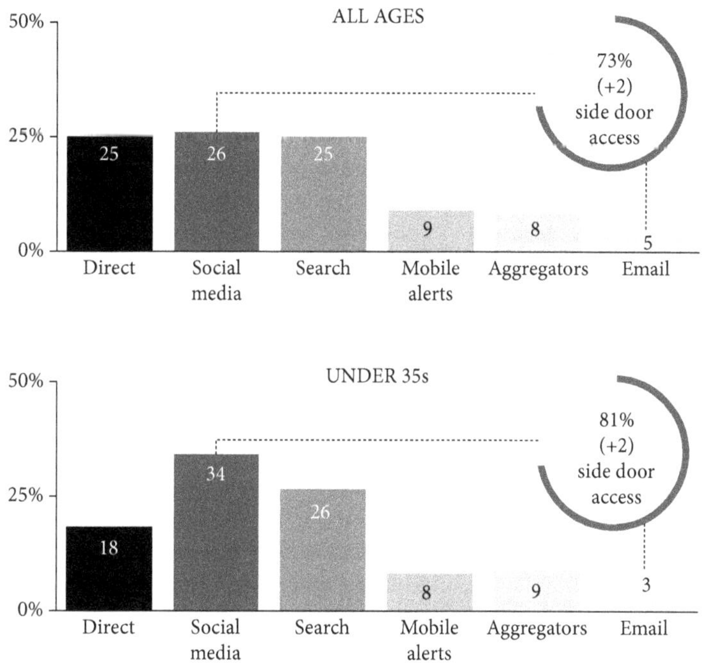

Source: Reuters Institute's 2021 'Digital News Report' (Q: Which of these was the main way in which you came across news in the last week? Base: all/U35 that came across news online last week in all 46 countries).[9]

B. The Declining Power of News Media

Partially associated with the rise of social media, the second change we address is the decreasing centrality of traditional media outlets. Legacy news media such as newspapers and broadcasters have also dealt with the digital transformation of the media environment and developed online news products. However, legacy players are today less effective in reaching audiences and hold a less relevant position in the news ecosystem. In the traditional media environment, they used to detain quasi-monopolistic positions in connecting audiences with media content, as well as in connecting advertisers with audiences. Depending on national and regional contexts, for audiences looking for media content there were few alternatives to newspapers and broadcasters, as well as for advertisers looking for audiences. Instead, today the competition for audience's attention is fierce, and digital platforms are able to attract most digital advertising revenues as they provide advertisers with wider audiences and more targeted

[9] Newman et al (n 5).

and cheaper advertising.[10,11] The Italian case can serve as an example of the weaker position of legacy media, which seems to be even worsened by the consequences of the COVID-19 pandemic. Because of the economic downturn that followed the breakout of the pandemic and the general implementation of lockdown measures, newspaper and broadcasting advertising decreased by 15 per cent and 8 per cent respectively in the first nine months of 2020. Instead, online advertising grew (+7 per cent). Major online platforms, which already attract approximately 80 per cent of online advertising expenditures in Italy, are the only players that have benefitted from this increase (+11 per cent), while publishers have had significant losses in this market (–7 per cent).[12] Despite its growth, digital advertising is a market where news organisations face serious challenges in competing with digital intermediaries, and so far the revenues generated cannot compensate for the losses in their legacy business.[13] It is worth noting that legacy news media are still a reputable source of news and their content also circulates on other media, including social media, but their ability to reach and monetise audiences online is tempered by digital intermediaries' primacy and effectiveness in this domain.

Other examples of the declining position of legacy news media can be found in Table 5.1, which shows longer-term changes in newspaper circulation, TV advertising and newspaper advertising in a selection of European countries. The data illustrates how both newspaper circulation and advertising revenues have dramatically declined in all the selected countries (particularly dramatically in, eg, Italy and Poland). At the same time, television advertising trends are mixed, with some countries (eg, Italy) facing more severe decreases, while others enjoy more stable or even positive trends (eg, the UK). This data exemplifies how legacy organisations, especially newspapers, need to find new ways to get in touch with audiences and to monetise their news operations. Indeed, digital advertising expenditures have grown for several years, but as reported in several industry studies, major digital platforms are able to attract the most advertising revenue, and legacy players still face challenges in sustaining their digital operations. A 2016 study on the changing business of news in six European countries, for example, reported that, even after years of decline of print circulation and advertising, and almost two decades of investment in digital media, the business model of top newspapers was still excessively reliant on their declining legacy operations, and only 10–20 per cent of their overall revenues were coming from their digital operations.[14] Therefore, digital developments enabled legacy players to innovate and reach broader audiences (at least in the case of newspapers), but how to monetise this broad online reach is still an issue of major concern within the news industry.

[10] A Cornia, A Sehl and RK Nielsen, *Private Sector Media and Digital News* (Reuters Institute, 2016).
[11] RK Nielsen 'The Business of News' in T Witschge et al (eds) *The SAGE Handbook of Digital Journalism* (SAGE, 2016).
[12] AGCOM, 'Communication Markets Monitoring System: Covid 19 Monitoring' (Autorità per le Garanzie nelle Comunicazioni; Italy 2021), available at www.agcom.it/osservatorio-sulle-comunicazioni.
[13] Cornia et al, *Private Sector Media* (2016).
[14] ibid.

Table 5.1 Change in media use and advertising expenditure in traditional media in six European countries from 2010 to 2014/15 as percentages

	Finland	France	Germany	Italy	Poland	UK
Change in newspaper circulation 2010/15	-22%	-15%	-17%	-35%	-37%	-31%
Change in TV advertising 2010/14	-0.4%	-6%	-9%	-27%	5%	17%
Change in newspaper advertising 2010/15	-25%	-26%	-20%	-50%	-63%	-31%

Source: Cornia, Sehl, and Nielsen (2016) Private sector media and digital news. Oxford: Reuters Institute's Report.[15]

The decline of legacy news media potentially bears negative implications for democracy, as traditional broadcasters and, especially, newspaper organisations play a fundamental role in funding professional journalism.[16] Although journalism often plays an ambiguous role (eg when it produces partisan or sensational coverage), rather than the idealised and romanticised role that is implied in many professional, academic and media discourses, independent and professionally produced news plays an important democratic role, as it has long contributed to informing the public and helping citizens make sense of public affairs. Moreover, it has provided information, analysis and opinions on key political events and contributed to keeping elites accountable by exposing corruption and political misbehaviours.[17]

The limited ability of legacy news media to reach audiences and generate revenues online is thus worrisome, as newspaper and broadcasting organisations are still the actors that invest the most in professional journalism. In the UK, for example, newspapers and magazines alone have been estimated to account for 69 per cent of total investment in news production in 2011, commercial broadcasters a further 10 per cent, the BBC 21 per cent, and digital-born outlets only one per cent.[18] In other words, neither news outlets that have started their operations online nor digital intermediaries employ a significant share of professional journalists, nor are expected to play a major role in funding journalism in the near future. The decline of legacy media, therefore, concerns not only the news

[15] ibid.
[16] JT Hamilton, *All the News that's Fit to Sell: How the Market Transforms Information into News* (Princeton University Press, 2004).
[17] Nielsen and Fletcher, 'Democratic Creative Destruction?' (2020).
[18] Mediatique, 'The Provision of News in the UK' (Mediatique Report for Ofcom, 2012).

outlets in question but also, more generally, the very survival of professional journalism in itself,[19] at least in its current form. To be fair, social media can also benefit journalism, which for example can now rely on a more active contribution by audiences, which participate in news production and distribution through citizen journalism initiatives and social media sharing. However, the role of news organisations in favouring journalists' adherence to established professional standards can hardly be maintained in this modern, fluid environment where news organisations play only a marginal role.

III. The Implications of the Rise of Social Media and Decline of News Media

A. Platforms Affect Journalism, as News Media Become More Dependent on Them

As a result of the scenario described above, news organisations rely heavily on social media to reach new and wider online audiences. By doing so, they contribute to increasing the power social media platforms exert on journalism and the news industry.

Both public service media and commercial news outlets in Europe have strongly invested in news distribution on social media. In addition to investing in sponsoring their content on platforms and creating specific pages and accounts to push their news among social media users, news organisations have created new job profiles and established dedicated teams to develop and implement strategies for maximising the reach of their content on social media platforms. In 2018, for example, the BBC had seven social media editors in its core team, as well as several social media editors working for specific topic pages, and approximately 15 journalists working for the user-generated content team.[20] Each publisher has developed its own social media publication strategy based on their specific editorial and commercial aims. News organisations strongly focused on traffic and advertising like the Italian newspaper *La Repubblica*, for example, published an average of 72 news posts per day on Facebook in 2018, while newspapers more focused on subscriptions such as the German *Süddeutsche Zeitung* or the British *The Times* published respectively 30 and 19 posts per day.[21]

The reason news organisations invest so much in social media distribution is that platforms provide them with an easy, effective and cheap way to increase

[19] A Cornia, A Sehl and RK Nielsen, 'Comparing Legacy Media Responses to a Changing Business of News: Cross-National Similarities and Differences across Media Types' (2019) 6–8 *International Communication Gazette* 686.

[20] A Sehl, A Cornia and RK Nielsen, *Public Service News and Social Media* (Reuters Institute, 2018).

[21] Cornia et al (n 4).

the online reach of their content and attract new and broader audiences, especially among younger age groups. Overall, the aim is to monetise this expanded online reach by referring social media users to the news organisations' websites, to monetise them with digital advertising or by trying to convert them into digital subscribers of the news outlet.[22] Therefore, social media brings *opportunities* for publishers, and this is the reason why news organisations engage in social media publishing, contributing de facto to strengthening the role of platforms as the new intermediaries between institutional, political, business and social actors, and users.

But social media also brings high risks for legacy media. First, news media risk becoming too dependent on platforms, which are increasingly able to influence news organisations' decisions and editorial choices. As we have seen, Twitter, TikTok, Instagram and especially Facebook drive significant traffic to news organisations' websites but, in order to maximise these numbers, news outlets have to adapt to the social media logic, tailoring their strategies to the workings of social media platforms and being ready to respond to the dynamics of social media platforms. For example, recent research demonstrated that established newspaper organisations have significantly invested in audiovisual units within their newsrooms to respond to Facebook's decision to prioritise online videos on its newsfeed in 2014.[23] Audiovisual content was not part of their core operations, but new strategies were focused on this format, as it was driving more engagement and reach on Facebook. Similarly, several European newspapers and broadcasters have strongly increased their frequency of publication to respond to the 2018 algorithm change that was expected to deprioritise news content on Facebook.[24] By adjusting their social media tactics, editorial strategies and organisational structures to respond to social media algorithm tweaks, news organisations are exposing the journalistic field to the influence of actors that are external to journalism. Additionally, several news outlets have been significantly affected by this algorithm change, which determined less visibility for their news content, a decrease in traffic referral, and a drop in users' engagement on the social media platform.[25] This testifies how a sudden and unilateral change in the workings of platforms' algorithms can have implications for news organisations that strongly rely on news distribution on social media.

More broadly, if publishers rely too much on platforms, they risk, in the long run, losing control of their distribution channels and of the direct contact with their public. In 2016, Emily Bell, director of the Tow Center for Digital Journalism, emphasised that news organisations risk reducing their role to that of mere content

[22] ibid.
[23] EC Tandoc Jr and J Maitra 'News organizations' use of Native Videos on Facebook: Tweaking the journalistic field one algorithm change at a time' (2018) 20 *New Media & Society* 1679.
[24] Cornia et al (n 4).
[25] ibid.

providers for platforms – ie producers of professional content that is then used by big tech corporations to offer engaging stories to their own users. In other words, they risk delegating to platforms the relationship with the audience. As Bell puts it:

> Publishers have lost control over [news] distribution. … Now the news is filtered through algorithms and platforms which are opaque and unpredictable. … Social media hasn't just swallowed journalism, it has swallowed everything: … political campaigns, banking systems, personal histories, the leisure industry, retail, even government and security.[26]

Therefore, social media platforms are affecting journalism because they bring both exciting opportunities and high risk for publishers. Publishers know platforms are winning the battle over advertising revenues and people's attention and are equally aware of the risks associated with social media distribution, but they struggle to find a balance between short-term opportunities and long-term risks,[27] which is apparent in the following quote from an interview made by the author of this chapter with a manager of France Télévisions:

> With platforms, there is the risk of losing control over your distribution process and, possibly, over the relationship we have with our audience. At the same time, if we don't go there, we risk losing a large part of the audience: young people who don't watch TV (Eric Scherer, Director of Future Media, France Télévisions, France. Interview published in: Sehl, Cornia, Nielsen, 2016).[28]

From this, it is clear how news organisations feel the pressure to adapt to the social media platforms' workings. If they do not do so, they fear losing a large part of the audience that they have increased difficulties with reaching through their own channels (print copies, broadcasts, news websites, news apps, etc). Adapting to the social media logic could be, in the short run, quite rewarding. In recent years, for example, several digital-born outlets such as Now This or BuzzFeed News have entered and found a position in an already crowded news market thanks to a period of intense and effective use of social media. However, it is evident that the more news organisations rely on social media platforms for news distribution, the more they become dependent on them and subject to their volatile policies. This further exposes news outlets and their journalistic outputs to the influence of powerful tech corporations that, rather than adhering to the journalistic professional standards that have long contributed to the better functioning of our democracies, predominantly seek to attract users' attention and monetise it with digital advertising.

While news organisations have struggled for decades to find an acceptable balance between their public service mission (represented by the editorial

[26] E Bell, 'Facebook is Eating the World' (2016) *Columbia Journalism Review*, available at www.cjr.org/analysis/facebook_and_media.php.

[27] Nielsen and Ganter, 'Dealing with Digital Intermediaries' (2018).

[28] A Sehl, A Cornia and RK Nielsen, *Public Service News and Digital Media* (Reuters Institute, 2016).

side of news organisations) and their commercial imperatives (represented by the business side),[29] platforms have only just started to deal with the problems associated with their increasingly central role in the public sphere (for example, they have inconsistently addressed issues like political advertising and disinformation in recent years). This means that they have not yet developed clear and transparent ethical and professional standards that can safeguard the health of our democracies. It is important to note that, in several instances, the news content produced by professional journalism and established news outlets also challenges democratic standards, and there are many cases where this balance between public purposes and commercial imperatives was not found, or was temporarily lost. However, the tension between editorial and commercial goals has long been at the core of news organisations' operations, which led to the establishment of expectations, codes of practice, ethical standards, and institutional actors devoted to enforcing rules and assessing infringements.

B. Platforms Affect Public Discourse, as Society Becomes More Reliant on Them

Another democratic concern relates to the increasing ability of social media platforms to affect the public discourse on public matters. This is not just because news organisations distribute their news on social media platforms, but also because several sectors of our society increasingly rely on social media to communicate and interact with the public.[30] Politicians use social media to communicate with both existing supporters, potential voters and journalists; business companies use them for advertisement and to provide their perspective on crises and other events that might affect their image; institutional actors use them to facilitate the spread of public information and widen the access to public services; social movements use them to raise public awareness for their causes and to organise protests. A large part of the communicative events that populate our public sphere are now taking place on social media platforms. Thanks to social media, progressive campaigns such as #MeToo and #BlackLivesMatter, but also extremist groups and disinformation producers, have managed to circumvent traditional gatekeepers such as newspapers and broadcasters to get public attention and in turn influence the public debate.[31]

Consequently, the gatekeeping function in our society is no longer a prerogative of media organisations and professional journalists, as it used to be in the mass-media-dominated age. Then, the decisions on which events were worthy of public attention and which voices deserved to be included in news reports were

[29] A Cornia, A Sehl and RK Nielsen '"We no longer Live in a Time of Separation": A Comparative Analysis of How Editorial and Commercial Integration Became a Norm' (2020) 21 *Journalism* 172.

[30] J van Dijck, T Poell and M de Waal, *The Platform Society* (Oxford University Press, 2018).

[31] Nielsen and Fletcher (n 8).

taken by journalists and other professionals, presumably in adherence to professional and ethical standards. Instead, it is now platforms that increasingly affect what type of content and which messages reach public attention by the way they set their algorithms, regulations, terms of services and partnerships.

Social media platforms' algorithms, in particular, play a key role in selecting which information is considered most important to users.[32] Google's PageRank algorithm, for example, defines the relevance of a web page by calculating the number and quality of hyperlinks to this page, in addition to many other indicators of our online behaviour that are used to offer personalised results to our searches. Similarly, Facebook's News Feed algorithm determines what content will be prominent, based on online activities of 'friends' and 'friends of friends', in addition to other indicators of preferences and tastes. Clearly, whether algorithmic selection is well-balanced or biased towards certain types of information, opinions and perspectives, it has an impact on our participation in public life. Our perception of the climate of opinion and of the balance of power between political contestants and ideas could be affected by structural biases if, for example, the results that emerge when we search a political topic on Google prioritise a certain perspective, or if the social media posts we are exposed to on Facebook overrepresent a political camp.

But the influence of social media platforms' on our public life goes beyond the way algorithms are set. Consider the debates and polemics that have followed Facebook and Twitter decisions to ban political advertising on their platforms ahead of the 2020 US election and the suspension of Donald Trump's accounts following the 2021 Capitol Hill attack. These are just two among many recent examples of how standards and expectations on how digital intermediaries should perform their gatekeeping role have not yet been transparently and consensually established. They also demonstrate a lack of clearness on whether and how social media should grant visibility to contested actors and topics. As Emily Bell puts it, this profound shift in how gatekeeping works in society is worrisome, as 'we are handing the controls of important parts of our public and private lives to a very small number of people, who are unelected and unaccountable'.[33]

The relationship between the news and its audience has also changed. Social media clearly have the potential to empower audiences, which can now play a more active role in the construction and circulation of news content, as well as in the construction of the public discourse.[34] When journalists and mass media had the prerogative of producing and distributing news, the audience role was mainly limited to that of the passive receiver and had rare and limited opportunities to make their voices heard (examples include writing letters to the editor

[32] T Gillespie 'The Relevance of Algorithms' in T Gillespie, PJ Boczkowski and KA Foot (eds), *Media Technologies: Essays on* Communication, Materiality, and Society (The MIT Press, 2014).
[33] Bell, 'Facebook is Eating the World' (2016).
[34] Van Dijck et al, *The Platform Society* (2018).

or participating in polls or in news media boycotts). Although only a minority actually engages with citizen journalism, wiki journalism and other forms of journalism that are based on the substantial participation of the audience in the new production process, audiences today have many more opportunities to play an active role. They often participate in news distribution by sharing, rating and recommending specific news articles, and they can make their voices heard by commenting or repurposing professionally produced content.

However, the emergence of a social media environment where the link between the content-producer and the channel of distribution is less evident has created the conditions for an increased circulation of disinformation and manipulated information. Recent research suggests that people are less likely to correctly attribute a story to a specific news brand when they access it via search or social compared to when they access it directly on the news outlet's website.[35] In other words, people tend to ignore the sources of many stories they find on social media. Together with the multiplication of online sources and the declining role of traditional and professionally bound intermediaries such as journalists and news media, this contributes to the circulation of disinformation, ie false information which is knowingly shared to cause harm, to pursue hidden political interests, or to make a profit.

C. Do Platforms Create More Information Inequality and Polarisation?

A third implication of the move towards a media environment increasingly dominated by social media and digital intermediaries is that these changes can possibly exacerbate existing inequalities in news consumption patterns and contribute to increasing the fragmentation and the political polarisation of news audiences. Both are theoretically plausible hypotheses that have been at the centre of public debates in recent years and might have profound implications for the functioning of our democracies, although – as we are going to see – empirical evidence is inconclusive, and does not fully corroborate such hypotheses.

The high-choice news avoidance thesis suggests that, in the move from a traditional media environment dominated by a few legacy newspapers and broadcasters to a digital environment marked by the multiplication of news sources and the possibility to personalise media consumption diets, people's attention is going away from news about politics and current affairs, mainly towards entertainment. In other words, presented with an almost unlimited choice of content to consume, users interested in political news and current affairs tend to follow them more while those less interested can avoid them more easily than before.

[35] A Kalogeropoulos, R Fletcher and RK Nielsen, 'News brand attribution in distributed environments: Do people know where they get their news?' (2019) 21 *New Media & Society* 583.

The move towards a high-choice media environment, therefore, might contribute to the fragmentation of media audiences by increasing the divide between groups that take full advantage of an increased number of news outlets and other online fora where politics and current affairs are discussed, on the one hand, and other groups that regularly avoid news content because more alternatives are present, on the other hand. This might potentially undermine the bases of deliberative democracy, which rest on principles such as equality of access to information and the maintenance of a shared basis for deliberation, a common understanding of basic facts that allow public discussion and political negotiations.[36]

Recent studies, however, suggest that although the news avoidance thesis is theoretically pleasing and plausible, its assumptions are contrasted by other possible arguments.[37] Social media, for example, might favour incidental exposure to news, meaning that people who use social networking sites for entertainment purposes only, for example, can still encounter news content shared by other users. Other structural features of social media might moderate the effect of individual preferences that is assumed in the news avoidance thesis: social media and search engine algorithms tend to also direct people towards already popular products and topics, and this might favour encounters with news items even when this type of content is not intentionally sought.

Both the news avoidance thesis and its counterarguments were tested in a study that analysed survey data on news avoidance in Norway from 1997 to 2016, a period that saw a profound transformation of the media environment.[38] Findings suggest that – despite the revolutionary transformation of media consumption patterns during these two decades – news avoidance has increased marginally. However, the study also found that although the general increase in news avoidance was modest, some inequalities in how different groups use political media have actually increased. Gender and age gaps exist (meaning that women and younger cohorts tend to consume less news) but have not increased in the move towards an increasingly digital and social media environment. Instead, the result showed a clear increase in gaps along educational lines: the proportion of news avoiders has considerably increased among the less-educated groups. This raises concerns related to the equality of access to information for groups with low socio-economic status.

Similar concerns populate the debate on whether social and digital media leads towards the creation of echo chambers, filter bubbles and increasingly polarised societies. Echo chambers are communicative spaces where ideas are mutually

[36] CR Sunstein, *#Republic: Divided Democracy in the Age of Social Media* (Princeton University Press, 2017).

[37] R Karlsen, A Beyer and K Steen-Johnsen, 'Do High-Choice Media Environments Facilitate News Avoidance? A Longitudinal Study 1997–2016' (2020) 64 *Journal of Broadcasting & Electronic Media* 794.

[38] ibid.

reinforced by like-minded people and messages that confirm pre-existing views and beliefs. The tendency to connect with similar people (homophily) and to insulate our own beliefs and views from rebuttal (to avoid cognitive dissonance) has always been part of human nature. However, the argument raised by influential scholars like Cass Sunstein is that digital media create more opportunities for users to expose themselves to certain types of content and opinions.[39] Today, indeed, there are myriad digital spaces such as niche websites, blogs, social media pages or groups where people can gather with others who share similar interests and views. The echo chamber thesis postulates that these spaces can turn into enclosed communicative environments that magnify messages and insulate them from rebuttal.

Another concept which is increasingly debated refers to filter bubbles. Activist and author Eli Pariser describes filter bubbles as the ecosystem of personalised information created by digital algorithms for each individual.[40] Based on past online behaviour, connections and other key information – for example the ones that govern the selection of posts on our social media feeds or the ranking of our search results – algorithms try to estimate what content is more relevant for us in order to offer a personalised and effective service. As a result, users encounter more frequently content and views that they are expected to like and, less frequently, content and opinions they dislike or disagree with. The concern at the basis of this thesis is therefore that digital and social media might isolate individuals in their own ideological bubbles and prevent them from encountering new and unexpected perspectives and information, limiting de facto the diversity of content they are exposed to and the amount of experience they share with other members of the society. Filter bubbles differ from more traditional forms of selective exposure to media content because the personalisation mechanisms operated by algorithms are almost invisible to most users. A viewer of a politically partisan news channel knows that the outlet that they are watching offers very specific viewpoints. Instead, most people are not fully aware that the Google results they see or the posts that appear on their feed on Facebook are algorithmically selected, structurally biased, and assembled to meet the platform's expectations about what they want.

Although disputable, the high-choice news avoidance, echo chambers and filter bubbles theories pose serious concerns for the health of our democracy. As emphasised by Sunstein,[41] democratic deliberation requires serendipitous encounters with information and opinions that people would have not chosen in advance. In the twentieth century, audiences would encounter news on politics and current affairs even if they were only interested in entertainment or sport, eg when watching the top stories of a news bulletin while waiting for the sports news or catching a news bulletin before the start of their favourite TV show. This

[39] Sunstein, *#Republic* (2017).
[40] E Pariser, *Filter Bubbles: What the Internet is Hiding from You* (Penguin, 2011).
[41] Sunstein (n 36).

was favoured by the very structure of the media environment before the rise of digital and social media: a media environment characterised by a more limited number of less specialised media sources that tended to blend different topics and genres. Instead, in a high-choice media environment characterised by fragmented audiences, personalised information, filter bubbles and echo chambers, part of the audience might regularly avoid news content or could predominantly encounter like-minded voices and perspectives. Moreover, Sunstein emphasises how democratic deliberation requires shared experiences which, unlike personalised news assemblages, provide a form of social glue. As echo chambers and filter bubbles entail like-minded people influencing one another and being exposed to content that confirms their pre-existing beliefs and isolates them from opposing viewpoints, these phenomena are believed to favour the polarisation of opinions, the tendency to adopt extreme viewpoints, and the propensity for disliking people that support opposing political parties. As Sunstein notes, 'if diverse groups are seeing and hearing quite different points of view, or focusing on quite different topics, mutual understanding might be difficult, and it might be increasingly hard for people to solve problems that society faces together'.[42]

Similar to the high-choice news avoidance thesis, empirical studies on filter bubbles and digitally enhanced echo chambers also offer unconclusive and mixed results. A 2016 review of scholarly research on these topics, for example, concluded that, in spite of the serious concerns voiced by many influential scholars and observers, there is no empirical evidence that supports any strong concerns about filter bubbles. The authors note that the personalisation on news outlets' websites and apps was in its infancy in 2016, and personalised content only constituted a marginal information source for most Internet users. The authors also recognise that the debate about filter bubbles and echo chambers is nevertheless important, and if the personalisation affordances of digital platforms would improve and personalised content would become the main source of information for many, substantial problems for our democracy could indeed arise.[43] A more recent review of the empirical research on filter bubbles and polarisation, however, confirms that there is little empirical evidence supporting the filter bubble thesis and the idea that social media and algorithmic selection lead to the balkanisation of opinions and more extreme viewpoints.[44] For example, social media users often see on these platforms news from outlets that they would not normally use and are often exposed to news stories on topics they are not typically interested in. Additionally, empirical studies have shown that social media users are exposed to more sources of news than people who do not use social media. Other studies have

[42] ibid 68.

[43] FJ Zuiderveen Borgesius et al, 'Should We Worry about Filter Bubbles?' (2016) 5 *Internet Policy Review* 1.

[44] R Fletcher and J Jenkins, 'Polarization and the News Media in Europe' (study for the Panel for Future of Science and Technology, European Parliamentary Research Service, 2020).

found that conversations about the news on Twitter are often cross-cutting, meaning that they tend to include different perspectives and voices.

The conclusion that new technologies do not intrinsically lead towards ideological segregation is also supported by a study on the level of online and offline political polarisation of news audiences in 12 countries, which, for example, demonstrated that online news audience polarisation was higher in most of the selected countries (meaning that online news outlets have stronger right- or left-leaning audiences than offline outlets), but this trend was not sharp, as the difference was statistically significant only in a limited number of cases, and there were a few cases of countries where the audiences of online outlets were actually more politically diverse than the audiences of offline outlets in the same country.[45] These findings suggest that political polarisation is a phenomenon that deserves public attention and scrutiny, but it is not an inevitable outcome of the move from a traditional media environment towards a high-choice digital media environment marked by the rise of social media platforms. The personalisation possibilities offered by digital media can certainly contribute to polarising societies, but the outcome of this process also depends on factors, such as historical developments and political cultures, that go beyond the level of technological development or the level of social media use in a given country.

IV. Conclusion

This chapter addresses two major changes taking place in our news environment: the increasingly important role of social media platforms as source of news for many people; and the simultaneous decline of legacy news organisations, which are today less effective in reaching audiences and sustaining their editorial activities with the revenues they generate, either online or offline. We argued that these two major changes can have serious implications for our democracy. Clearly, the declining role of news organisations can endanger our society's ability to rely on professional journalism. Indeed, legacy news organisations have always played a key role in funding journalism, and they still do so, employing a large majority of professional journalists. Social media platforms are only indirectly responsible for the decline of legacy news media, but we should recognise that they are taking over many of the functions that were traditionally undertaken by news organisations.

In fact, social media now constitutes the main gateway to news for many people, the platform of choice for many social and political actors seeking visibility for their messages and causes, and a particularly effective and cheaper way for advertisers to promote their products and services. Platforms are thus increasingly competing

[45] R Fletcher, A Cornia and RK Nielsen, 'How Polarized Are Online and Offline News Audiences? A Comparative Analysis of Twelve Countries' (2020) 23 *The International Journal of Press/Politics* 169.

with news media not only in the economic realm (as they are able to attract most online revenues), but also in performing the gatekeeping function that has long ensured that information is adequately selected and prepared for dissemination. Although news production is still mainly fulfilled by professional journalists and news organisations, many people access the news through the services provided by digital intermediaries and, if news media keeps on relying so strongly on social media to increase their online reach, they risk losing control of their news distribution channels and of the direct relationship with their audiences.

Additionally, the gatekeeping function is increasingly performed by algorithms that are aimed at providing users with personalised information, ie information that is expected to be relevant and in line with the preferences of individual users. However, algorithmic news selection raises relevant concerns, as many observers suggest that – if personalised services will become more widespread – existing inequalities in accessing information and news could worsen, and more fragmented and polarised societies could emerge.

Well-functioning democracies require universal access to information, serendipitous encounters with alternative topics and perspectives, and a shared experience and knowledge that serve as social glue and favour deliberative processes. It is thus of crucial importance that developments related to the gatekeeping function that is increasingly played by social media are closely researched, their implications are widely debated, and clear and widely accepted professional and ethical standards on how social media should deal with political messages and current affair news are established.

PART 2

Fundamental Rights and Platforms' Governance

6

Structural Power as a Critical Element of Social Media Platforms' Private Sovereignty

LUCA BELLI*

I. Introduction

This chapter discusses how large social media platforms are acquiring a form of private sovereignty, exercising a form of structural power as they define and implement their private ordering systems.[1] Its goal is to stress the existence of a new conception of sovereignty[2] that is intrinsically associated with the definition of the contractual regulations, technical architectures and adjudication capabilities of digital platforms. It will use the concept of 'structural power' elaborated by Susan Strange in her 1988 book, *States and Markets* to illustrate how platforms create private ordering systems. Ultimately, it will argue that such systems allow platforms to elude oversight from national governments, de facto giving rise to private type of sovereignty.

These considerations seem particularly relevant in the context of the current raise of digital sovereignty narratives at the state level.[3] Indeed, this chapter invites

* The author would like to acknowledge Dr Monica Horten for the useful conversations on how the 'structural power' concept can be used to understand the dynamics of Internet intermediaries. A compelling work in this sense is M Horten, *Closing of the Net* (Polity Press, 2016).

[1] For a digression on private ordering, see G-P Calliess and P Zumbansen, *Rough Consensus and Running Code. A Theory of Transnational Private Law* (Oxford/Portland, Hart, 2012); L Belli and J Venturini, 'Private ordering and the rise of terms of service as cyber-regulation' (2016) 5 Internet Policy Review, available at doi.org/10.14763/2016.4.441.

[2] Sovereignty is a complex concept which arose as an attempt to frame the internal structure of a state. Peter Malanczuk provides a useful discussion of sovereignty and its evolution, arguing that the sovereign enjoys the 'supreme power' to decide who is 'bound by the laws which he made'. See P Malanczuk Akehurst, *Modern Introduction to International Law*, 7th edn (Routledge, 1997).

[3] For an analysis of the concept of digital sovereignty, see J Pohle and T Thiel, 'Digital sovereignty' (2020) 9 *Internet Policy Review*, available at doi.org/10.14763/2020.4.1532. For a succinct reconstruction, also with reference to the digital context, see E Celeste, 'Digital Sovereignty in the EU: Challenges

the reader to consider from a different perspective the concept of (digital) sovereignty, paying closer attention to the role that non-state actors play by designing and implementing private structures that construct sovereignty.

The first section of this chapter will provide some preliminary considerations on the regulatory role of technology and the strategic function of private orderings established by major corporations. It will highlight in particular how these features are well known by governments of countries leading the development of digital technology since several decades. It will stress that the possibility that technological behemoths – notably, social media platforms – evolve into entities able to structure and exercise their own sovereignty and elude nation-state power has started to be appreciated only recently.

The second section will build upon previous works on platform regulation, where the conceptualisation of platforms as 'quasi sovereigns' was first pondered by this author together with several co-authors.[4] Based on these conceptualisations, this section will contend that social media platforms behave as private cyber-sovereigns, enjoying quasi-normative, quasi-executive and quasi-judicial power. The quasi-normative power is exercised through the unilateral definition of terms and service – or 'law of the platform'[5] – and the technical interfaces utilised to present them, sometimes in a remarkably biased fashion,[6] as well as by defining what personal data will be collected about users. This latter element might be compared with the power of legislative assemblies to lay and collect taxes: in the platform environment, however, such taxes are imposed on platform users, rather than citizens, and paid with data, rather than money. The quasi-executive power can be identified in the unilateral implementation of the platforms' terms and conditions, decisions and business practices via the platforms' technical architecture. Lastly, the quasi-judicial power is exercised by establishing the alternative

and Future Perspectives' in F Fabbrini, E Celeste and J Quinn (eds), *Data Protection Beyond Borders: Transatlantic Perspectives on Extraterritoriality and Sovereignty* (Hart, 2021). For a digression on why emerging economies might be keen on building digital sovereignty narratives, see L Belli, 'BRICS Countries to Build Digital Sovereignty' in L Belli (ed), *CyberBRICS: Cybersecurity Regulations in the BRICS Countries* (Springer, 2021).

[4] See L Belli and P De Filippi, 'Law of the Cloud v Law of the Land: Challenges and Opportunities for Innovation' (2012) 3 *European Journal of Law and Technology*, available at ssrn.com/abstract=2167382; L Belli and J Venturini, 'Private ordering' (2016); L Belli, PA Francisco and N Zingales, 'Law of the Land or Law of the Platform? Beware of the Privatisation of Regulation and Police' in L Belli and N Zingales (eds), *Platform Regulations How Platforms are Regulated and How They Regulate Us* (FGV Direito Rio, 2017); L Belli and C Sappa, 'The Intermediary Conundrum: Cyber-regulators, Cyber-police or both?' (2017) 8 *Journal of Intellectual Property, Information Technology and Electronic Commerce Law* 183.

[5] Belli, Francisco and Zingales, 'Law of the Land' (2017).

[6] This is the case of the so-called 'dark patterns', a concept first introduced by Harry Brignull: 'What are Dark Patterns?' (2018), available at darkpatterns.org. The author defined these misleading user interface designs as 'tricks used in websites and apps that make you do things that you didn't mean to, like buying or signing up for something'. An excellent overview of what are dark patterns is provided in A Mathur, J Mayer and M Kshirsagar, '*What Makes a Dark Pattern … Dark?: Design Attributes, Normative Considerations, and Measurement Methods*', Proceedings of the 2021 Conference on Human Factors in Computing Systems (2021), available at dl.acm.org/doi/10.1145/3411764.3445610.

dispute resolution mechanisms that solve controversies based on the platforms' unilaterally defined contractual conditions.

This section will draw upon Susan Strange's work on states and markets.[7] The British political scientist convincingly argued that sovereign entities exercise power not only through the ability to compel someone to do something and through 'classic' manifestations of power – ie through the creation of regimes that regulate societies – but also through the power to shape the structures defining how everything shall be done – ie defining the frameworks within which people, corporations and even states relate to each other. Importantly, this chapter contends that Susan Strange's considerations can also be extended to technology. By shaping how people or corporations can interact between themselves, how they can do business or communicate, technology in general and social media platforms, in particular, can deploy an enormous structural power that regulates effectively how the societies where such technology is utilised will function.

While not well known in legal circles, Susan Strange's work is particularly relevant, as it offers an illuminating reading of how power can be exercised not only by public powerful actors (sovereign states), but also by private constructions (markets). At the same time, the concept of structural power is particularly useful in understanding how technological structures – or 'architectures'[8] to use a term dear to Lawrence Lessig – can shape the relationship between technology users, be them physical or juridical persons, thus providing a telling illustration of the regulatory capabilities of the structural power.

In this sense, Strange's concept of structural power is useful in providing an additional perspective from which we can see the concept of architecture as envisaged by Lessig. The latter argues that architectures are constraints that both in the physical[9] and digital realm structure (cyber)spaces, determining whether specific behaviours are allowed by design, and thus playing a regulatory function. The conceptualisation formulated by the former allows us to consider the capacity to regulate by architecture as a real form of power through which, I will argue, sovereignty can be exercised.

Regulation by architecture is possible in the physical world, but the level and scale of control achieved by the digital architectures of online platforms is impossible to achieve in the offline world, even with the most sophisticated design choices. Moreover, the algorithms that enable platforms' functionalities – for instance, establishing the order according to which information will be displayed on the platform's timeline – do not need implementation, as they are

[7] S Strange, *States and Markets* (London, Pinter, 1988).

[8] The term is utilised in the conception proposed by Lawrence Lessig. See L Lessig, 'The Law of the Horse: What Cyberlaw Might Teach' (1999) 113 *Harvard Law Review* 501; L Lessig, *Code: And Other Laws of Cyberspace Version 2.0* (Basic Books, 2006).

[9] An example offered by Lessig is the architecture of the city of Paris, which was reorganised with large avenues by Baron Haussmann to prevent rebellious people from taking control of the city centre, as previously happened during the third French Revolution of 1848. See Lessig, *Code* (2006).

'self-executing norms'[10] that can be constantly updated to fit new needs and purposes defined unilaterally by the designer. This context will be used to illustrate how platforms concentrate quasi-normative, -executive and -judicial power, which are instrumental to underpin their private sovereignty.

The final section will argue that the tendency towards the establishment of complex private orderings, giving rise to the platforms' private sovereignty, may be the expression of a convenient compromise between platforms, eager to continue self-regulating and escape public oversight, and governments, eager to avoid responsibility to regulate. The latest evolution towards such private sovereignty is epitomised by the recently established private supreme court by Facebook, the Oversight Board,[11] which may be seen as a clear attempt to construct new institutions, providing a façade of accountability, and sopping and distracting stakeholders, while de facto corroborating platforms' private sovereignty, evading public scrutiny and, ultimately, benefitting shareholders.

II. The Regulatory Function of Technology: Unequally Appreciated by Different Actors

To understand how social media platforms are shaping their structural power and how this can be seen as a new form of private sovereignty, it is essential to first acknowledge the regulatory function of technology. On the one hand, technology always embeds the values of its creators and, therefore, can be a powerful vector to project such values even beyond the national borders of its country of origin. On the other hand, technology can be repurposed and utilised for applications that may considerably differ from the original objectives of its creators. Hence, exactly as other tools enabling regulation, technology can promote or restrict specific behaviours, but as it is not set in stone, it can also be updated, consequently modifying the type of behaviours that it fosters or hinders.

While this reasoning applies to any technology, digital technology maximises these features as it is much more scalable and easily updatable than any other technology. A single new technology can be adopted in few years by millions – or even billions – of individuals and businesses and its software structure can be relatively easily updated, compared to other technologies. These features make it particularly relevant to carefully ponder how digital technology affects the ways in which individuals' and businesses' legal sphere is shaped by such technologies. Indeed, rarely the impact of technology is neutral.

[10] L Belli, *De la Gouvernance à la régulation de l'Internet* (Berger-Levrault, 2016) 140–44.

[11] Oversight Board, 'Ensuring respect for free expression, through independent judgment', available at www.oversightboard.com.

A. Some Lessons from (Internet) History

The history of how Internet technology evolved is a telling example. The research community that conceived the Internet envisaged it as a technology enabling decentralised networking, thus increasing resilience in communications, while removing points of control.[12] However, the evolution witnessed over the past decade proves that, even if openness and decentralisation were the initial objectives, points of control have quickly emerged.[13] The current concentration and platformisation of the digital environment provide telling examples not only of the regulatory function of technology but also of how the application of a given technology may radically redefine the philosophy behind its initial conception.

Importantly, the potential of digital technologies to regulate and shape society – should they be adopted at scale – as well as their extremely strategic value, was understood by some stakeholders many decades ago. In the late 1970s, Zbigniew Brzezinski, a high-ranked US official who acted as security advisor to US President Jimmy Carter, famously acknowledged the regulatory and control capabilities of digital technology and the power that would reside in the 'elite' developing it.[14] Conspicuously, he stressed that

> the gradual appearance of a more controlled and directed society … dominated by an elite whose claim to political power would rest on allegedly superior scientific knowhow. Unhindered by the restraints of traditional liberal values, this elite would not hesitate to achieve its political ends by using the latest modern techniques for influencing public behavior and keeping society under close surveillance and control.[15]

This delineates an early awareness of the instrumental role of technology to regulate as well as the strategic value of being the producer of the most advanced and utilised technologies. Importantly, such structural power of technology started to be explicitly acknowledged in a period of intense ideological clashes, such as the Cold War. Those years witnessed the emergence of a clear understanding of technology's potential to be utilised as a vector to spread and implement the values that are embedded in it. Already in the 1960s, some countries had started devoting enormous public investments to fund technological research and development and, at the same time, many policy-makers, academics and business leaders started to realise the regulatory potential of technology. This potential could have been directed – and still can be – towards fostering democratic values, unrestricted

[12] For a historical account of the first phases of the Internet technical and normative evolution, see Belli, *De la Gouvernance* (2016) 133–90.

[13] J Goldsmith and T Wu, *Who Controls the Internet? Illusions of a Borderless World* (Oxford University Press, 2006). See also OECD, *The Role of Internet Intermediaries in Advancing Public Policy Objectives* (OECD Publishing, 2011); N Tusikov, *Chokepoints: Global Private Regulation on the Internet* (University of California Press, 2016).

[14] Z Brzezinski, *Between Two Ages America's Role in the Technetronic Era* (The Viking Press, 1970) 96.

[15] ibid.

communications, and free flow of information, but could also at the same time increase surveillance and information gathering on a massive scale.

In light of the above considerations, it is not a coincidence that, in this period, the first data protection regulatory frameworks started to take shape, while also the first efforts to facilitate transnational data flows. The fear of abusive use of technology, on the one hand, and the economic interests of the main technology producers, on the other hand, were the main drivers of such efforts.[16]

This double nature of digital technology – facilitating free communication, trade and development, while enabling surveillance and control – seems to have already been recognised by the most attentive stakeholders in the late 1970s. Such a recognition is epitomised by the parallel elaboration and subsequent adoption of the first two international documents prompting personal data regulation at international level. On the one hand, the Guidelines on the Protection of Privacy and Transborder Flows of Personal Data,[17] adopted in 1980 by the Organisation for Economic Co-operation and Development (OECD), aimed at regulating transnational flows of personal data, which were already seen as an essential strategical and economical asset by the most technologically advanced countries within the OECD. On the other hand, the Council of Europe Convention for the Protection of Individuals with regard to Automatic Processing of Personal Data[18] (usually referred to as 'Convention 108') was elaborated in the same period and adopted in 1981, having in mind the need to 'extend the safeguards for everyone's rights and fundamental freedoms, and in particular the right to the respect for privacy, taking account of the increasing flow across frontiers of personal data undergoing automatic processing'.[19]

The policy-making efforts mentioned above are particularly relevant in two different ways. First, they let us understand that the regulatory potential of technology has been well known since at least the 1970s and the most advanced countries have tried to shape their policies, aware of how technology can regulate society, for at least 40 years. Second, the early attempts to create a regulatory framework that can orientate the evolution of technology also proves the

[16] Art 1 of the 1978 French Data Protection Act encapsulates tellingly the fears and hopes that the rise of digital technology arose in society at the time: '*L'informatique doit être au service de chaque citoyen. Son développement doit s'opérer dans le cadre de la coopération internationale. Elle ne doit porter atteinte ni à l'identité humaine, ni aux droits de l'homme, ni à la vie privée, ni aux libertés individuelles ou publiques*.' See *loi* n° 78-17 du 6 janvier 1978 relative à l'informatique, aux fichiers et aux libertés, available at www.cnil.fr/fr/la-loi-informatique-et-libertes.

[17] Organisation for Economic Cooperation and Development, 'Guidelines On The Protection Of Privacy And Transborder Flows Of Personal Data' (OECD, 1980), available at www.oecd.org/sti/ieconomy/oecdguidelinesontheprotectionofprivacyandtransborderflowsofpersonaldata.htm.

[18] Council of Europe Convention for the Protection of Individuals with regard to Automatic Processing of Personal Data 1981 ETS no 108, available at rm.coe.int/1680078b37. The Convention opened for signature in January 1981 and was the first legally binding international instrument in the data protection field. The updated version of the Convention 108 was adopted in 2018, becoming the 'Convention 108+', and is available at rm.coe.int/leaflet-data-protection-final-26-april-2019/1680943556.

[19] ibid.

awareness that, paradoxically, the lack of public regulation and the encouragement of self-regulation is a clear regulatory choice.

Indeed, the absence of public regulation does not mean that society will not be regulated, but rather that the private entities will be delegated the task to regulate society through the self-regulatory tools (contractual or technological) they develop. Both documents acknowledged the potential impact of information technologies on individual rights and on businesses, and strived to define frameworks to facilitate the transborder use of such technologies without undermining neither rights nor business opportunities.

B. Towards Private Structural Power: A Deliberate Regulatory Choice

Another page of Internet history is particularly helpful to illustrate how the regulatory potential of technology and the structural power exercised by private entities is not something unknown to policy-makers – although it might have been ignored by some – and has underpinned very concrete national strategies.

When the Clinton administration established its Framework for Global Electronic Commerce in 1997, the intention to delegate Internet regulation to contractually based self-regulatory regimes was clear and explicit. The Framework argued that 'The success of electronic commerce will require an effective partnership between the private and public sectors, with the private sector in the lead'.[20] However, while understanding fully the 'explosive growth' that private sector involvement had provided to digital technologies and the capacity of private intermediaries to define private regimes, the abovementioned document naively – or falsely naively – considered that 'private fora' would have been an effective solution to 'take the lead in *areas requiring self-regulation such as privacy, content ratings, and consumer protection* and in areas such as standards development, commercial code, and fostering interoperability'.[21]

This illustrates that it is not absurd to posit that the capacity of Internet intermediaries in general, and social media platforms in particular, to structure the digital world via their technical architectures and contractual regimes has formed a pillar of US economic, foreign and regulatory policy since the 1990s. The establishment of private ordering systems was indeed deemed an effective way to regulate an environment where classic sovereignty was still struggling to be implemented. In this context, Susan Strange's concept of structural power becomes a useful framework for better understanding these dynamics.

Over the past few decades, several US administrations effectively maintained a centralised power over core regulatory functions of strategic markets by fostering

[20] B Clinton and A Gore, 'A Framework for Global Electronic Commerce' (World Wide Web Consortium, 1997), available at www.w3.org/TR/NOTE-framework-970706.

[21] ibid, notably the section on 'A Coordinated Strategy'; emphasis added.

global private corporations that could cultivate 'the perception of market-based private ordering'[22] while de facto acting as proxies for the implementation of US values and regulation on a global scale, with no need for direct US government intervention.[23] In this sense, a compelling case was already provided by Nico Krisch in 2005, emphasising the role of private actors with global range – such as the 'Big Three' credit rating agencies, S&P, Moody's and Fitch – as instances of the 'privatization of international rule', globally disseminating US-centric standards and practices.[24] Likewise Christopher M Bruner offered an interesting analysis of how the US Government has successfully 'instrumentalized private actors' to regulate quintessentially global sectors through private ordering while being able 'to obscure the government's own responsibility for adverse outcomes, shifting blame onto the private sector'.[25]

In this perspective, it is important to stress that, due to the inexistence or ineffectiveness of global institutions and regimes allowing to regulate specific sectors, the establishment of global private players acquires a particular relevance, as it is does not only represent an engine of economic expansion but also a proxy for global reach of domestic regulation. It is, therefore, important to keep in mind that delegation of regulatory functions to private intermediaries may allow to find efficient and effective solutions to regulate specific policy areas,[26] but we must recognise that efficiency and effectiveness are not synonyms of justice and rule of law.[27] In this context, while experimentation with private ordering can be very beneficial for efficiency and effectiveness purposes, ultimate oversight can only be public, if one wants to guarantee that fundamental rights, due process and the rule of law are respected.

While this section has argued that, over the past decades, dominant state actors may have utilised large private actors as regulatory proxies, the next section analyses why social media platforms may successfully exploit their structural power to acquire a set of capabilities that is normally seen only in sovereign nations. These features were likely promoted by governments facilitating the establishment of such technology companies as a strategy to assert global jurisdiction by proxy, but

[22] CM Bruner, 'States, Markets, and Gatekeepers: Public-Private Regulatory Regimes in an Era of Economic Globalization' (2008) 30 *Michigan Journal of International Law* 125.

[23] A telling example in this sense is the parallel copyright regime developed by YouTube, which can be deemed the most utilised content distribution platform. This example is particularly useful to illustrate the extraterritorial application of a national regulatory regime – in this case, US copyright legislation – de facto turning the platform into a private proxy for global application of national regulation. See Belli, Francisco and Zingales (n 4) 54–59.

[24] N Krisch, 'International Law in Times of Hegemony: Unequal Power and the Shaping of the International Legal Order' (2005) 16 *The European Journal of International Law* 369.

[25] In his paper Bruner discusses two useful examples: the regulation of national credit risk through the creation of private credit rating agencies; and the regulation of the domain name industry through the creation of the Internet Corporation for Assigned Names and Numbers. See Bruner, 'States, Markets, and Gatekeepers' (2008).

[26] See OECD (n 17).

[27] Belli, Francisco and Zingales (n 5).

may now have given rise to entities that are not even controllable by such governments and are concretely trying to assert their own private sovereignty.

Section III will argue that digital platforms can be seen as private cyber-sovereigns, able to establish private ordering systems within the digital frontiers delineated by their software architectures. Indeed, the structure they define allows them to enjoy quasi-normative, judicial and executive power, which underpin their private sovereignty.

III. Private Ordering to Structure Digital Platforms' Sovereignty

As digital platforms are increasingly omnipresent in our personal and business lives, public debate and policy-makers' attention is increasingly turning towards the role that these intermediaries play, the influence they exercise, and how they do so. While it may seem an overstatement to argue that social media platforms behave as private sovereigns, this section will illustrate that, in many ways, these private actors have integrated many functions previously reserved for state actors. Furthermore, the way platforms structure their contractual norms, technical architectures and interfaces may be seen as a form of structural power, in the conception put forward by Susan Strange.

Importantly, Strange's work offers a compelling argument of why sovereign entities exercise power by defining the structures and substructures based upon which people, corporations and even states can relate to each other. Exactly as the architect of a labyrinth can define where walls are and which doors can be open or closed, controlling how individuals or animals inside can move, the holder of structural power can define the infrastructural, normative, trade and communications structures that allow any actor using them to have social, economic or even political interactions. In this sense, structural power is instrumental to the exercise of sovereignty.

It also important to emphasise that the concept of (digital) sovereignty entails a certain complexity.[28] Public law and international relations are grounded on the assumption that states are the only actors having legitimacy to enjoy sovereignty. National and international law are grounded on the assumption that sovereign power is held by the state as the only political organisation able to effectively structure the governance of society. Public law traditionally prescribes that such structure is defined via a set of bodies that exercise the legislative, jurisdictional and executive powers – supposedly, in an independent fashion while mutually checking ad balancing each other.

[28] J Pohle and T Thiel, 'Digital sovereignty' (2020); Celeste, 'Digital Sovereignty in the EU' (2021); Belli, 'BRICS Countries to Build Digital Sovereignty' (2021).

While Max Weber famously considered that states are 'political enterprises'[29] characterised by 'the monopoly of the legitimate use of physical force within a given territory',[30] Carl Schmitt argued that, rather than a monopoly of coercion, the sovereign enjoys the monopoly to decide.[31] These assumptions are core concepts utilised by public law to describe national institutions and governance, but they become less certain when considered from a global and international perspective, rather than a purely domestic one. In this sense, the above-mentioned 1997 Framework for Global Electronic Commerce adopted a very pragmatic stance, recognising the inefficiency of the regulation set by national sovereigns and the need to rely on private actors to effectively regulate a digital environment designed to be transborder and global.

Hence, since the 1990s, there seems to have emerged an increasing understanding – or at least acceptance – that global phenomena must update traditional conceptions of sovereignty to fit the emerging role of private actors and their capacity to structure the sectors where they operate in a remarkably effective – though not necessary just – fashion. At the global level, indeed, no entity may claim the monopoly of force or the legitimacy to unilaterally establish binding rules, make decisions and enforce them. In this context, private actors have long taken the lead and bridged the gap left by the lack of international public authority, instituting private ordering systems that effectively structure power relations, building private regimes in a wide range of sectors, spanning from finance to organised crime.[32] It is precisely recognising these characteristics that, as convincingly argued by Bruner, 'hegemon governments' may opt to regulate indirectly – or by proxy[33] – issuing instructions to less powerful states via private standard setters.[34]

By nature, the Internet environment and, particularly, its application layer, which is largely composed of privately developed software platforms, lends itself very well to the surge of private authority to provide law and order. Indeed, the very commercialisation of the Internet was driven by the belief that 'the private sector should lead'[35] the expansion of electronic commerce over the Internet on a global basis. In this light, it is no surprise that the digital platforms that populate cyberspace have long-established private ordering mechanisms. While not necessarily compatible with democratic values and fundamental rights principles,[36]

[29] M Weber, 'Politics as a Vocation' in HH Gerth and C Wright Mills (eds), *From Max Weber: Essays in Sociology* (Routledge, 1948).

[30] ibid.

[31] C Schmitt, *Political Theology: Four Chapters on the Concept of Sovereignty* (MIT Press, 1985) 5.

[32] RB Hall and TJ Biersteker (eds) *The Emergence of Private Authority in Global Governance* (Cambridge University Press, 2002).

[33] Belli, Francisco and Zingales (n 5).

[34] See Bruner (n 22).

[35] See Clinton and Gore, 'A Framework' (1997).

[36] See particularly, L Belli and N Zingales 'Platform value(s): A multidimensional framework for online responsibility' (2020) 36 *Computer Law & Security Review*, available at doi.org/10.1016/j.clsr.2019.105364.

private ordering is a more efficient and reliable option for private actors, but also more diplomatically convenient for the 'hegemon governments' of the day willing to globally regulate the online world, rather than relying on unilateral imposition of domestic norms or ineffective intergovernmental institutions.

The initial ineffectiveness of state coercion and difficulty to enforce the law in the digital environment have prompted, on the one hand, the state to rely on private players as a proxy of national legislation and, on the other hand, digital intermediaries to fill the gaps left by the state ineffectiveness, by establishing contractual regimes and technical architectures aimed at effectively regulating individual behaviours online.

From this perspective, the technical architectures on which social media platforms rely for their function may be seen as digital 'territories' on which platform exercise their private sovereignty. Such territories are populated by individuals that must abide to the rules of the platforms, and where justice is given via adjudicating systems and decisions that are implemented via enforcement mechanisms unilaterally established by the private entities exercising 'sovereignty' within the digital frontiers delineated by the platform's technical architectures.[37]

A. Quasi-Normative Power

Every social media platform typically regulates the behaviour of its users through terms of service or terms and conditions. The main feature of these standard contracts – commonly referred to as adhesion contracts or boilerplate contracts – is that the conditions they include are not negotiated.[38] On the contrary, the contractual clauses are unilaterally predetermined by one party, which in our case is the platform provider. While, terms of service are legally considered as any other contract, signifying the expression of the willingness of all the parties, it is natural to consider this contractual typology as the quintessential expression of one-sided control.

For this reason, standard contracts are recurrently criticised,[39] due to the unilateral character of the provisions, the absence of negotiation between the parties, and the quasi-inexistence of the bargaining power of the adhering party. In this sense, the position of platform users – especially those of dominant platforms – is remarkably vulnerable, as assenting to the unilaterally established contractual regulation is the only option they have to utilise a service that, in some cases, may be vital. This seems to be particularly the case with dominant social

[37] See Belli (n 10) 202, 219.

[38] See the seminal work of O Prausnitz, *The standardization of commercial contracts in English and continental law* (Sweet & Maxwell, 1937).

[39] See most notably: MJ Radin, *Boilerplate: The Fine Print, Vanishing Rights, and the Rule of Law* (Princeton University Press, 2012); NS Kim, *Wrap Contracts: Foundations and Ramifications* (Oxford University Press, 2013).

media networks, notably in low- or middle-income countries, where acceptance of these platforms' contractual conditions may occur purely out of 'powerlessness and resignation',[40] and fear that otherwise one may be socially excluded.[41]

Indeed, due to important network effects triggered by those platforms, which are maximised by the fact that dominant social networks are the only apps to be 'zero rated'[42] – ie the data consumption related to such applications is not considered in the mobile access plan of users – in virtually all low- and middle-income countries.[43] Hence, in countries where everyone 'is on the platform', as they are the only subsidised means of communication, it is even more difficult for a user to 'take it or leave it'.

Furthermore, it is common practice for social media platforms to include contractual provisions allowing the unilateral modification of their – already unilaterally established – terms of service without even including obligations to notify users in case of modifications.[44] This situation, which has been tellingly described by Shubha Ghosh as 'contractual authoritarianism',[45] is further exacerbated by the structural power that digital platforms manifest by unilaterally implementing their private ordering through the definition of their digital architectures in a way that exclusively allows users to behave according to the will of the platform.

Hence, platforms enjoy a quasi-normative power in the form of a capacity to unilaterally establish the contractual provisions that will regulate the behaviour of their users, defining what activities they are allowed to perform, but also what personal data will be collected about them and how such data will be processed.[46]

[40] NA Draper and J Turow, 'The corporate cultivation of digital resignation' (2019) 21 *New Media & Society*, available at doi.org/10.1177/1461444819833331.

[41] L Belli and N Zingales, 'WhatsApp's New Rules: Time to Recognize the Real Cost of 'Free' Apps' (Medianama, 16 February 2021), available at www.medianama.com/2021/02/223-whatsapp-time-to-recognize-real-cost-of-free-apps.

[42] L Belli, 'Net neutrality, zero rating and the Minitelisation of the internet' (2017) 2 *Journal of Cyber*, available at doi.org/10.1080/23738871.2016.1238954.

[43] According to a study crowdsourced in 2018 by the UN Internet Governance Forum Coalition on Net Neutrality, in 98 out of 100 countries surveyed the only apps that are always zero-rated are part of the Facebook group. See Dynamic Coalition on Network Neutrality, 'Zero Rating Map' (Zero Rating, 2019), available at www.zerorating.info.

[44] Already in 2016, a study conducted by the Center for Technology and Society at Fundação Getulio Vargas in partnership with the Council of Europe analysed the terms of service of 50 online platforms, highlighting that only 30% of the analysed platforms explicitly committed to notifying users about changes in their contracts; 56% had contradictory or vague clauses, for instance, foreseeing that users will be notified only if the terms of service changes were considered 'significant' by the platform; while 12% of the platforms state explicitly that there would not be notification in the event of contractual changes regardless of their relevance. See J Venturini et al, 'Terms of Service and Human Rights: An Analysis of Online Platform Contracts' (Revan, 2016), available at hdl.handle.net/10438/18231.

[45] See S Ghosh, 'Against Contractual Authoritarianism' (2014) 44 *Southwestern Law School Review* 239, available at www.swlaw.edu/media/2916.

[46] See Belli and Venturini, 'Private ordering' (2016); Belli and Sappa, 'The Intermediary Conundrum' (2017).

The most salient feature of adhesion contracts commonly utilised by platforms is indeed that users can only decide to be subject to the pre-established terms.[47] In this context, the terms of service have the force of a 'law of the platform'[48] or even their 'constitution',[49] which is established and modifiable uniquely by the platform provider.

While the use of contractual regulation is not per se a new phenomenon, the extent to which this is used by digital platforms and social media in particular, and the combination of this feature with an extraordinarily frequent use of user interfaces defined as 'dark patterns', has the potential to enormously expand in scope and scale the impact of such private regulation. Indeed, the relatively new 'dark patterns' phenomenon aims at manipulating user behaviour, and ultimately subverting user intent,[50] via especially deceptive designs. Such design strategies can be seen as a further attempt to structure how users can behave, thus additionally undermining individual autonomy,[51] demonstrating the concrete impact on user behaviour of a surreptitious architecture – to use Lessig's terminology – and how the elaboration and implementation of such architectures allows platforms to exercise structural power. In this sense, the platforms' monopoly of decision is further configured by the unilateral capability to design interfaces making it impossible – or at least extraordinarily difficult and burdensome – for the user to express a 'choice' that is different than the one de facto imposed by the platform.

Lastly, yet importantly, the software architecture and interface defined by the platform provider allows it to define in an exhaustive manner the type and quantity of user data to be collected. In this sense, if we agree with the authors and institutions that, over the past decade, have incessantly stressed that 'data is the new oil'[52] and that personal data are 'the new currency of the digital world',[53] a 'new asset class'[54] and 'the world's most valuable resource',[55] then we must

[47] See Belli and De Filippi, 'Law of the Cloud' (2012); Radin, *Boilerplate* (2013); Kim, *Wrap Contracts* (2013).

[48] See Belli, Francisco and Zingales (n 5).

[49] E Celeste, 'Terms of Service and Bills of Rights: New Mechanisms of Constitutionalisation in the Social Media Environment?' (2019) 33 *International Review of Law, Computers & Technology* 122.

[50] See Mathur, Mayer and Kshirsagar, '*What Makes a Dark Pattern … Dark?* (2021).

[51] See Commission Nationale Informatique et Libertés, 'Shaping Choices in the Digital World' (2020), available at linc.cnil.fr/sites/default/files/atoms/files/cnil_ip_report_06_shaping_choices_in_the_digital_world.pdf.

[52] The phrase was coined by the British mathematician Clive Humby, in 2006, and was subsequently made popular by the World Economic Forum 2011 report on personal data. See World Economic Forum, 'Personal Data: The Emergence of a New Asset Class' (2011).

[53] M Kuneva, 'Keynote Speech' (European Commission Roundtable on Online Data Collection, Targeting and Profiling, Brussels, 31 March 2009), available at ec.europa.eu/commission/presscorner/detail/en/SPEECH_09_156.

[54] See World Economic Forum, 'Personal Data' (2011).

[55] 'The world's most valuable resource is no longer oil, but data' *The Economist* (6 May 2017), available at www.economist.com/leaders/2017/05/06/the-worlds-most-valuable-resource-is-no-longer-oil-but-data.

acknowledge that the power to define the quantity of data that will be collected from every user, de facto equals the power to levy taxes, paid with personal data. This latter point has been also acknowledged embryonically, in a recent decision of the Italian Competition Authority, AGCM, stressing that data provided to Facebook by its users 'represents payment for the use of the service'.[56]

B. Quasi-Executive Power

Digital platforms can enforce their private ordering through several technical measures. In this sense, the structural power they exercise becomes evident as they enjoy the unique capacity to define the software architectures of that shape the way platforms function. These software structures have a performative nature, as they do not simply define what behaviours are admitted within a platform, but they operationalise such prescriptions by building a structure that only allows users to behave as prescribed.[57] Indeed, the labyrinth metaphor is useful to describe also how the technical architectures and design interface of platforms work. The capability to monitor users, to collect specific types of data about them and to shape their behaviours and interactions is indeed baked into the structure of the platforms.

These features are well known by numerous policy-makers that have, for at least a decade, acknowledged explicitly the pivotal role of private intermediaries in advancing public policy objectives,[58] due to their position of control. The effectiveness of regulating by structure is the main reason why policy-makers are increasingly delegating traditional regulatory and police functions to the platforms that design and control digital environments.[59] Such tendency is visible in policies stimulating intermediaries' 'voluntary commitments'[60] to regulate and police the platforms and networks under their control, in accordance with the public policy objectives, to avoid being regulated by state actors.

Social media platforms have traditionally tried to avoid liability by 'voluntarily' banning content that may be deemed as illicit or 'harmful'.[61] These bans

[56] Autorità Garante della Concorrenza e del Mercato, 'IP330 – Sanzione a Facebook per 7 milioni' (*AGCM*, 17 February 2021), available at www.agcm.it/media/comunicati-stampa/2021/2/IP330-.

[57] See L. Belli (n 10) 143–44.

[58] See OECD (n 17).

[59] See particularly Belli, Francisco and Zingales (n 5); Belli and Sappa (n 4).

[60] See, for instance, the Code of Conduct on illegal online hate speech, developed by Facebook, Twitter, YouTube and Microsoft, together with the European Commission, which establishes a series of commitments to combat the spread of illegal hate speech online in Europe: 'Code of Conduct on Countering Illegal Hate Speech Online', available at ec.europa.eu/justice/fundamental-rights/files/hate_speech_code_of_conduct_en.pdf.

[61] See Part IV of this volume. See also E Celeste, 'Digital Punishment: Social Media Exclusion and the Constitutionalising Role of National Courts' (2021) 35 *International Review of Law, Computers & Technology* 1.

are enshrined – through usually vague terminology – in the platforms' terms of service or community guidelines, and are subsequently enforced either manually or algorithmically. Manual implementations are conducted by specific platform employees – the so-called 'moderators' – who actively monitor users' compliance.[62] As such, manual enforcement is performed by dedicated teams of individuals that dominant platforms often establish to monitor the activities of users and ensure compliance with the platform's own contractual regulation.[63] For example, Facebook can remove any content that is determined to violate its contractual conditions thanks to hundreds of reviewers. Any user considered by Facebook as having posted such content may be subject to the suspension or blocking of their account.[64] The same procedure is established by most platforms, which explicitly foresee the possibility to terminate user accounts without previous notice and without allowing users to challenge the decision.[65]

When establishing the logical architecture of their systems, social media can embed self-performing policing functions within the very algorithmic structure of their platforms. As such, the digital structure of the platform is designed to prohibit activities, for example, automatically filtering out copyrighted material or paedo-pornographic content.[66] Facebook's strategy to tackle misinformation tellingly exemplifies how technology is utilised, and how technology can be combined with human efforts to implement contractual provisions, but it also illustrates the limits of such efforts. Conspicuously, the social network's most recent Community Standards Enforcement Report explains that

> when we fight misinformation, we use a combination of technology and human review by third-party fact-checkers. When it comes to articles, we use technology to, first, predict articles that are likely to contain misinformation and prioritize those for fact-checkers to review. Second, once we have a rating from a fact-checker, we use technology to find duplicates of that content.[67]

[62] As an example, in May 2017, Facebook announced the adding of '3,000 people to [Facebook's] community operations team around the world – on top of the 4,500 we have today – to review the millions of reports we get every week'. See M Zuckerberg, 'Official announcement' (Facebook, 3 May 2017), available at <https:/www.facebook.com/zuck/posts/10103695315624661> accessed 22 July 2021.

[63] For instance, Facebook recently announced that, during March 2021 alone, it removed more than 1,100 accounts tied to spreading deceptive content in a variety of countries as part of its effort to root out disinformation efforts. See Facebook, 'March 2021 Coordinated Inauthentic Behavior Report' (About Facebook, 6 April 2021), available at about.fb.com/news/2021/04/march-2021-coordinated-inauthentic-behavior-report/> accessed 22 July 2021.

[64] See Facebook, 'Terms of Service' (2021), available at www.facebook.com/policies/?ref=pf.

[65] For instance, such provisions can be found in 88% of the platforms analysed by the study on Terms of Service and Human Rights, conducted by the Center for Technology and Society at FGV, which has also demonstrated that none of the analysed platforms commits to notifying users before proceeding with account termination. See Venturini et al, 'Terms of Service and Human Rights' (2016).

[66] See ch 10 (Frosio) in this volume.

[67] See Facebook, 'Seeing the Truth' (About Facebook, 13 September 2018), available at about.fb.com/news/2018/09/inside-feed-tessa-lyons-photos-videos.

However empirical evidence of automated technology's erroneous decisions and over-removal is abundant.[68] Indeed, automated technology cannot be implemented at scale as only humans can understand the nuanced ways humans communicate and the difference, for instance, between satire and threats.

Hence, while the definition of the platforms' software architectures is largely utilised to implement platforms policies and assert platforms' monopoly to decide within their digital frontiers, it seems hard to claim that such tools are exempt from critique, notably regarding their full compatibility with due process and other fundamental rights principles.

C. Quasi-Judicial Power

It also seems relevant to reiterate that platforms can put in place alternative dispute resolution processes, adjudicate disputes between users based on their self-defined contractual regulation, and subsequently implement the results of the adjudication via technical means.[69] Online dispute resolution (ODR) is a form of alternative dispute resolution increasingly adopted by social media platforms as it takes advantage of the efficiency and transborder nature of digital technologies. These systems are generating increasing interest from a wide range of stakeholders and, in 2019, the Coalition on Platform Responsibility of the United Nations Internet Governance Forum (IGF) has elaborated a set of Best Practices on Platforms' Implementation of the Right to an Effective Remedy, which may be seen a multistakeholder efforts to foster a responsible use of such ODR tools by digital platforms.[70]

ODR systems are far from being a novelty and, as an example, ecommerce platform eBay pioneered ODR in 1999. Since the late 1990s, the platform has invited its users to voluntarily settle their disputes, by offering assisted negotiation software, initially developed by the start-up SquareTrade.[71] If a settlement

[68] For an overview of tools and techniques utilised to implement 'takedowns' of illicit content, exploring mistakes 'made by both "bots" and humans,' see JM Urban, J Karaganis and BL Schofield, 'Notice and Takedown in Everyday Practice' (2017) UC Berkeley Public Law Research Paper No 2755628, available at ssrn.com/abstract=2755628. The Electronic Frontier Foundation has also provided a useful compilation of erroneous automatic implementations of social media terms of services in its online repository: 'TOSsed Out', available at www.eff.org/tossedout.

[69] See Belli (n 10) 202–09; Belli and Venturini (n 1).

[70] The Recommendations are structured in four sections exploring the safeguards: (a) prior to the adoption dispute resolution measures; (b) in connection with the adoption dispute resolution measures; (c) relating to dispute resolution mechanism; (d) and relating to the implementation of the remedy. See Coalition on Platform Responsibility of the United Nations Internet Governance Forum, 'Best Practices on Platforms' Implementation of the Right to an Effective Remedy' (2019), available at www.intgovforum.org/multilingual/index.php?q=filedepot_download/4905/1550.

[71] See E Katsh 'ODR: A Look at History – A Few Thoughts About the Present and Some Speculation About the Future' in MS Abdel Wahab, E Katsh and D Rainey (eds), *Online Dispute Resolution: Theory and Practice: A Treatise on Technology and Dispute Resolution* (Eleven International Publishers, 2011).

could not be reached, the claim escalated to adjudication while the sum involved in the disputed transaction was frozen, thus ensuring the enforcement of the final decision.[72]

Facebook has been researching ODR systems for several years and, in 2016, began offering its users software tools to resolve disputes over offensive posts, including insults and upsetting images. The social media network created message templates that facilitate users' attempts to explain the reasons why they wish to have some specific content removed. For example, users can select options, such as 'it's embarrassing' or 'it's a bad photo of me,' and they are also asked to state how the content they object made them feel, such as angry, sad or afraid, as well as the level of the emotions they report.

Besides these examples, ODR systems have been adopted by a variety of platforms that usually include – or may even impose[73] – such mechanisms to solve conflicts amongst users based on 'the law of the platform.' As such, it can be argued that digital platforms do not simply enjoy a quasi-normative power to unilaterally define their contractual regulation and the quasi-executive power to unilaterally enforce it technically, but they also enjoy the quasi-judicial power to take decisions based on the how their contractual norms are applied by their self-defined ODR systems.[74]

Probably the only governance element that digital platforms had not dared reproduce within their private ordering structures was a supreme court. As of 2020, however, as Part IV of this volume will analyse in depth, this taboo has been lifted, thanks to Facebook's new structural power experiment: the Oversight Board, which Mark Zuckerberg himself once defined as 'the Facebook Supreme Court.'[75]

IV. Conclusion

The combination of quasi-normative, -executive and -judicial powers ascribes a particularly authoritative position to social media platforms, concentrating remarkable power in their hands. Importantly, such concentration of private sovereignty does not originate exclusively from the platforms themselves; it can also be

[72] ibid.

[73] The above-mentioned study demonstrated that 34% of the 50 most utilised digital platforms imposed ODR systems as the only method for dispute resolution, in their terms of service. See Venturini et al (n 44).

[74] For a more detailed analysis of the quasi-judicial power of social media platforms, especially in the context of online content moderation, see Part IV of this volume.

[75] Mark Zuckerberg initially utilised such a formula, most likely regretting it and backpedalling at a later stage. See T Room, 'Facebook unveils charter for its "Supreme Court," where users can go to contest the company's decisions' *The Washington Post* (17 September 2019), available at www.washingtonpost.com/technology/2019/09/17/facebook-unveils-charter-its-supreme-court-where-users-can-go-contest-companys-decisions.

regarded as the expression of a consolidated tendency towards the privatisation of traditionally public functions, resulting from public policy. As pointed out previously, many examples already corroborate the tendency to delegate to platforms the design and implementation of – supposedly – efficient solutions to particularly thorny questions, to which policy-makers may not be able or willing to answer.

Facebook's Oversight Board is also an example in this sense. Heralded by the social network as an independent entity with a core function of content moderation oversight, the Board is able to 'reverse Facebook's decisions about whether to allow or remove certain posts on the platform'.[76] The triple purpose of the new supreme body is to hear and judge appeals from users regarding content that the social network has taken down from the platform, to review policy decisions submitted by Facebook to the Board, and to elaborate policy recommendations. Importantly, the Board has been designed to be a global body, with the aspirational goal to define global standards for social networking platforms. The fact that Facebook has established its own supreme court offers rather explicit evidence of the existence of its structural power, including regarding the establishment of new institutions. The establishment of the Board also represents the social media's understanding that such an institution represents the best possible effort to satisfy all stakeholders, calling for regulation to solve existing problems – or perhaps the best possible strategy to distract them from the elaboration of regulation.

This private constitutional effort may signal the willingness to create self-regulation mechanisms able to protect fundamental values and principles. However, it may also be considered a remarkably effective diversion, explicitly conceived to generate attention around a well-structured distraction, while the company maintains its business model unchanged. Indeed, public regulation of what content is admissible or not would almost certainly hamper the business of the social media company, based on the continuous user stimulation to share content – and associated personal data – and the permanent collection of personal and frequently sensitive information about its users. Public regulation outlawing specific content would, consequently, impose censoring such content, obliging companies to impede users from sharing the content and, therefore, losing the data associated to it.

Tellingly, the most controversial content moderation decisions by Facebook usually do not affect censoring problematic content, but *not* censoring it. The decision to maintain even patently false claims by elected politicians or virtually any kind of claims contained in political advertisements is not a decision on which the Board may have any remit as it is a platform policy to maintain content rather than taking it down. This clearly explains the (ir)relevance of the new Board for content moderation purposes, and how meaningfully one truly can expect it to increase

[76] See Facebook, 'Draft Charter: An Oversight Board for Content Decisions' (2019), available at about.fb.com/wp-content/uploads/2019/09/draft-charter-oversight-board-for-content-decisions-2.pdf.

the platform's responsibility. While the body and its process deserve credit, the real impact for which it has been designed is purposely limited.

Furthermore, one should remember that, while private ordering systems may offer interesting solutions to deal with complex online interactions, they are clearly not democratic institutions, accountable to anyone other than their company's shareholders. Considering that social, economic and, ultimately, democratic interactions increasingly depend on digital platforms, and notably on social media, one would expect stronger stances by policy-makers regarding their regulatory obligations and more resistance to letting platforms be the new private overlords. In this sense, it is surely worth exploring additional mechanisms to enhance digital platforms accountability, as the lack of adequate overview and properly defined – and duly enforced – limits to platform power gives rise to collateral effects such as blatant fundamental rights abuses[77] and irreversible distortions of competition in the market.[78]

Social media platforms are central to the entire digital ecosystem, which in turn, has become central to, if not indissociably intertwined with, the structure of offline activities. Increasingly, the ways in which platforms operate affect individuals' ability to develop their opinion and personality, shape their offline lives and engage in social, political and economic interactions. Given the scale of their impact, it is crucial to understand that platforms' architectural and regulatory choices are not neutral. On the contrary, their choices represent a clear example of structural power. The values that drive such choices affect both our personal lives and the functioning of our democracies and markets.[79] The question that should be addressed by future research is therefore a truly constitutional one: what is the most appropriate strategy to subject platforms' private sovereignty and structural power to fundamental rights values, democratic oversight, labour protection and competition regulation?

[77] In March 2018, the chairman of the UN Independent International Fact-Finding Mission on Myanmar, told reporters that Facebook had played a 'determining role' in facilitating the incitement of violence against Rohingya Muslims in Myanmar. See 'UN: Facebook has turned into a beast in Myanmar' (BBC, 13 March 2018), available at www.bbc.com/news/technology-43385677.

[78] See, for instance J Crémer, Y-A de Montjoye and H Schweitzer, 'Competition policy for the digital era' (Publications Office of the European Union, 2019); UK Competition and Markets Authority, 'Online Platforms and Digital Advertising' (CMA, 2019).

[79] See Belli and Zingales (n 36).

7

No Place for Women: Gaps and Challenges in Promoting Equality on Social Media

MARIANA VALENTE*

I. Introduction

In 2015, the Brazilian journalist A. F. wrote an article about sexism in the geek world.[1] Self-identifying as a geek, the young woman provided first-hand accounts of how it was to be female in certain online communities and the sorts of exclusions she went through. It did not take long before users of a Brazilian forum picked up on her article, discussed ways to abuse her, and someone allegedly broke into a scoring company database and obtained her home address. A.F. had to leave her home after receiving threats and being mailed all sorts of packages, from sex shop items to living animals. Her abusers even sent her neighbours t-shirts with her picture and slurs. In the forums, users said they would not stop until she committed suicide. A.F. reported this to the police and delivered the evidence, but the police took no action. She lost freelance opportunities because some editors were afraid to publish her. She also self-censored and had second thoughts before addressing gender subjects.

Five years later, in 2020, Brazil elected the highest ever number of women for local offices – though that figure was as low as 13 per cent of Brazilian mayors. Many analysts consider social media to have played a significant role in this.[2] However, gender-based violence directed at women candidates on social media

* I thank Fernanda Martins, Ester Borges, Clarice Tavares, Blenda Santos, Catharina Pereira, Jade Becari, Victor Pavarin, Anita Gurumurthy and Nandini Chami for discussions and help in developing some of the arguments presented in this chapter.

[1] I followed the case closely and had several academic interactions with the person in question. She allowed referring to her case but prefers not to have her name disclosed.

[2] L de Oliveira Ramos et al, Candidatas em jogo: um estudo sobre os impactos das regras eleitorais na inserção de mulheres na política (FGV Direito SP, 2020), available at bibliotecadigital.fgv.br/dspace/handle/10438/29826; AC Camargo, 'Género como condicionante da participação política no Brasil: trajetórias, capital político e o potencial das tecnologias' (2020) 9 *Revista Comunicando – Os novos caminhos da comunicação* 300.

was significant during the elections. In 2020, MonitorA, an observatory of political and electoral violence on social media conducted by InternetLab, a research centre based in São Paulo, Brazil, and AzMina, a Brazilian feminist media outlet, collected and analysed comments directed at 175 candidates for municipal elections, male and female, on Twitter, YouTube and Instagram.[3] In the first electoral round, female candidates received an average of 40 offensive comments on Twitter.[4] The objectionable content, in general, referred to physical, intellectual or moral aspects of their lives – who they *are*.[5] In contrast, male candidates were mostly criticized for what they *did* – frequently, their professional performance in political or public management positions. In the second round, the attacks extended to the supporters of the female candidates, containing even more violent, offensive and sexist content.[6]

When it comes to women's right to equality or enjoyment of fundamental rights, social media have been both the site for their expansion and new limitations. In different countries, civil society, academics, government officials and certain units inside social media companies have insisted particular focus be given to those processes. International organisations such as the United Nations, Internet policy-related forums such as the Internet Governance Forum and civil society spaces such as RightsCon have increasingly recognised and created space for this issue. Social media could support material equality and the conditions for the full expression of women's lives, personalities and choices. It can also provide the instruments and means for deepening existing inequalities. Norm-setting processes can support one way or the other.

Some countries have passed legislation against online violence connected to domestic violence and, more specifically, non-consensual dissemination of intimate images (NCII).[7] However, the legislation generally fails to address forms of violence linked to women's presence in online public spaces.[8] When it comes to social media, given the growing dominance of private actors in fulfilling or limiting fundamental rights, norm-setting also refers to their internal rules, which directly affect people's lives. The absence of working concepts and regulation strategies at

[3] AzMina Magazine and InternetLab, 'Monitora: Report On Online Political Violence On The Pages And Profiles Of Candidates In The 2020 Municipal Elections' (2021), available at www.internetlab.org.br/wp-content/uploads/2021/03/5P_Relatorio_MonitorA-ENG.pdf.

[4] The tweets were collected in the first electoral round, between 27 September and 27 October 2021; ibid 26.

[5] ibid 30.

[6] ibid 6. Among 3,100 tweets containing aggressive content and some engagement (like or retweet) involving monitored candidates in the first round, 40% were offences targeted at the female candidates, among which 42% involved moral insults and 27% fatphobia. When referring specifically to Joice Hasselmann, candidate for mayor of São Paulo, 55% of the tweets mentioned physical characteristics and used fatphobic terms.

[7] N Neris, J Pacetta Ruiz and M Giorgetti Valente, 'Análise comparada de estratégias de enfrentamento a "revenge porn" pelo mundo' (2017) 7 *Revista Brasileira de Políticas Públicas* 333.

[8] K Barker and O Jurasz, *Online Misogyny as Hate Crime: A Challenge for Legal Regulation?* (Routledge, 2018); D Lillian, 'A Thorn by Any Other Name: Sexist Discourse as Hate Speech' (2007) 18 *Discourse & Society* 719.

the state level feeds and is fed by social media's concurrent failure to address these forms of aggression unrelated to domestic violence.

This chapter addresses possible reasons for these failures and the related shortcomings in introducing gender constitutional protections to achieve equality and assure dignity to women. Section II addresses fundamental distinctions and the ambiguities present in the relationship between women's rights and social media. The complexity and multidirectionality of that relationship is an integral part of formulating policy that furthers women's fundamental rights. In section III, I consider how rules addressing platform liability for NCII in Brazil have reached a balance in rights and interests online. That case is instrumental to understanding how and why countries and social media themselves have been failing to reach a similar point regarding other forms of violence against women. Using field research from Brazil and drawing on discussions with research partners in India,[9] I aim to demonstrate that concepts such as hate speech are limited and encounter challenges when they do not correspond to local legal culture, concepts and practices. Because of that, and as a way to address legal developments in different jurisdictions, I suggest using instead the concept of 'misogynist public communication'.

II. Contrasting Online Misogyny

The results of the MonitorA project were similar to other international studies and civil society reports over the last decade: women in public positions – politicians, journalists, academics, activists – receive a disproportionate amount of online abuse. A 2021 Unesco study involving 901 female journalists from 125 countries found them to be under 'unprecedented attack'.[10] Nearly three-quarters experienced online hostility of some sort, and a quarter was threatened with death and sexual violence. The Filipino journalist Maria Ressa at one point received 90 hate messages per hour on Facebook alone – around 2,000 'ugly' comments per day. The Lebanese Al Jazeera presenter Ghada Ouiess receives at least one death threat every day she is on air.[11] The report states that online violence against women journalists is usually misogynistic and intimate, and extends to family, sources and colleagues. A 2017 study investigating 70 million comments posted to *The Guardian* website between 2006 and 2016 revealed that out of the 10 most targeted journalists, eight were women – while women consituted only 28 per cent

[9] I refer to research developed collaboratively between IT for Change (India) and InternetLab (Brazil), supported by the International Development Research Center (IDRC, Canada), in the project Recognize, Resist, Remedy. The project focuses on exploring legal-institutional and socio-cultural responses to online sexism and misogyny, with special attention to the challenges of postcolonial democracies in the Global South.

[10] J Posetti et al, 'The Chilling: Global Trends in Online Violence against Women Journalists' (UNESCO, 2021), available at en.unesco.org/publications/thechilling.

[11] ibid.

of writers for the newspaper.[12] Black, Asian and minority ethnic women are disproportionately affected, as was the case for black female candidates in the Brazilian MonitorA research.[13]

Online misogyny is not just a problem of women expressing their opinions publicly – misogyny and antifeminism are different and complementary concepts, as we will discuss. A 2020 survey from Plan International of over 14,000 girls and young women across 22 countries revealed that 58 per cent of them had personally faced some form of harassment on social media platforms.[14] In Brazil, that number is as high as 77 per cent. In addition, 39 per cent of the total reported threats of sexual violence, 39 per cent body-shaming, and 29 per cent received racist comments (41 per cent in Brazil). As a result, they suffered from lower self-esteem or confidence, mental and emotional stress, feeling physically unsafe, and problems with family, friends, school or finding jobs.[15] A Pew Research study shows that US men generally receive more harassment than women (43 per cent to 38 per cent), but 47 per cent of women say they think it happened because of their gender, versus 18 per cent of men.[16] Women are also far more likely to be sexually abused online (33 per cent of women under 35, versus 11 per cent of men of the same age).[17]

Gender-based online harassment tactics take different forms. They include threats and intimidation, hateful speech, impersonation or online identity theft, extortion, manipulating one's image, creating false information about them, doxing (sharing private information), distributing non-consensual intimate images, stalking, sending unwanted nude photos, or violent content. They might be coordinated actions over periods of time and will often be combined with offline acts. Online forms of violence have also leveraged domestic violence in their attempts to intimidate, dominate and isolate victims. Therefore, around the world, women have additionally faced technology-based surveillance and privacy breaches.[18]

[12] B Gardiner, '"It's a Terrible Way to Go to Work:" What 70 Million Readers' Comments on the Guardian Revealed about Hostility to Women and Minorities Online' (2018) 18 *Feminist Media Studies* 592.

[13] AzMina Magazine and InternetLab (n 2). In Latin America, the expression 'political violence' has been used particularly in Latin America to account for (unfortunately frequent) politically motivated violence towards persons holding or aspiring to public elected offices – whether online or offline – affecting sub-altern groups, including women. The assassination of Rio de Janeiro city councillor Marielle Franco in 2018 was a brutal milestone that demonstrated how far political violence can go. In online spaces, and particularly on social media, women politicians report not only harassment and hostility, but also direct and indirect threats.

[14] Plan International, 'Free to be online?' (2020), available at plan-international.org/publications/freetobeonline.

[15] ibid.

[16] Pew Research Center, 'The State of Online Harassment' (2021), available at www.pewresearch.org/internet/2021/01/13/the-state-of-online-harassment.

[17] ibid.

[18] M Dragiewicz et al, 'Technology Facilitated Coercive Control: Domestic Violence and the Competing Roles of Digital Media Platforms' (2018) 18 *Feminist Media Studies* 609, 4.

According to Debbie Ging and Eugenia Siapera, while misogyny refers to 'a more general set of attitudes and behaviors towards women', antifeminism is understood as 'a response to a distinct set of gender-political values that are not espoused exclusively by women'[19] – a position that is explicitly against gender equality. However, recent developments in digital technologies and social media have progressively blurred the line between antifeminism and misogyny. For example, online antifeminism in the anglophone world often involves misogynist sentiments, and one of its strategies has been the individualised, and frequently sexualised, attacks on individual women.[20] The Irish writer Angela Nagle describes how antifeminism is a cross-cutting presence in the alt-right movement, with varying levels of misogyny.[21] Eugenia Siapera argues that, ultimately, antifeminism and misogyny express the same position: that biology and reproduction functions determine women's role in society; hence, because their options and destinies are seen as limited, women are accordingly not afforded full autonomy or humanity.[22]

At the same time, the distinction between the two concepts still holds. The spread of non-consensual intimate images (NCII), for instance, is a form of gender-based violence that expresses misogynistic values, but its perpetrators might not espouse explicit antifeminism.[23] Also, while legal systems in the world encompass and punish certain manifestations of misogyny,[24] antifeminism per se

[19] D Ging and E Siapera, 'Introduction' in D Ging and E Siaspera (eds), *Gender Hate Online: Understanding the New Anti-Feminism* (Palgrave Macmillan, 2019) 2.

[20] 'While pre-internet antifeminism tended to mobilize men around issues such as divorce, child custody and the feminization of education, using conventional political methods such as public demonstrations and petitions, the new anti-feminists have adopted a highly personalized style of politics that often fails to distinguish between feminists and women.' Ging and Siapera (ibid) 2. Worldwide, antifeminist misogynist groups have attracted public attention after high-profile events such as the Oregon, Isla Vista and Toronto killings. Also in the Brazilian context, at least two mass murders have been linked to such groups, in Suzano (2019) and Realengo (2011). See L Coelho, 'Sol, Luciana, Elidia, Massacres de Suzano e Realengo: as 23 vítimas do terrorismo misógino', *Ponte Jornalismo* (9 March 2021), available at ponte.org/sol-luciana-elidia-massacres-de-suzano-e-realengo-as-23-vitimas-do-terrorismo-misogino.

[21] A Nagle, *Kill All Normies: Online Culture Wars From 4Chan And Tumblr To Trump And The Alt-Right* (Zero Books, 2017).

[22] E Siapera, 'Online Misogyny as Witch Hunt: Primitive Accumulation in the Age of Techno-Capitalism' in D Ging and E Siapera (eds), *Gender Hate Online: Understanding the New Anti-Feminism* (Palgrave Macmillan, 2019) 31.

[23] NCII is gendered violence: it is evident that, with few exceptions, the female sex is affected. Brazilian case law research I coordinated in 2016 revealed that women were the plaintiffs in around 90% of cases involving NCII – even when, in many of these cases, images depict heterosexual couples. MG Valente et al, *O Corpo é o Código: Estratégias Jurídicas de Enfrentamento Ao Revenge Porn No Brasil* (InternetLab, 2016).

[24] For example, in Brazil, a 2015 law (Law n. 13.104) provides that feminicide, that is, homicides committed against women in the context of domestic law or upon contempt or discrimination against women, is punished with a higher penalty than simple homicides. The Mexican Criminal Code (DOF 23-12-1974) has had a similar provision since 2012 (DOF 14.06.2012), describing what constitutes a 'gender-related motivation' in detail, for example, that the victimised woman had been threatened by the aggressor before. Several Latin-American countries have passed laws defining political violence against women that mobilise notions of misogyny. See United Nations/CEPAL, 'Observatorio de Igualdad de Género de América Latina y el Caribe', available at oig.cepal.org/en/laws/violence-laws.

is not unlawful, even if, through feminist lenses, it damages gender equality. Below, I will address in detail how the relationship between women's fundamental rights and the Internet, particularly social media, is complex and cannot be determined by violence, antifeminism and misogyny alone.

A. An Internet of Ambiguities: Women's Activism, Social Media and Violence

In the 1990s, theorists envisioned the Internet as a radically inclusive place, where gender, race and class differences had a less important role or would be crushed altogether:[25] it was seen as having an enormous liberating potential for women.[26] However, more recent literature has questioned that view. Even Emma Jane, whose statement, 'misogyny's gone viral' (referring to her observation of the rise of online misogyny in the past few years), is frequently quoted, refers back to her own experience in 1998 to argue that misogyny has always been there, if not as widespread.[27] Whitney Phillips refers to the period between 2008 and 2012, when what she says is called an 'Internet culture' or a 'meme culture' was formed on the platform 4chan.[28] The forum was at that time populated by mostly male, white, middle-class individuals, and the hateful content that was an integral part of its humour did not affect them personally. That 'Internet culture', then, though universalised as *the* Internet culture, is the particular culture of a particular demographic.[29] A similar demographic was prevalent online in the 1990s. However, groups of feminists would look ahead and embrace the idea of cyberfeminism:[30] activist, intellectual and artistic visions that digital technologies could be extremely liberating, that is now largely considered to be excessively optimist.[31] In the 2000s, the scenario became more complex,[32] and feminist takes on the Internet began to incorporate discussions such as intersectionality, unequal participation in the development of digital technologies, violence and discrimination.[33]

[25] The famous John Perry Barlow's 'A Declaration of the Independence of Cyberspace' (1996) states that the cybersphere would be a world where 'all may enter without privilege or prejudice accorded by race, economic power, military force, or station of birth.'

[26] J Wajcman, 'Feminist Theories of Technology' (2010) 34 *Cambridge Journal of Economics* 143.

[27] E Jane, *Misogyny Online: A Short (and Brutish) History* (SAGE, 2016) 18.

[28] W Phillips, 'It Wasn't Just the Trolls: Early Internet Culture, 'Fun,' and the Fires of Exclusionary Laughter' (2019) 5 *Social Media + Society*.

[29] ibid.

[30] Based on Donna Haraway's metaphor of the cyborg. See D Haraway, 'A Manifesto for Cyborgs: Science, Technology, and Socialist Feminism in the 1980s' (1987) 2 *Australian Feminist Studies* 1.

[31] Judy Wajcman, 'Feminist Theories of Technology' (2010).

[32] C Branco de Castro Ferreira, 'Feminismos web: linhas de ação e maneiras de atuação no debate feminista contemporâneo' [2015] *Cadernos Pagu* 199.

[33] J Wajcman, 'Reflections on Gender and Technology Studies: In What State Is the Art?' (2000) 30 *Social Studies of Science* 447.

Field research in Brazil has highlighted the significant role played by the Internet in the founding of feminist collectives in the outskirts of São Paulo, overcoming geographical limits.[34] It also showed how international trends connected to fourth-wave feminism,[35] particularly the Slut Walk, impacted local feminism (which had become 'institutionalised' in the previous decades), leading to the re-occupation of streets in the 2010s.[36] The links between online and on-site mobilisation are tight, both in Brazil and elsewhere.[37] But social networks have also been important for the feminist movements per se as centres for discursive elaboration,[38] building on communication strategies that existed before the advent of digital technologies[39] and impacting the traditional media in turn.

The paradox is that, while the Internet has become a critical avenue for women to express themselves and engage in public life, it has also emerged as a space of heightened hostility against feminism and against women who simply speak.[40] At least part of online gender-based violence can be understood as a reaction to these processes of bringing visibility to women's organising. Part of its desired effects is against activism and activists. Therefore, there are structural ties between online feminist activism and online gender-based violence.

The English-speaking literature frequently approaches this problem as a conflict between fourth-wave feminism (or the pejorative term 'social justice warriors')

[34] J Medeiros, 'Microssociologia de Uma Esfera Pública Virtual: A Formação de Uma Rede Feminista Periférica Na Internet' (FESPSP, 2016), available at www.fespsp.org.br/seminarios/anaisV/GT4/Microsocioesf_JonasMedeiros.pdf.

[35] E Lawrence and J Ringrose, 'From Misandry Memes to Manspreading: How Social Media Feminism is Challenging Sexism' (2016) Seminar: A Collaborative Critical Sexology and Sex-Gen-inthe-South, Critical Sexology (United Kingdom, 2016).

[36] J de Medeiros and F Fanti, 'A Gênese da 'Primavera Feminista' no Brasil: A Emergência de Novos Sujeitos Coletivos' project presented at the Public Sphere and Political Culture subgroup of CEBRAP's Núcleo Direito e Democracia (CEBRAP, 2018).

[37] 'The women's marches in the U.S. in 2017, the demonstrations in Spain in May 2018 against a non-guilty gang rape verdict and the 2018 on-street political activism in Ireland around the Repeal the 8th campaign, all suggest that connective and collective action (Bennett and Segerberg 2012) can be engaged in mutually productive interplay. Indeed, the range of creative initiatives undertaken by the Irish Repeal movement serve as excellent examples of both Paulo Gerbaudo's (2012) and Jeffrey Juris' (2012) analyses of the political uses of social media to reappropriate public space'. D Ging, 'Bros v. Hos: Postfeminism, Anti-Feminism and the Toxic Turn in Digital Gender Politics' in D Ging and E Siapera (eds), *Gender Hate Online: Understanding the New Anti-Feminism* (Palgrave Macmillan, 2019).

[38] Medeiros, 'Microssociologia de Uma Esfera Pública Virtual' (2016).

[39] In 1970s Brazil, in the middle of a military dictatorship that persecuted and tortured activists, feminists struggled to influence the media and communications involved the development of alternative media to circulate marginalised issues and voices. That was the case of the newspapers *Brasil Mulher* (1975–79), *Nós Mulheres* (1976–78), and *Mulherio* (1981–87). MA de Almeida Teles, *Breve história do feminismo no Brasil e outros ensaios* (Alameda, 2017); M Valente and N Neris, 'Are We Going to Feminise the Internet?' (2019) 15 *Sur – International Journal on Human Rights* 102.

[40] Nancy Fraser's perspective on the public sphere, critiquing of Jürgen Habermas' earlier formulation of the concept, helps to better understand this paradox – there is a plurality of publics competing with each other. N Fraser, 'Rethinking the Public Sphere: A Contribution to the Critique of Actually Existing Democracy' (1990) *Social Text* 56.

and the alt-right, channers, trolls or man-rights groups.[41] Online violence against women indeed takes outrageously similar forms worldwide, as the story about A.F. at the beginning of this chapter illustrates. However, local characteristics of sexism and activism demand that different narratives be considered, involving, in the case of Brazil, colonialist powers, a deep entrenchment with racism,[42] and the deeply unequal access to technology.

Lola Aronovich, a feminist journalist who has written a prominent blog since 1998, has been attacked online and offline by organised misogynist groups since 2011. Her main aggressor was definitively arrested in 2018 after being briefly detained in 2009 for racism in online spaces.[43] Débora Diniz, a feminist academic who is outspoken on reproductive rights, which are almost absent in Brazil, left the country after receiving a large number of online threats. There is evidence that her abusers were connected to Lola's abusers, who also targeted former gay congressman Jean Willys and writer and favela activist Anderson França – both of whom exiled due to the online and physical threats they received.[44] The profile of violence seems to have risen since the election of far-right President Jair Bolsonaro in 2019.

However, despite the similarities, the local resistance to networked feminism does not seem to have developed as a result of fourth-wave or even postfeminism reactions. Instead, it is interwoven with Brazil's longstanding history of violence against human rights activists. A chan-like, misogynist culture influenced by their international counterparts is also found in Portuguese and English-speaking Brazilians. However, the police's low investigating capabilities, wide-spread violence, and extreme gender and racial inequality in political representation also play a part. Violence is a mark of Brazilian colonial history: sexual violence against enslaved African women was a colonial tool.[45] Since Brazil's redemocratisation in 1988, social movements have conquered anti-discrimination legislation and pushed courts to recognise the acquired rights. Misogyny, however, is still not recognised as a specific form of discrimination from a constitutional perspective.

In the next section, I will address possible structural relations between gender and technology to broaden the scope of the narratives around why and how

[41] For example, see Nagle, *Kill All Normies* (2017); Ging, 'Bros v. Hos' (2019). Some authors also consider the role of culture or material economic vulnerabilities that exacerbate conflict – see Siapera, 'Online Misogyny as Witch Hunt' (2019). I will not tackle that problem in depth here; what I observe, however, is that violence in Brazil is characteristic of social relations and finds its roots in colonial history.

[42] For a detailed account on how those differences intertwine, see L Gonzalez, *Por um feminismo afro-latino-americano* (Zahar, 2020).

[43] R Baptista, 'Senti que existe justiça, diz Lola sobre vitória em ação contra misógino' *Tilt Uol* (Recife, 24 November 2020), available at www.uol.com.br/tilt/noticias/redacao/2020/11/24/lola-aronovich-celebra-vitoria-judicial-em-caso-contra-mascu.htm.

[44] D Phillips, 'New generation of political exiles leave Bolsonaro's Brazil "to stay alive"' *The Guardian* (11 July 2019), available at www.theguardian.com/world/2019/jul/11/brazil-political-exiles-bolsonaro.

[45] See, again, Gonzalez, *Por um feminismo afro-latino-americano* (2020).

online gender-based violence takes place. Drawing on a story about the evolution of the idea that violence could happen online, I also argue that normative ideas at societal level impact policy and governance processes – and are an integral part of overcoming the risks to fundamental rights posed to women on social media.

B. Bodies in Code and Code in Bodies

Defining online acts as violence is central to interpreting pre-existing legislation and constitutional rights as enforceable against online attacks. Since 2012, the United Nations Human Rights Council has adopted resolutions affirming that people's offline rights must be protected online.[46] In each jurisdiction, that understanding has required a mix of legislative reform and legal interpretation. Academics and civil societies groups from different fields have made efforts to influence both.

It used to be thought that because society and technology are interlinked, measures to counter online misogyny would need to address both. That position has been contested. Since 2010, the number of attackers, targets, channels and attack modes has expanded drastically,[47] suggesting that the Internet inaugurated a new phenomenon, or simply shed light on one that women had always dealt with privately. It is impossible to assess what kind of hostility was present in private disconnected spaces, but feminist activism and theory support the idea that these practices stem from a long tradition of gender inequality and sexual oppression.[48]

Explanations that focus exclusively on social media's 'inherent' qualities such as anonymity, decentralisation, lack of control and algorithmic curation – the medium – are connected to techno-determinist views that technological development has pre-established, universal social effects.[49] On the other hand, focusing primarily on pre-existing inequalities in social, political and economic power and strategies to maintain this power in different societies – the foundations of the *message* – connects to another communication studies tradition, that of the 'social construction of technology', which preconised that nothing is inevitable in technological developement.[50]

Is this new wave of misogyny a product of the new medium, or is technology simply the means of expressing pre-exisiting misogyny? How does an answer to

[46] A/HRC/38/L.10/Rev.1, 2018; A/HRC/32/L.20, 2016; A/HRC/res/26/13, 2014; A/HRC/res/20/8, 2012.

[47] Jane, *Misogyny Online* (2016) 35.

[48] ibid.

[49] M Simões, S Las Heras and A Augusto, 'Gênero e Tecnologias Da Informação e Da Comunicação No Espaço Doméstico: Não Chega Ter, é Preciso Saber, Querer e Poder Usar' (2011) 8 *Cultura, Tecnologia e Identidade* 155.

[50] R Williams, *Television: Technology and Cultural Form*, 3rd edn (Routledge, 2015). TJ Pinch and WE Bijker, 'The Social Construction of Facts and Artefacts: Or How the Sociology of Science and the Sociology of Technology Might Benefit Each Other' (1984) 14 *Social Studies of Science* 399.

this question determine how we tackle the problem? Some contemporary authors have rejected both views as simplistic and unidirectional, proposing instead that social studies involving technology adopt an intermediary stance, that of 'reciprocal conditioning'[51] and the idea of 'mutual shaping'. As a result, the distinction between social or technical purity is eliminated: technologies are products of choices and become part of the social fabric. Technological transformation is a contingent and heterogeneous process in which technology and society are mutually constituted.[52] Long-time, pre-existing social, economic and cultural features are embedded in how technologies are built and how people appropriate them; their affordances – such as anonymity, formats such as memes, speed and disinhibition – are appropriated by and affect the behaviour of users, and vice versa.[53]

Social theories of technology have not traditionally been concerned with gender relations, but feminists and gender studies have highlighted the social and historical association between technology and masculinity.[54] Historian of technology Janet Abbate tells a detailed story of how notions about the computing profession and computing itself acquired different gender meanings over the decades, from undervalued feminine work during World War II to a highly valued, male-centered profession in later decades.[55] Recent studies connect the predominantly white and masculine environments in which digital technologies are developed with architectures and policies that take misogyny for granted; others relate technology-enabled misogyny to global economic shifts causing a decline in the real value of wages and sentiments of 'aggrieved entitlement' in some white men – a masculinity-in-crisis narrative.[56]

Mutual shaping means that online gender-based violence is an integral part of the making and the effects of technologies and social media. Policy responses have been delayed by an absence of recognition of such acts online and recognising them as violence per se – and therefore as something to push back against. The very concept of violence is socially and legally disputed; a minimum cross-culturally

[51] Simões, Las Heras and Augusto, 'Gênero e Tecnologias Da Informação e Da Comunicação No Espaço Doméstico' (2011) 2–3.

[52] Wajcman, 'Feminist Theories' (2010) 149.

[53] One example is Adrienne Massanari's work, particularly '#Gamergate and The Fappening: How Reddit's Algorithm, Governance, and Culture Support Toxic Technocultures' (2017) 19 *New Media & Society* 329. Grounding on actor-network theory, she analyses how Reddit's design, algorithm and policies have served misogynist activism, without assuming that they caused it.

[54] In the 1980s, the focus of feminist research and debates involving technology turned towards new themes. Sandra Harding pointed out that the feminist critique of science moved from a discussion of how women can access existing technologies to question how the science that seems so enmeshed in masculine projects serves emancipatory ends (S Harding, *The Science Question in Feminism* (Cornell University Press, 1986)). Furthermore, the debates in feminist technology studies received contributions from theoretical developments occurring, on the one hand, in the social studies of technology (SST) and, on the other hand, from the postmodern turn in gender theory. See Wajcman (n 26).

[55] J Abbate, *Recoding Gender: Women's Changing Participation in Computing* (MIT Press, 2012).

[56] Ging (n 37) 48, citing Messner and Montez de Oca and Michael Kimmel. See also Siapera (n 22).

valid concept would be that of non-legitimate or contestable physical harm, but most theorists of violence see the deep contextual character of violence.[57] In 2015, when the Association for Progressive Communications launched the anti-online gender-based violence Take Back the Tech campaign, online groups attacked it.[58] They argued that the campaign used an empty narrative and that equating online acts with violence would harm freedom of expression.[59] Around the same time, I was involved in legal research about NCII in Brazil. We discovered that lawyers and prosecutors had not been using the domestic violence legal framework for such cases.[60] It was still not common to understand NCII as violence and attach to it the same legal consequences.

Naming these online acts as violence is also a performative act. Besides unleashing legal consequences, it activates the attention that culture gives to everything forbidden, transgressive and illegal.[61] Notably, in the realm of institutional struggles for women's rights, the simple understanding of an act as violence, without having to prove, for instance, physical harm produced offline, mobilises a series of consequences.

Saying that online violence is violence per se does not understate its effects on women's rights online or offline. The consequences are social, psychological, financial and political, and they are felt online – self-censoring, withdrawing from online spaces, writing pseudonymously – and offline.[62] Victims also spend time and money on legal and physical protection and miss opportunities due to fear. In a broader, societal sense, bystanders feel effects too – deliberately or subconsciously, misogyny's tools are used to keep women 'in their place'[63] – and beyond individualised threats and other forms of attacks, discourses produce effects in the world.[64] Therefore, misogyny is a form of censorship. It imposes very high costs to speaking out[65] and produces concrete subordination and exclusion from

[57] The Brazilian anthropologist Maria Filomena Gregoria understands violence not necessarily as an abusive act that generates physical damage, but as abusive acts subject to moral and social condemnation or criminalisation ('Limites da sexualidade: violência, gênero e erotismo' (2008) 51 *Revista de Antropologia* 575). Along a similar line, the British social anthropologist Henrietta Moore refers to violence as an effective form of social control: instead of a breach of social order, violence is a signal of maintenance of fantasies of power and identity, involving gender, race and class, in a process that acquires different meanings over time and context. ('The problem of explaining violence in the social sciences' in P Harvey and P Gow (eds), *Sex and Violence: The Psychology of Violence and Risk Assessment.* (New York, Routledge, 1994) 138–55).

[58] 'Take Back The Tech | Take Control of Technology to End Gender-Based Violence', available at takebackthetech.net.

[59] Valente et al *O Corpo é o Código* (2016).

[60] ibid.

[61] M Valente and N Neris, 'Para falar de violência de gênero na internet: uma proposta teórica e metodológica' in G Natansohn and F Rovetto (eds), *Internet e feminismos: olhares sobre violências sexistas desde a América Latina* (Salvador, EDUFBA, 2019) 32–33.

[62] Jane (n 27).

[63] Ging and Siapera, 'Introduction' (2019) 2.

[64] M Matsuda, 'Public Response to Racist Speech: Considering the Victim's Story' (1989) 87 *Michigan Law Review* 2320.

[65] This is Zeynep Tufekci's argument in *Twitter and Tear Gas: The Power and Fragility of Networked Protest* (Yale University Press, 2018).

accessing and controlling the means of production and socio-economic participation in techno-capitalism.[66] In the next section, I will discuss a Brazilian example of a policy that successfully addressed imbalances related to women's rights on social media platforms; I will then dwell on how violence in public online spaces is still largely unaddressed.

III. Image-Based Violence and Platform Governance

Because the social and the technological are mutually constitutive and online violence harms women concretely, the law's role in national territories should involve finding solutions affecting both the level of society and platform governance. Legislating for image-based violence against women in Brazil is a good example of how those levels interplay and point to further difficulties for countries and between the national and transnational levels.

In 2013, two young women on opposite sides of the country committed suicide after having intimate images exposed, causing a national commotion. The episodes triggered immediate demands to criminalise the act of sharing NCII; in 2018, a new criminal offence was passed in Congress.[67] As controversial as criminalisation strategies are, it is quite straightforward that this legislative change addressed important demands. Before that, NCII victims had to resort to defamation laws to have their aggressors punished and thereby prove their *honour* was violated – honour is a legal category that has quite a several implications for women's freedoms.[68] Moreover, defamation laws are hard and expensive to prosecute under. The new offence is now considered a crime against sexual liberties, which is an important recognition and influences judges' legal reasoning.[69]

Finding ways to hold disseminators of NCII accountable was the obvious first step in global legal discussions. In many countries, laws criminalising NCII were approved around this time.[70] However, because the problem was deeply rooted in social media and messaging apps, there was an expectation that victims would turn to the tech companies for a resolution.

When the two young women committed suicide in 2013, Brazil debated its Marco Civil da Internet (translated both as Internet Bill of Rights and as Internet Civil Framework) in Congress.[71] The Marco Civil is an ambitious piece of

[66] Ging and Siapera (n 19) 22.

[67] Código Penal 1940, 218-C. Introduced by Law 13718, 2018.

[68] In 2021, the Brazilian Supreme Court declared that the argument of the 'self-defense of honor' is unconstitutional. It had been used for many decades by men to avoid punishment for feminicides following betrayals or acts considered detrimental to these men's honors.

[69] In our research, we found cases in which judges absolved aggressors because their victims supposedly 'had no honor to be protected', and compensations being defined by the amount of honor a woman was considered to have; Valente et al (n 23).

[70] Neris, Ruiz and Valente, 'Análise comparada de estratégias' (2017).

[71] Brasil, Marco Civil da Internet 2014 [12965].

legislation. One of its most important features is defining a judicial procedure as the necessary step to recognise online service providers' liability. The model has been referred to as a 'human rights model' because of it protects the freedom of expression of Internet users by calibrating incentives against the abuse in content removal claims.[72]

After the suicides, a clause introducing a special intermediary liability rule for NCII was included in the bill: when victims report abuse, online service providers become co-liable if they fail to remove the content in a reasonable time.[73] The rationale of the principle is that, as a rule, content removal involves hard decisions between the free expression of users who posted and other concurring rights, so judges would be in the best position to decide. However, when it comes to NCII, no freedom of expression claims are upheld when someone's intimate image is being disseminated without consent. Therefore, deciding to take down such content should be quite straightforward for platforms; they should be provided with incentives for expeditious removals, given the importance of protecting the victims' dignity.

It sounds right. The Marco Civil would appear to be the first legislation in the world to have a specific intermediary liability rule for NCII. Our research in 2016 concluded that the new rule had an immediate effect – in interviews, lawyers claimed to have perceived a change in platforms' response to NCII removal requests in Brazil.[74] One concern voiced by academics and activists at the time was that the legislation could have the undesired effect of being used against consensual sexual imagery. There is no evidence of that having been the case.

Often, platform regulation fails to recognise differences and promote equity. The Marco Civil story illustrates how platform governance regulation can be sensitive to gender dynamics and women's rights, and consider them in conjunction with other human rights in online settings.

A. Women in Public: Addressing Non-Intimacy in Online Gender-Based Violence

It was not just the law that recognised NCII as a problem to be solved – most large platforms also did. From 2014 onwards, large social media and search engine services introduced specific policies for handling that such content through, for instance, the use of filters or providing ways to facilitate reporting and takedown.

[72] For an account that recognises benefits in that model but also points to its shortfalls, see C Iglesias Keller, 'Policy by Judicialisation: The Institutional Framework for Intermediary Liability in Brazil' (2020) 0 *International Review of Law, Computers & Technology* 1.

[73] Brasil Marco Civil da Internet (n 71) 21.

[74] Valente et al (n 23). However, the Marco Civil solution is short on solving NCII running on messaging apps, where the media is stored on users' devices and on websites that cannot be easily under the reach of Brazilian justice.

However, other forms of violence impacting women's public and equal presence on social media have met more difficulties.

It has been difficult to conceptualise the different forms of attack that women experience online. Terms such as 'harassment', 'abuse', 'cyberviolence' and 'gendered cyberhate'[75] conceal the different experiences women have, which at their worst involve sexually violent rhetoric and even death threats. Until some years ago, many of these acts were referred to as 'flaming' or 'trolling'. Whitney Philips criticises these terms for being vague and understating the importance of the problem.[76]

I propose using the concept of 'misogynist public communications' to address the violence that occurs in speech or other forms of communication that publicly express disdain for women or femininity. Concepts are only valuable to the extent they help to explain and organise phenomena, and they will inevitably be tested through use. The intention behind this term is to avoid referring to 'hate speech'. Hate speech is a legal concept present in the largest social media platforms' policies, but not necessarily part of the national legislation where these platforms operate. For instance, in Brazil and India, hate speech is not defined in legislation and is rarely used in court decisions;[77] it has been used as a weapon in the public debate to refer to aggressive or offensive speech against individuals of any gender.

Inherent in these suggestions is the aim of avoiding terms that refer to existing legal categories or legal concepts, so as to describe a problem to which different solutions can be sought. While hate speech, for instance, immediately points to the notion of suppression or, in the online environment, content removal, a broader, less tightly defined concept invites discussions about different solutions. For instance, the category of 'dangerous speech', developed by Susan Benesch to account for expression that could cause harm,[78] could be a useful framework for some of the forms of violence we discuss here under misogynist public communication – as well as solutions based on compliance instead of deterrence.[79] Misogynist public communication encompasses communicative forms that may not be

[75] Jane (n 27).

[76] W Phillips, *This Is Why We Can't Have Nice Things: Mapping the Relationship between Online Trolling and Mainstream Culture* (MIT Press, 2015).

[77] For a discussion on the category of hate speech in Indian Law, see NS Nappinai, 'Role of the Law in Combating Online Misogyny, Hate Speech and Violence Against Women and Girls' (2021), Rethinking Legal-Institutional Approaches to Sexist Hate Speech in India, IT for Change, available at itforchange.net/sites/default/files/1883/NS-Nappinai-Rethinking-Legal-Institutional-Approaches-To-Sexist-Hate-Speech-ITfC-IT-for-Change.pdf.

[78] S Benesch, 'Dangerous Speech: A Proposal to Prevent Group Violence' (2013), Dangerous Speech Project, available at dangerousspeech.org/wp-content/uploads/2018/01/Dangerous-Speech-Guidelines-2013.pdf.

[79] A Sinha, 'Regulating Sexist Online Harassment: A Model of Online Harassment as a Form of Censorship' (2021), Rethinking Legal-Institutional Approaches to Sexist Hate Speech in India, IT for Change, available at itforchange.net/sites/default/files/1883/NS-Nappinai-Rethinking-Legal-Institutional-Approaches-To-Sexist-Hate-Speech-ITfC-IT-for-Change.pdf.

considered troubling separately, but are violent when aggregated; it also addresses part of the problem of political violence addressed above. 'Public', here, does not refer to the discussion on whether social media are to be considered legally and politically public or private spaces; it refers to 'in public' and, as I will address next, in opposition to the problem of *domestic* violence.

The women's movement, especially since the 1980s, has shaped a legal and institutional agenda against domestic violence which is reflected in law and culture worldwide. However, misogynist public communications are rarely addressed in national legislation,[80] and many of the laws responding to, for instance, hate speech and discrimination do not refer to gender or sex.[81] Violence against women is broadly normalised; the difficulty in coming up with frameworks that recognise women's dignity in public communications is connected to yet another layer of normalisation: the very idea of what a woman can be a victim to falls prey to gendered assumptions. The public space is still not seen as a place for women. Because gender notions rely on interpretations of biological functions, normalisation of gender difference is also the normalisation of forms of misogyny – some of them more than others, perhaps. It is also why discussions are focused on binaries, thus excluding non-binary people.

Ideas of femininity have been forged across time and contexts. Referring to European history, Silvia Federici argues that femininity is a construction of the transition from feudal-agricultural to industrial production, which masks the task of biological and social reproduction as a natural destiny.[82] Women were (violently) banned from public spaces, associated with emotionality and lack of control, stripped of social power and legal autonomy, and their knowledge systems were devalued, prohibited and terrorised through the witch hunt. Likewise, violent acts of misogyny reproduce subjugation, control and exclusion from the digital sphere and might produce other effects (for instance, online misogyny within alt-right groups).

The lack of a legal vocabulary for addressing misogynist public communication implies that judges lack the language and tools required; instead, general terms such as 'defamation' and 'harm' are frequently applied.[83] Complexities go beyond

[80] Lillian, 'A Thorn by Any Other Name' (2007).

[81] Barker and Jurasz, *Online Misogyny as Hate Crime* (2018). Brazil's anti-discrimination law (Law n. 7716/89) addresses discrimination perpetrated in relation to race, colour, ethnicity, religion and national precedence. Although Brazil has signed and ratified several international treaties on violence against women, in addition to having one of the most advanced bodies of legislation in the world to combat domestic violence against women, there is a gap in the legislation to deal with other forms of discrimination. Since 2014, over 40 bills addressing women's participation in politics were proposed, although only a few mentioned the issue of political violence.

[82] S Federici, *Caliban and the Witch: Women, the Body and Primitive Accumulation* (Autonomedia, 2004).

[83] At InternetLab we have been looking for databases of Courts of Appeal cases in Brazil since 2018. We are collecting those in which there was a mobilisation of misogynistic or similar terms and threats to physical integrity in a virtual environment shared by more people than just the aggressor and the victim (such as WhatsApp groups and Facebook posts). The methodology has had to be adapted several times to account for the lack of vocabulary that would lead us to useful search terms.

the absence of a legal framework. In the case of Brazil, even when clear misogynist terms are used as slurs, the incidents are rarely recognised as involving any form of discrimination against women. Many of them are treated as domestic violence if involving a current or former partner. However, as they occurred in 'public' online spaces – in Facebook posts, WhatsApp groups, Instagram stories, etc – they also affect the social imagination about how women can be read and treated. They are, in fact, what I call 'misogynist public communication'.

B. Aggregate Harm

Cases of mass attacks – known in English as 'dog-piling' – involve 'additive' practices that produce harm. These mob or *en masse* assaults, often incited by influential individuals and working cross-networks, raise legal discussions that go much beyond the well-known dilemma in drawing lines between freedom of expression and hate or generally unallowed speech.

The most voted-for councilwoman in the city of São Paulo, Erika Hilton, is a trans, black woman who received an enormous amount of slurs and threats during the 2020 elections.[84] Ten months later, many of the tweets identified as offensive are still online. Many of them, individually, do not violate Twitter's terms of service, and taken separately, would not even be considered to break the law. The Australia-based professor Emma Jane, having interviewed several targets of gendered cyberhate, argues that attacks involving mass messages can drive women to breaking point – not just because of the content of the messages, but also the investment of time and energy to read, report, block and take action.[85]

We are frequently speaking of content that, in aggregate, produces a sense of persecution and an atmosphere of threat, even if individual posts do not strictly violate the law or terms of service. It is also often the case that a victim will fail in many jurisdictions to prove that a threat was credible under existing legal frameworks. The Philippines-based journalist Maria Ressa argues that simply blocking, muting, reporting, deleting and ignoring is not a solution: 'You don't know when it will jump out from the virtual world and sneak into the physical world'.[86]

C. Political Weaponisation

The political weaponisation of gender discussions worldwide undermines the discussion and obliviates the fundamental rights issues at stake.[87] For example,

[84] AzMina Magazine and InternetLab (n 2).
[85] Jane (n 27) 62.
[86] Posetti et al, 'The Chilling' (2021) 19.
[87] Flavia Biroli, Engenia Siapera, Debbie Ging and Angela Nagle are academics who write about the ties between the alt-right, antifeminism and online misogyny in their contexts.

on Facebook, what is protected is 'gender' – not women or femininity. That means that the phrase 'I hate men', even in the context of calling out sexism, is treated the same way as 'I hate women' in a misogynist post. Instead of having social media incorporate equality and full flourishment of personality and human dignity, they are instrumentalised by a weaponised expression of gender dilemmas. A May 2021 analysis of social media policies[88] involving Facebook, Instagram, LinkedIn, Snapchat, Twitter, TikTok and YouTube reveals that all refer to 'hate speech' or 'hate promotion' and provide lists of characteristics considered protected against such hate.[89] These policies never refer to misogyny itself and fail to acknowledge 'women' specifically – as with most legislation on hate.

Countries also seem not to have been able to regulate platforms to make them more accountable for the misogyny that runs on their services. But, again, that problem is related to how general culture, legal culture and legal concepts fail to recognise the specificities of misogynist public communication.

IV. Conclusion: The Path Beyond

Regulating social media is at the top of policy priorities today. It goes without saying that the law is not the only instrument needed to address women's constitutional rights to dignity and full equality. The previous discussion on how women have appropriated social media and how that has led to enhanced women's rights in different territories is a small example of how activist, artistic and educational strategies are at the centre of change. In this chapter, I have explored how these strategies intertwine with legal discussions. Without a shared social understanding of violence that encompasses women's experiences online, much of the existing regulation goes unenforced.

At the same time, the law is a central strategy in making problems visible and minimising inequalities,[90] one that civil society cannot give up on – even if it will not solve issues alone. The same must be said about social media policies. Recent proposals to curb content moderation are clouding the very fact that social media platforms are all different, deal with an immensity of content daily and invite political discussion and the development of personalities. The full enjoyment of rights, including women's rights to express themselves, requires policies and moderation committed to such rights and accountable to societies – including those in the South, and including smaller markets.

[88] InternetLab researchers Ester Borges and Clarice Tavares must be acknowledged for their work on this.

[89] They include age, race, ethnicity, class, religion, sexual orientation, caste, disability or serious illness status, migratory status, national origin, and gender identity.

[90] P Williams, 'Alchemical Notes: Reconstructing Ideals from Deconstructed Rights' (1987) 22 *Harvard Civil Rights – Civil Liberties Law Review* 401.

Legislators are starting to come up with regulations that go beyond the usual content-centred measures. In the past few decades, much of the discussion about online protection of multiple human rights has involved finding a balance in intermediary liability.[91] Recent proposals such as the Digital Services Act in the European Union present different approaches: establishing accountability duties that refer to transparency and proactive action. Legislators are also experimenting with co-regulation, for example, by setting targets to which platforms must flexibly comply.[92] Worldwide, discussions involve ideas of due process in content moderation online, architectures of choice and protection and algorithmic accountability. Women's rights must be nominally recognised as an integral part of these efforts.

I addressed how the development of digital technologies is inscribed in larger societal structures and how online misogyny is part of a mutual shaping scheme. Usually, legal solutions targeting individuals are addressing misogyny in society, but largely through an individual perspective. Solutions targeting platforms imply that the technical leads to the social too. The connections between those strands are underdeveloped.

Finally, I should mention policies for full participation of women in the technological sector – in universities, companies and civil society organisations. The conditions for developing technologies and making them accountable – and sensitive to local contexts – are also connected to feminist ethics, and legislative efforts must incorporate that. As Jane puts it, 'security and privacy functionalities are being designed by people who overwhelmingly fit the profile of individuals with the lowest risk assessments'.[93] Open source is more connected to feminism than is usually acknowledged,[94] and gender and wider social inequalities are deeply connected with recent developments in techno-capitalism. Women's participation in the labour market is linked to the unpaid work of social reproduction and subjected to biologisation processes. More than mainstreaming gender, the message is that radical commitment to women's rights and their full humanity is needed at every stage of regulating technologies in our societies. This is far from simple, and we are yet to reach solutions. For instance, how do we deal with the fact that perhaps not hate itself, but the 'stickiness' of debates and controversies, drive profits to social media companies?[95] Certainly, law alone will not suffice.

[91] See ch 10 (Frosio) in this volume.

[92] See ch 13 (Iglesias Keller) in this volume.

[93] Jane (n 27).

[94] S Federici, 'Feminism and the Politics of the Commons' (2011) The Commoner, available at thecommoner.org/wp-content/uploads/2020/06/federici-feminism-and-the-politics-of-commons.pdf.

[95] Ging (n 37) 62.

8

Social Media, Electoral Campaigns and Regulation of Hybrid Political Communication: Rethinking Communication Rights

EUGENIA SIAPERA AND NIAMH KIRK

I. Introduction

Since the Cambridge Analytica scandal and the 2016 electoral campaign of Donald Trump, there have been ongoing calls for regulation of electoral advertisements on social media. Most countries have only recently begun the process of developing and introducing new regulations to enhance transparency around political advertising. But many continue to rely on the electoral regulations developed in the pre-digital era that have little bearing on the new media environment and the creativity it facilitates. The development of regulation for elections both at national and EU level has largely been responsive to the issues that arose in the Brexit referendum in the UK and the US elections of 2016, without really taking broader issues into account. Thus, the focus is on preventing foreign interference, disinformation and the need for transparency around who is paying for advertisements. Key aspects include whether election monitors are able to verify if payers are appropriately registered as political actors on electoral or lobbying registers, how much is being spent, and whether this complies with electoral spending regulations. While these are all necessary policies, they are only part of what political actors can do in the digital sphere. In terms of the conceptualisation of the citizen-user of these platforms in regulation, two approaches have emerged.[1] The first sees citizen-users as passive consumers of information in need of protection, while the second conceptualises citizen-users as active consumers in need of enhanced

[1] E Siapera, N Kirk and K Doyle, 'Netflix and Binge? Understanding New Cultures of Media Consumption' (2019), available at www.bai.ie/en/media/sites/2/dlm_uploads/2019/12/Netflix-and-Binge-Final-Report.pdf.

access to information. Neither of these approaches, we argue, fully represent the dynamics of user engagement with social media.

The media and information environment are fundamentally transformed, and opened up in a wide range of ways by which political actors and lobbyists can raise the salience of and frame political issues.[2] The new media environment, which Chadwick understands as hybrid,[3] has complicated the standard political communication model of politicians, journalists and citizens. The hybrid media system is a fusion of old and new media (and media logics), where information flows are shaped by various actors that can modify, enable or disable others' engagement with a particular issue. The new actors in the hybrid media environment are more diverse than before digitisation – from citizens and activists to digital journalists and foreign state actors and lobbyists – giving rise to a complex and dynamic system where unpredictability is the new normal. In this environment, political actors develop creative and sophisticated political campaigns, often adapting to or working around any limitations placed upon them by states or platforms.

The hybrid media system and the associated hybrid political communication are linked with imaginative and inclusive political campaigns articulating demands for social justice, such as the #BlackLivesMatter movement, transcending national boundaries and reigniting calls for justice and equality. The same hybrid political communication, however, is linked to a communication malaise, where baseless conspiracy theories, racist and misogynist speech, and secret political 'psyops' circulate unchallenged. Additionally, hybrid political communication takes place in proprietary social media platforms, which operate for profit, and whose architecture is structured around their business and revenue models.

In this context, we argue that regulation at a national and supranational level has not risen to the challenge because its focus is too narrow, the concept of the citizen-user is underdeveloped, and its emphasis is on enforcement and monitoring mechanisms (section II). Concerned mainly with technicalities and chasing an ever-changing set of tools and practices used by actors with funds and the motivation to interfere in the political process, its main objective is to limit and control potentially malicious actors rather than to strengthen and empower citizens. We posit that regulation is structured around key tensions between fundamental rights and interests, but ultimately relies on a polarised and simplified version of citizenship and political communication that fails to capture the complex reality of digital political communication (section III). To reconcile the tensions in such a way that captures the complexity of political communications today, we contend that we should begin with a (re)consideration of communication rights for the digital era (section IV). We conclude by presenting communication rights as a key addition to the process of constitutionalisation of social media. However, we argue

[2] S Meraz and Z Papacharissi, 'Networked framing and gatekeeping' in T Witschge, CW Anderson, D Domingo and A Hermida (eds), *The Sage Handbook of Digital Journalism* (Sage, 2016) 95–112.

[3] A Chadwick, *The hybrid media system: Politics and power* (Oxford University Press, 2017).

that these rights will need to be reconceptualised in ways that are commensurable with the present political-economic and socio-technical context (section V).

II. Political Communication in the Digital Sphere

While regulation looks to capture the values and norms surrounding political communication, the reality is that, given recent technological, political and socio-cultural developments, the political and communicative context has shifted dramatically from the one within and for which regulation emerged, ie the nation state and representative democracy. In its place, we witness the emergence of a hybrid media system, in which political communication takes many forms and new political actors and communicative norms emerge. The idea of hybridity is important, because as Chadwick[4] notes, it alludes to the coexistence and fusion of the old and the new, rather than a replacement. While Chadwick,[5] Castells[6] and others find great promise in digital media and political communication, our discussion below identifies important inequalities, concluding that despite its widening and diversification, the hybrid political communication in the digital sphere is an unequal space.

Traditional models of political communication, and especially the literature around electoral campaigns, make reference to three sets of political actors: politicians/political organisations, journalists/media and citizens.[7] Political communication during elections emerges from politicians and political parties, goes through the media and is received by citizens who are expected to formulate a political opinion based on the communications that reach them. In a well-functioning public sphere, citizens should be able to deliberate on issues, while the media should act both as a platform for public opinion and as advocates for specific perspectives. As an ideal, communication flows through the triangle of politicians, media and citizens are multidirectional. This prototype of communication seems to underlie approaches to electoral regulation. While there were already critical voices discussing the infiltration of the public sphere by commercial interests and professional communicators,[8] digital media alongside other political and social developments in late capitalism have disrupted the ideal described above. As Dommett and Bakir note,[9] while in the analogue era the main resource for shaping or distorting the information environment was wealth and direct payments for promotion of messages, the digital era has expanded the range of options that

[4] ibid.
[5] ibid.
[6] M Castells, *Communication power* (Oxford University Press, 2017).
[7] B McNair, *An introduction to political communication* (Routledge, 2011).
[8] J Habermas, *The structural transformation of the public sphere* (MIT Press, 1989).
[9] K Dommett and ME Bakir, 'A Transparent Digital Election Campaign? The Insights and Significance of Political Advertising Archives for Debates on Electoral Regulation' (2020) 73 (Supplement 1) *Parliamentary Affairs* 208.

can be used to pollute or overwhelm the media ecology: time, expertise, digital media production skills and software, access to metrics to optimise using tools such as Crowdtangle, and network and distribution tools such as Hootsuite. In this context, a wide range of political actors can access 'free media' without concern for editorial control over the message. The category of political communicators had already expanded significantly beyond the nation state with the rise of satellite television, but digital platforms enabled it to expand not only geographically but also horizontally. This proliferation of actors is identified by Chadwick, who pointed out the ways in which political actors can emerge unexpectedly and can have an impact on the process of political communication. Social movements, citizen journalists, witnesses and social media personalities/influencers can all be seen as political actors insofar as they can affect the political decision-making process.[10] The disintermediation of political communication, that is, the ability of digital platforms to bypass journalism and news media, allowing politicians to communicate directly with the public, has led to the adoption of such new forms by politicians themselves, undermining traditional political journalism. This has also had the effect of undermining the agenda-setting role of politicians and political journalism, as publics can and do bring to the fore issues that matter to them. In Ireland, the issue of water charges emerged as crucial for publics but was largely overlooked by politicians and political journalism.[11]

With new communicators/political actors, new political communication practices and forms emerged. Personal narratives and affective communication have more currency on digital platforms, and stories are shared more widely than fact-based communication.[12] Deliberating on arguments is no longer the privileged form of political communication. For example, in Ireland, sharing personal stories on abortion-related issues through the 'In Her Shoes' Facebook page became a focal point in the referendum to repeal the 8th Amendment to the Irish Constitution, which prohibited abortions. The power of digital storytelling and the affective rhythms generated by publics in agreeing, disagreeing, commenting, liking and so on, are important new communicative tools playing a significant political role.[13] The algorithmic structuring of digital media tends to reinforce provocative, sensational posts and image- and video-based communication, which is then used by those who are looking to influence the political decision-making process.[14] Multimedia contents, memes, threaded stories, etc interweave personal

[10] McNair, *An introduction to political communication* (2011); S Allan, *Citizen witnessing: Revisioning journalism in times of crisis* (John Wiley & Sons, 2013); M Castells, *Networks of outrage and hope: Social movements in the Internet age* (John Wiley & Sons, 2015).

[11] H Silke, E Siapera and M Rieder, 'Hybrid Media and Movements: The Irish Water Movement, Press Coverage, and Social Media' (2020) 14 *International Journal of Communication* 3330.

[12] L Bennett and A Segerberg, *The logic of connective action: Digital media and the personalization of contentious politics* (Cambridge University Press, 2013).

[13] Z Papacharissi, *Affective Publics* (Oxford University Press, 2015).

[14] C Pérez-Curiel and P Limón-Naharro, 'Political influencers. A study of Donald Trump's personal brand on Twitter and its impact on the media and users' (2019) 32 *Communication & Society* 57.

and political narratives, drawing in publics in ways that differ drastically from the political and electoral campaigning of the broadcast era. The affective shift in digital media and the rise of affective publics, that is, networked publics that feel their way into politics by way of digital media,[15] throw into question assumptions of citizens as individual, rational agents, fully responsible for their choices. Rather, in the hybrid political communication, citizens are part of affective formations, connecting and disconnecting from others and their stories, investing or divesting their affective energies.

A final aspect of the emerging hybrid political communication refers to the question of temporality. While political communication encompasses all forms of politically relevant communication, there are variations in its rhythms, which ebb and flow following the tempos set by the electoral cycle. However, because of social media's constant invitation to communicate, in a context ruled by an attention economy,[16] political communication has moved to a state of permanent campaigning. For example, in their work on Narendra Modi, the Prime Minister of India and leader of the Bhartiya Janata Party, Rodrigues and Nieman[17] showed that Modi and his party are constantly campaigning, using social media in agenda-building processes. 'Agenda-building' refers to the process by which political actors create support for specific issues or causes, vying for the attention of publics and public policy-makers.[18] Rodrigues and Nieman found this to be so because digital platforms enable them to bypass legacy media and because they have built extensive networks engaging and amplifying their posts. An important aspect here concerns the rise of right-wing populist politicians who adopt and adapt digital media in pursuing their political objectives. Publics can oppose, support, undermine or propagate political content in this perpetual campaigning.

A key aspect of the hybrid political communication is that, despite early views on widening democratisation, it is ridden with inequalities. While, as noted earlier, political actors have multiplied and diversified, the result was less equal participation in political communication and an intensification of competition over communication power.[19] Secondly, while the proliferation of affect has made political communication more relatable, it has also opened the way for manipulation and exploitation, possibly because of affective priming effects.[20] Thirdly, the

[15] Papacharissi, *Affective Publics* (2015).

[16] TH Davenport and JC Beck, *The attention economy* (Ubiquity, 2001).

[17] Usha M Rodrigues and Michael Niemann, 'Social Media as a Platform for Incessant Political Communication: A Case Study of Modi's "Clean India" Campaign' (2017) 11 *International Journal of Communication* 3431.

[18] R Cobb, J-K Ross and MH Ross, 'Agenda building as a comparative political process' (1976) 70 *The American Political Science Review* 126; S Young Lee, 'Agenda-building theory' in C Carroll (ed), *The SAGE encyclopaedia of corporate reputation* (SAGE Publications, 2016) 28–30.

[19] M Castells, *Communication power* (Oxford University Press, 2017).

[20] KC Klauer and J Musch, 'Affective priming: Findings and theories' in KC Klauer and J Musch (eds), *The psychology of evaluation: Affective processes in cognition and emotion* (Lawrence Erlbaum Associates Publishers, 2003) 7–49. This refers to the finding that people's evaluative behaviour can be altered when positive or negative affective cues are presented first. Therefore if people are systematically primed negatively before their evaluation of a particular object, they are more likely to evaluate it negatively.

altered temporality and always-on character of the hybrid political communication favours those with time and resources, which in turn is likely to privilege organised and resource-rich political actors. Finally, the platformisation of political communication implies that the communicative space is structured by and through the interests of platforms.[21] It is evident therefore that hybrid political communication is an unequal space/process and not a level playing field.

Summarising these developments, we can see that a multiplication of political actors and forms of communication, alongside a temporal expansion of political campaigning above and beyond election periods are key characteristics of hybrid political communication. When it comes to political actors, therefore, we observe that citizens can at any time become political actors, both driving political campaigns and as supporters or opponents, actively engaging in the political process. In this context, it is neither the technologies themselves nor the behaviours of actors/users that determine political communication. Rather, technological affordances, such as low entry costs, virality, visibility, affective reactions[22] and actor/user behaviours combine to give rise to this dynamic ecosystem, that constantly shifts and evolves along with actors and technologies. This dynamism does not take place in a vacuum but follows broader socio-political developments – in this respect, as Wolfsfeld et al[23] put it, 'politics comes first', that is, that the behaviours of political actors are motivated primarily by political objectives and not by the technologies they can use. On the other hand, communicative technologies may expand or contract the communicative possibilities available. We note therefore that this new dynamic ecosystem reveals a complex picture when it comes to political actors, which include not only politicians and political journalists/media, but also citizens as political actors both driving political campaigns and participating in affective publics aligning or diverging from such campaigns. However, the hybrid political communication as a space and as a process is profoundly unequal as actors compete intensely for communication power, with organised and better resourced actors likely to accumulate more power. All this complicates the picture of citizens, political actors and the digital public sphere implicit in the regulatory approaches. Additionally, it questions the narrow focus on periods of election and points to the need to consider political communication in its entirety. The issue that emerges from this analysis therefore does not concern the protection or responsibilisation of the citizen, nor what rules must cover electoral campaigning, but rather what rules must be created for this kind of political communication to ensure that it remains democratic. In the next section, we offer a description and a critique of the current regulatory landscape.

[21] T Poell, D Nieborg and J van Dijck, 'Platformisation' (2019) 8 *Internet Policy Review* 1.

[22] d boyd, 'Social network sites as networked publics: Affordances, dynamics, and implications' in Z Papacharissi (ed), *Networked self: Identity, community, and culture on social network sites* (Routledge, 2010) 39–58; T Bucher and A Helmond, 'The Affordances of Social Media Platforms' *The SAGE handbook of social media* (SAGE, 2017) 233–53.

[23] G Wolfsfeld, E Segev and T Sheafer, 'Social media and the Arab Spring: Politics comes first' (2013) 18 *The International Journal of Press/Politics* 115.

III. Regulating Online Political Advertisements: The Current Landscape

A. EU Governance

The EU has refrained from interfering in national legislation on elections, leaving such matters to Member States. Responding to the perceived threats emerging from Brexit and the Trump campaign, largely mis/disinformation and foreign interference, and aiming to develop a common approach while accepting the variances in the electoral systems throughout the EU, the European Commission established a voluntary Code of Practice on Disinformation (CoPD). The Code was signed by Microsoft, Mozilla, Google, Facebook and Twitter along with a range of digital advertising companies in September 2018. TikTok signed up in 2020 having established a base in Europe.[24]

The EU response to the issue of regulating online political advertising, with particular focus on social media, is situated within the political response to disinformation, rather than being addressed separately, as part of electoral and campaigning politics. It is formulated to address 'bad actors' advertising disinformation – rather than establishing a level playing field for all political actors to campaign and advertise. It is administered by the European Regulators Group for Audiovisual Media Services (ERGA) rather than an electoral commission. The EU Code of Practice on Disinformation contains 15 commitments organised under five pillars:

A. scrutiny of ad placements (aimed at demonetising online purveyors of disinformation);
B. political advertising and issue-based advertising (aimed at making sure that political advertisements are clearly identified by the users);
C. integrity of services (aimed at identifying and closing fake accounts and using appropriate mechanisms to signal bot-driven interactions);
D. empowering consumers (aimed at reducing the risks of social media 'echo chambers' by making it easier for users to discover and access different news sources representing alternative viewpoints);
E. empowering the research community (aimed at by granting researchers access to platforms' data that are necessary to continuously monitor online disinformation).

It is Pillar B that most directly addresses political and issue-based advertising around elections. The requirements under the Code of Practice are very broad, and a review of their implementation in Europe during the EU parliamentary elections 2019

[24] European Commission Code of Practice on Disinformation, available at digital-strategy.ec.europa.eu/en/policies/code-practice-disinformation.

highlighted the need for greater specificity. As it stands, the code allows social media platforms to develop their own definitions of political advertising and choose whether to disclose issue-based advertising. If they do, platforms are free to decide and define what political issues are at any given time. While the EU performs regular monitoring exercises, checking the application and effectiveness of the Code of Practice, these efforts are hampered by the lack of access to social media platforms' data. Indeed, if the research community were offered access to protected datasets of advertisements for independent scrutiny the degree of transparency would be considerably higher.[25]

More broadly, the language of the Code places emphasis on the platforms' obligations towards individual users. It includes labelling of information about who paid for an advertisement, who benefitted, and any micro-targeting data selected.[26] It is important to note that prior to none of the EU policy recommendations has the labelling or signage been tested on users for efficacy. This lack of understanding or research into users perhaps contributes to the contradiction in how citizen-users are conceptualised in the EU regulatory approach. While, on the one hand, users are understood as passive or agnostic regarding the sources and purpose of content in their information environments, they can, on the other hand, be 'activated' and encouraged to engage with information sources through the placement of labels and provision of further information. It remains unclear, however, what users are expected to do with this information and how the provision of details about advertising addresses the individual or collective harms caused by unregulated political marketing. The focus is to see if platforms will comply with the Code and how the Code can be improved to ensure greater transparency from signatories, but regrettably without any consideration of the impact or effect on the end users. Indeed, while there is a requirement, for example, to clearly label a political ad as 'political', it is not clear if or what types of labelling work for users.

B. National Regulation: The Example of Ireland

At a national level, political advertising on social media is focused on advertisers' compliance with electoral spending regulations. Each EU country has its own national level regulations on digital political campaigns. Much depends on the

[25] N Kirk, E Culloty, E Casey, L Teeling, K Park and J Suiter, 'ElectCheck2019: A Report on Political Advertising Online During the 2019 European Elections' (Broadcasting Authority of Ireland, 2019); N Kirk and L Teeling, 'Code Check: A Review of Platform Compliance with The EC Code of Practice on Disinformation' (Broadcasting Authority of Ireland, 2020). The issue of providing datasets to researchers for further scrutiny is detailed further in the ElectCheck and CodeCheck reports which describe the challenges to electoral monitoring in the absence of access to whole datasets of advertisements applied for and published during an electoral campaign.

[26] As noted by Kirk et al (ibid) and Kirk and Teeling (ibid), only basic demographic information is provided, age, gender and locations and the wide variety of other options or the use of lookalike audiences is not disclosed.

media system, in particular on the relationship between politics and the media sector, and the degree of professionalisation of the media sector.[27] In the case of Ireland, understood as a liberal media system, these regulations fall under the purview of the Standards in Public Office Commission (SIPO) and the focus is mainly on the period of elections. Electoral regulation in Ireland is primarily concerned with transparency and balance. Media, especially public service broadcasters, have to adhere to strict guidelines of balance between political parties, while there is also a moratorium on electoral campaigning for 24 hours before the election. While print media can publish political advertisements, political advertising is prohibited on television and radio. In terms of transparency, current legislation makes provisions for disclosure of advertising spend of over €130, political donations of over €100, and a registration process for donors and lobbyists.

When it comes to enforcement, the monitoring of the European Parliament election in 2019[28] and the Irish general election in 2020[29] showed that the spend on the vast majority of online advertisements fell far below the €130 figure, with most political actors spending between €1-99, and placing multiple advertisements throughout the campaigns. Therefore, there is a substantial amount of money spent by political parties and other actors on electoral campaigns that have little or no oversight. Similarly, when it comes to lobby groups, Kirk and Teeling note that there are no requirements on Irish political actors to disclose details of advertising beyond election campaigns, such as issue-based advertising on topics like environmentalism or homelessness.[30]

There have been calls for reform of the electoral regulation in Ireland ahead of the referendum on the 8th Amendment to the Irish Constitution in 2018, which eventually eliminated the contested prohibition of abortion in Ireland. Indeed, Irish civil society already understood the impact of digital advertising in the Brexit referendum and recognised the lacuna in regulation here: Irish political parties and lobby groups do not have to disclose details of their *digital* electoral campaigning, as the current legislation only regulates traditional media, such as newspapers, radio and television. The Transparency Referendum Initiative,[31] a civil society organisation, the Elect Check and Code Check projects, as well as the now lapsed Online Advertising and Social Media (Transparency) Bill,[32] have all called for substantive reform to enhance transparency in online election campaigns, both by

[27] D Hallin and P Mancini, *Comparing media systems: Three models of media and politics* (Cambridge University Press, 2004).

[28] Kirk et al, 'ElectCheck2019' (2019).

[29] N Kirk, 'Political Advertising Online during the 2020 General Election' (UCD Connected Politics Lab, 13 February 2020), available at www.ucd.ie/connected_politics/blog/political advertising online duringthe2020generalelectioncamping.

[30] N Kirk and L Teeling, 'A review of political advertising online during the 2019 European Elections and establishing future regulatory requirements in Ireland' (2021) 36 *Irish Political Studies* 1.

[31] Transparency Referendum Initiative, available at tref.ie.

[32] Online Advertising and Social Media (Transparency) Bill 2017, 150/2017.

the platforms used and from political parties.[33] In addition to transparency, calls for reform identified several areas of concern including the definition of political advertising, monitoring and enforcement mechanisms, and the development of a governance system, such as an Electoral Commission with the role to oversee the conduct of political actors during election periods.[34] To contextualise the Irish case among other European countries, we note that there is no homogenous electoral landscape, and each country has a specific history of development and varying rules and regulations around election advertising across media.[35]

This brief exposition of some of the regulatory issues concerning disinformation, online political campaigning and advertising reveal a fraught terrain. While there is increasing recognition that the field should be regulated, there is little agreement on how to do it, or even what the main problem is.

C. Platform Governance

Social media platforms have adopted different approaches to political advertising, and the situation is constantly evolving. In response to the Code of Practice on Disinformation, one of the first measures taken by social media companies was to restrict who could advertise, with each company implementing some form of verification system to enhance transparency of who is paying for and benefitting from advertising. Additionally, information about the location of the advertiser is also included in the data collected to address the issue of foreign interference. However, such measures are problematic on three grounds. Firstly, because limiting those who can advertise to only those with official documentation and safe to openly advertise their political positions may result in excluding marginalised groups, such as racialised minority groups, who are then effectively prohibited from engaging in the political sphere. Secondly, the variances in definitions of political advertising and what constitutes sufficient labelling for user transparency pose substantial challenges to both users and researchers monitoring election campaigning advertising.[36] Thirdly, while some notable changes were introduced after the 2019 European elections, there has been no research evaluating the effectiveness of labelling procedures. In other words, despite the calls for labelling of advertisements on users' timelines and platforms' response in adding notices that advertisements are 'political' or 'issue-based' as well as providing some added information when users choose to explore, we still do not know the extent to which

[33] Kirk and Teeling, 'Code Check' (2020).

[34] Department of the Taoiseach, 'Public Consultation on Regulation of Transparency of Online Political Advertising Summary of Submissions Received' (2019), available at www.gov.ie/en/publication/86da72-regulation-of-online-political-advertising-in-ireland-submissions.

[35] J-F Furnémont and D Kevin, 'Regulation of Political Advertising: A comparative Study with Reflection on the situation in South-East Europe' (Council of Europe, 2020), available at rm.coe.int/study-on-political-advertising-eng-final/1680a0c6e0.

[36] Kirk and Teeling, 'A review of political advertising' (2021); Kirk and Teeling (n 25).

such measures make any difference. Whether users notice the labels and recognise the advertisements as electoral or political and pursue further information on payers and amount spent is unclear. As such, while we know platforms benefit from the current process of labelling advertisements as political in that they can demonstrate compliance with the Code of Practice, there is little interrogation of the benefit to users. Since a key demand has been for more transparency, a proposal that has emerged concerns the creation of digital repositories of advertisements, which users (and journalists) can check to examine which advertisements were paid and by whom. Platforms are developing policy responses to address compliance with the Code of Practice on Disinformation rather than addressing the wider issues around political or electoral campaigning.

It is beneficial to analyse the response adopted by the most popular platforms in this context: Twitter, Facebook (including Instagram), and Google (including YouTube). Twitter made some substantial changes following the audits during the 2019 European elections. Like Google and Facebook, it provided an online library of advertisements in the Twitter Transparency Centre.[37] However, it was highly problematic in that it was not possible to identify all the political advertisements that were placed in a specific country. Later, in November 2019, the company announced it would ban all political advertising based on the 'belief that political message reach should be earned, not bought'.[38] In an extended thread on Twitter the company's CEO, Jack Dorsey, underlined that a host of technological developments poses challenges to civic and political discourse online.[39] Twitter maintained the Transparency Centre with the historic political advertisements until early 2021 when it quietly removed it and replaced it with a link to a 'downloadable' list of advertisements in.txt format.[40] Unlike Facebook and Google, it no longer provides an online library of adverts that can be used for monitoring purposes. Twitter's definition of political advertisements is highly limited, largely focusing on elections and campaigning, and omits a potentially wide range of political communications from a range of actors that occur beyond election time.

Twitter's position seems to rely on what Meraz and Papacharissi[41] refer to as 'networked framing and salience', ie the process by which messages acquire prominence in social media because of their resonance, and not only because they are artificially boosted like advertisements or because they are disseminated by prominent political actors. Nevertheless, messages by well-known political actors

[37] Twitter 'Ads transparency', available at business.twitter.com/en/help/ads-policies/product-policies/ads-transparency.html.

[38] Twitter, 'Ad Content Policies: Political Content', available at business.twitter.com/en/help/ads-policies/ads-content-policies/political-content.html.

[39] J Dorsey, 'Ban on Political Advertising Thread' (Twitter, 30 October 2019), available at twitter.com/jack/status/1189634360472829952?lang=en.

[40] Twitter, 'Ad Transparency Archive', available at business.twitter.com/content/dam/business-twitter/help/ads-transparency-archive/political.txt.

[41] Meraz and Papacharissi, 'Networked Framing and Gatekeeping' (2016) 95–112.

are more likely to constitute political communication and to reach broader audiences. Hence, although Twitter's advertising ban is meant to empower networked citizens and to level the political communication playing field, its approach ultimately favours already established political actors with large numbers of followers. Twitter's 'earned not bought' approach to visibility is a challenge particularly for new, independent candidates who cannot rely on large established party accounts to promote them. The European elections in 2019 saw a record number of independent candidates run for office, most of whom relied on social media and digital advertising to reach new audiences that traditional canvassing may not have achieved. Additionally, this approach does little to tackle endemic inequalities or redress the marginalisation of some communities on digital platforms. Rather, it empowers the already powerful, while marginalised groups must work harder to compete for visibility.[42]

Facebook, on the other hand, enhanced its online advertising repository, including some additional labels and information on whether advertisements were also published on Instagram. However, much of the information provided, such as the amount spent, the reach/impressions and the demographics of people who saw the advertisement (rather than who was targeted with it) remains too broad to extract meaningful insights. Google made no tangible changes to its online ad library, but did add other regions to the database beyond the US and Europe.

Common to each of the regulatory levels is a contradiction of how users are conceptualised; two divergent understandings of citizens/users, which lead to different and at times contradictory applications of regulation. It often seems that regulatory discussions take place in the absence of a more in-depth understanding of citizens or users and the broader context of a changing political communication. While the discussion on online advertising regulation tends to oscillate between passive and empowered citizens, and respectively between platforms/technologies as determining user behaviours or as mere tools in the hands of users, the reality is more complex. Research into technology and society suggests a codetermining relationship such that technologies and their users mutually shape one another, though not in circumstances of their own choosing.[43]

While platforms are seen broadly as compliant with the EU Code of Practice, or working towards it, it is difficult to see what, if any, improvements this compliance has resulted in in the domain of political communication. Critically, this is not a regulatory instrument designed to address the electoral process or political communication, but to tackle disinformation. At best, it seems that this approach has generated a new layer of bureaucracy, consisting of transparency reports, monitoring efforts and associated reports, observatories, and fact-check

[42] Y Gerrard, 'Social media content moderation: six opportunities for feminist intervention' (2020) 20 *Feminist Media Studies* 748.

[43] W Bijker and J Law (eds), *Shaping technology/building society: Studies in sociotechnical change* (MIT Press, 1994).

organisations, but the overall outcome for citizens and their rights is unclear. In each of the EU-wide, national and platform approaches to regulation, neither the individual and collective online harms nor specific threats to democracy are well defined and therefore meaningfully addressed. In each of these regulatory arenas, political advertising is conceptualised as image or video with text that is paid to be distributed beyond a user's followers. However, this is a limited approach, rooted in analogue advertising styles, and fails to consider the transformation of political communication and the resourcing of electoral campaigning in the digital era, which we discuss below. Furthermore, while the EU, state-level and platforms suggest that regulations are designed to enhance fundamental rights of users and, in turn, democracies, this is not possible within the current framework because, as we outline below, tensions between fundamental rights arise when policies are put into practice.

IV. Tensions between Fundamental Rights

The question of regulation of online advertising and related platform governance approaches presupposes an analysis of the extent to which they comply with or even enhance the fundamental rights of European citizens. Overall, the literature addressing the issue of electoral advertising on social media tends to address three core areas regarding fundamental rights: freedom of expression; free and fair elections; and privacy. Within these, three key tensions are revealed: between regulating political advertising and freedom of expression; between unregulated political advertising and fair elections; and between citizens' privacy and the requirement for transparency. This section examines these tensions, revealing that the previously mentioned conceptualisation of the citizen-user is present at EU, national and platform level: citizens are conceived as either passive subjects in need of protection or increasingly responsible individuals in complete control of information flows.

In the absence of detailed information from social media platforms about the application of their policies that aim to uphold fundamental rights to validate and analyse, it is only possible to address what each of the companies say. The CEO of Facebook, Mark Zuckerberg, has commented many times that the approach of his company is underpinned by a belief that freedom of expression empowers the powerless, and expressed resistance to the idea of further limitation to what content can be published (beyond those that are already illegal).[44] Dobber, Fathaigh and Zuiderveen Borgesius[45] seem to agree with Facebook, pointing out that 'a political

[44] Facebook, 'Mark Zuckerberg Stands for Voice and Free Expression' (17 October 2019), available at about.fb.com/news/2019/10/mark-zuckerberg-stands-for-voice-and-free-expression.

[45] T Dobber, RÓ Fathaigh and F Zuiderveen Borgesius, 'The regulation of online political micro-targeting in Europe' (2019) 8 *Internet Policy Review* 8.

party's and online platform's right to impart information' and 'a voter's right to receive information' are potentially protected by the freedom of expression, albeit not in an absolute manner.[46] In prioritising freedom of expression, this view relies on an understanding of citizens as empowered, able to both express themselves and judiciously manage information that comes their way.

On the other hand, EU and state regulation focuses on the need for fair elections, and the need to prevent wealthy interests from manipulating the public sphere by flooding it with their messages or presenting false information either about themselves or to smear other candidates. The high-profile examples of the Brexit referendum[47] and the Trump presidential campaign in 2016[48] made clear the need to develop and implement rules for the protection of citizens from manipulation. The issue of microtargeting has emerged as particularly relevant here especially in terms of how social media algorithms choose what information is shown and to whom. Gerards argues that algorithms are 'non-transparent, non-neutral human constructs' that use computational mathematical formulas to make decisions that operate in black boxes.[49] Regulation must therefore come in to protect citizens from manipulation and the unaccountable operations of algorithms.

Microtargeting and algorithms are not only an issue for fair elections but also for privacy and freedom of expression. To enable algorithmic systems to microtarget citizens, platforms collect and process data about them and their behaviour on platforms. Gerards stresses the conflict that the vast collection of user data has with privacy. For Gerards, this is what constitutes the threat to freedom of expression and access to information as algorithms, using our data, select links to present to users on search engines.[50] Algorithms that limit our access to information by blocking or deprioritising content some may find offensive, based on the morality of groups users are not members of, can have discriminatory effects, for example in microtargeting of advertisements, say by categories such as gender.[51] Green and Issenberg argue that omitting people from political or electoral communications is counter to the spirit of the freedom to access and free and fair elections.[52]

[46] All nations have electoral campaigning legislation and that the freedom of expression sometimes conflicts with other fundamental rights such as freedom from persecution on the bases of gender, religious affiliation or race.

[47] C Fuchs, *Nationalism 2.0: The Making of Brexit on Social Media* (Pluto Press, 2018).

[48] E Franklin Fowler, TN Ridout and M Franz, 'Political Advertising in 2016: The Presidential Election as Outlier?' (2016) 14 The Forum 445.

[49] J Gerards, 'The fundamental rights challenges of algorithms' (2019) 37 *Netherlands Quarterly of Human Rights* 205.

[50] ibid.

[51] Gerard also notes issues with procedural justice – all parties in a case should have equal access to all the information and the court should evaluate all the evidence – it is not possible where the evidence is out of reach or one party or both. This issue arose during the investigations into Brexit.

[52] J Green and S Issenberg 'Inside the Trump bunker, with days to go' (Bloomberg Businessweek, 27 October 2016), available at www.bloomberg.com/news/articles/2016-10-27/inside-the-trump-bunker-with-12-days-to-go.

Microtargeting means political actors can ignore certain voter groups they deem unimportant ('redlining') or demobilise supporters of competing parties.[53] Here, freedom of expression and the right to access information conflict, and neither is a clear priority.

The second tension emerges between the issue of user data privacy and the need for transparency in political campaigning. While the Code of Practice stipulates that platforms share data to allow for independent monitoring of their efforts, this has not happened. The Code is primarily assessed through platforms' own self-reports and assessment. The lack of data-sharing is justified by platforms on the basis of the requirement to be GDPR-compliant and to protect the data of their users. In contrast, the calls for transparency by researchers and civil society organisations requires access to some users' information to ensure the electoral process is not undermined. Furthermore, this position rests on the premise that citizens who access, for example, digital libraries of online advertisements, or who find out how algorithms operate via monitors, will be empowered to make more informed political choices; again, this is presumed in the absence of any evidence.

On the other hand, platforms discuss their algorithms as user-based, and as tools to allow users to make the most out of their platforms. For example, in a recent article, Nick Clegg, the former British deputy prime minister and current Vice President of Global Affairs and Communication for Facebook, wonders: 'people are portrayed as powerless victims, robbed of their free will. Humans have become the playthings of manipulative algorithmic systems. But is this really true?' His answer is that 'Data-driven personalized services like social media have empowered people with the means to express themselves and to communicate with others on an unprecedented scale', stressing that 'people should be able to choose for themselves, and that people can generally be trusted to know what is best for them'.[54] While Clegg is not against external oversight and regulation, it is clear in this article that his view of citizens is very different from the protective approach implied in existing and proposed regulations. The issue of protecting citizens constitutes the main justification for EU and state regulation of online political advertising, while platform approaches tend to be underpinned by the values around freedom of expression and privacy for user data.

So far, we have argued that EU, state and platform regulatory approaches fail to address transformed political communication processes, that the conceptualisation of political advertising and citizens across regulation is problematic and that the varying prioritisation of citizens fundamental rights expose irreconcilable tensions within the current tiers of regulatory framework. Furthermore, the regulatory

[53] ibid

[54] N Clegg, 'You and the Algorithm: It takes two to tango' (Medium.com, 31 March 2021), available at nickclegg.medium.com/you-and-the-algorithm-it-takes-two-to-tango-7722b19aa1c2.

environment fails to include the perspectives of marginalised communities and people which campaigns such as #Brusselssowhite and #whomakestherules? seek to highlight. Next, we illustrate how a communication rights approach could address the emerging limitations and tensions.

V. Rethinking Communication Rights

In this section we propose that a more comprehensive approach to political advertising is necessary. This should address new political campaigning practices, within and beyond elections. To accomplish this, a regulatory approach could engage with communication rights as a key mechanism that can facilitate the participation of all citizens in political communication in the digital era. A communication rights approach is important because of three main factors: firstly, it historicises debates on regulation of the media sphere; secondly, it explicitly thematises inequality and justice; and thirdly, it challenges the current individualistic approach to rights. As such, it moves towards a needs-based approach that takes into account the differential impact of communication rights for some communities and the significance of communication rights for the articulation of political demands. The adoption of a communication right approach therefore constitutionalises the regulation of political campaigning on social media by centralising the democratic principles of fairness and equity of elections, and freedom of expression and participation in politics. Moreover, we argue that the digital era requires the explicit addition and further development and elaboration of communication rights to be included in the arsenal of constitutional rights.

Communication rights and the right to communicate have their basis on Article 19 of the 1948 UN Declaration of Human Rights, which refers to the right of freedom of expression. However, this was taken further in a series of discussions in the 1970s, which highlighted that countries of the Global South did not and could not exercise the right to communicate because of an unequal informational world order. Concerns around media dominance, inequalities of access and limitations to freedom of expression's impact on democracy parallel today's concerns. To address these issues UNESCO established a new Commission headed by the Irish politician Sean MacBride, which published its report, 'Many Voices, One World', in 1980. The report urged that the right to communicate, involving 'the right to be informed, the right to inform, the right to privacy, the right to participate in public communication' and their implications be further explored.[55] While the McBride report and its recommendations were never endorsed, mainly because the US and the UK disagreed and left UNESCO, the debate on communication rights and the

[55] S MacBride, 'Many voices, one world: towards a new, more just, and more efficient world information and communication order' (UNESCO, 1980), available at unesdoc.unesco.org/ark:/48223/pf0000040066 265.

best way to define, achieve and enforce them still remain,[56] and, we would add, acquired a new impetus in the current context.

Elaborating further, Uppal et al argue that communication must be understood as a right

> without which it is impossible to fully exercise citizenship, in the sense that exercising control and power over individual and collective communication practices is a condition for exercising other citizen rights such as political participation through voting, influencing policy making and accessing information.[57]

The discourse on communication rights has always been about creating an equitable information environment and empowering those who are marginalised, excluded and exploited, so that they can participate in public communication on an equal footing. For Cammaerts, communication rights represent 'a participatory and citizen-oriented approach to information and communication, embedded in an open and transparent democratic culture'.[58] This is translated into a wide range of demands, from access to communication infrastructures to articulations of the common good, knowledge-sharing and decommodification of information, and from independence and ethical approaches to journalism to support for participatory and community media. While Cammaerts was primarily discussing broadcast and print media, these ideas are more than relevant for social media. Within this framework there is a need to democratise the process of engaging with political debate online by creating a more equitable space for a wide range of communities to participate and by enabling people to engage and debate political issues as well as to promote their own political concerns. This idea has also been raised by Leurs in relation to migrant communication rights and the benefits of engaging with communication rights as a bottom-up expression of human rights.[59]

It is noted that there is a similarity between this participatory approach and the citizen empowerment-responsibilisation discourses by platforms and occasionally found in regulatory initiatives, especially in the calls for transparency (the right to know) and media literacy campaigns. Indeed, Chakravartty argues that the normative logic of communication rights can turn into neoliberal rationality, where people's right to participate in communication, to inform and be informed, is translated into an individualised right exercised through using social

[56] U Carlsson, 'From NWICO to global governance of the information society' in O Hemer and T Tufte, *Media and glocal change: Rethinking communication for development* (UNESCO, 2005) 193–214.

[57] C Uppal, P Sartoretto and D Cheruiyot, 'The Case for Communication Rights: A Rights-Based Approach to Media Development' (2019) 15 *Global Media and Communication* 323, 327.

[58] B Cammaerts, 'Citizenship, the public sphere and media' in B Cammaerts and N Carpentier (eds), *Reclaiming the media: communication rights and democratic media roles. European communication research and education association series* (Intellect, 2007) 1, 5.

[59] K Leurs, 'Communication rights from the margins: Politicising young refugees' smartphone pocket archives' (2017) 79 *International Communication Gazette* 674.

media platforms.[60] Dean's work on communicative capitalism is instructive here.[61] Discussing the proliferation of communication on social media, Dean notes that this involves a shift from communication as a message intending to reach specific others to communication as a contribution to the circulation of contents. In this context, participation in communicative networks stands in for political participation in the sense of participating in struggles. The right to know has become associated with transparency, and this in turn is reduced to calls for warning labels and more data while avoiding hard or unpopular decisions.[62] Finally, we note that initiatives towards media literacy, that are both necessary and important, often take the form of individual learning through people's own actions, as for example found in the recent 'Be Media Smart' campaign in Ireland with its motto 'Stop, Think, Check'.[63] Here it is the citizen's responsibility to take ownership of their own actions around social media content. But education, and media literacy as education, is something that society owes to its citizens, and it is far more comprehensive than the morsels of information contained in media campaigns. In short, while the discourse on communication rights has articulated an important critique pointing to media inequalities it has so far failed to address them, because rights have been interpreted as individual rights and therefore the potential to address race, gender and class-based inequalities in the sphere of communication has been lost.

The question for regulation and for civil society therefore is firstly to reimagine communication rights in ways that do not reduce them to individual rights and secondly to link communication rights to the original demands for equality and justice. While it is not easy to imagine how this might take place, there are at least two fruitful avenues that could be explored: one, as suggested by Gangadharan, emerges from civil society campaigns related to media justice.[64] The second avenue may lie in the role of state and supranational institutions, which bear the responsibility for addressing inequalities. In particular, Gangadharan discussed media justice campaigns in the US, and outlined their successes in specific cases of problematic and stereotypical media representations and in forcing telecom companies to provide broadband access to rural communities.[65] To these we could add the successful mobilisation against facial recognition technologies for surveillance, that led to a moratorium. In these terms, civil society mobilisations

[60] P Chakravartty, 'Communication Rights and Neoliberal Development: Technopolitics in India' in C Padovani and A Calabrese (eds), *Communication Rights and Social Justice. Global Transformations in Media and Communication Research* (Palgrave Macmillan, 2014).

[61] J Dean, 'Communicative capitalism: Circulation and the foreclosure of politics' (2005) 1 Cultural Politics 51.

[62] ibid.

[63] Media Literacy Ireland, 'Be Smart Media Campaign', available at www.bemediasmart.ie.

[64] S Pena Gangadharan, 'Media justice and communication rights' (2014) in C Padovani and A Calabrese (eds), *Communication Rights and Social Justice. Global Transformations in Media and Communication Research* (Palgrave Macmillan, 2014) 203–18.

[65] ibid.

around questions of media justice have an important role to play in articulating where some of the communication fault lines exist, which can then be addressed through regulation. Secondly, media and communication inequalities need to be seen as part of broader social inequalities of gender, race and class, and addressed as such. It is crucial to note here that regulation of political content does not harm all communities equally and this is something that must be considered in relevant policy initiatives. Communication rights are not merely an add on to other rights, but the principal means by which to claim other fundamental rights.

VI. Conclusion

This chapter began with a discussion of the specific provisions of electoral campaign regulation internationally, focusing on the EU, and nationally, focusing on Ireland, while also considering the question of disinformation from the perspective of platform governance. We examined the regulation in its technical dimensions and in terms of its rationale or prevailing logics, arguing that it is structured on the basis of certain key tensions between specific fundamental rights. In these tensions we identified an oscillation between two prevailing understandings of the citizen-user: one that constructs the figure of the user as vulnerable and in need of protection and a second that constructs them as empowered and responsible. We argued that none of these understandings is appropriate because the reality of hybrid political communication is more complex. The discussion of the hybrid political communication revealed that it is structured along four main inequalities: (i) an intensification of competition over communication power; (ii) a focus on affect which opens political communication up to manipulation; (iii) a permanently active temporality; (iv) an architecture that was designed by platforms for their own benefit. All these, we argue, privilege the resource-rich.

It is clear therefore that unless regulatory approaches take into account the broader context of hybrid political communication, they are bound to have a limited contribution in countering problematic aspects such as disinformation. The Code of Practice and related instruments that focus on election periods are inadequate to address the issues generated by the always-on campaigning in hybrid political communication. We therefore propose a rethinking of the current regulatory approach that involves a shift from the fundamental rights approach and its tensions to a communication rights-based one. The development and further elaboration of communication rights in the twenty-first century should be part of the agenda for constitutionalising social media. The articulation of communication rights emerged in the post-colonial period of the 1970s, initiated by the Non-Aligned Movement, which sought to address inequalities in communication structures and access to them in the global world system. Although these proposals were never implemented as originally intended, the rich discourse around communication rights has been generative, because it formulated demands for inclusion and participation, decommodification of communication, articulations of the common good and communication ethics, and public access to and control of information and communication infrastructures. At the same time, however, an important critique emerged, revolving around the ways in which communication rights have been appropriated by neoliberal logics of self-empowerment via market-based solutions. Often, the discourse of platforms resembles that of communication rights because, as we argue, they have been interpreted as individual rights rather than as calls to address communicative inequalities as manifestations of race, gender and class inequalities.

While this discussion might be seen as distant from the immediate and pressing needs to protect 'our democracies' from the (real or imagined) dangers of disinformation, during (and beyond) elections, from 'bad actors' and 'deep fakes', we argue that unless democracies are strengthened within, through addressing the deep divisions of inequality that spill over in the sphere of communication, any regulation is bound to be little more than a sticking plaster.

9

Data Protection Law: Constituting an Effective Framework for Social Media?

MORITZ HENNEMANN*

I. Introduction

The 'hunger' for data by social media is regularly framed rather negatively – most prominently by Zuboff, who coined the term 'surveillance capitalism'[1] – and social media platforms are indeed processing a huge amount of personal data every second. This setting obviously offers the possibility of – though does not automatically lead to – misuses of data.[2] The probability of misuse is (also, but not solely) determined by the legal framework for data-processing. In Europe, the EU General Data Protection Regulation of 2016 (GDPR)[3] has established manifold obligations for data-processors – spanning from consent requirements to a new right to data portability. For this reason, the GDPR has so far been promoted as

* The drafting of this chapter is supported by the Bavarian State Ministry of Science and Culture. The chapter builds upon earlier publications and unpublished conference papers, especially P Boshe, M Hennemann, and R von Meding, 'African Data Protection Laws – Current Regulatory Approaches, Policy Initiatives, and the Way Forward' (2022) 3 *Global Privacy Law Review*, forthcoming; M Hennemann, P Boshe, and R von Meding, 'Datenschutzrechtsordnungen in Afrika – Grundlagen, Rechtsentwicklung und Fortentwicklungspotenziale' (2021) *Zeitschrift für Digitalisierung und Recht* 193; M Hennemann, 'Das Schweizer Datenschutzrecht im Wettbewerb der Rechtsordnungen' in BP Paal, D Poelzig, and O Fehrenbacher (eds), *Festschrift Ebke* (CH Beck, 2022) 371; M Hennemann, 'Wettbewerb der Datenschutzrechtsordnungen? – zur Rezeption der Datenschutz-Grundverordnung' (2020) 84 *Rabels Zeitschrift für ausländisches und internationales Privatrecht* 864; M Hennemann, 'Data Protection and Antitrust Law: The German Cartel Office's Facebook Case and its European Aftermath' (unpublished conference paper for 'Big Tech & Antitrust', Information Society Project, Yale Law School, October 2020); BP Paal and M Hennemann, 'Big Data im Recht – Wettbewerbs- und daten(schutz)rechtliche Herausforderungen' (2017) *Neue Juristische Wochenschrift* 1697; M Hennemann, 'Datenportabilität' (2017) *Privacy in Germany* 5.

[1] S Zuboff, *The Age of Surveillance Capitalism* (Public Affairs, 2019).

[2] This chapter is focused on the processing of personal data (for which data protection regulation generally applies); it is not concerned with the use (or sharing) of non-personal data (cf in this regard M Hennemann, 'Datenlizenzverträge' (2021) *Recht Digital* 61).

[3] Regulation (EU) 2016/679 of the European Parliament and of the Council of 27 April 2016 on the protection of natural persons with regard to the processing of personal data and on the free movement of such data, [2016] OJ L 119 pp 1ff.

a normative tool for the constitution and implementation of effective regulatory framework for Big Tech – and the business model of social media was used as the prime case for a modern and strong European data protection law. The GDPR was and is perceived by the EU legislator to be the 'Gold Standard'.[4] A huge number of countries worldwide have – partly on that basis – followed or were inspired by the GDPR approach: for example, Brazil[5] and Switzerland.[6] This is a process the European Union actively pushed for – and at the same time (and maybe surprisingly to some) is supported by social media companies themselves, including, inter alia, Facebook's CEO Mark Zuckerberg.[7]

Against this background, the chapter will analyse to what extent and by which means modern data protection law regulations, with a special focus on the EU, do (or do not) efficiently regulate – and thereby constitutionalise – social media. In this context, however, it must not be forgotten that social media are not only acting to the detriment of fundamental rights (including data protection), but might also serve as one of the biggest enablers of, inter alia, the right to informational self-determination. On the one hand, the chapter will demonstrate that social media is bound by data protection law rules in various ways, taking the GDPR and particularly the rules on consent into consideration. On the other hand, it will contend that the existing rules do not 'tie' social media too strongly, or even too efficiently. This finding is first and foremost based on a legal analysis of the existing statute law and its (prevailing) interpretation in Europe, and especially in Germany, but also on (behavioural) economics. The chapter will selectively point to respective interdisciplinary insights, for example with regard to the privacy paradox. In this context, the more fundamental question shall be discussed of whether and to what extent existing data protection rules might even favour the business model of social media. Finally, the chapter will briefly turn to global developments in data protection law rulemaking.[8] By pointing to the global 'race to the GDPR' the chapter will underline the fact that the degree of (in)efficiency of the GDPR in regulating social media also has a global dimension.

[4] JP Albrecht, 'Das neue EU-Datenschutzrecht' (2016) 32 *Computer und Recht* 88, 98; cf also G Butarelli, 'The EU GDPR as a clarion call for a new global digital gold standard' (2016) 6 *International Data Privacy Law* 77.

[5] cf T Hoeren and S Pinelli, 'Das neue brasilianische Datenschutzrecht – Eine kritische Betrachtung im Vergleich mit der DS-GVO' (2020) *Zeitschrift für Datenschutz* 351.

[6] cf M Griesinger, 'Ein Überblick über das neue Schweizer Datenschutzgesetz (DSG) – Anforderungen und Voraussetzung des revidierten Schweizer Datenschutzgesetzes für die Datenschutz-Compliance von Unternehmen' (2021) *Privacy in Germany* 43; Hennemann, 'Das Schweizer Datenschutzrecht' (2022).

[7] M Zuckerberg, 'The Internet needs new rules. Let's start in these four areas' (30 March 2019), available at www.washingtonpost.com/opinions/mark-zuckerberg-the-internet-needs-new-rules-lets-start-in-these-four-areas/2019/03/29/9e6f0504-521a-11e9-a3f7-78b7525a8d5f_story.html?noredirect=on.

[8] cf in this regard Hennemann, 'Wettbewerb der Datenschutzrechtsordnungen?' (2020); PM Schwartz, 'Global Data Privacy: The EU Way' (2019) 94 *NYU Law Review* 771; WG Voss, 'Cross-Border Data Flows, the GDPR, and Data Governance' (2020) 29 *Washington International Law Journal* 485.

II. Data Protection Regulation and Social Media

Data protection law – at least in Europe – has a strong constitutional basis. It is largely construed on the right to privacy, the right to informational self-determination, and the right to data protection. Some modern constitutional documents mention this fundament more or less explicitly (eg Article 8 ECHR); in other cases, it is derived from an interpretation by courts and academia (ie German Basic Law). It is important to underline that the fundamental rights of privacy, informational self-determination and data protection are not mirroring a coherent dimension of protection; rather, they represent different, sometimes overlapping notions and goals. Whereas privacy is, generally speaking, understood as the 'right to be let alone' (first spelled out by Warren and Brandeis), informational self-determination (famously formed by the German Constitutional Court in its *Volkszählungsurteil*)[9] is linked to the fact that a person can be 'construed' through and 'mirrored' by its personal data. This individual shall be 'in control' and therefore (ideally) knows who processes his or her own data and for what purposes – a concept followed by the GDPR and corresponding instruments.

The right to data protection originally often targeted state-to-citizen relationships (see however the Council of Europe Resolution (73) 22 providing protection of the privacy of individuals vis-à-vis electronic data banks in the private sector), and the processing of personal data by public bodies is still the benchmark until today. However, when converting such constitutional layers into statutory law, modern data protection laws have extended their scopes and shifted their focus to business-to-consumer constellations. As a consequence of this shift, constitutional values – and corresponding legal instruments – are infiltrating private-to-private relationships. Mutual relationships and the exchange of information in this context are traditionally governed by contractual agreements. Data protection law has thus added a new regulative layer to this setting.

The business model of social media is today regulated in a variety of ways, from contract law[10] (including unfair terms regulation) and competition law[11] to information society and media law.[12] First and foremost, however, this business model is inherently linked to – and dependent on – data protection law. 'Gaining' and 'using' personal data goes to the heart of the data economy in general and to (advertisement-driven) social media in particular. Personal data are an

[9] BVerfG, 15 December 1983, 1 BvR 209/83 – *Volkszählungsurteil*.

[10] It is worth noticing that the 2019 EU Digital Content Directive has strengthened the valuable contract law layer of the contractual user-platform relationship.

[11] cf BP Paal and M Hennemann, *Big Data as an Asset: Daten und Kartellrecht* (study conducted for the interdisciplinary research cluster ABIDA – Assessing Big Data, 2018), available at www.abida.de/sites/default/files/Gutachten_ABIDA_Big_Data_as_an_Asset.pdf.

[12] cf from a German perspective, BP Paal and M Hennemann, 'Meinungsbildung im digitalen Zeitalter: Regulierungsinstrumente für einen gefährdungsadäquaten Rechtsrahmen' (2017) 72 *Juristenzeitung* 641.

indispensable prerequisite for close to every service offered by and on social media platforms. A factor that has drawn eminent attention by law enforcement agencies, eg the German national competition authority, Federal Cartel Office (FCO). In a dispute involving Facebook, the latter affirmed that: 'it appears to be indispensable to examine the conduct of dominant companies under competition law also in terms of their [data-processing] procedures, as especially the conduct of online businesses is highly relevant from a competition law perspective'.[13]

A. Central Pillars of the Regulatory Framework

In the EU, any social media provider must therefore ensure that personal data are legally processed. Not a simple task, as any processing is, from the outset, forbidden if no distinct justification (legal ground) for processing is given. Article 6, para 1 GDPR reads:

> Processing shall be lawful only if and to the extent that at least one of the following applies: (a) the data subject has given consent to the processing of his or her personal data for one or more specific purposes; (b) processing is necessary for the performance of a contract to which the data subject is party or in order to take steps at the request of the data subject prior to entering into a contract; … (f) processing is necessary for the purposes of the legitimate interests pursued by the controller or by a third party.

Any data-processing goes along with manifold further obligations:[14] inter alia, detailed information duties (Articles 13 and 14 GDPR), elaborated data management systems (Article 5, para 2 and Articles 15–21 GDPR), privacy by design and privacy by default principles (Article 25 GDPR), and technical measures regarding data security (Article 24 and 32 GDPR).

The consent of the data subject in particular – prime justification for data-processing, also as an act of informational self-determination – is linked to distinct prerequisites. Consent must be freely given, on an informed basis (Article 4(11) GDPR) and with respect to 'one or more specific purposes' (Article 6, para 1(1) GDPR). When asking for consent (in a written form), such 'request … shall be presented in a manner which is clearly distinguishable from the other matters, in an intelligible and easily accessible form, using clear and plain language' (Article 7, para 2 GDPR). Furthermore, Article 7, para 4 GDPR tries to tackle the genuine and regular link between monetary-free services and a consent declaration:

> When assessing whether consent is freely given, utmost account shall be taken of whether, inter alia, the performance of a contract, including the provision of a service, is conditional on consent to the processing of personal data that is not necessary for the performance of that contract.

[13] *FCO v Facebook, Inc & Ors*, 6 February 2019, Case B6-22/16 – Case Summary (15 February 2019), p 8.

[14] The following lines do only highlight major obligations and do therefore not include a full account of all the obligations set by the GDPR.

Finally, data subjects have a right to data portability according to Article 20 GDPR. Data subjects may request their data 'in a structured, commonly used and machine-readable format and have the right to transmit those data to another controller without hindrance from the [first] controller'. Recital 68 GDPR spells out the aim of this provision: 'To further strengthen the control over [the subject's] own data'. Data subjects are offered the opportunity to overcome potential lock-in-effects, which might derive from the fact that it is too burdensome to change data controllers if personal data has to be provided manually all over again to a second controller.[15] This instrument is therefore – to be precise – not a 'true' data protection law tool, but a modified competition law tool.[16] Data subjects shall make their choice for or against a specific controller independently of factual disadvantages – to the benefit of a product-related competition. That the right is 'serving' not data protection but competition is also underlined by the fact that its execution does not necessarily affect the contractual relationship to the original controller: consent is not withdrawn, and the underlying contract is not terminated. From an abstract viewpoint, the 'risk' for the data subject actually increases, as its personal data is now processed by more than one data controller.

Furthermore, Article 20 GDPR does not guarantee that data in itself is portable (in the sense of interoperable), as Recital 68 GDPR confirms:

> Data controllers should be encouraged to develop interoperable formats that enable data portability. … The data subject's right to transmit or receive personal data concerning him or her should not create an obligation for the controllers to adopt or maintain processing systems which are technically compatible.

Hence, the policy debate on interoperability is ongoing, but, nonetheless, Article 20 GDPR serves as a functional starting point that might be further shaped by subsequent EU data law legislation – and subsequently also contribute to a more effective protection of connected fundamental rights.

B. An Effective Framework?

At first sight, the GDPR seems to set 'tight' limits for social media platforms. The situation is, however, and as always, more complicated.

i. The Legal Perspective: 'Hard' or 'Soft' Regulation?

This is first and foremost true for the GDPR and related national instruments, but also with regard to the interplay with competition law. The data protection law framework might be even 'tighter' if dominant undertakings – which prominent

[15] Hennemann, 'Datenportabilität' (2017) 6.
[16] ibid 5 for details.

social media platforms regularly are – are at stake. In other words: do we have to 'read' competition law parameters into data protection law?[17] The German federal competition authority (FCO) answers this question affirmatively: 'data protection law considers corporate circumstances like market dominance, the concrete purpose and the amount of data processed in its justifications'.[18] The effects of such an approach can inter alia be demonstrated by a central element of data protection law: the consent of the data subject.

At first sight, the consent requirement does not seem to be a major obstacle for the data-driven economy. Consent is regularly given. Empirical evidence underlines that consent rates might have dipped after the coming into force of the GDPR (in this case – 12.5 per cent), but that – due to a more coherent set of those still opting in – 'the remaining consumers are trackable for a longer period of time'.[19] Social media platforms seem to have a rather rock-solid basis for their data-processing. For two reasons, however, this fundament might erode away. First, consent declarations might be subject to unfair standard terms regulation, though this seems to be rarely enforced so far.[20] Second, vis-à-vis dominant undertakings, the consent might not be given 'freely'.[21] The FCO has given prominence to this perspective in a recent case involving Facebook.[22] The FCO argued that no valid consent to Facebook's data-processing was given by users.[23] The validity was denied with reference to the lack of voluntariness of the consent. Voluntariness is not only defined by an absence of force, but might also be challenged in situations of 'imbalance'. Recital 43 sentence 1 GDPR supports this approach in general:

> In order to ensure that consent is freely given, consent should not provide a valid legal ground for the processing of personal data in a specific case where there is a clear imbalance between the data subject and the controller, (...).[24]

Some also point to the rule of Article 7, para 4 GDPR in this regard.[25] The FCO's approach was not fully shared by the follow-on case law[26] or a significant part

[17] See in this regard also E Bueren, 'Kartellrecht und Datenschutzrecht – zugleich ein Beitrag zur 10. GWB-Novelle und zum Facebook-Verfahren' (2019) *Zeitschrift für Wettbewerbsrecht* 403, 419f; BP Paal, 'Marktmacht im Daten(schutz)recht' (2020) 18 *Zeitschrift für Wettbewerbsrecht* 215.

[18] *FCO v Facebook* (n 13), p 11.

[19] G Aridor, Y-K Che and T Salz, 'The Effect of Privacy Regulation on the Data Industry: Empirical Evidence from Gdpr' (NBER Working Paper No. w26900, 30 March 2020), available at ssrn.com/abstract=3563968.

[20] cf M Hennemann, 'Personalisierte Medienangebote im Datenschutz- und Vertragsrecht' (2017) *ZUM* 544, 548 ff.

[21] cf in detail Paal, 'Marktmacht' (2020) 231 ff.

[22] *FCO v Facebook* (n 13).

[23] ibid 1 ff.

[24] However, the sentence continues by pointing to 'in particular … public authorit[ies]' and situations where 'it is therefore unlikely that consent was freely given in all the circumstances of that specific situation'.

[25] cf for the discussion Paal (n 17) 215.

[26] cf OLG Düsseldorf, 26 August 2019, VI-Kart 1/19 (V) – *Facebook/Bundeskartellamt*, II. B. 1. b) bb. (3.1) (p 10) and (4.2) (c) (cc) (3.1) (p 28); Federal Court of Justice, 23 June 2020, KVR 69/19 = [2020] GRUR-RS 20737.

of the scholarship, and so in this context is questionable in its rigidity. However, if the FCO's route will be taken again in the future, this will lead to imposing a very 'tight' limit for data-processing, especially by dominant social media platforms. These undertakings could not process data on the basis of consent, but would have to rely on other legal grounds to pursue data-processing. Considering the rather small number of legal grounds, one should be aware of the far-reaching consequences of this.

In this context, it shall be noted that the FCO also denied the lawfulness of Facebook's activities *in casu* based on other legal grounds (especially Article 6, para 1(b) and (f) GDPR).[27] This approach was only partly confirmed by the German Federal Court of Justice (FCJ), but without linking it to the dominant position of the undertaking, pointing instead to the specific data-processing (ie transfer to third parties) at stake.[28]

ii. The Economic Perspective: Stabilising Market Power through the GDPR?

From an economic point of view, the effects of the GDPR are not as straightforward as one might expect. It is hard to ascertain if the GDPR has made market conditions less favourable for Big Tech. Rather, these large and financially strong companies seem to have arranged themselves quite neatly in relation to the GDPR standards. Since they cannot avoid this type of regulation, some might therefore prefer to have only this standard regime worldwide, instead of having to comply with different sets of legislation (discussed above). This leaves us with a moment to pause and to reflect on the economic effects of the GDPR.

First and foremost, Big Tech's wish for more 'copies' of the GDPR is driven by the desire not to be confronted with too many different forms of regulation. A coherent global regime offers options for economies of scales. Companies often favour a uniform approach that reduces implementation and therefore transaction costs (legal costs, etc), which is also true in relation to content moderation.[29] GDPR-compliant mechanisms must be developed if one is active on the EU market, and such tools might then also be used for other parts of the world.

Second, despite the EU's narrative, the GDPR still leaves quite some room for the data economy to manoeuvre. That is not to say that the GDPR does not install boundaries for data-processing or is not enforced by data protection authorities, but – as seen above – the 'tightness' of the GDPR rules are questionable. More importantly, the GDPR – as Gal and Aviv have pointed to – rather counterintuitively, and unintentionally, supports dominant undertakings.[30] On the one hand,

[27] *FCO v Facebook* (n 13) 10 ff.
[28] Federal Court of Justice, 23 June 2020, KVR 69/19 = [2020] GRUR-RS 20737.
[29] See ch 16 (Celeste, Palladino, Redeker and Yilma) in this volume.
[30] See the seminal work by MS Gal and O Aviv, 'The Competitive Effects of the GDPR' (2020) 16 *Journal of Competition Law & Economics* 349.

the GDPR follows a 'one size fits all' approach that favours larger undertakings, as compliance costs are proportionally a bigger burden for SMEs. On the other hand, consent as a justification for data-processing means data can be easily exploited, as consent is regularly and, according to the prevailing view[31] vis-à-vis a dominant undertaking, freely given. However, if one adopts the alternative view (following the FCO's judgment on the voluntariness of consent) one would face a different picture, with significant economic effects. The denial of a consent option would have the potential to break up concentrated data-driven markets.[32] Dominant undertakings would only have a limited access to personal data and, consequently, non-dominant undertakings would gain a significant advantage[33] and a realistic opportunity to challenge the dominant undertaking's market position.[34]

The fact that data subjects are more or less trapped into the 'privacy paradox' adds a further layer in favour of undertakings asking for content. The notion of 'privacy paradox' applies when data subjects generally value the theoretical notion of data protection, but do not act accordingly. This becomes especially apparent with regard to informed consent. Data subjects rarely read the small print. It is often time-consuming, burdensome and sometimes inefficient to engage with the enormous amount of information data-processors present to them. Data subjects are facing an information overload, a collateral effect the legislator seems to have underestimated. It is important to recognise that this practice challenges the very heart of the EU data protection concept, which assumes that the data subject is in control of its data and acts knowingly on the basis of information provided. The declaration of consent is theoretically an enabler of self-determination, but this is not materially true in many cases.

Third, it is currently not clear whether the GDPR has sufficiently tackled lock-in-effects to the benefit of dominant undertakings in data economies,[35] a phenomenon which also favours Big Tech.[36] In particular, the GDPR's right to data portability has not become the game-changer that was promised. From an interpretative perspective, the actual wording of Article 20 GDPR raises a number of questions. It is still unclear what is meant by 'the personal data …, which he or she has provided': does 'personal data' encompasses only data that the subject actively provided, or does it also cover data that is 'tracked' when using a specific service (ie location data)? Furthermore, Article 20, para 4 GDPR states that the right to data portability 'shall not adversely affect the rights and freedoms of others'. This substantial limitation of the right is highly relevant in relation to social media; for example, chat feeds regularly include the personal data of other data subjects,

[31] cf also Bueren, 'Kartellrecht und Datenschutzrecht' (2019) 427.
[32] Paal (n 17) 243 ff.
[33] cf eg J Crémer, Y-A de Montjoye and H Schweitzer, *Competition policy for the digital era* (2019) 4, 7ff, available at ec.europa.eu/competition/publications/reports/kd0419345enn.pdf.
[34] Paal (n 17) 243 ff.
[35] Crémer, de Montjoye and Schweitzer, *Competition policy* (2019) 8.
[36] ibid 2.

and the right will often only cover small elements of the personal data provided to the platform. Finally, empirical evidence suggests that the right to data portability is not well known among data subjects and so is not exercised in a significant number of cases.[37]

To sum up, the GDPR seems to stabilise rather than tackle market power. Against this background, the calls in favour of the GDPR by dominant undertakings (as the one by Zuckerberg) are even more understandable – and are not primarily motivated by altruistic thinking or, presumably, a thorough concern for data protection.

III. The Global Race to the GDPR and its Constitutionalising Function

So far, this desire for uniformity is not unimaginable.[38] First, with regard to the global business model of social media platforms, a uniform approach might serve practical purposes. Second, a uniformity is also empirically observable. The GDPR has established itself as a global trendsetter,[39] including in the Global South.[40] This is the case despite the conceptual shortcomings of the GDPR (discussed above).[41] We can also observe various harmonisation or gradual convergence processes worldwide[42] – a tendency actively pushed for by the EU. This trend benefits from the so-called Brussels Effect identified by Bradford[43] and complementing GDPR instruments, such as its extraterritorial scope of application (Article 3, para 2(a) GDPR) and adequacy decisions (Article 45 GDPR).[44]

It is a pressing policy question whether the EU should operate along these lines. Using competition law language, one might ask whether the EU as a

[37] R Luzsa, 'Datenportabilität: Bedeutungsvoll, aber kaum bekannt' (bidt Blog, 5 October 2020), available at www.bidt.digital/blog-datenportabilitaet; P Walshe, *Privacy in the EU and US: Consumer experiences across three global platforms* (2019), available at eu.boell.org/sites/default/files/2019-12/TACD-HBS-report-Final.pdf.

[38] The following paragraph is based upon my article on the global 'competition' between data protection laws; see Hennemann, 'Wettbewerb der Datenschutzrechtsordnungen?' (2020).

[39] cf for a European perspective, Hennemann, 'Wettbewerb der Datenschutzrechtsordnungen?' (2020); cf for the US perspective, Schwartz, 'Global Data Privacy' (2019) 771.

[40] cf eg for the development on the African continent, Boshe, Hennemann, and von Meding, 'African Data Protection Laws' (2022); J Bryant, 'Africa in the Information Age: Challenges, Opportunities, and Strategies for Data Protection and Digital Rights' (2021) 24 *Stanford Technology Law Review* 389.

[41] cf eg W D'Avis and T Giesen, 'Datenschutz in der EU' (2019) 35 *Computer und Recht* 24; Gal and Aviv, 'Competitive Effects' (2020); C Krönke, 'Datenpaternalismus' (2016) 55 *Der Staat* 319; E Schmidt-Jortzig, 'IT-Revolution und Datenschutz' (2018) *Die Öffentliche Verwaltung* 10; W Veil, 'Die Datenschutz-Grundverordnung: des Kaisers neue Kleider' (2018) 10 *Neue Zeitschrift für Verwaltungsrecht* 686.

[42] For details see Hennemann, 'Wettbewerb der Datenschutzrechtsordnungen?' (2020).

[43] A Bradford, 'The Brussels Effect' (2012) 107 *Northwestern University Law Review* 1.

[44] cf F Fabbrini, E Celeste and J Quinn (eds), *Data Protection beyond Borders: Transatlantic Perspectives on Extraterritoriality and Sovereignty* (Hart, 2021).

'dominant' legislator should use pull-and-push effects[45] to press its regulation onto the 'legislative market' (and whether it is 'misusing' its position). This is not only questionable with respect to conceptual shortcomings, but also in principle – as legal transplants might go along with elements of 'legal imperialism' and – as 'lock-in-effects' do – structurally hinder other, maybe even more adequate or culturally sensible, legislative approaches.[46] From a constitutional law perspective, however, one might argue that this approach successfully 'constitutionalises' to a considerable extent data economies, including social media, worldwide – as giving data protection regulation a fundamental rights basis is increasingly the standard to be followed.

IV. Conclusion and Outlook

The responsibilities EU data protection law places upon social media are not in every respect as powerful as expected by legislators and data protection activists. The information- and consent-based 'one size fits all' model of the GDPR might be successful and 'easily transplantable'[47] on a global scale – and might 'constitutionalise' social media globally on a theoretical level. The actual effects of this regulatory approach so far, however, raise doubts as to its suitability. Assuming that the GDPR (and similar legislation elsewhere) will not be amended substantially in the near future, improvements are only possible through legal interpretation by academics and the courts, and this approach has not so far been used to its full extent. For example, a far-reaching unfair standard terms control of consent declarations could make the GDPR a more effective framework vis-à-vis dominant social media undertakings.

[45] cf to this notion Hennemann, 'Das Schweizer Datenschutzrecht' (2022).
[46] See for a further analysis, Hennemann, 'Wettbewerb der Datenschutzrechtsordnungen?' (2020).
[47] Schwartz (n 8) 809.

PART 3

States and Social Media Regulation

10

Regulatory Shift in State Intervention: From Intermediary Liability to Responsibility

GIANCARLO FROSIO

I. Introduction

As I have argued elsewhere,[1] the legal framework regulating online intermediaries has changed considerably in the past few years. Recent legal developments can be situated within a trend towards the expansion of the liabilities – and responsibilities – of online intermediaries. In particular, public enforcement lacking the technical knowledge and resources to address an unprecedented challenge in terms of global human semiotic behaviour would coactively outsource online enforcement to private parties. In doing so, intermediary regulation has shifted from intermediary liability to responsibility. This process pushes towards an amorphous notion of responsibility that incentivises online intermediaries' self-intervention to police allegedly infringing activities on the Internet, while departing from longstanding, legislatively mandated liability rules approaches, such as the knowledge-and-take-down and the no-monitoring obligation principles.[2]

The regulatory and enforcement (section VI) shift that is presently occurring depends on theoretical (section II), market (section III), policy (section IV) and technological (section V) changes. This chapter will investigate these changes and their effects. These emerging innovation policy choices reversed an earlier approach that provided online intermediaries with substantial liability exemptions to incentivise their capacity to develop Internet infrastructure and applications. Today, due to changed market conditions, policy-makers might want to switch the

[1] See G Frosio, 'Why Keep a Dog and Bark Yourself? From Intermediary Liability to Responsibility' (2018) 26 *International Journal of Law and Information Technology* 1; G Frosio and M Husovec, 'Intermediary Accountability and Responsibility' in G Frosio (ed), *The Oxford Handbook of Online Intermediary Liability* (Oxford University Press, 2020) 613–30.

[2] See, for a discussion of this departure, Giancarlo Frosio, 'The Death of 'No Monitoring Obligations': A Story of Untameable Monsters' (2017) 8(3) *JIPITEC* 199–215.

enormous transaction costs of online content regulation to online intermediaries as they might be the least-cost avoiders, in particular given their economies of scale. Meanwhile, online content sanitisation is increasingly becoming the sole domain of private – and opaque – algorithmic technologies. Burdened by expansive enforcement obligations, online intermediaries resort to the widespread deployment of algorithmic enforcement tools, which remain the only option at their disposal that will not jeopardise their business models.

As per the effects of this policy development, privately enforced intermediary responsibilities challenge the rule of law and a vast array of fundamental rights, but also run counter to any constitutionalisation process of online regulation. A centripetal move towards digital constitutionalism – although partially occurring at multiple levels, as this book highlights – might still be overshadowed for now by the counterpoising centrifugal move caused by private ordering and intermediary responsibility. State intervention has been increasingly delegating online enforcement and regulation to private parties, thus fragmenting responses and standards, rather than consolidating and 'constitutionalising' Internet governance. Of course, the regulatory framework is in constant flux, to the extent that it might become ever more difficult to identify consistent trends. The recently proposed Digital Services Act,[3] for example, might formalise private ordering measures into legislatively mandated obligations, in light of the principle of proportionality and fundamental rights, thus promoting constitutionalisation of platform regulation.

II. Theory: From Welfare to Moral Theories

The theoretical perspective justifying Internet governance and online intermediaries' regulation has been subject to profound revisions in the last few decades. In general, bringing pressure to innocent third parties that may enable or encourage violations by others is a well-established strategy to curb infringement. This strategy is expected to decrease the amount of online content infringement. There are two major theoretical approaches that underpin intermediaries' liability: moral and utilitarian. According to the moral approach, encouraging infringement is immoral, therefore the law should punish that behaviour in all instances, regardless of negative externalities that might derive from the liability regulatory framework.[4] The moral approach characterised more primitive, earlier responses

[3] See Proposal for a regulation of the European Parliament and of the Council on a Single Market For Digital Services (Digital Services Act) and amending Directive 2000/31/EC, COM(2020) 825 (hereafter 'DSA Proposal').

[4] See eg R Spinello, 'Intellectual Property: Legal and Moral Challenges of Online File Sharing' in R Sandler (ed), *Ethics and Emerging Technologies* (Palgrave Macmillan, 2013) 300; M Manesh, 'Immorality of Theft, the Amorality of Infringement' (2006) 2006 *Stanford Technology Law Review* 5; R Spinello, 'Secondary Liability in the Post Napster Era: Ethical Observations on MGM v. Grokster' (2005) 3 *Journal of Information, Communication and Ethics in Society* 121.

to intermediary regulation. The utilitarian, or welfare, approach instead attempts to balance competing rights and the interests at stake. It was established by Reiner Kraakman in a 1986 seminal article that set the basis for a 'gatekeeper theory', which seeks to use third parties to help enforce the law and regulate infringers according to a strict cost-benefit analysis.[5] According to Kraakman:

> Successful gatekeeping is likely to require (1) serious misconduct that practicable penalties cannot deter; (2) missing or inadequate private gatekeeping incentives; (3) gatekeepers who can and will prevent misconduct reliably, regardless of the preferences and market alternatives of wrongdoers; and (4) gatekeepers whom legal rules can induce to detect misconduct at reasonable cost.[6]

Originally designed to be used in security regulations, Kraakman's theoretical framework was later applied to online infringement.[7] First, sanctions should only be enforced upon intermediaries to prevent infringing conduct by third parties if the level of infringement would be exceptionally high because socially acceptable sanctions against direct infringers would not deter them. Second, the intermediaries must be unwilling to prevent infringement on their own – and may even foster it. Third, the intermediaries can effectively suppress infringement with minimal capacity for direct infringers to circumvent them. Finally, intermediaries must be able to prevent infringement by third parties without a high social or economic cost.[8] This cost-benefit analysis would be highly relevant in the case of dual-use technologies, ie technologies that are used to infringe others' rights and also allow social beneficial users.

Welfare approaches to intermediaries' obligations in online enforcement and content moderation have been dominant over the past few decades, giving life to safe-harbour legislation and liability exemptions. However, in recent times, as highlighted by some scholars, a resurgence of moral approaches to online liability has been trying to push more responsibility onto online intermediaries, often in the form of private ordering and voluntary measures, rather than statutory mandated liability based on welfare law and economics analysis.[9] Policy approaches might be returning to implement moral theories of intermediary liability, rather than utilitarian or welfare theories. In this case, justification for policy intervention would be based on responsibility for the actions of users as opposed to considerations based on market efficiency or balance innovation vs harm. In turn, this strategy poses challenges from a fundamental and user-right perspective. However, as the

[5] See R Kraakman, 'Gatekeepers: the Anatomy of a Third-Party Enforcement Strategy' (1986) 2 *Journal of Law, Economics and Organization* 53.

[6] ibid 61.

[7] See W Fisher, CopyrightX: Lecture 11.1, 'Supplements to Copyright: Secondary Liability' (18 February 2014) 7:50, available at www.youtube.com/watch?v=7YGg-VfwK_Y.

[8] ibid.

[9] See M Husovec, *Injunctions against Intermediaries in the European Union: Accountable but Not Liable?* (Cambridge University Press, 2017). See also Frosio and Husovec, 'Intermediary Accountability and Responsibility' (2020) 613–30; Frosio, 'Why Keep a Dog and Bark Yourself?' (2018).

next section examines, a cost-benefit analysis focusing on transaction costs of enforcement in light of changed market conditions and Internet market geopolitics also play a role in shifting responsibility on least-cost avoiders and in shaping recent policy responses.

III. Market: From Innovators to Moderators

In response to the rise of the Internet in the 1990s, legislators took the decision that access and hosting providers should enjoy liability exemptions for the unlawful acts of third parties on their networks. It was a brave new world. The internet infrastructure was yet to be built – and, even after it was, the Internet would have remained an empty shell, absent the right incentives to encourage high-tech innovators to develop millions of applications. It was a highly unpredictable business venture. Most companies were doomed to failure, and just a few survived those early years. Thus, policy-makers understood that both access providers, which had to set up the Internet infrastructure, and hosting providers, which had to populate that infrastructure with applications, had to be lured into the new market with the guarantee of liability exemptions for anything that could go wrong – and their users could do wrong. In the US, these market conditions justified the very broad safe harbours provided to access providers, for any content, and to hosting providers for the speech they gave a platform to, as well as the more limited safe harbours enjoyed by hosting providers for copyright-infringing content.[10] Outside the US, other jurisdictions followed suit with very similar legal arrangements, although, in the EU at least, with more limited liability exemptions for hosting providers at large, regardless of whether they carry speech- or copyright-infringing content.[11] In fact, most international jurisdictions were eager to attract investments and innovation from the US companies that dominated the nascent Internet market, and concluded that the most beneficial policy option was to provide these companies with the same conditions they enjoyed at home, at least temporarily while the Internet developed. Therefore, given the great uncertainty regarding the future growth of the Internet, innovators were exempted from the obligation of policing Internet activities.[12]

Today, market conditions have profoundly changed. The Internet is established and has grown beyond any expectation, becoming the most pervasive medium in people's daily life. Rather than providing incentives to develop Internet infrastructure and applications, policy-makers, governmental institutions and law

[10] See Communications Decency Act of 1996, 47 USC § 230; The Digital Millennium Copyright Act of 1998, 17 USC § 512 (DMCA).

[11] See eg Directive 2000/31/EC of the European Parliament and of the Council of 8 June 2000 on certain legal aspects of information society services, in particular electronic commerce, in the Internal Market, 2000 OJ (L 178) 1–16 ('eCommerce Directive' or ECD).

[12] Hence, the no general monitoring obligations principle enacted by most jurisdictions.

enforcement agencies are increasingly concerned with content moderation due to the relentless capacity of the Internet to disseminate content that might infringe people's rights – and create social unrest at an unprecedented speed. At the same time, on the one hand, regulators face the conundrum of the enormous costs of online content moderation that have grown exponentially with the growth of the Internet. On the other hand, only large high-tech companies own the infrastructure and technology that can manage the massive content moderation volumes of the digital society. Thus, a sound policy solution might be to switch the enormous transaction costs of online content regulation to online intermediaries as they might serve as Calabresi-Coase's 'least-cost avoiders',[13] in particular given their economies of scale. Meanwhile, market geopolitics of the platform economy also play a role in this process, which is tightly linked to changes in incentives that might guide state intervention. For this very reason, this policy trend that turns innovators into responsible moderators has been emerging markedly in Europe as Europe has a limited control over Internet resources, thus has fewer concerns in switching transaction costs of enforcement on online intermediaries, mostly US conglomerates.

IV. Policy: From Intermediary Liability to Responsibility

Traditionally, platform liability regulation has struggled to find a proper balance between competing rights that might be affected by online intermediaries activities and obligations. Early regulatory approaches established limited liability frameworks including exemptions for online intermediaries, which in turn provided strong safeguards for users' fundamental rights. Following in the footsteps of initial legislation enacted in the United States,[14] the European Union introduced obligations on Member States to protect information service providers from liability,[15] as well as the possibility of seeking injunctions against them to prevent infringements.[16] Similar legal arrangements have, since then, been set up by several international jurisdictions.[17]

[13] See G Calabresi, 'Some Thoughts on Risk Distribution and the Law of Torts' (1961) 70 *Yale Law Journal* 499; R Coase, 'The Problem of Social Cost' (1960) 3 *Journal of Law and Economics* 1.

[14] See n 10.

[15] See ECD (n 11).

[16] See ECD (n 11) Arts 12–15; Directive 2001/29/EC of the European Parliament and of the Council of 22 May 2001 on the Harmonisation of Certain Aspects of Copyright and Related Rights in the Information Society, 2001 OJ (L 167) 10–19 ('InfoSoc Directive') Art 8(3); Directive 2004/48/EC of the European Parliament and of the Council of 29 April 2000 on the Enforcement of Intellectual Property Rights, 2004 OJ (L 195) 16 ('Enforcement Directive') Art 11.

[17] See for a review of safe harbour legislations, World Intermediary Liability Map (WILMap) (a project designed and developed by Giancarlo Frosio and hosted at Stanford CIS), available at wilmap.law.stanford.edu.

In recent times, however, the ethical implications of online service providers' (OSPs) role in contemporary information societies are raising unprecedented social challenges, as proven by examples like the PRISM scandal, the debate on the 'right to be forgotten', or the banning of former US President Trump from social media. Hence, academia, policy-makers and society increasingly ascribe a public role to online intermediaries. According to Shapiro, 'in democratic societies, those who control the access to information have a responsibility to support the public interest. … these gatekeepers must assume an obligation as trustees of the greater good'.[18]

As a result, policy discourse is increasingly shifting from liability to enhanced 'responsibilities' for intermediaries under the assumption that OSPs' role is unprecedented for their capacity to influence the informational environment and users' interactions within it.[19] This is happening via a number of policy developments, including private ordering and voluntary measures, which come as a consequence of an emergent emphasis on corporate social responsibility. At the same time, these developments also depend upon newly enhanced cooperation between states and private parties in online enforcement that often trespasses into public deal-making and jawboning.

As noted, however, private enforcement 'downgrades the law to a second-class status, behind the "leading role" of private companies that are being asked to arbitrarily implement their terms of service'.[20] Voluntary measures make intermediaries prone to serve governmental purposes under murky, privately enforced standards, rather than transparent legal obligations. This process might be pushing an amorphous notion of responsibility that incentivises intermediaries' self-intervention to police allegedly infringing activities on the Internet.

A. Corporate Social Responsibility

A move from intermediary liability to platform responsibility has been occurring first with special focus on intermediaries' corporate social responsibility (CSR) and their role in implementing and fostering human rights. The discourse has increasingly focused on the moral responsibilities of OSPs in contemporary societies and aims at building ethical frameworks for the understanding of OSPs' responsibilities. Thus, responsible behaviour beyond the law finds justification in

[18] A Shapiro, *The Control Revolution: How the Internet is Putting Individuals in Charge and Changing the World We Know* (Public Affairs, 2000) 225.

[19] See eg European Commission, 'Tackling Illegal Content Online. Towards an enhanced responsibility of online platforms' COM(2017) 555 final, 28 September 2017, § 6 (noting 'the constantly rising influence of online platforms in society, which flows from their role as gatekeepers to content and information, increases their responsibilities towards their users and society at large').

[20] 'EDRi and Access Now withdraw from the EU Commission IT Forum discussions' (EDRi, 16 May 2016), available at edri.org/edri-access-now-withdraw-eu-commission-forum-discussions.

intermediaries' corporate social responsibilities and their role in implementing and fostering human rights.[21]

According to Taddeo and Floridi, given their prominent role, online intermediaries are increasingly expected to act according to current social and cultural values, which gives rise to 'questions as to what kind of responsibilities OSPs should bear, and which ethical principles should guide their actions'.[22] In search of a model to define OSP responsibilities, Taddeo and Floridi distinguish them on the basis of the different kinds of information that they control.[23] They identify three important set of ethical problems: the organisation and managing of access to information; censorship and freedom of speech; and users' privacy.[24] Whether OSPs bear any moral responsibilities for circulating on their infrastructures third-party generated content that may prove harmful, rather than whether OSPs should be held morally responsible for their users' actions, remain the major issue at stake.[25] Some commentators have argued that it may be desirable to ascribe moral responsibilities to OSPs with respect to the circulation of harmful material,[26] although the focus might be on their responsibility towards the reasoning processes in reaching decisions, rather than on their outcomes.[27] Finally, copious literature argued that OSPs might have moral responsibility with respects to users' privacy, while being responsible for a devaluation of privacy.[28]

With the emergence of the CSR, arguments have been made that obligations pertaining to states, such as those endorsed by the UN Human Rights Council declaration of Internet freedom as a human right,[29] should be extended to online platforms as well.[30] In particular, the preamble of the Universal Declaration of Human Rights appears to support corporate obligations to protect human rights where it states that 'every individual and every organ of society' should strive to promote these rights.[31] Other international instruments to that effect have been

[21] See E Laidlaw, Regulating Speech in Cyberspace: Gatekeepers, Human Rights and Corporate Responsibility (Cambridge University Press, 2015); D Broeders et al, 'Does Great Power Come with Great Responsibility? The Need to Talk About Corporate Responsibility' in M Taddeo and L Floridi, *The Responsibilities of Online Service Providers* (Springer, 2017) 315–23.

[22] M Taddeo and L Floridi, 'New Civic Responsibilities for Online Service Providers' in M Taddeo and L Floridi, The Responsibilities of Online Service Providers (Springer, 2017) 1.

[23] M Taddeo and L Floridi, 'The Debate on the Moral Responsibility of Online Service Providers' (2015) 22 *Science and Engineering Ethics* 1575.

[24] ibid 1580.

[25] ibid 1584–85.

[26] See eg H Tavani and F Grodzinsky, 'Cyberstalking, Personal Privacy, and Moral Responsibility' (2002) 4 *Ethics and Information Technology* 123.

[27] See M Thompson, 'Beyond Gatekeeping: The Normative Responsibility of Internet Intermediaries' (2016) 18 Vanderbilt Journal of Entertainment and Technology Law 783, 783–84.

[28] See Taddeo and Floridi, 'Moral Responsibility' (2015) 16–18.

[29] See Human Rights Council of the United Nations, Resolution on the Promotion, Protection and Enjoyment of Human Rights on the Internet (2012).

[30] See eg F Wettstein, 'Silence as Complicity: Elements of a Corporate Duty to Speak out Against the Violation of Human Rights' (2012) 22 *Business Ethics Quarterly* 37; Stephen Chen, 'Corporate Responsibilities in Internet-Enabled Social Networks' (2009) 90(4) Journal of Business Ethics 523.

[31] See Universal Declaration of Human Rights, GA Res 217A (III), UN Doc A/810 at 71 (1948), Preamble.

identified in the Declaration of Human Duties and Responsibilities,[32] the preamble of the UN Norms on the Responsibilities of Transnational Corporations and Other Business Enterprises,[33] and the UN Guiding Principles on Business and Human Rights.[34] Recently, the United Nations Human Rights Council adopted a resolution on the promotion, protection and enjoyment of human rights on the Internet, which also addressed a legally binding instrument on corporations' responsibility to ensure human rights.[35]

One downside of the CSR approach is that, while trying to create an environment in which companies will act in a responsible way, the expectations are often vague and thus hard to measure or evaluate.[36] To mitigate these limitations, some projects developed best practices that might be implemented by intermediaries in their terms of service, with special emphasis on protecting fundamental rights.[37] For example, under the aegis of the Internet Governance Forum, the Dynamic Coalition for Platform Responsibility aims to delineate a set of model contractual-provisions.[38] This provisions should be compliant with the UN 'Protect, Respect and Remedy' Framework as endorsed by the UN Human Rights Council, together with the UN Guiding Principles on Business and Human Rights.[39] Appropriate digital labels should signal the inclusion of these model contractual provisions in the Terms of Service of selected platform providers to 'help Internet users to easily identify the platform-providers who are committed to securing the respect of human rights in a responsible manner'.[40] Again, the Global Network Initiative (GNI) put together a multistakeholder group of companies, civil society organisations, investors and academics to create a global framework to protect and advance freedom of expression and privacy in information and communications technologies. The GNI's participants – such as Facebook, Google, LinkedIn, Microsoft and Yahoo! – committed to a set of core documents, including the GNI Principles, Implementations Guidelines and Accountability, Policy & Learning Framework.[41] Similarly, Ranking Digital Rights is an initiative that ranks Internet

[32] See UNESCO Declaration of Human Duties and Responsibilities (Valencia Declaration) (1998).

[33] See UN Norms on the Responsibilities of Transnational Corporations and Other Business Enterprises (13 August 2003).

[34] See United Nations, Human Rights, Office of the High Commissioner, Guiding Principles on Business Human Rights: Implementing the United Nations 'Protect, Respect, and Remedy' Framework (2011) ('UN GPBHRs').

[35] See United Nations Human Rights Council, The Promotion, Protection and Enjoyment of Human Rights on the Internet, A/HRC/RES/26/13 (20 June 2014).

[36] See ch 11 (Elkin-Koren) of this volume.

[37] See eg J Venturini et al, Terms of Service and Human Rights: Analysing Contracts of Online Platforms (CoE, FGV Direito Rio, Editora Revan, 2016).

[38] See Dynamic Coalition on Platform Responsibility: a Structural Element of the United Nations Internet Governance Forum, available at platformresponsibility.info.

[39] See UN GPBHRs (n 34).

[40] See Dynamic Coalition on Platform Responsibility (n 38).

[41] See Global Network Initiatives, Principles, available at globalnetworkinitiative.org/principles/index.php.

and telecommunications companies according to their virtuous behaviour in respecting users' rights, including privacy and freedom of speech.[42]

B. State-Driven Cooperation in Online Enforcement

In light of the widespread acceptance of CSR, states have been pushing new forms of cooperation with private parties, such as online intermediaries, to alleviate the burden on the public of online sanitisation of allegedly infringing – or merely dangerous – content without deploying prescriptive norms and mandatory obligations. For quite some time, the European Commission's regulatory efforts have been emphasising voluntary and proactive measures to remove certain categories of illegal content and allow intermediaries to fulfil enhanced duties of care reasonably expected from them,[43] with special emphasis on enforcement of intellectual property rights (IPR) infringement.[44] For states, coercing intermediaries into 'voluntary' measures has doubtless advantages by allowing to circumvent the EU Charter on restrictions to fundamental rights, avoiding the threat of legal challenges, and taking a quicker reform route. In the EU, the 'Communication on Online Platforms and the Digital Single Market' puts forward the idea that 'the responsibility of online platforms is a key and cross-cutting issue'.[45] Again, in 'Tackling Illegal Content Online', the Commission made this goal even clearer by openly pursuing 'enhanced responsibility of online platforms' on a voluntary basis and noting that 'the constantly rising influence of online platforms in society, which flows from their role as gatekeepers to content and information, increases their responsibilities towards their users and society at large'.[46] This terminology plainly evokes the mentioned move from intermediary liability to intermediary responsibility in platform governance.

Under this framework of enhanced responsibilities, online intermediaries and platforms would be invested by a duty to ensure a safe online environment for users,[47] hostile to criminal and other illegal exploitation, which should be deterred and prevented by: (1) allowing prompt removal of illegal content; (2) adopting effective *proactive* measures to detect and remove illegal content online,[48] rather

[42] See Ranking Digital Rights, available at rankingdigitalrights.org. See also R MacKinnon, *Consent of the Networked: The Worldwide Struggle for Internet Freedom* (Basic Books, 2012).

[43] See eg European Commission, Public consultation on the regulatory environment for platforms, online intermediaries, data and cloud computing and the collaborative economy (24 September 2015) 21–23.

[44] See European Commission, Public Consultation on the Evaluation and Modernisation of the Legal Framework for the Enforcement of Intellectual Property Rights (9 December 2015) D.1.

[45] European Commission, 'Online Platforms and the Digital Single Market: Opportunities and Challenges for Europe' (Communication) COM(2016) 288 Final, 9.

[46] See European Commission (n 19) s 6.

[47] ibid s 3.

[48] European Commission (n 19) s 3.3.1.

than limiting themselves to reacting to notices; and (3) encouraging the use of automated monitoring and filtering technology.[49] In particular, 'online platforms must be encouraged to take more effective voluntary action to curtail exposure to illegal or harmful content, such as incitement to terrorism, child sexual abuse and hate speech'.[50] This should occur, in particular, by setting up a privileged channel with 'trusted flaggers', competent authorities and specialised private entities with specific expertise in identifying illegal content,[51] regardless of 'being required to do so on the basis of a court order or administrative decision, especially where a law enforcement authority identifies and informs them of allegedly illegal content'.[52] In sum, online platforms should be able to prevent and contrast online illegal activities by allowing rapid content take-down, setting up proactive intervention, deploying automated filtering technologies, and adopting effective notice and actions mechanisms, which might not necessarily require users to identify themselves when reporting content that they consider illegal.[53]

The 2019 UK Government's 'Online Harms' White Paper reinforces this approach of adding responsible duties beyond those provided in the liability framework by proposing a new duty of care towards users, holding companies to account for tackling a comprehensive set of online harms, ranging from illegal activity and content to behaviours which are harmful but not necessarily illegal.[54] The goal of the proposal is to set out 'high-level expectations of companies, including some specific expectations in relation to certain harms'.[55] The violation of the duty of care would be assessed separately from liability for particular items of harmful content. This 'systemic form of liability' essentially superimposes a novel duty to cooperate on the providers and turns it into a separate form of responsibility, which is enforceable by public authorities by means of fines.[56] At the same time, it leaves the underlying responsibility for individual instances of problematic content intact.

C. Public Deal-Making and Jawboning

Sometimes state-driven cooperation in online enforcement is more subtle and resembles closely what has been termed a public-private 'invisible handshake'.[57]

[49] ibid s 3.3.2. See also Recommendation from the Commission on Measures to Effectively Tackle Illegal Content Online, C(2018)1177final, 1 March 2018, para 37.

[50] European Commission (n 45) 9.

[51] European Commission (n 19) § 3.2.1.

[52] ibid § 3.1.

[53] ibid § 3.2.3.

[54] See Department for Digital, Culture, Media & Sport and Home Department, 'Online Harm' (White Paper, Cp 59, 2019).

[55] ibid 67.

[56] ibid 59.

[57] M Birnhack and N Elkin-Koren, 'The Invisible Handshake: The Reemergence of the State in the Digital Environment' (2003) 8 *Virginia Journal of Law and Technology* 6.

This is the case when enhanced voluntary enforcement measures adopted by online intermediaries is the result of public deal-making. According to Rebecca Tushnet, in the US at least, online intermediaries enjoy 'power without responsibility',[58] given that, as a result of liability exemptions, online intermediaries effectively have power to decide about the content which users post but do not have a responsibility towards their users to respect their speech rights in some particular form. This responsibility gap,[59] then, invites the Government to pressure for removal of information without following a proper process. In *Against Jawboning*, Bambauer cites Representative James Sensenbrenner, pressing the US Internet Service Provider Association to adopt putatively voluntary data retention scheme in the following terms: 'if you aren't a good rabbit and don't start eating the carrot, I'm afraid we're all going to be throwing the stick at you'.[60] So, public deal-making finds its economic justification in the interest of platforms to avoid new forms of regulation. Cost and uncertainty in resisting pressures serve as a strong incentive for online intermediaries to play along.

D. Market-Driven Private Ordering and Voluntary Measures

Finally, online platforms' increased responsibilities might result from market-driven private ordering and voluntary measures, either implemented in the intermediary's self-interest or because of rational business decisions based on dealings with the right-holders. As per the first category, a number of factors might lead online intermediaries to expand their own responsibility.[61] First, it might be the need of improving users' experience as users might be misled or defrauded by illegal content, such as in the case of abusive or spam content.[62] Second, online platforms might want to enhance their credibility and reputation, which helps attract advertising or other investments, as in the case of Yelp, which incorporated a right-to-reply into its review service after public pressure from the business community.[63]

On the other hand, increased platform responsibility might result from market dynamics, when right-holders cut deals with platforms, or leverage their existing business relationships. For example, voluntary enforcement schemes were usually initiated when intermediaries such as Internet access providers tried to vertically

[58] R Tushnet, 'Power Without Responsibility: Intermediaries and the First Amendment' (2008) 76 *George Washington Law Review* 986, 986.

[59] ibid.

[60] See also D Bambauer, 'Against Jawboning' (2015) 100 *Minnesota Law Review* 51, 51–52.

[61] See M Husovec, *Injunctions Against Intermediaries in the European Union: Accountable But Not Liable?* (Cambridge University Press, 2017) 13.

[62] For an overview of industry practices and their corresponding business reasons, see E Goodman, 'Online Comment Moderation: Emerging Best Practices' (WAN-IFRA, 2013), available at www.wan-ifra.org/reports/2013/10/04/online-comment-moderation-emerging-best-practices.

[63] See C Miller, 'Yelp Will Let Businesses Respond to Web Reviews' *New York Times* (10 April 2009).

integrate into markets where they had to do business with major right-holders and license their content.[64] In exchange, the right-holders might ask to implement some sort of enforcement strategy.

Later, this chapter will review several of these private ordering enforcement measures in practice, such as private DNS content regulation, website blocking, online search manipulation and proactive filtering, graduate response, and payment blockades. Of course, such private solutions are agreed upon secretly by the parties involved. Implementation terms are customarily confidential. Therefore, they are not subject to any public scrutiny, even though such measures might limit the fundamental rights of users affected, causing obvious tensions with due process.

E. Countering Private Ordering Fragmentation via Constitutionalisation of Internet Governance

However, there are counter-posing forces at work in the present Internet governance struggle. A centripetal move towards digital constitutionalism for Internet governance alleviates the effects of the centrifugal platform responsibility discourse. Efforts to draft an Internet Bill of Rights can be traced at least as far back as the mid-1990s.[65] Two full decades later, aspirational principles have begun to crystallise into law. Gill, Redeker and Gasser have described more than 30 initiatives spanning from 1999 to 2015 that can be labelled under the umbrella of 'digital constitutionalism'.[66] These initiatives show great differences – and range from advocacy statements to official positions of intergovernmental organisations to proposed legislation – but belong to a broader proto-constitutional discourse seeking to advance a relatively comprehensive set of rights, principles and governance norms for the Internet.[67]

Recently, the European Parliament may have strengthened this process of constitutionalisation of Internet governance, de facto tuning down previous approaches that might have instead emphasised private ordering solutions. The proposed Digital Services Act (DSA) apparently seeks a more balanced approach in digital policies where all competing fundamental rights and interests of stakeholders involved receive equal safeguards. Starting with the resolution on the 'Digital Services Act and fundamental rights issued posed',[68] the DSA Proposal

[64] See Frosio and Husovec (n 1) 625–26.

[65] See L Gill, D Redeker and U Gasser, 'Towards Digital Constitutionalism? Mapping Attempts to Craft an Internet Bill of Rights' (Berkman Center Research Publication No 2015-15, 9 November 2015).

[66] ibid 1; see also O Pollicino and G Romeo (eds), *The Internet and Constitutional Law* (Routledge, 2016); E Celeste, 'Digital Constitutionalism: A New Systematic Theorisation' (2019) 33 *International Review of Law, Computers & Technology* 76.

[67] See Gill, Redeker and Gasser, 'Towards Digital Constitutionalism?' (2015) 1.

[68] European Parliament, 'Resolution on the Digital Services Act and fundamental rights issues posed' [2020/2022(INI)] 20 October 2020, Provisional edition, P9_TA-PROV(2020)0274, available at www.europarl.europa.eu/doceo/document/TA-9-2020-0274_EN.html ('EP Resolution on the DSA and FRs').

highlights from the inception the central role of fundamental rights in online regulation, and for the DSA in particular.[69] In addition, the DSA Proposal would like to created EU-wide coordinated mechanisms to oversee compliance by online intermediaries with the DSA regulation, with special emphasis on standards for content management and algorithmic technologies deployed to that end.[70] In this sense, the DSA Proposal would move in the direction of a substantive and procedural 'constitutionalisation' of Internet governance in the EU by structuring, standardising and homogenising content moderation processes that have been recently promoted under a private ordering approach.

V. Technology: From Human to Algorithmic Enforcement

Algorithmic enforcement is a further effect of recent regulatory trends imposing enhanced responsibility on online intermediaries and platforms.[71] The described emerging regulatory move from intermediary liability to responsibility – together with new legislative obligations and judicial trends – would like to force online intermediaries to implement Internet architectural changes leading to sanitisation of allegedly infringing content – possibly legit freedom of expression – by design. As Lessig and others have explained, the code is the law of cyberspace.[72] Therefore, enforcement can become implicit by modifying the architecture of the Internet.[73] Given the unsustainable transaction costs related to manual checking of infringing content and linking to infringing content,[74] online intermediaries will be forced to change the Internet architecture and deploy algorithmic tools to perform monitoring and filtering, and limit their liability.[75]

There is a number of negative externalities that algorithmic enforcement might bring about. First, it leads to privatisation of enforcement and delegation of public

[69] See also, on the increasing influence of human and fundamental rights on the resolution of intellectual property (IP) disputes, C Geiger, 'Constitutionalising Intellectual Property Law?, The Influence of Fundamental Rights on Intellectual Property in Europe' (2006) 37 *International Review of Intellectual Property and Competition Law* 371; and C Geiger, 'Reconceptualizing the Constitutional Dimension of Intellectual Property – An Update' in P Torremans (ed), *Intellectual Property and Human Rights*, 4th edn (Kluwer Law International, 2020) 117.

[70] See DSA Proposal (n 3) Arts 38–48.

[71] See, in general, G Frosio, 'Algorithmic Enforcement Online' in P Torremans (ed), *Intellectual Property Law and Human Rights* (Wolters Kluwer, 2020) 709–44.

[72] See L Lessig, *The Code and Other Laws of Cyberspace* (Basic Books, 1999) 3–60.

[73] See J Reidenberg, 'Lex Informatica: The Formulation of Information Policy Rules Through Technology' (1998) 76 *Texas Law Review* 553.

[74] See G Frosio, 'It's All Linked: How Communication to the Public Affects Internet Architecture' (2020) 37 *Computer Law & Security Review* 1.

[75] See, for a discussion of this very issue in connection to the enactment of Art 17 of Directive 2019/790/EU, G Frosio, 'Reforming the C-DSM Reform: a User-Based Copyright Theory for Commonplace Creativity' (2020) 52 *International Review of Intellectual Property and Competition Law* 709.

authority. Automated and algorithmic content moderation implies a number of policy choices, which are operated by platforms and rightsholders and subject freedom of expression and online cultural participation to a new layer of 'private ordering'.[76] In practice, in the case of copyright enforcement, for example, automated filtering determines online behaviour far more 'than whether that conduct is, or is not, substantively in compliance with copyright law'.[77] A legal system switching the liability equilibrium on online intermediaries – which can more than any other manipulate Internet architecture – can actually lead to fundamental architectonical changes to limit that liability. As Calabresi-Coase's 'least-cost avoiders',[78] OSPs will inherently try to lower transaction costs of adjudication and liability and, in order to do so, might functionally err on the side of overblocking. This process is likely to bring about pervasive over-enforcement, which becomes invisible and leads users to get accustomed to a highly censored online ecosystem.[79]

Also, online intermediaries' regulatory choices – occurring through algorithmic tools – can affect profoundly enjoyment of users' fundamental rights, such as due process, freedom of expression, freedom of information, and right to privacy and data protection.[80] In this context, tensions have been highlighted between algorithmic enforcement and the European Convention of Human Rights (ECHR) and the Charter of Fundamental Rights of the European Union (EU Charter).[81] In particular, as the CJEU made clear in *Scarlet* and *Netlog*, automated filtering tools cannot properly balance intellectual property rights and other competing fundamental rights, such as freedom of expression, freedom of business and privacy.[82] In particular, present algorithmic filtering tools impinge upon freedom of expression as they might be unable to identify uses made by applying exceptions and limitations, or might not discern the public domain status of works.[83] Again, algorithmic

[76] See M Sag, 'Internet Safe Harbors and the Transformation of Copyright Law' (2017) 93 *Notre Dame Law Review* 1.

[77] ibid.

[78] See G Calabresi, 'Some Thoughts on Risk Distribution and the Law of Torts' (1961) 70 *Yale Law Journal* 499; R Coase, 'The Problem of Social Cost' (1960) 3 *Journal of Law & Economics*. 1.

[79] But see Elkin-Koren and Husovec arguing that technologies might be the only way to address concerns of over-blocking on scale and with necessary speed: N Elkin-Koren, 'Fair Use by Design' (2017) 64 *UCLA Law Review* 22; M Husovec, 'The Promises of Algorithmic Copyright Enforcement: Takedown or Staydown? Which is Superior? And Why?' (2019) 42 *Columbia Journal of Law & the Arts* 53.

[80] See, for detailed overview of fundamental rights and content moderation, G Frosio and C Geiger, 'Taking Fundamental Rights Seriously in the Digital Services Act's Platform Liability Regime' (study commissioned by Copyright for Creativity (C4C), 2020), available at ssrn.com/abstract_id=3747756.

[81] See Convention for the Protection of Human Rights and Fundamental Freedoms (European Convention on Human Rights, as amended) [1950] (ECHR); Charter of Fundamental Rights of the European Union 2012 OJ (C 326) 391 ('EU Charter'). See also eg *Akdeniz v Turkey*, App no 20877/10, 11 March 2014.

[82] See eg C-360/10 *Belgische Vereniging van Auteurs, Componisten en Uitgevers CVBA (SABAM) v Netlog NV* [2012] ECLI:EU:C:2012:85 [51]; Case C-70/10 Scarlet Extended SA v Société belge des auteurs, compositeurs et éditeurs SCRL (SABAM) [2011] ECLI:EU:C:2011:771 [53]. See also C-314/12, *UPC Telekabel Wien* [2014] EU:C:2014:192 ('*UPC Telekabel*').

[83] *Netlog* (ibid) [50].

enforcement appears to be inherently unsuitable to apply 'fair use' doctrines, which require an equity – thus inherently human – judgement.[84]

Finally, in online content sanitisation, algorithms take decisions reflecting policy assumptions and interests that have very significant consequences to society at large, yet there is limited understanding of these processes. Socially relevant choices online increasingly occur through automated private enforcement run by opaque algorithms, which creates a so-called 'black-box' society.[85] Algorithmic enforcement finds its primary Achilles' heel in algorithms' transparency and accountability, which continues to challenge democratic semiotic regulation online.[86]

VI. Practice: Private Enforcement in Action

In practice, miscellaneous forms of 'responsible' behaviours beyond the law have recently emerged via multiple enforcement tools applied by different categories of online service providers.[87] They reflect a globalised, ongoing move towards privatisation of law enforcement online through proactive actions and algorithmic tools that spans all subject matters relevant to intermediary liability online. Their common denominator is that that they go beyond the baseline legal expectations created by the legal liability framework. Inherently, their common trajectory is towards more proactive tackling of illegal or otherwise objectionable content. They are usually applied via codes of conducts and standardisation, while targeting a vast array of online intermediaries, such as: (1) DNS providers in the case of private DNS content regulation; (2) access providers for website blocking and graduate response; (3) search engines, in the case of online search manipulation; (4) hosting providers, deploying proactive monitoring and filtering strategies; and (5) online advertisement and payment providers, in the case of payment blockades and follow-the-money strategies.

Voluntary measures and private ordering schemes are often rationalised via state-driven Code of Conducts (CoCs) and standardisation processes. These have

[84] See D Burk and J Cohen, 'Fair Use Infrastructure for Copyright Management Systems' (2000) Georgetown Public Law Research Paper 239731/2000, available at ssrn.com/abstract=239731. See also AP Heldt, 'Upload-Filters: Bypassing Classical Concepts of Censorship?' (2019) 10 *Journal of Intellectual Property, Information Technology and E-Commerce Law*, available at www.jipitec.eu/issues/jipitec-10-1-2019/4877.

[85] F Pasquale, *The Black Box Society: The Secret Algorithms That Control Money and Information* (Harvard University Press, 2015).

[86] See, for some proposals promoting algorithmic transparency and accountability, Frosio, 'Reforming the C-DSM Reform' (2020) 740–43.

[87] In fact, these enforcement strategies are actually deployed through a larger spectrum of policy options that spans from legally mandated obligations to private ordering. Even the same type of enforcement arrangements can be the result of a private ordering scheme, ad hoc governmental policy administered by agencies, or the application of legislatively mandated obligations.

been emerging quite consistently in the EU, for example. The proposed DSA might take this standardisation further by legislatively mandating standards for content moderation, such as notice-and-action mechanisms, trusted flaggers schemes and CoCs.[88]

For quite some time, CoCs have been singled out as a useful tool for promoting content sanitisation online. The ECD already provided that Member States and the Commission must encourage the 'drawing up of codes of conduct at Community level by trade, professional and consumer associations or organisations designed to contribute to the proper implementation of articles 5 to 15'.[89] The wider deployment of CoCs has increasingly become an EU-brokered self-regulatory mechanism. Historically, the first was the Memorandum of Understanding in the area of trademark infringements.[90] Recently, the European Commission adopted CoCs against hate speech and against disinformation.[91] In particular, the European Commission has coordinated an EU-wide self-regulatory efforts by which online platforms should be directed to fight hate speech, incitement to terrorism and prevent cyber-bullying.[92] As an immediate result of this new policy trend, the Commission agreed with all major online hosting providers – including Facebook, Twitter, YouTube, Microsoft, Instagram, Snapchat and Dailymotion – on a CoC that endorses a series of commitments to combat the spread of illegal hate speech online in Europe.[93] The code spells out commitments such as faster notice and takedown for illegal hate speech that will be removed within 24 hours or special channels for government and NGOs' notice to remove illegal content.[94] In partial response to this increased pressure from the EU regarding the role of intermediaries in the fight against online terrorism, Facebook, Microsoft, Twitter and YouTube announced that they will begin sharing hashes (unique digital fingerprints) of apparent terrorist propaganda.[95]

The European Commission has been also trying to standardise procedures via soft law, with particular regard to notification mechanisms and technologies used to implement enforcement actions, by creating a set of expectations that should be followed by the intermediaries. On the one hand, the Communication

[88] See DSA Proposal (n 3) Arts 14–24.

[89] eCommerce Directive (n 11) Art 16.

[90] See European Commission, 'Memorandum of Understanding on online advertising and IPR' (May 2011), available at ec.europa.eu/growth/industry/intellectual-property/enforcement/memorandum-of-understanding-online-advertising-ipr_en.

[91] See European Commission, 'Code of Practice on Disinformation' (28 September 2018), available at ec.europa.eu/digital-single-market/en/news/code-practice-disinformation.

[92] See European Commission (n 45).

[93] See European Commission, 'European Commission and IT Companies Announce Code of Conduct on Illegal Online Hate Speech', Press Release (31 May 2016), available at europa.eu/rapid/press-release_IP-16-1937_en.htm.

[94] ibid.

[95] See 'Google in Europe, Partnering to Help Curb the Spread of Terrorist Content Online' (Google Blog, 5 December 2016), available at blog.google/topics/google-europe/partnering-help-curb-spread-terrorist-content-online.

'Tackling Illegal Content Online' endorses the view that 'in order to ensure a high quality of notices and faster removal of illegal content, *criteria* based notably on respect for fundamental rights and of democratic values could be agreed by the industry at EU level' through self-regulatory mechanisms.[96] On the other hand, the Communication mentions that this can be also done 'within the EU standardisation framework, under which a particular entity can be considered a trusted flagger'.[97] Sufficient flexibility to take account of content-specific characteristics and the role of the trusted flagger should be obtained via a number of additional criteria, including 'internal training standards, process standards and quality assurance, as well as legal safeguards as regards independence, conflicts of interest, protection of privacy and personal data, as a non-exhaustive list'.[98] In particular, especially in the domain of terrorist propaganda, extremism and hate speech, as mentioned, the European Commission 'encourages that the notices from trusted flaggers should be able to be fast-tracked by the platform', and user-friendly anonymous notification systems.[99] Actually, provisions legislatively mandating trusted flaggers schemes in online content moderation are now included in the DSA Proposal.[100]

A. DNS Providers: Private DNS Content Regulation

Domain Name System (DNS) providers have been enlisted in the fight against online piracy, so that enforcement would occur at the Internet backbone through the administration of the DNS.[101] This enforcement strategy mainly targets infringing behaviour known as domain-hopping that evades law enforcement by moving from one country code top-level domains(ccTLD) or generic top-level domain (gTLD) registrar to another, thus driving up time and resources spent on protecting IP rights or other rights. In this context, responsible behaviour would rely on stewards of the Internet's infrastructure and governance, such as ICANN, via a so-called 'trusted notifier' copyright enforcement programme, which resembles closely the 'trusted flaggers' approach endorsed by the European commission. In fact, ICANN contractual architecture for the new gTLDs embeds support for private, DNS-based content regulation on behalf of copyright holders – and, potentially, other 'trusted' parties – imposing on registry operators and registrars an express prohibition on IP infringement and obligations including suspension

[96] See European Commission (n 19) s 3.2.1.
[97] ibid.
[98] ibid.
[99] ibid s 3.2.1. and 3.2.3.
[100] See DSA Proposal (n 3) Art 19.
[101] See eg A Bridy, 'Addressing Infringement: Developments in Content Regulation in the US and the DNS' in Frosio (n 1) 631–46; S Schwemer, 'The regulation of abusive activity and content: a study of registries' terms of service' (2020) 9 *Internet Policy Review*, available at doi.org/10.14763/2020.1.1448.

of the domain name.[102] Through this contractual framework, ICANN facilitated voluntary enforcement agreements between DNS intermediaries and rightholders, such as the DNA's Healthy Domains Initiative.[103] The registry operators agrees, if 'the domain clearly is devoted to abusive behaviour … in its discretion [to] suspend, terminate, or place the domain on registry lock, hold, or similar status' within 10 business days form the complaint.[104] However, this voluntary enforcement scheme apparently lacks due process safeguards. As Bridy explains, 'in creating that architecture, ICANN did nothing to secure any procedural protections or uniform substantive standards for domain name registrants who find themselves subject to this new form of DNS regulation'.[105]

B. Access Providers

Access providers are also involved with content sanitisation and online enforcement on a voluntary basis. In particular, they might implement website blocking and graduate response schemes.

i. Website Blocking

Website blocking measures have been widely used in the field of intellectual property enforcement. These injunctions led to considerable case law in some of the Member States, with courts defining conditions, legal and technical modalities under which such orders should be available on the national level in the EU.[106] These measures were then sometimes adopted in the national law by means of administrative regulations which entrusted authorities with special powers to block websites under specific conditions.[107] However, a number of access providers also engaged in voluntary website blocking schemes.

'Soft law' arrangements have been established in several European jurisdictions. Perhaps the most prominent of these was the anti-child abuse programme

[102] See ICANN-Registry Agreement (2013) s 2.17 Specification 11; ICANN Registrar Accreditation Agreement (2013) s 3.18.

[103] See Meeting Transcript, 'MARRAKECH – Industry Best Practices – the DNA's Healthy Domains Initiative' 13, available at meetings.icann.org/en/marrakech55/schedule/wed-dna-healthy-domains-initiative/transcript-dna-healthy-domains-initiative-09mar16-en.pdf.

[104] See Donuts.Domains, 'Characteristics of a Trusted Notifier Program', available at www.donuts.domains/images/pdfs/Trusted-Notifier-Summary.pdf.

[105] A Bridy, 'Notice and Takedown in the Domain Name System: ICANN's Ambivalent Drift into Online Content Regulation' (2017) 74 *Washington and Lee Law Review* 1345, 1386.

[106] See, for a broad overview, G Frosio and O Bulayenko, 'Study on Dynamic Blocking Injunctions, commissioned by the European Intellectual Property Office' (EUIPO, 2021).

[107] See eg A Cogo and M Ricolfi, 'Administrative Enforcement of Copyright Infringement in Europe' in G Frosio (ed), *The Oxford Handbook of Online Intermediary Liability* (Oxford University Press, 2020) 586–602.

operated by the Internet Watch Foundation (IWF),[108] which, in 2002, started distributing its URL list for the purposes of implementing blocking or filtering solutions.[109] In Denmark and the UK, self-regulatory measures were established between stakeholders. In Denmark, the most notable arrangement is the Code of Conduct for handling decisions on blocking access to services infringing intellectual property rights, entered into between the telecommunications industry (TI) and the Rights Alliance.[110] There is a voluntary CoC in place between the major search engines that operate in the UK, including Google, Bing and Yahoo!, and other relevant stakeholders for demoting copyright-infringing websites. In Belgium, a general CoC adhered to by members of the Internet Service Providers Association (ISPA) Belgium sets up a central contact point within the judicial police to receive complaints about illegal activity on the Internet, including copyright infringement.[111] Meanwhile, German Internet access providers and rights holders have set up an independent Internet Copyright Clearing House under a jointly agreed CoC that provides that the access to so-called 'structurally copyright-infringing websites' can now be blocked out of court upon recommendation of the clearing house if the Federal Network Agency has no concerns under the EU Net Neutrality Regulation.[112] In Finland, there is a voluntary mechanism to block foreign websites, but its scope is limited to child pornography. The Finnish police maintains a record of foreign child pornography websites, which ISPs may use to prevent access to these websites.[113] A specific regulatory framework for the development of CoCs exists in Italy, which provides that Internet service providers can implement codes of self-conduct regulating the review of claims concerning (among others) unlawful behaviours of their clients. To that end business, professional or consumer associations or organisations promote the adoption of CoCs that transmit to the Ministry of Productive Activities and the European Commission.[114]

ii. Graduated Response

So-called 'graduated response' or 'three-strike' regulations are also a form of 'responsible' behaviour of access providers. These enforcement schemes are

[108] See Internet Watch Foundation (IWF), 'URL List Policy', available at www.iwf.org.uk/become-a-member/services-for-members/url-list/url-list-policy.

[109] ibid.

[110] The recent revised version of the CoC is dated 18 May 2020 and is available at rettighedsalliancen.dk (in Danish).

[111] See ISPA Code of Conduct, available at www.ispa.be/code-conduct-fr.

[112] Structurally infringing websites are websites whose business model is geared towards mass copyright infringements according to a unanimous recommendation of the 'clearing house'. See 'Joint solution for dealing with structurally infringing websites on the Internet: Internet access providers and rights holders set up independent "clearing house"', Press Release (CUII, 11 March 2021), available at cuii.info/fileadmin/files/20210311_PM_Gruendung_CUII.pdf.

[113] See Act on measures to prevent the distribution of child pornography (2006/1068).

[114] See Legislative Decree 70/2003, Art 18.

meant to block the household Internet connections of repeat infringers. In some instances, graduate response arrangements have been judicially or legislatively mandated. Often, they result from voluntary arrangements. French Hadopi Law and other countries such as New Zealand, South Korea, Taiwan and the United Kingdom, have mandated gradual response schemes, in fact managed by administrative agencies, rather than intermediaries.[115] Courts have also reviewed the legality of graduated response schemes and issued injunctions mandating such arrangements.[116]

However, industry-led self-regulation makes up the largest part of graduated response schemes as in the case of the 'six strikes' Copyright Alert System (CAS),[117] discontinued in January 2017.[118] CAS implemented a system of multiple alerts. After a fifth alert, ISPs were allowed to take 'mitigation measures' to prevent future infringement, including 'temporary reductions of Internet speeds, temporary downgrade in Internet service tier or redirection to a landing page'.[119] In Australia, an industry-negotiated graduated response Code was submitted to the Australian Communications and Media Authority (ACMA) for registration as an industry code, requiring Internet service providers to pass on an escalating series of infringements warnings to residential fixed account-holders who are alleged to have infringed copyright.[120] In Europe, Eircom was one of the first European ISPs to implement a voluntary Graduated Response Protocol under which Eircom would issue copyright infringement notices to the customer, after a settlement had been reached between record companies and Eircom.[121] The Irish Supreme Court later upheld the validity of the scheme against an Irish Data Protection Commissioner's enforcement notice requiring Eircom to cease its operation of the Protocol.[122] Also, an agreement has been negotiated between major British ISPs and rights-holders – with the support of the UK Government – under the

[115] See Law no 2009-669 of 12 June 2009, promoting the dissemination and protection of creative works on the Internet (aka HADOPI law) (FR); Copyright (Infringing File Sharing) Regulations 2011 (NZ); Copyright Act as amended on 22 January 2014, Art 90-4(2) (TW); Digital Economy Act 2010 (UK) (however, the 'obligations to limit Internet access' have not yet been implemented).

[116] See eg Sony Music & Ors v UPC Communications [2015] IECH 317; G Kelly, 'A Court-Ordered Graduated Response System in Ireland: the Beginning of the End?' (2016) 11 *Journal of Intellectual Property Law & Practice* 183. But see Roadshow Films Pty Ltd v iiNet Limited [2012] HCA 16 (rejecting the injunction).

[117] See A Bridy, 'Graduated Response American Style: "Six Strikes" Measured Against Five Norms' (2012) 23 *Fordham Intellectual Property, Media & Entertainment Law Journal* 1.

[118] D Kravets, 'RIP, "Six Strikes" Copyright Alert System' (ArsTechnica, 30 January 2017).

[119] See Center for Copyright Information, 'Copyright Alert System (CAS)', available at web.archive.org/web/20130113051248/http://www.copyrightinformation.org/alerts.

[120] See Communications Alliance Ltd, C653:2015 – Copyright Notice Scheme Industry Code (April 2015), available at www.commsalliance.com.au/__data/assets/pdf_file/0005/48551/C653-Copyright-Notice-Scheme-Industry-Code-FINAL.pdf.

[121] See EIR, Legal Music – Frequently Asked Questions, available at www.eir.ie/notification/legalmusic/faqs.

[122] See EMI v Data Protection Commissioner [2013] IESC 34 (IR).

name of Creative Content UK.[123] This voluntary scheme would implement four educational-only notices or alerts sent by the ISPs to their subscribers based on IP addresses supplied by the rights-holders, where the IP address is alleged to have been used to transmit infringing content.[124] Graduated response mechanisms have been broadly questioned for their negative implications on users' rights, and their limited positive externalities in curbing infringement.[125] In fact, due to their lack of effectiveness, graduated response strategies have lost much of their original appeal.

C. Search Engines: Online Search Manipulation

A number of voluntary measures applied by search engines go under the name of online search manipulation or demotion.[126] They might apply to multiple online allegedly illicit activities, although copyright enforcement has been a primary goal of these measures. Google have been demoting allegedly pirate sites since 2012. First, Google altered its PageRank search algorithm and demoted websites according to the number of DMCA-compliant notices received for each website.[127] Later, in 2014, Google started to demote autocomplete predictions returning search results containing DMCA-demoted sites.[128] Such measures became widespread and have been increasingly agreed upon by stakeholders via CoCs. For example, under the aegis of the UK Intellectual Property Office, representatives from the creative industries and leading UK search engines developed a Voluntary Code of Practice dedicated to reducing the visibility of infringing content in search results, especially by demoting search entries from the first page.[129]

In addition, voluntary search manipulation measures have been traditionally implemented with regard to manifestly illegal content. Rather than waiting for legislatively mandated obligations, online hosting providers have increasingly pursued self-regulatory initiatives in this field. Child pornography, of course, is one such early example.[130] Also, Google has adopted specific self-regulatory

[123] Creative Content UK, available at www.creativecontentuk.org.
[124] ibid.
[125] See eg, for further reference, Frosio (n 1) 19–20.
[126] See eg K Grind et al, 'How Google Interferes With Its Search Algorithms and Changes Your Results' *Wall Street Journal* (15 November 2015), available at www.wsj.com/articles/how-google-interferes-with-its-search-algorithms-and-changes-your-results-11573823753.
[127] See A Bridy, 'Copyright's Digital Deputies: DMCA-plus Enforcement by Internet Intermediaries' in J Rothchild (ed), *Research Handbook on Electronic Commerce Law* (Edward Elgar Publishing, 2016) 200.
[128] ibid.
[129] See Intellectual Property Office, 'Press Release: Search Engines and Creative Industries Sign Anti-Piracy Agreement' (20 February 2017), available at www.gov.uk/government/news/search-engines-and-creative-industries-sign-anti-piracy-agreement.
[130] See eg Department for Digital, Culture, Media & Sport, Interim code of practice on online child sexual exploitation and abuse (15 December 2020) Principle 6.

measures for revenge porn, which Google delists from Internet searches.[131] Other major platforms followed Google's lead. After being ordered by a Dutch court to identify revenge porn publishers in the past,[132] Facebook decided to introduce photo-matching technology to stop revenge porn and proactively filter its reappearance.[133] Finally, search manipulation and demotion started to be applied to curb extremism and radicalisation, such as in the case of the UK Interim code of practice on terrorist content and activity online.[134] Plans of a pilot scheme to tweak search to make counter-radicalisation videos and links more prominent have also been announced.[135]

D. Hosting Providers: Proactive Monitoring and Filtering

Proactive monitoring and filtering has more recently been implemented via legislative obligations, at least in the EU,[136] but it first appeared as a private ordering measure following rightholder and government pressures to purge the Internet of alleged content infringements or illegal speech. In the midst of major copyright lawsuits launched against them,[137] YouTube and Vimeo felt compelled to voluntarily implement filtering mechanisms on their platforms: Google launched Contend ID in 2008,[138] and Vimeo adopted Copyright Match in 2014.[139] Both technologies rely on digital fingerprinting to match an uploaded file against a database of protected works provided by rightholders.[140]

[131] See J Walters, 'Google to Exclude Revenge Porn from Internet Searches? *The Guardian* (21 June 2015), available at www.theguardian.com/technology/2015/jun/20/google-excludes-revenge-porn-internet-searches.

[132] See Agence France-Press, 'Facebook Ordered by Dutch Court to Identify Revenge Porn Publisher' *The Guardian* (26 June 2015), available at www.theguardian.com/technology/2015/jun/26/facebook-ordered-by-dutch-court-to-identify-revenge-porn-publisher.

[133] See E Grey Ellis, 'Facebook's New Plan May Curb Revenge Porn, but Won't Kill It' (Wired, 6 April 2017).

[134] See eg Department for Digital, Culture, Media & Sport, Interim code of practice on terrorist content and activity online (15 December 2020) Principle 2.

[135] See B Quinn, 'Google to Point Extremist Searches Towards Anti-radicalization Websites' *The Guardian* (2 February 2016), available at buff.ly/20J3pFi.

[136] See Directive 2019/790/EU of the European Parliament and of the Council of 17 April 2019 on copyright and related rights in the Digital Single Market and amending Directives 96/9/EC and 2001/29/EC [2019] OJ L 130/92 ('C-DSM Directive') Art 17 (providing inter alia that selected providers are subject to proactive monitoring and filtering obligations in case they fail to conclude licensing agreements and are given necessary information to trigger such technologies). See also Frosio, 'Reforming the C-DSM Reform' (2020) 709–50.

[137] See *Viacom Int'l v YouTube Inc*, 676 F3d 19 (2nd Cir 2012); *Capitol Records LLC v Vimeo*, 826 F3d 78 (2nd Cir 2015).

[138] See YouTube, 'How Content ID Works', available at support.google.com/youtube/answer/2797370?hl=en.

[139] See C Welch, 'Vimeo Rolls Out Copyright Match to Find and Remove Illegal Videos' (The Verge, 21 May 2014), available at www.theverge.com/2014/5/21/5738584/vimeo-copyright-match-finds-and-removes-illegal-videos.

[140] YouTube (n 138).

You Tube and Facebook have been using other matching tools to filter 'extremist content'.[141] In this context, tech companies plan to create a shared database of hashes that can identify images and videos promoting terrorism, which would then be removed.[142] Meanwhile, the European Commission would like to provide a regulatory framework for these initiatives by stressing the need for Internet platforms to speed up the removal process of hate speech. The Communication 'Tackling Illegal Content Online' reinforces this point on the agenda by endorsing 'automatic stay-down procedures' to fingerprint and filter out content which has been already identified and assessed as illegal.[143] In addition, with special emphasis on tackling the dissemination of terrorist content online, hosting providers should take 'proportionate and specific proactive measures, including by using automated means, in order to detect, identify and expeditiously remove or disable access to terrorist content'.[144] These automated means should also 'immediately prevent content providers from re-submitting content which has already been removed or to which access has already been disabled because it is considered to be terrorist content'.[145] A recommendation for preventing dissemination of terrorist content online endorses similar principles and includes an obligation for digital platforms to remove 'terrorist content or disable access to terrorist content in all member states as soon as possible and in any event within one hour of receipt of the removal order', which will encourage hosting providers to use proactive algorithmic filtering for their moderation in order to make the strict deadline for removal.[146]

Similar initiatives also relying on hashing technologies have been implemented in the area of child abuse material. Microsoft's PhotoDNA has been widely used to find the images and stop their distribution.[147] The technology is being used by the Internet Watch Foundation, which operates its dedicated Internet crawler,[148] and private firms, such as by Microsoft, Twitter, Google and Facebook, for some of their own products.[149]

[141] See J Menn and D Volz, 'Excusive: Google, Facebook Quietly Move Toward Automatic Blocking of Extremist Videos' (Reuters, 25 June 2016), available at www.reuters.com/article/us-internet-extremism-video-exclusive-idUSKCN0ZB00M.

[142] O Solon, 'Facebook, Twitter, Google and Microsoft Team up to Tackle Extremist Content *The Guardian* (6 December 2016), available at www.theguardian.com/technology/2016/dec/05/facebook-twitter-google-microsoft-terrorist-extremist-content.

[143] See European Commission (n 19) § 5.2.

[144] European Commission, 'Recommendation on measures to effectively tackle illegal content online' C(2018) 1177 final.

[145] ibid.

[146] See Regulation of the European Parliament and the Council on preventing the dissemination of terrorist content online' [2021] 2018/0331(COD) Art 3.

[147] See Microsoft, 'PhotoDNA', available at www.microsoft.com/en-us/photodna.

[148] See 'Using Crawling and Hashing Technologies to Find Child Sexual Abuse Material – the Internet Watch Foundation' (NetClean, 11 February 2019), available at /www.netclean.com/2019/02/11/using-crawling-and-hashing-technologies-to-find-child-sexual-abuse-material-the-internet-watch-foundation.

[149] See Wikipedia, 'PhotoDNA', available at en.wikipedia.org/wiki/PhotoDNA.

E. Advertisement and Payment Providers: Payment Blockades and Follow-the-Money Strategies

Payment blockades and 'voluntary best practices agreements' between major corporate copyright and trademark owners and online payment processors have been widely applied.[150] For example, across 2011 and 2012, American Express, Discover, MasterCard, Visa and PayPal, PULSE, and Diners Club entered into a best practice agreement with 31 major right-holders as part of the Payment Processor Initiative run by the International AntiCounterfeiting Coalition (IACC).[151] Both the US Government, with its 'Joint Strategic Plan for Intellectual Property Enforcement',[152] and the European Commission's Communication, 'Towards a Modern, More European Copyright Framework', have endorsed similar 'follow-the-money' strategies.[153] As the Commission puts it, the goal is 'to engage with platforms in setting up and applying voluntary cooperation mechanisms aimed at depriving those engaging in commercial infringements of intellectual property rights (IPRs) of the revenue streams emanating from their illegal activities'.[154] According to the Commission, 'follow-the-money' mechanisms should be based on a self-regulatory approach through the implementation of Code of Conducts, such as the Guiding Principles for a Stakeholders' Voluntary Agreement on Online Advertising and IPR.[155] As stated by the principles, 'the purpose of the agreement is to dissuade the placement of advertising on commercial scale IP infringing websites and apps (eg on mobile, tablets, or set-top boxes), thereby minimising the funding of IP infringement through advertising revenue'.[156] Of course, in the case of payments blockades, intermediaries might have business incentives that make them more likely to yield to pressure, and less proactive in considering negative externalities for fundamental rights, such as due process and freedom to conduct a business.

VII. Conclusions

Current Internet policy – especially in Europe – is silently drifting away from fundamental user safeguards online, while sealing an 'invisible handshake'

[150] See A Bridy, 'Internet Payment Blockades' (2015) 67 *Florida Law Review* 1523.

[151] See 'Best Practices to Address Copyright Infringement and the Sale of Counterfeit Products on the Internet' (16 May 2011). See also Bridy, 'Internet Payment Blockades' (2015) 1549.

[152] See Office of the Intellectual Property Enforcement Coordinator, 'Supporting Innovation, Creativity & Enterprise: Charting a Path Ahead (US Joint Strategic Plan for Intellectual Property Enforcement FY 2017–2019)' (2017).

[153] See European Commission, 'Towards a Modern More European Copyright Framework' (Communication) COM(2015) 260 final 10–11.

[154] See European Commission (n 45) 8.

[155] See European Commission, 'The Follow the Money Approach to IPR Enforcement – Stakeholders' Voluntary Agreement on Online Advertising and IPR: Guiding Principles', available at ec.europa.eu/docsroom/documents/19462/attachments/1/translations/en/renditions/native.

[156] ibid.

between rights-holders, online intermediaries and governments. Public enforcement lacking technical knowledge and resources to address an unprecedented challenge in terms of global human semiotic behaviour would coactively outsource enforcement online to private parties. This is occurring via state-driven and market-driven private ordering measures, such as private DNS content regulation, website-blocking, graduated response, online search manipulation, monitoring and filtering, payment blockades and follow-the-money strategies, in light of a newly emphasised notion of CSR.

Although privatisation of online enforcement and adjudication has been consolidating as a trend for quite some time now, counterposing forces are also at work, as evidenced by the recent Digital Services Act and Digital Markets Act proposals. With these initiatives, the state might try to regain a more central and supervisory role in Internet and platform governance by creating legislatively mandated standards and regulatory national and supernational infrastructures that limit private ordering fragmentation, while guaranteeing more tightly users' fundamental rights. Avoiding a dystopian future depends on the protection of users' fundamental rights online, with emphasis on due process, freedom of expression and privacy, against the apparently relentless forces of privately administered algorithmic content moderation, adjudication and enforcement.

11

Government–Platform Synergy and its Perils

NIVA ELKIN-KOREN*

I. Introduction

Social media have become the dominant modern public sphere in which users can express their opinions, shape their identity, communicate to build social relationships, and organise for collective action.[1] Some speech shared by users might be harmful, such as disinformation, terrorist propaganda or revenge porn. Social media platforms, which host speech originated by users, control the uploading of content as well as the visibility of it. Consequently, platforms have become a focal point for limiting the online spread of potentially harmful speech, offering effective tools for identifying and removing content.

Public authorities increasingly rely on platforms in law enforcement efforts.[2] In an attempt to tackle allegedly illegal content, governments collaborate with digital platforms in a variety of ways. These include coordinated efforts to prevent foreign election interference, countering terrorist and extremist content, or combating COVID-19 misinformation. Of particular interest for this chapter is the practice of flagging allegedly illegal content, and requesting its voluntary removal based on the platforms' Terms of Use (ToU). Thus, rather than obtaining a warrant to prevent a crime which takes place within private infrastructure, governmental agencies act as a trusted flagger, expecting, and some would even say encouraging, platforms to exercise their own (private) power to tackle potentially harmful speech.

* I thank Michael Birnhack, Ellen Goodman, Uri Hacohen, Amélie Heldt, Daphne Keller and Mickey Zar for their helpful comments, and Yuval Tuchman for his invaluable research assistance.

[1] As highlighted in Part 1 of this volume.

[2] See N Elkin-Koren and E Haber, 'Governance by Proxy: Cyber Challenges to Civil Liberties' (2016) 82 *Brooklyn Law Review* 105, 112–20; See also, L Goldstein, 'How a Secretive Cyber Unit Censors Palestinians' (The American Prospect, 12 July 2021), available at prospect.org/world/how-secretive-cyber-unit-censors-palestinians.

This chapter argues that increasing governmental reliance on platform policies creates a distinct type of informal collaboration. This *sui generis* collaboration is bypassing democratic checks, which are intended to safeguard civil liberties and the right of self-governance by restraining the exercise of governmental coercive power.[3] The proactive flagging of content by national governments enables governments to censor online content, avoiding any judicial review or public scrutiny, and thereby bypassing the rule of law, separation of powers and due process.

Flagging by government does not legally mandate the removal of content. It does not follow, however, that platforms are free to exercise discretion in removal decisions. Two decades ago, Michael Birnhack and I called this type of informal collaboration between government and online intermediaries the *invisible handshake*, where major market players, which rely on government on a wide array of issues, are likely to comply with informal expectations by governmental agencies to promote their own commercial self-interest.[4]

Twenty years later, online intermediaries have become powerful multinational platforms. The socio-technological affordances and business practices of digital platforms increasingly shape the enforcement practices of public authorities. The growing dependency of governments on for-profit digital platforms for law enforcement purposes therefore creates a new type of synergy which threatens to undermine the independence of governmental discretion.

All in all, the collaboration between governments and digital platforms introduces new ways of exercising power which are situated in a constitutional twilight zone. It enables governments to escape constitutional constraints, and at the same time it also strengthens the power of unaccountable global platforms to mediate not simply private interactions (generally governed by private law), but also the relationship between government and citizens (generally governed by public law). This synergy creates a new type of power that resides neither in government alone, nor in platforms, but rather merges their capacities through informal coordination. As further demonstrated in this chapter, recent attempts to constitutionalise such collaboration fall short of addressing this synergy, which may require fresh thinking on how to secure civil liberties in the twenty-first century.

This chapter describes the emerging synergy between governments and platform in law enforcement efforts and demonstrates its ramifications by analysing a case study of content removal practices applied by the Cyber Unit at the Israeli State Attorney's office. Since 2015, the Cyber Unit has encouraged platforms to remove allegedly illegal speech, by issuing complaints to major social media platforms based on the alleged violation of their contractual community guidelines. A recent petition to the Israeli High Court of Justice sought to challenge the constitutional basis of this practice, but failed.[5] While the Court recognised the

[3] See Elkin-Koren and Haber, 'Governance by Proxy' (2016) 164–65.

[4] MD Birnhack and N Elkin-Koren, 'The Invisible Handshake: The Reemergence of the State in the Digital Environment' (2003) 8 *Virginia Journal of Law and Technology*.

[5] HCJ 7846/19 *Adalah v Israeli State Attorney (Cyber Unit)* IsrSC 1 judgment of 12 April 2021.

regulatory implications of such practices for indirectly governing speech in the public sphere, it failed to hold the Government fully accountable for its actions. Moreover, the Court overlooked the potential synergy between governments and platforms, whereby government and platforms may influence one another.

The chapter analyses the blind spot of the standard constitutional framework, and its shortcomings in addressing a government-platform synergy in governing speech. Gaining a better understanding of this synergy could help us think about how to restrain this new form of emerging power. Section II describes the practice of governmental removal requests, and argues that it generates unaccountable use of power. Section III demonstrates the limits of the current constitutional framework for tackling these practices, by critically discussing the recent decision by the Israeli Supreme Court. Section IV highlights the novel challenges introduced by the emerging synergy between government and platforms. Section V concludes.

II. Governmental Speech Enforcement by Platforms

A. Content Moderation by Digital Platforms

The power of social media platforms to shape public discourse and govern the online public sphere is widely acknowledged.[6] Platforms entertain enormous power to shape the public sphere through their content moderation policies.[7] By invoking legal duties established by their self-drafted ToU, and applying content moderation strategies to manage online postings by users, digital platforms practically determine which expression would become available or not, and what would be accessible to whom and how.

Platforms routinely screen content shared by users on their systems, to ensure it complies with appropriate norms. These practices include 'the screening, evaluation, categorization, approval or removal/hiding of online content according to relevant communications and publishing policies … to support and enforce positive communications behaviour online, and to minimize aggression and anti-social behaviour'.[8] Speech norms are defined by the platform as contractual obligations which apply to all users of the service (ie, community guidelines) often intended to ensure that the service remains attractive to a wide range of potential users and

[6] K Klonick, 'The New Governors: The People, Rules, and Processes Governing Online Speech' (2018) 131 *Harvard Law Review* 1598; AP Heldt, 'Merging the "Social" and the "Public": How Social Media Platforms Could Be a New Public Forum' (2019) 46 *Mitchell Hamline Law Review* 997; R Van Loo, 'Rise of the Digital Regulator' (2017) 66 *Duke Law Journal* 1267.

[7] G Tarleton, *Custodians of the Internet: Platforms, Content Moderation, and the Hidden Decisions that Shape Social Media* (Yale University Press, 2018).

[8] T Flew, 'Internet Regulation as Media Policy: Rethinking the Question of Digital Communication Platform Governance' (2019) 10 *Journal of Digital Media & Policy* 33.

also to ensure compliance with some legal duties defined by law (ie, regulatory restraints).

Platforms face increased regulatory pressure to remove potentially harmful content.[9] Lawmakers in the European Union, for instance, have recently adopted Article 17 of the Digital Single Market (DSM) Directive, which requires hosting platforms to ensure from the outset the unavailability of copyright-infringing content posted by users, in order to avoid strict liability.[10] Germany's Network Enforcement Act of 2018 requires a swifter response from online platforms to remove 'manifestly unlawful' content within 24 hours of a complaint being filed, meaning platforms must actively engage in content moderation at the outset.[11] The EU Commission explicitly recommended that platforms take proportionate and specific proactive measures against terrorist content including the use of automated measures.[12] In a similar vein, the United States Congress, in the 2021 Appropriations Act, directed the Federal Trade Commission (FTC) to provide recommendations on the use of AI against specified online harms, including fraud, deep fakes, harassment, hate crimes, terrorist content and election-related disinformation.[13]

Harmful content could be either flagged by individual users or by trusted third parties such as civil society organisations or public authorities. Flaggers alert the platform on potentially harmful content, making use of the 'notice and takedown' procedures. These procedures have been developed by platforms since the late 1990s, as a response to the safe harbour regime, which offered online intermediaries immunity from liability for content posted by users in exchange for content moderation.[14]

Content might also be proactively screened by either human moderators or automated tools. With the volume of content growing exponentially, social

[9] DK Citron, 'Extremist Speech, Compelled Conformity, and Censorship Creep' (2018) 93 *Notre Dame Law Review* 1035; H Bloch-Wehba, 'Automation in Moderation' (2020) 53 *Cornell International Law Journal* 41.

[10] Article 17(1), European Parliament (26 March 2019).

[11] Deutscher Bundesrat: Drucksachen [BR-Drs] 536/17 (30 June 2017).

[12] Directive 2017/541 of the European Parliament and of the Council of 15 March 2017 on Combating Terrorism and Replacing Council Framework Decision 2002/475/ JHA and Amending Council Decision 2005/671/JHA, 2017 OJ (L 88) 6, 9 (EU). The Commission proposed a duty to remove terrorist content within one hour of being posted. On 28 April 2021 the European Parliament adopted the regulation on addressing the dissemination of terrorist content online, which will apply as of 7 June 2022. REGULATION (EU) 2021/784 OF THE EUROPEAN PARLIAMENT AND OF THE COUNCIL of 29 April 2021 on addressing the dissemination of terrorist content online.

[13] HR 133 – 116th Congress: HR 133: Consolidated Appropriations Act, 2021 [Including Coronavirus Stimulus & Relief] (2019), available at www.govtrack.us/congress/bills/116/hr133.

[14] The US Digital Millennium Copyright Act (DMCA), for instance, requires platforms to expeditiously remove alleged copyright-infringing materials upon receiving notice from rights holders (17 USC § 512). Similarly, in the EU, safe harbour provisions under the E-Commerce Directive 2000/31 exempt hosting platforms from liability for content posted by their users, provided that they did not modify that content and were not aware of its illegal character. Once notice is received, the platform is obliged to promptly remove the content. See M Husovec, *Injunctions against Intermediaries in the European Union – Accountable But Not Liable?* (Cambridge University Press, 2017).

platforms were forced to supplement and even replace human review with automated systems.[15] Thus, all major social media platforms deploy machine learning (ML) systems to improve the speedy detection of potentially harmful content, to filter unwarranted content before it is posted, to identify and track similar content, and to block access to it or remove it from the platform. The shift to automated moderation systems has been primarily driven by scale.

B. Governmental Actions against Allegedly Harmful Speech

Government agencies have come to rely on social media platforms in law enforcement efforts, seeking their cooperation in evidence-gathering and information-sharing,[16] or in limiting the spread of illegal content.[17] Such efforts may aim to enforce the law pertaining to illegal content, or might be preventative, aiming to mitigate risks to national security or public safety (eg, incitement of terrorism).[18]

In an effort to slow down the spread of potentially harmful content, some government agencies make use of the notification procedures set out by platforms to request the removal of allegedly unlawful postings ('removal by flagging'). When governments systematically make use of such procedures, they act as trusted flaggers, alerting the platform that some postings are violating the platforms' community guidelines and ToU. Trusted flaggers often enjoy a privileged notification channel, which may include bulk reporting tools and priority review.[19] They must demonstrate a distinct expertise and a high rate of accuracy when flagging content.[20]

In the UK, for instance, the Counter-Terrorism Internet Referral Unit (CTIRU)[21] identifies content which allegedly violates the terms of service of social

[15] R Gorwa et al, 'Algorithmic Content Moderation: Technical and Political Challenges in the Automation of Platform Governance' (2020) 7 *Big Data & Society*; Cambridge Consultants, 'Use of artificial intelligence in online content moderation' (2019), available at www.ofcom.org.uk/__data/assets/pdf_file/0028/157249/cambridge-consultants-ai-content-moderation.pdf.

[16] H Bloch-Wehba, 'Global Platform Governance: Private Power in the Shadow of the State' (2019) 72 *SMU Law Review* 27.

[17] See Birnhack and Elkin-Koren, 'The Invisible Handshake' (2003); Elkin-Koren and Haber (n 1); see also C Montgomery, 'Can Brandenburg v. Ohio Survive the Internet and the Age of Terrorism: The Secret Weakening of a Venerable Doctrine' (2009) 70 *Ohio State Law Journal* 141, 168–78 (describing how law enforcement has encouraged voluntary action by ISPs and communications service providers).

[18] AP Heldt, 'Upload-Filters: Bypassing Classical Concepts of Censorship?' (2019) 10 *Journal of Intellectual Property, Information Technology and Electronic Commerce Law* 56, para 1; see also Bloch-Wehba, 'Global Platform Governance' (2019).

[19] See, for instance, YouTube Trusted Flagger program, at support.google.com/youtube/answer/7554338?hl=en. See generally, SF Schwemer, 'Trusted Notifiers and the Privatization of Online Enforcement' (2019) 35 *Computer Law & Security Review*.

[20] See European Commission, 'Tackling Illegal Content Online' (Communication) COM(2017) 555 final. The Commission urged platforms to cooperate with trusted flaggers by improving such channels. See the Commission Recommendation on measures to effectively tackle illegal content online, C(2018)1177 final, at 6.

[21] Established in 2010 by the Association of Chief Police Officers (ACPO) (a non-governmental body which was later replaced by the National Police Chiefs' Council (NPCC) (also a private company, which

media platforms and requests that they remove the content on a voluntary basis.[22] Similarly, in Israel, a comprehensive and elaborate practice of enforcement of speech regulation through digital platforms was deployed by the Cyber Unit at the State Attorney's Office. Established in 2015, the Cyber Unit aims to coordinate governmental efforts to tackle crime and terrorism in cyberspace.[23] The Unit systematically files removal requests with digital platforms, targeting allegedly illegal content, such as postings which instigate violence against judges or other public servants, threats against minors, or materials which incite terrorism.[24] The content in question is brought to the attention of the Cyber Unit by various government agencies, typically by Israeli security agencies. The Unit then conducts an internal process for reviewing the legality of the content in question and the propriety of seeking its removal.[25] It then files removal requests with the relevant social media platforms, search engines or hosting facilities. Platforms generally treat governmental requests separately, and may include them as a unique category in their transparency reports, often without providing further details on specific requests.

Requests are made based on the platforms' own content moderation policy, as reflected in its ToU, so-called community standards or community guidelines. Platforms arguably exercise discretion over whether such content violates their ToU and subsequently which action to take regarding such content.

This type of enforcement strategy was dubbed 'voluntary enforcement' by some, referring to the discretionary power sustained by platforms on whether to remove the content or not.[26] Yet, as further discussed below, the political economy of the relationship between government and digital platforms suggest that this might not be the case.

C. Accountability Twilight Zone

The *removal by flagging* enforcement strategy demonstrates the risks involved in the informal public-private collaboration. Such strategy presumably involves mere coordination between the different stakeholders, although, in practice, it results in the exercise of unaccountable power – public and private – which may threaten fundamental civil rights and the rule of law.[27]

coordinates anti-terrorist efforts), and run by the police, this initiative acts to remove terrorist material content from digital platforms.

[22] CTIRU focuses on UK-based materials, but also compiles lists of URLs for material hosted outside the UK to be blocked by the relevant service providers. See wiki.openrightsgroup.org/wiki/Counter-Terrorism_Internet_Referral_Unit.

[23] The Ministry of Justice, 'About Cyber Unit' (Govil, 11 May 2021), available at www.gov.il/en/departments/general/cyber-about.

[24] See Arbel Commission Report (November 2020): 'a committee to form means of protecting the public and civil servants from harmful publication and bulling on the internet'.

[25] The Israeli Ministry of Justice (n 23).

[26] H Wismonsky, 'Alternative Enforcement for Content Related Offences in Cyberspace' in A Harel (ed), *Law And Justice? Criminal Procedure In Israel – Failures And Challenges* (Nevo, 2018) (Hebrew).

[27] See G De Gregorio, 'Democratising Online Content Moderation: A Constitutional Framework' (2020) 36 *Computer Law and Security Review* 105374.

i. Unaccountable Public Power

The removal by flagging strategy blurs the public-private distinction, thus enabling government to evade some constitutional restraints on the use of coercive power.

The flagging of content by a governmental agency to provoke removal of online speech on social media may harm individual fundamental rights. It enables the Government to effectively restrain freedom of expression with barely any checks and balances. It may silence some speakers (eg, social activists, political opponents) thus depriving the general public of access to legitimate speech. Moreover, when governments rely on removal by flagging, the scope of permissible speech is effectively defined by the guidelines of the social media platforms, which often cover a wider range of objectionable speech than those provided by law. Such discrepancy between the platforms' definitions of harmful speech and illegal content defined by public authorities may lead to either over-removal or under-enforcement of speech norms.

When the Government attempts to restrict speech, it is required to demonstrate authority in law, which is often subject to constitutional checks.[28] For instance, the US Constitution restrains the use of governmental power to restrict speech,[29] so that any attempt to do so would be subject to strict scrutiny under the First Amendment.[30] Yet when speech is removed by private companies, it does not provoke that constitutional protection. Only governmental actions are subject to constitutional scrutiny and restrained to assure their legitimacy and safeguard from abuse of power.[31]

Removal by flagging allows the exercise of unaccountable power, which threatens civil liberties. It undermines the basic mechanisms by which enforcement agencies become accountable to the public, namely: explicit authority defined by law, and subject to judicial review.[32] Rather than obtaining a warrant to prevent an offence that takes place on private infrastructure,[33] governmental agencies acting as a trusted flagger, are encouraging platforms to exercise their own (private) power to tackle potentially harmful speech. Consequently, governments are able to censor online content, absent any judicial review or public scrutiny, undermining fundamental democratic principles of the rule of law, separation of powers, due process and transparency, which were intended to safeguard civil liberties.

[28] See E Haber and A Reichman, 'The User, the Superuser, and the Regulator: Functional Separation of Powers and the Plurality of the State in Cyber' (2020) 35 *Berkeley Technology Law Journal* 431, 439.

[29] US Constitution. amend I ('*Congress* shall make no law … abridging the freedom of speech').

[30] See for example *Sable Communications of California v FCC*, 492 US 115, 126 (1989).

[31] See KN Brown, 'Public Laws and Private Lawmakers' (2016) 93 *Washington University Law Review* 615, 618.

[32] Users may of course file a suit in court. Yet, they may often be unaware of the limits set on the availability of their content. Even if they are, they are unlikely to appeal. Studies have shown, that in practice users rarely exercise their right to appeal a removal decision by platforms. See JM Urban, J Karaganis and BL Schofield, 'Notice and Takedown: Online Service Provider and Rightsholder Accounts of Everyday Practice' (2017) 64 *Journal of the Copyright Society of the USA* 371; see also ch 15 (Heldt) in this volume.

[33] See Birnhack and Elkin-Koren (n 4) para 144; HCJ 7846/19 (n 5) [48]–[54] (Melcer J).

Indeed, governments claim that flagging does not amount to governmental exercise of power, as it leaves the removal at the sole discretion of private actors, whose content moderation practices are governed by private law.[34] Yet, while social media platforms are multinational companies with some leverage over governments, they are also operating under the threat of regulation that may impose stricter duties.[35] Public authorities can also nudge private businesses to perform law enforcement tasks, at the shadow of other regulatory powers, involving competition, tax or labour law.[36] As a result, governmental policies which affect content removal by platforms might effectively airbrush out some expressions from the public sphere. Balkin calls this 'soft censorship'[37] and Bambauer refers to it as 'jawboning', namely 'enforcement through informal channels, where the underlying authority is in doubt'.[38]

In brief, the flagging strategy has given rise to the exercise of unaccountable power, which is threatening civil liberties.[39]

ii. Unaccountable Private Power

Social media platforms, too, might not be held accountable for unjustified removal of content. In the US, platforms are immune from liability pertaining to users' content under section 230 of the Communication Decency Act (CDA).[40] Under US constitutional law the Government is restrained from undertaking any regulatory measures that would intervene in platforms' discretion. As private entities, digital platforms are free to entertain full discretion regarding the content they carry.

Users whose content was removed by the platforms have very little recourse to contest the removal.[41] This is due to the safe-harbour provisions under the CDA and DMCA, in the US, and also in the EU.[42] It is also due, however, to contractual bars, including limitation of liability clauses, and broad removal discretion often defined by the boilerplate ToU.[43]

[34] See Elkin-Koren and Haber (n 2) 107, 138.
[35] ibid; See Birnhack and Elkin-Koren (n 4).
[36] See Heldt, 'Merging the "Social" and the "Public"' (2019); Citron, 'Extremist Speech' (2018); ibid.
[37] See JM Balkin, 'Free Speech is a Triangle' (2018) 118 *Columbia Law Review* 2011, 2314.
[38] DE Bambauer, 'Orwell's Armchair' (2012) 79 *University of Chicago Law Review* 863.
[39] See Giovanni De Gregorio, 'Democratising Online Content Moderation' (2020).
[40] See US Code § 230. An important exception is liability for copyright, which is governed by the Digital Millennium Copyright Act (1998), § 512 (DMCA). See SK Mehra and M Trimble, 'Secondary Liability, ISP Immunity, and Incumbent Entrenchment' (2014) 62 *American Journal of Comparative Law* 685.
[41] See D Keller, 'Who Do You Sue? State and Platform Hybrid Power Over Online Speech' Aegis Series Paper No 1902 (Hoover Institution, 2019), available at www.hoover.org/sites/default/files/research/docs/who-do-you-sue-state-and-platform-hybrid-power-over-online-speech_0.pdf.
[42] See safe harbour under the E-Commerce Directive 2000/31.
[43] N Elkin-Koren et al, 'Social media as contractual networks: A bottom up check on content moderation' (2022, forthcoming) *Iowa Law Review*, available at papers.ssrn.com/sol3/papers.cfm?abstract_id=3797554.

Reform proposals have suggested increasing the platforms' liability for the harms caused by the content they host,[44] imposing mandatory transparency requirements on platforms,[45] and introducing legislation that allows the government and law enforcement agencies to actively intervene in the moderation of content by the platforms, and to supervise their censorship.[46] Such reform initiatives might face constitutional challenges in the US. Additionally, they may bolster the silent collaboration – the 'invisible handshake' – between the government and the platforms, further deepening the accountability crisis.

III. The Limits of the Constitutional Framework in the Digital Political Economy

A recent petition before the Israeli Supreme Court, has challenged the removal by flagging practice. It demonstrates the limits of the current constitutional framework for addressing the challenges involved in the new synergy between governments and platforms. In *Adalah v Cyber Unit*[47] the Israeli Supreme Court, in its capacity as a High Court of Justice,[48] addressed a petition filed by several NGOs against the enforcement strategy of the Cyber Unit at the Attorney General Office.[49] Below I briefly discuss the background, analyse the opinion of the Court and highlight some of its limitations.

[44] Executive Orders, of both President Trump and President Biden, manifesting a commitment to restrain excessive power entertained by social media platforms.

[45] For example, the Digital Services Act Package aims to introduce more transparency and accountability in platforms' activities. See European Commission, Commission Work Programme, A Union that strives for more, COM(2020) 37, 29 January 2020; M Maccarthy, 'Transparency Requirements for Digital Social Media Platforms: Recommendations for Policy Makers and Industry' (Transatlantic Working Group, 2020), available at www.ivir.nl/publicaties/download/Transparency_MacCarthy_Feb_2020.pdf.

[46] One example is the Singaporean Protection from Online Falsehoods and Manipulation bill from October 2019, which facilitates the blocking of sites promoting fake news pursuant to a governmental order; see BBC News, 'Facebook expresses "deep concern" after Singapore orders page block' (19 February 2020), available at www.bbc.com/news/world-asia-51556620.

[47] HCJ 7846/19 (n 5).

[48] See The Knesset official website, 'Lexicon of Terms – The High Court of Justice' (1 January 2003), available at www.knesset.gov.il/lexicon/eng/bagatz_eng.htm.

[49] Adalah – The Legal Center for Arab Minority Rights in Israel and ACRI – The Association for Civil Rights in Israel. An amicus brief of The Movement for Freedom of Information in Israel argued that the question of authority at the centre of the petition should be examined, also taking into account the fact that the Cyber Unit operates in the absence of transparency, and this is reflected in the lack of documentation of the expressions the Cyber Unit seeks to remove; See in this matter HCJ 7846/19 (n 5) [27] (Melcer J).

A. Flagging by the Government: A Constitutional Challenge

Petitioners brought a constitutional challenge[50] against the removal requests issued by the Government, claiming that the exercise of governmental power is void as it lacks any explicit authority, in contrary to the rule of law and the principle of legality.[51] The principle of legality permits public authorities to exercise governmental powers only when they are explicitly authorised by law.[52] Petitioners argued that the Government lacked such authority to engage in a robust, systematic flagging practice, which amounted to governmental enforcement, and therefore these governmental actions should be rendered *ultra vires*.[53]

Several statutory provisions under Israeli law authorise courts to order the removal of particular expressions, or to restrict its distribution for a particular cause, including online gambling, child pornography, advertising of prostitution services, drug trafficking, and acts of terrorist organisations.[54] Other legal provisions authorise courts to restrict the publication of sensitive information, such as the identity of victims of sexual assaults, or the identity of different actors in adoption procedures.[55] Enforcement actions in those instances require a court order and are thus subject to judicial review. For all other matters, there is currently no explicit, direct statutory authority for requesting the takedown of online content. Interestingly, the Cyber Unit claimed that this lacuna in the law was not intentional,[56] and therefore the Government was authorised by law to act against illegal content, including inducement of violence, terrorism, racism, sexual harassment and threats.[57]

The Government further claimed that the flagging did not amount to the exercise of governmental power, since the Cyber Unit merely informed platforms of

[50] In the absence of a constitution, Israeli fundamental rights are listed in several basic laws, including the Basic Law: Human Dignity and Liberty. The fundamental right to freedom of expression and the right to due process are not listed explicitly under the Basic Law, but were interpreted by the Israeli Supreme Court as such in a numerous previous proceedings.

[51] HCJ 7846/19 (n 5) [39]–[41] (Melcer J).

[52] The principle of legality reflects the subordination of the administrative authority to the rule of law. Accordingly, the executive branch is authorised to perform only those actions that the law authorized it to perform, rendering all other actions void. See discussion about the 'principle of legality' in D Barak-Erez, *Administrative Law* (The Israel Bar-Publishing House, 2010) (Hebrew) 97–110.

[53] Petitioners further argued that the flagging practice by the Cyber Unit blurs the distinction between investigative powers (assigned to the police under s 59 of the Criminal Procedure Law) and prosecution powers assigned to the Attorney General.

[54] HCJ 7846/19 (n 5) [4]–[5] (Melcer J); Law on Authorities for the Prevention of Committing Crimes Through Use of an Internet Site 5777-2017 SH 2650 (Isr).

[55] See s 352 of Israel Penal Law 5737-1977 SH 864; See s 34 of The Child Adoption Law 5741-1981 SH 1028.

[56] HCJ 7846/19 (n 5) [6], [15] (Melcer J).

[57] Draft Bill for the Removal from the Internet of Content whose Publication Constitutes an Offense 5777-2016 HH (Gov)1104 (Isr), available at fs.knesset.gov.il//20/law/20_ls1_365358.pdf. This bill, proposing to authorise courts to issue orders in such circumstances, faced strong opposition from digital platforms and civil society organisations and eventually failed. See generally T Schwartz Altshuler and R Aridor-Hershkovitz, 'Israel's Proposed "Facebook Bill"'(Lawfare, 29 August 2018), available at www.lawfareblog.com/israels-proposed-facebook-bill.

alleged violations of their own terms of service, leaving it to the platform to decide how to act upon such reports. The final decision on whether to restrict access, remove or block it remains at the sole discretion of the platform.[58] Consequently, the Cyber Unit dubbed this practice 'voluntary enforcement', implying that platforms reserve full discretion on content removal issues.

The Court dismissed the petition, holding that it suffered from two essential flaws: first, it failed to include the digital platforms as respondents; and second, it lacked sufficient evidentiary basis for claiming that the Government violated fundamental rights and therefore required special, rather than general, authority in law.[59]

Writing for the majority, Melcer J examined the removal by flagging practice from a regulatory perspective, concluding that this practice did not fall neatly under either a *command and control* framework,[60] where rules are crafted by the Government and enforced top-down on market actors, nor under a *self-regulation* framework, where actors agree to craft and undertake certain binding rules.[61]

Melcer J concluded that the flagging practice was indeed a *governmental action*.[62] Building on the *New School Regulation* approach introduced by Professor Jack Balkin,[63] the Court described the regulatory scene as a triangle comprised of three players – governments, platforms, and citizens[64] – in which the Government indirectly shapes the behaviour of citizens via platforms.

Dubbing the flagging practice *reverse regulation*, Melcer J maintained that it constituted the exercise of governmental power, where the final decision on how to act remained in the hands of those subject to the regulation.[65] The threat that the

[58] HCJ 7846/19 (n 5) [40], [54] (Melcer J).

[59] ibid [31]–[41] (Melcer J); ibid [1]–[10] (Hayut CJ).

[60] 'Command and control' refers to vertical top-down regulation, where the Government sets the rules and undertakes enforcement measures to ensure compliance; ibid [46] (Melcer J). See also J Black, 'Critical Reflections on Regulation' (2002) 27 *Australian Journal of Legal Philosophy* 1: 'Such form of regulation usually refers to state regulation using legal rules backed by sanctions'. See definition in R Baldwin et al, *A Reader on Regulation* (Oxford University Press, 1998): 'set of authoritative rules, often accompanied by some administrative agency, for monitoring or enforcing compliance'.

[61] This regulatory approach risks to unduly bind the discretion of a regulatory agency; see generally J Braithwaite, 'Enforced Self-Regulation: A New Strategy for Corporate Crime Control' (1982) 80 *Michigan Law Review* 1466. See also S Yadin, *Regulation: Administrative Law in the Age of Regulatory Contracts* (Bursi, 2016) (Hebrew).

[62] In a short concurring opinion, Hayut CJ also concluded that the flagging practice constitutes a governmental action, since it was a 'systematic, deliberate, extensive and organized' activity which fulfilled a public function and therefore amounted to the exercise of authority on behalf of the state. Yet, she maintained that the two fundamental flaws (lack of evidence on violation of fundamental rights and failure to designate the digital platforms as party in the petition) justified a preliminary rejection of the petition. ibid [4] (Hayut CJ).

[63] See Balkin, 'Free Speech is a Triangle' (2018).

[64] Balkin argues that rather than applying direct regulation to citizens, government collaborates with platforms on speech governance which eventually shape free speech norms to citizens.

[65] Note that in the US, private actors might be held liable for violating the First Amendment under the state action doctrine when they act on behalf of the Government or perform a function that is normally done by the Government. See *Manhattan Cmty Access Corp v Halleck*, No 17-1702, slip op at [2](17 June 2019).

Government might (ab)use its regulatory coercive power to apply some binding rules to platforms raises a concern that platforms may not exercise independent discretion and would not act voluntarily. Moreover, platforms may seek to maintain a good relationship with the authority for other reasons involving competition, labour law, tax cuts and the like. Interestingly, the Court held that such a concern remained theoretical due to the uniquely powerful status of multinational digital platforms,[66] and absent evidence to the contrary, it was possible that these multinational platforms act independently, exercise their own independent discretion and operate without fear.[67] Subsequently, the Court found no demonstration of actual violation of fundamental rights, and therefore held that the Government could rely on its general statutory authorisation to satisfy the legality principle by relying on its residual power[68] under section 32 of the Basic Law: The Government.[69]

The Court noted, however, that if there were evidence of violation of fundamental rights, or if petitioners could demonstrate that platforms did not, in fact, exercise independent discretion in removing content, then a more specific statutory language authorising the government to engage in such practice would be required.[70] At the same time, however, the Court held that the flagging practice should be viewed as a *governmental action*, to which I turn next.

B. Flagging Content as a Governmental Action

The main significance of the decision is the holding that the removal by flagging practice constitutes a governmental action. The Court dismissed the Government's claim that by simply informing platforms of illicit content, rather than demanding its removal, the Government simply acted like any other private actor.[71]

Holding that the systematic issuing of takedown notices constitutes a governmental action might carry important implications for the rule of law. It may fill a critical gap in current constitutional analysis, which generally leaves the collaboration between governments and platforms in a legal twilight zone, where no accountability applies.[72] The exercise of governmental authority must be accountable to the electorate and subject to the rule of law,[73] because the Government

[66] HCJ 7846/19 (n 5) [48]–[54] (Melcer J); see further Haber and Reichman, 'The User, the Superuser, and the Regulator' (2020) 440.

[67] HCJ 7846/19 (n 5) [50]–[54] (Melcer J).

[68] ibid [31]–[35], [50] (Melcer J); ibid [5] (Hayut CJ).

[69] s 32 of the Basic Law: The Government (2001).

[70] HCJ 7846/19 (n 5) [69] (Melcer J).

[71] ibid [51] (Melcer J).

[72] See K Langvardt, 'Regulating Online Content Moderation' (2018) 106 *Georgetown Law Journal* 1353 (describing content removal by the platforms as the swiftest regime of censorship the world has ever known, and offers several approaches to legislation-based solutions).

[73] J Freeman, 'Private Parties, Public Functions and the New Administrative Law' (2000) 52 *Administrative Law Review* 813.

has a unique capacity to coerce behaviour and undermine individual freedom.[74] By restraining government power and assuring the protection of civil rights by government agencies, democracies safeguard against tyranny.[75] Holding the Government accountable to the flagging practice and its consequences subject this practice to the checks and balances on the use of coercive power.

First, this approach assists in holding the Government accountable to uphold fundamental principles of *separation of powers*. The democratic principle of separation of powers seeks to ensure adequate checks in the exercise of governmental power to facilitate oversight and safeguard against misuse of abuse of power.[76] This constitutional principle intends to provide practical safeguard against the excessive concentration of political power in one branch of the Government.[77] Each branch was made 'answerable to different sets of constituencies and subject to different temporal demands'.[78] Institutionalising such a differentiation between executive, legislative and judicial powers is expected to 'harness political competition into a system of government that would effectively organize, check, balance, and diffuse power'.[79]

In practice, governmental takedown requests entail that the prosecution is not only performing the traditional enforcement role reserved for the executive branch, which is to identify alleged violation of the law and bring violators to justice. It is also exercising discretion as to which content violates the law, and act to remove such content from the public sphere. Indeed, petitioners claimed that the flagging practice violated basic principles of constitutional law, since the Government unilaterally determined the scope of freedom of expression and whether a criminal offence was committed, without referring the matter to a court of law, nor allowing those affected by their decision to respond. While such determination is usually performed by the court, the flagging practice merges executive duties and judicial discretion. Indeed, the prosecution has discretion as to which cases to prosecute.[80] Yet, exercising such discretion would usually invoke due process rights of the accused parties to contest such determination in a court of law. The Government discretion would therefore be subject to judicial review, either *ex ante*, when law enforcement agencies seek to acquire a court order, or ex post, when contested by the subject of such order.[81] In the case of the flagging-takedown procedure, by

[74] See Haber and Reichman (n 28); see also M Yemini, 'Missing in State Action: Toward a Pluralist Conception of the First Amendment' (2020) 23 *Lewis & Clark Law Review* 1149, 1170 (critically discussing the 'libertarian premise' that government has such a unique capacity).

[75] See *The Federalist no 51* at 291–92 (J Madison) (C Rossiter ed, 1961); Madison discusses the way a republican government can serve as a check on the power of factions, and the tyranny of the majority.

[76] See H Heclo, 'What Has Happened to the Separation of Powers?' in BO Wilson and PW Schramm (eds), Separation of Powers and Good Government (Rowman & Littlefield, 1994) 131, 133–34.

[77] DJ Levinson and RH Pildes, 'Separation of Parties, Not Powers' (2006) 119 *Harvard Law Review* 2312.

[78] JD Michaels, 'An Enduring, Evolving Separation of Powers' (2015) 115 *Columbia Law Review* 515.

[79] Levinson and Pildes, 'Separation of Parties' (2006) 2313.

[80] HCJ 7846/19 (n 5) [27], [44] (Melcer J).

[81] Elkin-Koren and Haber (n 2) 135–42.

contrast, the only check on the exercise of discretion by the prosecution (executive branch) is the (allegedly) independent discretion of the digital platforms. Yet, governmental actions should not be allowed to bypass legal oversight, simply by delegating discretion to platforms, especially when action taken by platforms is likely to be (in)voluntary.[82] Digital platforms are profit-maximising companies, which might be dependent on the Government for various stakes. Consequently, such review, if any, is insufficient as a check on the use of coercive power by the Government.

By focusing attention on governmental action, the ruling of the Israeli Supreme Court reinforced the role of judicial review over the implementation of removal by flagging at its various stages. This practice has created a new type of collaboration by coordination that is not grounded in any special law, and therefore makes it more difficult to hold governments accountable to the consequences of such practice. The Court's holding might help future petitioners to hold the government accountable based on the scope of governmental authority defined by law. Indeed, the Court recommended (though did not mandate) that the scope of executive power would be defined in a new primary legislation and that the practices of the Cyber Unit be subject to regular monitoring.[83]

A second principle that might be invoked by the treatment of the flagging practice as governmental action is transparency to promote public oversight. Freedom of information laws seek to ensure that governments be held accountable to their citizens by mandating transparency. Indeed, responding to an *amicus curiae* brief submitted by the Freedom of Information Association, the Court noted several procedural flaws in the Cyber Unit operation, including a lack of clear and transparent procedures regarding takedown practices, and a failure to keep records of the takedown requests issued. Consequently, the Court called for the adoption of appropriate procedures to ensure more transparency regarding the practices of the Cyber Unit, including the publication of details of the Work Procedure of the Cyber Unit, documenting the removal requests and consider institutionalising an ongoing monitoring operation.[84]

C. The Constitutional Blind Spot

The constitutional lens focuses on unaccountable exercise of public power, seeking to ensure that no undue pressure is made on private bodies to comply with governmental commands without sufficient checks.

[82] For a different approach taken by the European Court of Human Rights see the recent EU decision on human rights regarding surveillance: *Big Brother Watch and Others v The United Kingdom* App no 58170/13, 62322/14, 24960/15 (ECtHR, 25 May 2021).

[83] HCJ 7846/19 (n 5) [72]–[73] (Melcer J).

[84] HCJ 7846/19 (n 5) [72]–[73] (Melcer J); ibid [11] (Hayut CJ).

But power, in the context of government–platform collaboration, acquires an additional dimension, which is not fully captured by this type of traditional constitutional analysis. The reasoning provided by the Court for dismissing the petition demonstrates some perils in the emerging synergy between governments and digital platforms, which are raising new types of challenges to democratic principles and fundamental rights.

Specifically, the Court dismissed the petition on the ground that it lacked evidence of actual harm, ie that the takedown notices issued by the government resulted in the infringement of fundamental rights, particularly freedom of expression.[85] By this holding, the Court evaded the difficult question of whether the removal by flagging practice should be considered constitutional from the outset. One of the main risks of the informal collaboration between digital platforms and governments in law enforcement efforts is that such collaboration creates synergy between public power and private power, without adequate mechanisms to restrain it.

A fundamental premise in liberal democracies is that public and private are distinct spheres.[86] This distinction is considered a necessary precondition for liberty itself because it defines the private sphere as sacred, to be free from government intervention. Under constitutional law, it is the exercise of governmental authority that must be accountable to the electorate and subject to the rule of law,[87] because the Government has a unique capacity to coerce behaviour and undermine individual freedom.[88] By restraining the power of the Government and ensuring governmental agencies protect civil rights, democracies safeguard against tyranny.[89]

For the purpose of legal scrutiny, most scholars agree that there ought to be a meaningful difference between public and private spheres, and that constitutional restraints should apply only to the former.[90] In fact, 'no matter how blurred the line between public and private and no matter how difficult to design an intellectually defensible test to distinguish them',[91] the public-private divide seems to retain its dominance in constitutional law.

[85] ibid [31]–[35], [50] (Melcer J); ibid [9]–[11] (Hayut CJ); the Court listed other reasons to support its finding that no sufficient evidence was provided to demonstrate harm to free expression. For a critical discussion of these reasonings see T Shadmy and Y Shany, 'Protection Gaps in Public Law Governing Cyberspace: Israel's High Court's Decision on Government-Initiated Takedown Requests' (LAWFARE, 23 April 2021), available at www.lawfareblog.com/protection-gaps-public-law-governing-cyberspace-israels-high-courts-decision-government-initiated.

[86] GE Metzger, 'Privatization as Delegation' (2003) 103 *Columbia Law Review* 1367.

[87] Freeman, 'Private Parties' (2000).

[88] See Yemini, 'Missing in State Action' (2020) 1170 (discussing the 'libertarian premise' that government has such a unique capacity).

[89] See, for example *The Federalist* (n 75).

[90] Freeman (n 73) 842.

[91] ibid; see also Metzger, 'Privatization as Delegation' (2003) 1369 (explaining that 'private actors are so deeply embedded in governance that "the boundaries between the public and private sectors" have become "pervasively blurred"') [internal citation omitted].

The public-private divide also underlies concerns about regulatory measures pertaining to content moderation by social media platforms. One reason to limit regulatory intervention in content moderation is a deep distrust of the Government, and the concern that it could exercise powers against dissidents and shut down opponents' speech.[92] Another concern is that digital platforms, which rank among the largest companies in the world, could gain control over governmental processes and tilt regulatory policies to serve their interests. A related concern is that governments may have a vested interest in harnessing the capabilities of platforms to govern online speech, so as to achieve particular goals while circumventing constitutional barriers.[93]

While the constitutional perspective could partially address some of the challenge arising from the exercise of unaccountable public power, the challenges raised by the synergy between the Government and platforms are more difficult to tackle under current constitutional standards. Next I discuss some of these new challenges.

IV. Public–Platform Synergy

Collaborative governance, which relies on partnerships between public authorities and private actors to achieve regulatory goals is rather common.[94] In collaborative governance, private actors develop their own system of compliance within a regulatory framework set by the Government. As observed by Ari Waldman, 'the government plays the role of a "backdrop threat"', encouraging compliance by setting a liability exemption when actors adopt adequate measures, provide certifying compliance protocols, or threatening sanctions if things go wrong.[95]

Moving beyond mere coordination, removal by flagging involves more profound interaction and integration between digital platforms and governments, where the boundaries between them are blurred and considerations, actions, and processes might merge. What makes public–platform collaboration unique is the way it is consolidated in the speech governance infrastructure deployed by platforms, in ways that might make public and private actions inseparable.

Platforms initially deployed human moderators to identify harmful content, but with the amount of content growing exponentially they were forced to supplement, and even replace, human review with automated systems. Currently, all

[92] See N Suzor, 'Digital Constitutionalism: Using the Rule of Law to Evaluate the Legitimacy of Governance by Platforms' (2018) 4 *Social Media + Society* 4.

[93] See Elkin-Koren and Haber (n 2); Citron (n 9).

[94] J Freeman, 'Collaborative Governance in the Administrative State' (1997) 45 *UCLA Law Review* 1; O Lobel, 'New Governance as Regulatory Governance' in D Levi-Fur (ed), The Oxford Handbook of Governance (Oxford University Press, 2012) 7–65.

[95] AE Waldman, 'Privacy, Practice, and Performance' (2021) 110 *California Law Review*, available at ssrn.com/abstract=3784667 or dx.doi.org/10.2139/ssrn.3784667.

major platforms deploy automated tools to manage the massive volume of online speech.[96] Machine learning (ML) systems and artificial intelligence (AI) (used here interchangeably) improve the detection of potentially harmful content, filter such content before it is posted, identify and track similar content, and block access to it or remove it from the platform. As further explained below, this automated content moderation infrastructure embeds the synergy between government and platforms, and might carry serious implications for civil liberties.

A. Shaping Governmental Enforcement by Platform Design

In removal by flagging, governments issue notices to platforms, requesting the removal of allegedly illegal content. The scope of claims and removal requests would be shaped, however, by the platform choices, as reflected by the contractual terms and the technical design.

ML content moderation systems make use of algorithms and data to identify patterns and make predictions.[97] There are many choices in implementing enforcement by such ML systems, including which data to collect and to record, what could be flagged, how often, on which grounds, and what would be the consequences of such flagging. Such choices are made by platforms as system designers, responsible for developing and operation these systems.[98]

The system design of digital platforms creates affordances, which define the scope of enforcement. Such affordance may determine which content could be deleted, whether content would be subject to preventative monitoring, or whether personal data source of the content might be available.

ML systems designed to tackle illegal content could focus on classifying the content alone, checking whether it matches some classifiers which render it likely to be unwarranted. Systems might also attain the capacity to analyse individual personal data by drawing on their prior behaviour, to make predictions regarding the risk the content may pose based on the identity of the origin of the posting or their social network. Processing personal data of users might invoke fundamental rights, but might also enable ML systems to differentiate between different contexts more efficiently to determine the legitimacy of use. For instance, some use of copyright materials by students or teachers for the purpose of learning might be considered fair use.[99] The same may apply for disinformation, as demonstrated by a report by the Center for Countering Digital Hate (CCDH), which was

[96] See Gorwa et al, 'Algorithmic Content Moderation' (2020).

[97] D Lehr and P Ohm, 'Playing with the Data: What Legal Scholars Should Learn about Machine Learning' (2017) 51 *UCD Law Review* 653.

[98] See KJ Strandburg, 'Monitoring, Datafication, and Consent: Legal Approaches to Privacy in the Big Data Context' in J Lane et al (eds), *Privacy, Big Data, and the Public Good: Frameworks for Engagement* (Cambridge University Press, 2014).

[99] N Elkin-Koren, 'Fair Use by Design' (2017) 64 *UCLA Law Review* 1082.

recently cited by the White House, claiming that Russia and China are spreading anti-Western COVID-19 vaccine misinformation on social media.[100]

Arguably, digital platforms may adjust their systems as a response to regulatory pressure. Danielle Citron, for instance, described how speech standards mandated by countries in the EU, have subsequently shaped speech norms on social media platforms and have become a de facto speech standard in the US.[101] This may vary between countries, however, depending on their geopolitical and economic power and the regulatory leverage they are able to use.[102]

Government discretion in applying speech enforcement may often be constrained by enforcement affordances which are made available by platforms. This may undermine the ability of law enforcement agencies to act against illegal content, but also against impermissible restrictions of legitimate speech. One danger is that law enforcement agencies would eventually act only against illegal speech which digital platforms make it possible to tackle through their enforcement infrastructure.

B. Adjudicating Power

The algorithmic infrastructure which enables and implements the removal by flagging enforcement strategy does not merely execute the decisions which were made by law enforcement agencies. The system may also learn to further implement this decision on its own. Thus, the governmental enforcement power and adjudication discretion exercised in implementing it converge in the automated content moderation infrastructure.

Determination of judicial and semi-judicial issues regarding such illegal content, depend on the technical implementation in the ML content moderation systems.[103] Consider, for instance, the screening of online content, using digital hash technology, which converts images or videos into a hash (ie a digital signature) in a database of predefined illicit content. Using hashes, the system could identify iterations of the original content, thus enabling the identification of content which is similar, though not identical (resized images, or images with minor colour alterations). In making such determinations, platforms are actually interpreting the law.

By engaging in removal by flagging, the Government, which is entrusted with the public interest, is delegating an interpretation authority to private actors which

[100] MR Gordon and D Volz, 'Russian Disinformation Campaign Aims to Undermine Confidence in Pfizer, Other Covid-19 Vaccines, U.S. Officials Say' *The Wall Street Journal* (7 March 2021).

[101] See Citron (n 9).

[102] C Arun, 'Facebook's Faces' (2021), available at ssrn.com/abstract=3805210 or dx.doi.org/10.2139/ssrn.3805210.

[103] For instance, the definition of threshold of substantial similarity in copyright law or selecting a particular scoring for what counts as obscenity. See YouTube Content ID.

are driven by profits. In executing the governmental requests on their automated systems, the platforms become themselves the intermediaries between the laws (as interpreted by the enforcing agency which issued the removal request) and the citizens whose freedom of expression rights were intended to be safeguarded by law.

As I have argued elsewhere,[104] the different functions performed by digital platforms in content moderation, curating personalised content for targeted advertising and filtering allegedly illicit content, are all embedded in the same system. ML content moderation systems perform these functions through the labelling of users and content, application programming interfaces (API), learning patterns and software. Consequently, decisions on removal of speech, for (public) law enforcement purposes, are driven by the same data, algorithms and optimisation logic that underlie all other profit-maximising functions performed by digital platforms.

C. Amplifying the Power of the Executive in Speech Governance

The removal by flagging enforcement strategy may influence speech governance, beyond the silencing of particular expressions. ML systems amplify the impact of such silencing using filters designed to ensure that flagged content may not be uploaded again ('stay down policy').

Moreover, the recursive nature of the ML content moderation systems may impact not simply current removal decisions, but also future removals. ML enforcement tools typically contain four main features. The first is *labelling* of data as either legitimate or unwarranted. Another feature is a *predictive model*, which predicts whether any given content is illicit based on features learned in the training model. The third is automated decisions with respect to the *action* to be performed, and the performance of that action (eg post, recommend, remove, block, filter). Finally, a key feature of ML content moderation systems is a *feedback loop*. These systems are often capable of continual learning, which relies on a recursive feedback loop. Content identified as illicit is fed back into the model so that it will be detected the next time the system runs.

By systematically issuing removal requests, the Government could shape the speech norms embedded in the ML screening tools. When the Government issues a notice, and content is tagged as hate speech or terrorist propaganda, it may not only be subject to removal, but will likely also be screened by upload filters. Since ML systems are based on learning from historical data (path dependency),

[104] See N Elkin-Koren and M Perel, 'Separation of Functions for AI: Restraining Speech Regulation by Online Platforms' (2019) 24 *Lewis & Clark Law Review* 857.

a decision to classify content as harmful may increase the likelihood that future, similar posts will also be classified as such.

This vulnerability of the platform's content moderation systems to strategic flagging by governments[105] is demonstrated by the Chinese Government's use of YouTube's rules to silence human rights activists.[106] The YouTube channel of activists who collected and published video testimonies from family members of people imprisoned in China's internment camps in Xinjiang was recently removed by YouTube. The channel was removed following mass flagging campaigns allegedly orchestrated by the Chinese and Kazakh Governments, in which their supporters were instructed to flag the videos en masse, forcing YouTube to take the channel down.

Ultimately, the systematic issuing of removal requests may affect the technical definitions of what is considered illicit content, and may tilt the AI-based filters towards governmental perceptions of what counts as illegal. This process is taking place without any judicial review or public oversight. The effect of these digital definitions of speech is intensified by the fact that platforms are multinational companies, which could affect speech norms across nations.

Governmental flagging policy may thus influence what type of expressions will become available to members of the public, at a large scale, and consequently whether the public will be informed of certain information or opinions, and which issues may become the subject of public debates. Consequently, this type of indirect content moderation by governments may carry serious implications for democratic deliberation and free speech.[107]

D. Transparency and Oversight

Removal by flagging fails to offer sufficient oversight. Where governmental requests are not distinct and transparent, there is a smaller chance that they will be challenged by users.

Users whose expression was removed due to a governmental request may not be aware that such removal was the result of governmental action. Consequently, they are less likely to contest such removal to hold government accountable in court. Reporting governmental requests might also be confusing. Presumably, removals are performed under the platform's internal guidelines, so might not necessarily appear as a governmental removal request in the platform transparency report.

[105] This vulnerability to strategic misuse is typical of digital networks which are governed by a mixture of distributed input (of content or flagging – which is information on content) and a central moderating mechanism based on ML. It could be misused by strategic players, such as large corporations, governments or organised online crowds.

[106] E Guo, 'How YouTube's rules are used to silence human rights activists' (*MIT Technology Review*, 24 June 2021), available at www.technologyreview.com/2021/06/24/1027048/youtube-xinjiang-censorship-human-rights-atajurt.

[107] De Gregorio (n 27).

Moreover, even if the original request by the Government is listed as such, further actions taken by the platform to prevent reload of the posting, limit its spread, or any 'stay-down' preventative measures, are not necessarily listed as governmental efforts.

Speakers whose content has been removed are also less likely to even notice the removal. While controversial content posted online can become the subject of public debate, the absence of content is less visible. The removal of expressions as a result of flagging by public authorities is no exception.

Moreover, the lack of clear distinction between public and private actions could significantly weaken the ability of social media users to seek remedy when their content has been removed. The difficulty of distinguishing between the flagging of content by platforms and actions performed by state actors may impair the ability of users to bring a legal action against the Government and hold it accountable for illegal restraints on legitimate speech.[108]

Finally, even when the requests by the Government are treated separately, the embedded effect of flagging through upload filters and ML remains non-transparent, and makes it difficult for the public to ascertain its overall impact.

V. Conclusions

Governmental removal by flagging practices demonstrate the limits of the current constitutional framework in addressing the emerging challenges introduced by public–platform collaboration.

Arguably, platforms are powerful players, which operate quite independently of governments. Yet, platforms are also subordinated to the governmental regulatory powers and susceptible to pressure. Governments, in turn, also rely on platforms for executing law enforcement tasks, and the growing influence of multinational digital platforms over the public sphere suggests that governments might enter such collaborative initiatives with platforms from a disadvantage.

Approaching government–platform collaboration as governmental action, and holding the government accountable, is a first important step. Yet it only captures part of the larger matrix of synergies evolving between governments and platforms. It fails to take into account the transformation of power, and the implications of blurring the distinction between public and private.

The collaboration between governments and social media platforms on law enforcement initiatives is part of the growing synergy between governments and platforms. It requires a fresh thinking on the appropriate measures that could restrain this new performance of power in the digital sphere, and the best way to safeguard civil liberties. Recognising the challenge arising from this synergy is an essential step in ensuring that current regulatory reforms aimed at regulating digital platforms would serve the interests of society as a whole.

[108] See Elkin-Koren et al (n 43).

12

Social Media and State Surveillance in China: The Interplay between Authorities, Businesses and Citizens

YUNER ZHU

I. Introduction

20:55. 20 September 1987. Beijing. A small room populated with a dozen Chinese and German scientists, surrounding a Siemens Model 6670 computer. Its bulky monitor displays a draft email: 'Across the Great Wall, we can reach every corner in the world (Chinese: 越过长城，走向世界)'. This is the first international email sent from China.[1] Delightful and ambitious. It shows the very natural cyber-euphoria about the digital future – the worldwide web can enable everyone to relate to the world regardless of physical, cultural and ideological disparities. The world would collapse into a small village where nothing, not even the Great Wall, can break us apart.

The techno-euphoria was hijacked, however, by rising concern among authorities and pundits. Alarmed by the demise of the Soviet Union in which television and radio broadcasts played vital roles, many top leaders cling to having a China-only information network sealed off from the dangerous temptations of the worldwide web. The Great Firewall was in the making from then on. Unlike the Great Wall, this virtual firewall is quickly evolving, expanding, and gaining technological sophistication. China now has the most far-reaching and most extensive surveillance system in the world.

20:34. 23 July 2011. Wenzhou. Lightning strikes a moving train. The train comes to a halt and is rear-ended by another train. Four cars derail and fall off the viaduct. Four minutes later, a Weibo user issued the first post from the scene. Then came the second post, desperately crying for help.[2] In the following days, complaints

[1] W Zorn, 'How China Was Connected to the International Computer Networks' (2007) 15 *The Amateur Computerist* 36.

[2] M Wines and S LaFraniere, 'In Baring Facts of Train Crash, Blogs Erode China Censorship' *The New York Times* (28 July 2011), available at www.nytimes.com/2011/07/29/world/asia/29china.html.

flood into Weibo,[3] pushing the authorities to apologise and unearth the buried train wreck. This event, inscribed with large-scale civic engagement and the rising of rights consciousness on the Internet, became a milestone in China and affirmed Weibo as a potent platform for citizen activism despite draconian censorship.

As David Shambaugh put it, 'in China today, a daily battle is waged between the state and the society over "what is fit to know"'.[4] The advance of technology not only nourishes the public sphere envisioned by Habermas, but also incubates a surveillance society envisioned in George Orwell's *1984*. The cases above epitomise the constant tug-of-war between the regime's effort to rein on the Internet and civil society's effort to circumvent such control. As a large part of political life is moving online, the Chinese Government has made a wide range of institutional, legislative and developmental adaptations to fit with the digital modernity. This chapter endeavours to shed light on these adaptations and offers an explorative framework for studying digital surveillance in contemporary China. Specifically, it focuses on the surveillance activities taking place on social media, which is the major arena of Internet regulation, and assesses the overall strength and efficacy of the surveillance system.

II. Infrastructure and Legislation of State Surveillance

'Network surveillance' refers to a far-reaching information control regime that curbs, monitors and analyses online activities for the purposes of influencing, managing, directing or protecting people.[5] Publication control and access control are its two significant components. The former suppresses free speech while the latter restricts information access. In the following sections, I will elucidate how existing legislation provides the party-state with the legal bricks to consolidate its publication control and access control. I will also explain how this legislation is put into practice with the support of digital technologies and how ordinary citizens usually react to state surveillance.

A. Publication Control

i. Legislation

The primary policy framework of publication control is set out in three regulatory documents: the Regulation for the Internet Security Protection of Computer

[3] E Wong, 'China's Railway Minister Loses Post in Corruption Inquiry' *New York Times* (13 February 2011), available at www.nytimes.com/2011/02/13/world/asia/13china.html?module=inline; C Buckley, 'China Train Crash Censorship Scorned on Internet' Reuters (11 August 2011), available at www.reuters.com/article/us-china-train-censorship-idUSTRE7700ET20110801.

[4] D Shambaugh, 'China's Propaganda System: Institutions, Processes and Efficacy' (2007) 57 *The China Journal* 25.

[5] D Lyon, *Surveillance Studies: An Overview* (Polity Press, 2007).

Information Network (Security Regulation hereafter);[6] the Regulation for the Internet Information Services (Services Regulation hereafter);[7] and Cybersecurity Law.[8]

The two regulations consistently articulate nine types of unlawful online content:[9]

(a) information that incites the resistance and disruption of the implementation of the constitution, laws, and administrative regulations
(b) information that incites the subversion of the state and overthrow of the socialist system
(c) information that incites secessionism and sabotage of national unity
(d) information that incites hatred and discrimination among races and sabotage racial unity
(e) information that fabricates or distorts facts, spreads rumours, and disrupts social order
(f) information that propagates feudalistic, superstitious, obscene, pornographic, gambling, violence, murder and terror, and that instigates crimes
(g) information that openly insults others or fabricates facts to slander others
(h) information that damages the reputation of state organs
(i) information that violates the constitution, laws, and administrative regulations.

The Cybersecurity Law, as the most important Internet legislation,[10] extends the scope of unlawful content to include another two types:

(j) information that promulgates terrorism and extremism
(k) information that violates other people's privacy or intellectual property.

Such expansion reveals how the central goals of the Chinese leadership have changed as new threats surface over time. In the wake of the 11 September attacks and Uighur separatism's rise, counterterrorism has taken on greater strategic importance in the Chinese Government's political agenda.[11] Authorities have increasingly mentioned cyberspace as an emerging battlefield for the war on terror, which gave rise to the addition of point (j) to the unlawful content list.[12]

[6] Ministry of Public Security, 'Regulation for the Internet Security Protection of Computer Information Network', available at www.gov.cn/gongbao/content/2011/content_1860856.htm.

[7] State Council, 'Regulation for the Internet Information Services', available at www.gov.cn/gongbao/content/2000/content_60531.htm.

[8] National People's Congress Standing Committee, 'Cybersecurity Law', available at www.cac.gov.cn/2016-11/07/c_1119867116.htm.

[9] A new version of Information Service has been drafted and is still under revision with the comments received during the public consultation. In the new version, more regulations are rolled out targeting misinformation, Internet fraud, and online rumour, especially those related to natural disaster, pandemic, construction safety, food safety and the financial market.

[10] J Lee, 'Hacking into China's Cybersecurity Law' (2018) 53 *Wake Forest Law Review* 57.

[11] C Chung, 'China's 'War on Terror': September 11 and Uighur Separatism' (2002) 81 *Foreign Affairs* 8, available at www.jstor.org/stable/20033235.

[12] X Zang, 'The Second Conference on Combating Online Terrorism Is Held in Beijing Under the Framework of Global Anti-Terrorism Forum (Quanqiu Fankong Luntan Kuangjia Xia Dier Ci Daji

Besides, China has come under tremendous international pressure over the rampant piracy of intellectual property (IP) inside the domestic market.[13] In response to this, from 1982 onwards, a stack of IP protection legislation has been enacted, from trademarks to patents to copyright protection.[14] However, there was no legislation relating to online IP, which is much more intractable and intangible than its offline counterpart, until the Cybersecurity Law. Cybersecurity Law takes the first step towards criminalising IP violation and Internet terrorism.

That being said, the 11 unlawful content types are not being equally censored on social media. Some unlawful content types are subjected to more stringent censorship than others. To shed light on this, I will summarise the machinery of publication control and review some key empirical studies that reverse-engineer censorship apparatus in the next section.

ii. Machinery

In compliance with the regulations, all ISPs, from small discussion forums to mainstream social media platforms, have deployed censorship apparatuses on their platforms to scan the posts and prohibit unlawful content from circulating. Most ISPs have adopted a two-step publication control scheme, censoring the content before and after its publication.

According to King, Pan, and Roberts,[15] 66 per cent of websites have implemented pre-publication censorship. Pre-publication censorship checks submissions and prohibits sensitive content. The keyword-filtering algorithms first scan each submission for any blacklisted keywords, topics, images and hyperlinks.[16] For example, *Sina Weibo* (Figure 12.1) prohibits any post from explicitly

Wangluo Kongbu Zhuyi Yantao Hui Zai Jing Juxing)' Xinhua News Agency (21 October 2016), available at www.cac.gov.cn/2016-10/21/c_1119764953.htm; C Zhao, 'Cyberspace Has Become New Battlefield for International Counter-Terrorism Activities (Wangluo Kongjian Yi Chengwei Fankong Xin Zhendi)' *Guangming Daily* (14 June 2017), available at theory.people.com.cn/n1/2017/0614/c40531-29337673.html.

[13] 'China, U.S. Trade Barbs over WTO Piracy Case' Reuters (20 March 2009), available at www.reuters.com/article/us-china-usa-wto-idUSTRE52J3T920090320; WTO, 'China – Measures Affecting Trading Rights and Distribution Services for Certain Publications and Audiovisual Entertainment Products' (2009), available at www.wto.org/english/tratop_e/dispu_e/363r_e.pdf; L Liu and Q Yu, 'IPR Disputes Fuelled by Auto Makers' *China Daily* (6 September 2004), available at www.chinadaily.com.cn/english/doc/2004-09/06/content_371939.htm.

[14] D Bosworth and D Yang, 'Intellectual Property Law, Technology Flow and Licensing Opportunities in the People's Republic of China' (2000) 9 *International Business Review* 453, available at www.sciencedirect.com/science/article/pii/S0969593100000135.

[15] G King, J Pan and ME Roberts, 'Reverse-Engineering Censorship in China: Randomized Experimentation and Participant Observation' (2014) 345 *Science* 1.

[16] ibid; G King, J Pan and ME Roberts, 'How Censorship in China Allows Government Criticism but Silences Collective Expression' (2013) 107 *American Political Science Review* 326; T Zhu et al, 'The Velocity of Censorship: High-Fidelity Detection of Microblog Post Deletions', Proceedings of the 22nd USENIX Security Symposium (2013).

mentioning 'Liu Xiaobo (刘晓波)' or 'Gui Minhai (桂民海)', two prominent dissenters' names, regardless of what the post actually says ('Publication Prohibited' in the decision tree). More recently, automatic filtering systems have been upgraded to inspect images and videos. On the night Liu Xiaobo passed away, submissions containing candle emoji or photos were banned before publication to silence tributes.[17]

After passing the initial screening, some posts will be held for manual review if the algorithm finds them ambiguous and cannot correctly decode the contents. According to King, Pan and Roberts,[18] as many as 63 per cent of submissions withheld for manual review never appear online as intended. Even after the publication, posts can still be removed at any time by censors who patrol the platform for unlawful content.[19] According to Zhu et al[20] and King, Pan and Roberts,[21] post-publication censorship usually occurs within 24 hours after publication. The censorship apparatus, in this sense, is highly effective and responsive.

Figure 12.1 Decision tree of censorship on Sina Weibo

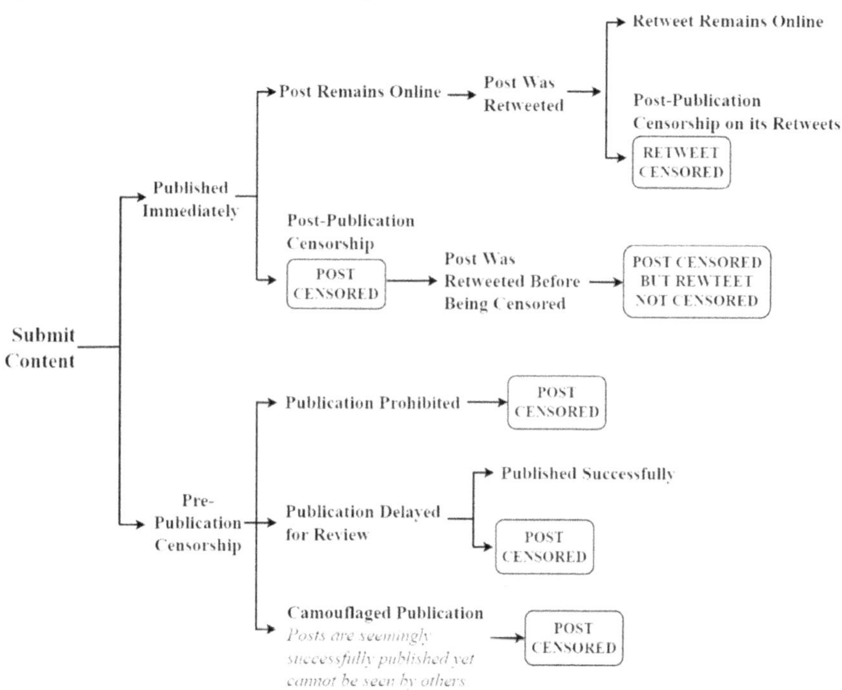

Generally speaking, keywords-based pre-publication screening has been largely automated whereas post-publication censorship still relies on human expertise, knowledge and judgement. So, in order to maintain the efficiency of censorship apparatus, ISPs have invested heavily, not only in their technological infrastructure but also in manpower. For example, ByteDance – the parent company of TikTok, Douyin and Jinri Toutiao – has established seven content auditing centres across China, amassing more than 20,000 censors to scrutinise content around the clock.[22]

In addition to the employed in-house censors, an increasing number of volunteer users are recruited into censorship teams to help filter out, identify, and evaluate suspected unlawful content. They are like an autonomous 'militia' raised from the public to supplement the regular and formally hired 'army' of in-house censors. On Sina Weibo, a total of 13,808 users are organised to form a community committee ('社区委员会委员') and up to 2,000 users are working as Weibo supervisors ('微博监督员').[23] Supervisors file reports against a great many possibly unlawful posts and some reports are dispatched to community committees who would cast their votes like in a judiciary to determine whether the alleged problems are in violation of relevant regulations. The posts that are labelled as unlawful by community committees' majority votes will be sent to in-house censors to decide whether the posts should be removed, banned from distribution, or hidden from the public. So, although in-house censors are the only actors who have the real power to delete posts, the censorship militia members can screen potentially objectionable content for in-house censors and the reports filed by censorship militia members are given priority over reports by ordinary users.

Sina Weibo has set a very high bar for this censorship militia. It requires Weibo supervisors to report at least 500 posts every month at an accuracy rate over 98 per cent, and requires committees to amass over 800 valid votes for each case within the 24 hours after the case is reported. Supervisors who fail to meet this minimum target will be disqualified and committee decisions that do not gather enough votes will be declared invalid. According to an ex-supervisor's account, an

[17] Agence France-Presse, 'China Censors "RIP" and Scrubs Emoji Tributes to Nobel Winner Liu Xiaobo' *Hong Kong Free Press* (14 July 2017), available at hongkongfp.com/2017/07/14/china-censors-rip-scrubs-emoji-tributes-nobel-winner-liu-xiaobo.

[18] King, Pan and Roberts, 'Reverse-Engineering Censorship in China' (2014).

[19] Y Lu, 'A Censor's Confession: Moderator Team Is What Define the Future of Internet' *The Initium* (14 March 2019), available at theinitium.com/article/20190314-mainland-internet-censors; Zhu et al, 'The Velocity of Censorship' (2013).

[20] Zhu et al (n 16).

[21] King, Pan and Roberts, 'How Censorship in China Allows Government Criticism' (2013).

[22] W Wang, 'Jinan: A Rising Capital of Internet Censorship' *Southern Weekly* (19 April 2019); Agence France-Presse, 'Top China News App Jinri Toutiao Self-Criticises after Government Crackdown' *Hong Kong Free Press* (11 April 2018), available at www.hongkongfp.com/2018/04/11/top-china-news-app-jinri-toutiao-self-criticises-government-crackdown; Lu, 'A Censor's Confession' (2019).

[23] O Lam, 'China's Sina Weibo Hires 1,000 Supervisors to Censor "Harmful Content" – Including Women's Legs' *Hong Kong Free Press* (15 October 2017); O Lam, 'Chinese Netizens Identify the Weibo Supervisor System as a Source of Arbitrary Censorship' *Global Voices* (2 September 2021).

average supervisor needs to spend about two hours a day on this work; a supervisor with three years' experience will take a few dozen minutes a day to complete their assigned work.[24]

To compensate for their hard work, Sina Weibo provides generous material rewards. The supervisor with the most monthly complaints will be rewarded with a RMB 5,000 bonus and the top 20 awardees will receive RMB 1,000–4,000. The supervisors who have fulfilled the minimum requirement of 500 reports per month but failed to make it into the top 20 will still be rewarded with a moderate bonus of RMB 200–1,000. Sina Weibo spent more than RMB 187 million on its bonuses for supervisors in 2017. Its investment does pay off. This 'militia' group is alleged to effectively identify and remove as many as 74 million unlawful posts at an extremely high accuracy rate (higher than 90 per cent in 2020), significantly enhancing the capacity of censorship apparatus.[25]

The censorship militia is the product of ISPs' experiments to coopt grassroots forces into the censorship system by nurturing an autonomous semi-judicial community to which ISPs can outsource some moderation tasks. This bold trial became a great success. Consequently, the grassroots militia is now a stable and potent extension of the in-house censorship team. They have been contributing to the publication control efficacy and give censorship apparatus a hybrid form integrating centralised and decentralised moderations at the same time.

iii. Target of Censorship

A clear division of labour can be observed between in-house censors and grassroots censorship militia. The in-house censors focus more on removing political harmful content ((a), (b), (c), (e), (h), (i) and (j) in the unlawful content list) while the grassroots militia is responsible for monitoring and reporting non-political harmful content. ISPs outsource fewer politicised tasks to grassroots censors, preferring to keep those in-house.

On Sina Weibo, voluntary supervisors focus more on removing pornographic content ((f) in the unlawful content list). It is only in late May 2019 that a small number of Weibo supervisors were allowed to participate in screening political harmful information. Even after that, Weibo supervisors still file many more reports on pornographic material than political content. In August 2021, for example, the ratio of reports on pornographic material to political harmful information was about 24:1.

On the other hand, community committees focus more on solving interpersonal conflicts between users. They give verdicts on a wide range of interpersonal conflicts, such as gender discrimination, regional discrimination, privacy-violation,

[24] D Xu, 'Working as a Weibo Supervisor: Report 0.2 Million Pornographic Posts per Month to Get Rewarded 4 IPhones and 2 IPads' *Time Weekly* (31 August 2021).

[25] L Zhuo, '2000 Weibo Supervisors: Works and Benefits' *The Initium* (2021).

IP-infringement, verbal attacks and slander ((d), (g) and (k) in the list). According to their monthly report, community committees cast votes relating to 619 controversial posts in July 2021, of which 43 per cent related to regional discrimination, 28.6 per cent to gender discrimination, and 10.2 per cent to verbal attacks.

However, community committees and Weibo supervisors are rarely involved in purging political harmful content. Furthermore, given the fact that several million allegedly pornographic posts are removed by Weibo supervisors each month and only a few hundred posts in relation to interpersonal conflicts are removed by community committees, the censorship on pornographic information is arguably much more stringent than those on interpersonal conflicts. This is also in agreement with what King, Pan and Roberts[26] have found – pornography is among the most censored topics on social media.

As for the political harmful content ((a), (b), (c), (e), (h), (i) and (j) in the unlawful content list), most deletions are executed by in-house censors following centralised moderation guidelines issued and updated every day by authorities. These can be further classified into two categories: content that is critical of governments and top leaders ((h) in the list); and content that mobilises resistant collective actions against governments.[27] Alongside this classification rise two contrasting theories about censorship, namely the state critique theory and the collective action theory. The first asserts the posts criticising government is the overarching target of censorship, while the second assumes suppressing prospective collective action is the foremost goal of censorship.

According to the legislation mentioned above, the state critique content includes only type (h) in the unlawful content list, whereas the latter category covers type (a), (b), (c) and (j). Based on the face value of legislation, the collective action information attracts more attention from authorities, takes up more space, and is elaborated with more detail than state critique information. The second theory is supported in this regard.

In addition, many scholars have conducted empirical research to physically measure the magnitudes of censorship in different topic areas. Zhu et al (2013)[28] find that users who show more interest in discussing state power are subjected to more censorship than politically apathetic ones. Bamman et al (2012)[29] unveil a list of sensitive keywords, including 'Fang Binxing', 'Ministry of Truth', 'Fa Lungong', 'communist bandit', 'Jiang Zeming' and 'Ai Weiwei'. Most sensitive keywords are related to state critique. Fu et al (2013)[30] detail another list of sensitive keywords, most of which are related to contentious political events that might

[26] King, Pan and Roberts (n 16).

[27] ibid; King, Pan and Roberts (n 15).

[28] Zhu et al (n 16).

[29] D Bamman, B O'Connor and N Smith, 'Censorship and Deletion Practices in Chinese Social Media' (2012) 17 *First Monday* 234, available at www.uic.edu/htbin/cgiwrap/bin/ojs/index.php/fm/article/view/3943.

[30] K Fu, C Chan and M Chau, 'Assessing Censorship on Microblogs in China' (2013) 17 *IEEE Internet Computing* 2, available at www.computer.org/csdl/mags/ic/2013/03/mic2013030042.html.

carry unfavourable opinions of the Government, such as the Bo Xilai scandal, human rights lawyer event, one-child policy, and two meetings. This group of studies has substantiated that the posts criticising the party-state are subjected to non-negligible censorship on social media, supporting rather than disputing the state critique theory.

Nevertheless, drawing on 3,674,698 posts from 1,382 websites about 85 topics, King, Pan, and Roberts[31] reveal that the discussions around collective action suffer more censorship than those criticising government, policies and news. They also find that the valence of discussion, be it pro-government or anti-government, does not affect the censorship. So, they argue that the main goal of censorship is to reduce the probability of collective action rather than suppress the criticism of the Government. In a 2014 paper based on an online experiment reviewing 100 Chinese websites, they reaffirm the posts with collective action potentials are subjected to more censorship than the posts criticising governments.[32]

The available evidence up to now has not been strong or consistent enough to derive a decisive conclusion as to whether state critique theory is more real and more robust than collective action theory, or vice versa. Both have been supported by substantive yet inconclusive evidence. However, it is safe to say that, in relation to harmful political content, both state critique and collective action content is subjected to significant censorship, although the magnitude of censorship will change with the times and the social conditions.

B. Access Control

With the help of effective censorship infrastructure and a sizeable group of human censors, the regime has a strong grip on the online communications within its jurisdiction. Yet, since the Internet is borderless by nature, people can still access and consume unlawful content published beyond the regime's jurisdiction. To close this loophole in the surveillance system, an intangible wall is erected. Licences and the Great Firewall are two prominent bricks in this wall. Licences block some ISPs from entering the Chinese information marketplace, while the Great Firewall prohibits Chinese people from accessing some overseas content.

i. Licence

According to the Service Regulation, non-commercial ISPs need to register with authorities, and commercial ISPs need to be licensed with authorities (Article 4). All organisations must seek approval from authorities for their engagement in Internet publishing activities.

[31] King, Pan and Roberts (n 15); King, Pan and Roberts (n 16).
[32] King, Pan and Roberts (n 15).

News services, as politically sensitive information services, are subject to more stringent control. In September 2005, the State Council Information Office and the Ministry of Information Industry (currently known as the Ministry of Industry and Information Technology (MIIT)), jointly issued the Regulation for the Internet News Service (News Regulation hereafter),[33] strictly stipulating that only state-owned news institutions were eligible for online political news production (Article 7 (2005); Articles 6 and 8 (2017)). Private companies can only provide a news circulation service and should never produce their original political news (Article 8 (2005); Article 6 (2017)). Foreign companies and Sino-foreign joint ventures are banned from providing any news services (Article 9 (2005); Article 7 (2017)) and should not collaborate with licensed institutions without approval from the State Council Information Office.

Taken together, this regulation stipulates that only official news institutions can produce political news; only Chinese institutions can circulate news; no foreign companies are allowed to engage in news service without approval from the central Government.

All online news providers are required to obtain the Online News Service Licence (互联网新闻信息服务许可证). Per the News Regulation, the news service licence clearly specifies whether the institution is licensed to produce or circulate news. In journalistic jargon, the licence for news production is the Type A Licence (A类牌照) and the licence for news circulation is the Type B Licence (B类牌照).

Licensing/registration control has profoundly reshaped the Chinese online media landscape. Only a small fraction of alternative news media[34] have been able to obtain licences, leaving the majority under constant scrutiny and prolonged risks of punishment.

In 2017, Jinri Toutiao (the most popular news application in China, owned by ByteDance with more than 200 million monthly active users and more than five million followers on Sina Weibo), Phoenix News, and Pear Video, were summoned by the Cyberspace Administrative Office[35] because of their unlicensed news services. After the overhaul, Jinri Toutiao removed its community news

[33] State Council Information Office and Ministry of Information Industry, 'Regulation for the Internet News Service', available at www.gov.cn/gongbao/content/2006/content_375814.htm.

[34] Alternative media can be defined as a residual category of media that do not belong to established mainstream media. In China, this term is usually used to refer to media that are not owned by the state and run by the party. It entails a vague connotation of media being relatively independent and autonomous operating via social media accounts, websites or mobile applications.

[35] Beijing Cyberspace Administrative Office, 'Beijing Cyberspace Administrative Office Surmmons Principals of Jinri Toutiao and Phoenix News Application (Beijing Wangxinban Yuetan Jinri Toutiao and Fenghuang Xinwen Shouji Kehuduan Fuze Ren)' Xinhua Net (29 December 2017); Y Zhang, 'Cyberspace Administrative Office Forces Pear Video to Overhaul It News Business As It Does Not Obtain the Required License (Li Shipin Bei Wangxinban Deng Bumen Zeling Quanmian Zhenggai Wei Qude Xiangguan Fuwu Zizhi)' China National Radio Net (5 February 2017), available at china.cnr.cn/ygxw/20170205/t20170205_523557970.shtml.

channel, closed 36 self-media accounts, and opened a new channel – New Era Channel[36] – to promote the official ideology proposed by President Xi. After this rearrangement, Jinri Toutiao successfully obtained the Type B Licence in 2019. On the other hand, Phoenix News, though not yet licensed, has the financial strength to recover quickly after every punishment and continues to operate its news service as usual.

However, alternative media and self-media have been subject to more heavy-handed punishments. A prominent example is Q Daily (好奇心日报), which was well-known for high-quality reports. It was forced to suspend its service for some months in 2018 and 2019 because of its lack of a licence.[37] Unlike Phoenix News, Q Daily did not have financial strength to survive the suspension and was finally dissolved in 2020. The punishment imposed on self-media is even harsher,[38] usually leading to permanent closure. Governments at different levels launched campaigns iteratively to wipe out unlicensed self-media accounts on social media. The far-reaching crackdown in 2019, for example, has resulted in a closure of 9,800 self-media accounts.[39] Major social media platforms were required to adopt regulatory measures to prohibit the owners of these self-media accounts from creating new accounts.[40] WeChat and Weibo sent 'mild' alerts to self-media accounts, warning them that if they produce content in relation to political, economic, military and diplomatic topics, they will violate laws and regulations and face punishment.

[36] Y Xu, 'Jinri Toutiao to Close Community News Channel and Set New Era Channel as Default (Jinri Toutiao Pingtai Xuanbu Guanbi Shehui Pindao Jiang Xin Shidai Pindao Shezhi Wei Moren Pindao)' *The Paper* (31 December 2017), available at www.thepaper.cn/newsDetail_forward_1930227.

[37] P Shen and S Yang, 'Q Daily to Stop Updating for Three Months Netizens Sigh: Media Are Only Allowed to Be the Party's Megaphone (Haoqixin Ribao Tingzhi Gengxin Sange Yue Wangmin Tan: Meiti Zhineng Zuo Chuanshengtong)' Central News Agency (28 May 2019), available at www.cna.com.tw/news/acn/201905280143.aspx; 'Q Daily Will Stop Updating All Platforms for One Month, Pledging to Face the Problem and Overhaul the Business Thoroughly' Sina Tech (3 August 2018), available at tech.sina.com.cn/i/2018-08-03/doc-ihhehtqh4353630.shtml.

[38] Saqilatu, 'Four WeChat Public Account Are Punished for Violating Internet Rules in Baotou. Two Are Permanently Closed! (Dong Zhen Ge Le! Baotou Sige Weixin Gongzhong Hao Weigui Bei Chuli, Liangge Yongjiu Fenghao)' *Inner Mongolia Daily* (28 November 2017), available at www.sohu.com/a/207175174_99958604; Lvliang Cyberspace Administrative Office, 'Internet Information Ecology Management: Kan Lvliang and Da Mei Lvliang Two WeChat Public Accounts Are Summoned' Yellow River News Net (7 March 2020), available at www.sohu.com/a/378228166_253235; Cyberspace Administration Office, 'Beijing Cyberspace Administrative Office Summons the Principals of Phoenix News Under the Guidance of Central Cyberspace Administrative Office (Guojia Wangxinban Zhidao Beijing Wangxinban Yeutan Fenghuang Wang Fuze Ren)' Chinese Internet Information Net (15 February 2020), available at www.cac.gov.cn/2020-02/15/c_1583303419227448.htm; Shangluo Cyberspace Administrative Office, 'Shangluo's Cyberspace Administrative Office Summons Four WeChat Public Accounts for Violating Internet Rules (Shangluo Shi Wangxinban Yifa Yuetan Sijia Weixin Gongzhong Hao)' Chinese Internet Information Net (21 January 2018), available at www.cac.gov.cn/2018-01/21/c_1122288520.htm.

[39] '"Combination Blow" Rectifies Self-Media Chaos' (Cyberspace Administration of China, 2019), available at www.cac.gov.cn/2019-03/20/c_1124259403.htm.

[40] ibid.

Licensing hangs like the sword of Damocles over the heads of all news professionals and organisations. Licences are a scarce resource monopolised by the Government and are only granted to those endorsed by the authorities. Licensing control is not consistently and proportionately exercised. Authorities never purge unqualified media entirely, but they instead launch sporadic inspections, taking down some while ignoring the others. The uncertainty amplifies the power. Besides, as administrative ligation is rare anywhere in China and petition is usually preferred over litigation,[41] authorities are seldom questioned to clarify what is accepted and what is not, why some accounts can obtain licences and others cannot, and why some unlicensed outlets are closed down permanently while others can keep operating as usual. Licence, as well as the uncertainty in the licensing procedure, enables asymmetric power, which gives surveillance its omnipresent form and can solicit loyalty in a more effective way.

ii. The Great Firewall

While the service licence blocks ISPs from entering the Chinese marketplace, the Great Firewall blocks ordinary citizens from freely entering overseas cyberspace. The Great Firewall is the nickname of China's nationwide firewall system that blocks China-based IPs from accessing the overseas Internet content that the authorities deem harmful or objectional to the state.[42] It is the pillar of China's surveillance system, laying the foundation for effective authoritarian control over Internet content.

a. Hierarchical Structure of the Internet

The Internet works as a hierarchy of interconnected networks of computers (Figure 12.2). Personal computers are clustered in the local area networks (LANs); the discrete LANs within the same city are connected to metropolitan area networks (MANs); then the discrete WANs in the same country are connected to nationwide backbone networks (NBNs); finally, only a few NBNs are granted the rights to open international gateways ('国际出入口信道' in Chinese) which work as aggregation points for Internet traffic going in and out of the country.

This hierarchical structure makes top-down control much easier. The gateways are like the online checkpoints inspecting the identities of 'cyber-travellers' who intend to cross the border. To block people's access to overseas websites, the state only needs to control gateways and ensure all backbone network operators are compliant with authoritative commands. Given that telecommunication is fully monopolised by state organs in China, controlling international gateways is painless for Chinese authorities.

[41] KJ O'Brien and L Li, 'Suing the Local State: Administrative Litigation in Rural China' (2004) 51 *The China Journal* 75.

[42] J Lee, 'Great Firewall', *The SAGE Encyclopedia of the Internet* (SAGE, 2018).

Figure 12.2 The hierarchical structure of the Internet. NBNs work at the top level, handling MAN to MAN transmissions and cross-border transmissions

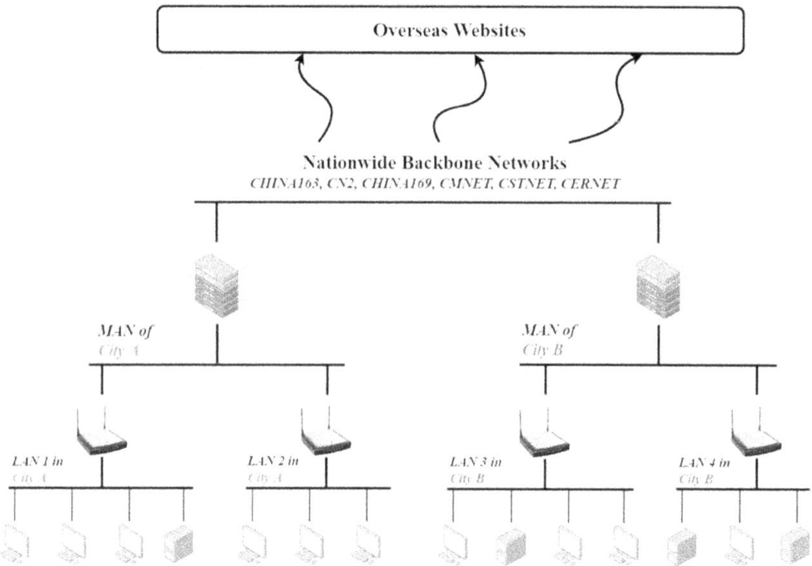

b. Legislation

Several laws and regulations contribute to legalising the functioning of the Great Firewall and outlawing the firewall-escaping actions.

According to Interim Provisions of the International Internet Connection of Computer Information Network (Interim Provisions hereafter),[43] computers can only be connected to the international Internet through gateways in the backbone networks (Article 6). It also stipulates that no unlicensed organisations or individuals should set up their own international gateways or use unapproved international gateways set up by others. Articles 8 and 10 further mandate that people can only use the licensed network services to reach the international Internet. Taken together, consumers can only rely on the big three operators to pass through the checkpoints to view overseas information. The use of unlicensed virtual private networks (VPNs) as well as the use of other unlicensed network services is outlawed. For anyone who violates these provisions, the public security bureaus will first cut off their Internet connection, warn them not to repeat the misconduct, and fine them up to RMB 15,000 (Article 14).

The Cybersecurity Law further consolidates this regulation by expanding the scope of criminality to include helping others escape the Great Firewall. Articles 27, 46 and 63 mandate that no one should provide technical support, promotion or

[43] State Council, 'Interim Provisions of the International Internet Connection of Computer Information Network', available at www.gov.cn/gongbao/content/2011/content_1860856.htm.

financial support to activities jeopardising cybersecurity. Dodging firewalls is also considered to be a jeopardising action.

However, it is only recently that these regulations have been used to punish firewall-dodging. In 2020, three persons were detained for three days for publishing tutorial articles on online forums introducing available VPNs.[44] Another seven persons were detained for two to three days for sharing or selling VPNs in interpersonal chats on WeChat.[45] Because the punishments are relatively mild, they do not substantially curb the wide use of VPNs.

C. Individual Responses to State Surveillance

Although the network surveillance regime, as introduced above, has put an extremely large number of people under close inspection through either publication control, access control or information monitoring means, it also leaves considerable leeway for tech-savvy individuals to evade such control.

Disobedient netizens can creatively devise many jargons of blacklisted keywords to circumvent censorship. 4 June is often referred to as 'number event' and the Red-Yellow-Blue nursery school suspected of abusing children is referred to as 'three colours'. Sensitive articles have been translated into different languages, or used emojis, morse code and local dialects during the early days of COVID-19 pandemic. Given that 67 per cent of the Chinese population has access to the Internet, creating more than 4.6 million websites,[46] it is impractical to scan every piece of information in full, and impossible to exhaust all possible variants of blacklisted keywords.

However, the fact that the surveillance system is permeable does not mean everyone will be motivated to permeate it. In a recent article, Margaret Roberts[47] enumerates three essential components of censorship resilience: awareness of censorship; incentives to seek out information; and resources to circumvent censorship. Echoing the first point, Pan and Siegel[48] assert that awareness of censorship is positively associated with an increase in incentives to seek out information – a type of backfire effect that is sometimes referred to as the 'gateway effect'. They find that Saudi Arabs' crackdowns on opposition leaders not only boost the engagement level of leaders' old followers but also attract new followers, who began interacting

[44] Case numbers: 芜公（定）决字〔2020〕第0371号，开公（湘）决字〔2020〕第0500号，怀鹤公（团结）决字〔2020〕第0361号.

[45] Case numbers: 京公（四）行罚决字〔2020〕199号，苍公(龙)行罚决字〔2020〕00387号，衢衢公(大)行罚决字〔2019〕51188号，铜公（彭）行罚决字〔2019〕1419号，贾公（夏）行罚决字〔2019〕410号，海公（城）行罚决字〔2019〕1517号，皋公（网）行罚决字〔2019〕1486号.

[46] CNNIC, 'Forty-Sixth Statistical Report on Internet Development in China' (2020), available at cnnic.com.cn/IDR/ReportDownloads/202012/P020201201530023411644.pdf.

[47] ME Roberts, 'Resilience to Online Censorship' (2020) 23 *Annual Review of Political Science* 22.1.

[48] J Pan and Siegel, 'How Saudi Crackdowns Fail to Silence Online Dissent' (2020) 114 *American Political Science Review* 109.

with the imprisoned leaders or only run searches for them after the crackdown. In China's context, Hobbs and Roberts[49] also reveal that an awareness of censorship will motivate citizens to acquire access to blocked information.[50] They observe that the sudden block of Instagram in China led those seeking entertainment to download not only VPNs but also other social networking applications, such as Twitter and Facebook, where they were very likely to be exposed to the political information blocked by authorities. Similarly, from an experiment involving 150 Chinese university students, Roberts[51] finds that Chinese censorship triggered further interest in consuming censored topics. Steinert-Threlkeld, Hobbs, Chang and Roberts[52] show how China's coronavirus crisis spurs firewall-escaping behaviours to access international news. Linking the censorship awareness to deteriorated trust in government, Stan Wong and Liang[53] found that people are not willing to seek assistance from the Government after experiencing censorship as censorship signals the Government's inability to address the issue being censored.

Drawing on the discussion around the 2019 Hong Kong protests on Weibo, Zhu and Fu[54] investigated the effects of censorship on individual expression on social media. They formulated four layers of censorship exposure where people can encounter it. It shows that people tend to stay silent when censorship in the global environment is intensive. In contrast, they tend to 'rebel' against censorship by voicing their opinions when they experience censorship themselves or witness censorship occurring to their friends or reference persons. The community also acts as a buffer to mitigate the influence of censorship on individuals. Outspoken crowds shield individuals from the fear of punishment, and outspoken friends could mitigate individuals' anger against censorship, liberating individuals from overconcern with censorship and empowering them to act for themselves.

Extant literature has proved that awareness of censorship, especially censorship against oneself or one's social media contacts, could backfire by raising interest in off-limits information, increasing distrust in government, and boosting motivation for expression. On the other hand, censorship reduces the willingness of expression of individuals who are politically apathetic or have no personal connections with people who get censored. Therefore, the latter group of individuals (apolitical and distant to the censorship sites) is more vulnerable to the chilling

[49] WR Hobbs and ME Roberts, 'How Sudden Censorship Can Increase Access to Information' (2018) 112 *American Political Science Review* 621.

[50] Pan and Siegel (n 48).

[51] ME Roberts, 'Reactions to Experience with Censorship', *Censored: Distraction and Diversion Inside China's Great Firewall* (Pri, 2018).

[52] ZC Steinert-Threlkeld et al, 'Crisis Is a Gateway to Censored Information: The Case of Coronavirus in China' (2020), available at preprints.apsanet.org/engage/apsa/article-details/5f76b5a3e9593d0018ff035e.

[53] SH Wong and J Liang, 'Dubious until Officially Censored: Effects of Online Censorship Exposure on Viewers' Attitudes in Authoritarian Regimes' (2021) 00 *Journal of Information Technology & Politics* 1, available at doi.org/10.1080/19331681.2021.1879343.

[54] Y Zhu and K Fu, 'Speaking up or Staying Silent? Examining the Influences of Censorship and Behavioral Contagion on Opinion (Non-) Expression in China' (2020) 23 *New Media & Society* 3634.

effects of censorship and more likely to stay silent on the issues that are subjected to the most scrutiny by censors.

III. Conclusions

As a cyber superpower with the largest online population, and five of the top ten Internet companies in the world, China's Internet policy has considerable influence on not only Chinese people but also other jurisdictions.[55] This chapter briefly summarises the technological, legislative and administrative efforts by Chinese authorities to uphold its surveillance system. The regime has been actively leveraging digital technology and coopting grassroots netizens to advance its surveillance apparatus. At the same time, a set of regulations to legalise the operation of surveillance apparatus has been rolled out: some define what constitutes unlawful content; some ban unlicensed news services; and some outlaw wall-escaping behaviours. The development of legislation has a consistent politico-economic theme: to strengthen authoritarian control over political messages, and to offer more protections over individuals' economic rights on the Internet.

The protections for individuals' commercial rights have been enhanced in recent years. For example, in compliance with the Cybersecurity Law, the major ISPs like Sina Weibo have implemented complaint-taking channels to solve conflicts in relation to privacy and intellectual property infringements. However, the legislation does not offer equivalent protections against government actions. Although several million posts labelled as politically harmful information on Sina Weibo are removed every month, only in a few instances are people granted the right to appeal or rebut the platform's decision. Most of time, the in-house censors can almost arbitrarily remove any content in the name of prohibiting politically harmful content without justification. To fully translate constitutional principles in light of digital modernity, more effort is required to promote legislation and institutions that safeguard citizens' rights to free speech and the balance among all actors involved, including the public agencies, ISPs and individual users.

At the same time, the chapter also reflects on how state surveillance and people are reacting to each other. Surveillance is the elephant in the room. It is omnipresent, restricting people's utterances and banning public access to some foreign websites. Yet, it is also permeable, leaving room for people to circumvent it as long as they have the time and resources. As the evidence shows, the influence of censorship is asymmetric. It can effectively tame apolitical individuals while having little and even reverse influence on people who are attentive to the sensitive issues and have personal contacts with people who get censored.

[55] J Pan, 'How Market Dynamics of Domestic and Foreign Social Media Firms Shape Strategies of Internet Censorship' (2017) 64 *Problems of Post-Communism* 167, available at doi.org/10.1080/10758216.2016.1181525; MC Eades, 'China's Newest Export: Internet Censorship' US News and World Report (30 January 2014).

After living with surveillance for a long time, most Chinese people have internalised its existence and can innately gauge what is likely to be censored.[56] Nevertheless, the calculation does not necessarily result in submission or compliance. A substantial group of people are resilient in the face of censorship and are willing to try various ways to pass their messages through the system and get their voices heard. Surveillance and counter-surveillance measures are evolving together, which drives an arms race between the state organs and disobedient civil society. This tug-of-war is still ongoing.

[56] J DeLisle, A Goldstein and G Yang, 'The Internet, Social Media, and a Changing China' in J DeLisle, A Goldstein and G Yang (eds), *The Internet, Social Media, and a Changing China* (University of Pennsylvania Press, 2016); SY Lee, 'Surviving Online Censorship in China: Three Satirical Tactics and Their Impact' (2016) 228 *China Quarterly* 1061; RE Stern and J Hassid, 'Amplifying Silence: Uncertainty and Control Parables in Contemporary China' (2012) 45 *Comparative Political Studies* 1230; G Wacker, 'The Internet and Censorship in China' in CR Hughes and G Wacker (eds), *China and the Internet: Politics of the digital leap forward* (Routledge, 2003).

13

The Perks of Co-Regulation: An Institutional Arrangement for Social Media Regulation?

CLARA IGLESIAS KELLER*

I. Introduction

To a great extent, the debate around constitutionalising social media boils down to choosing the right strategies to ensure efficient and legitimate enforcement of fundamental rights online. Since inherent intermediation hindered traditional means of law enforcement and enabled private ordering, self-regulation presented itself, at first, as the default intervention model for the online environment – either by rapid institutional choices,[1] or by governmental 'paralysis by analysis'.[2]

While the shortcomings of this benchmark are apparent,[3] state-centred alternatives have often proved inadequate. The limitations of the tools used by liberal democracies to govern the Internet have been acknowledged by the literature,[4] as their duties towards expression and communication liberties clash with traditional mechanisms for exerting direct control over digital technologies.[5] Statutory legislation and administrative measures have fostered a series of mechanisms that have their legitimacy questioned (for disproportionally restricting civil liberties) or prove inefficient (as mechanisms implemented are not able to address the harms

* For the comments and conversations that helped me make sense of the ideas in this chapter, I would like to thank Stephan Dreyer, Amélie Heldt, Blayne Haggart, Robert Gorwa, the POLDI Pogo Kolloquium and the authors in this volume for their feedback during our May 2021 Conference, 'Constitutionalising Social Media'. I also thank Alexander Reik for the support with literature research and Leonard Kamps for proofreading the manuscript.

[1] D Tambini, D L and CT Marsden, *Codifying Cyberspace: Communications Self-Regulation in the Age of Internet Convergence* (Routledge, 2008).

[2] N Cortez, 'Regulating Disruptive Innovation' (2014) 29 *Berkeley Technology Law Journal* 175, 176.

[3] R Mansell and WE Steinmueller, *Advanced Introduction to Platform Economics* (Edward Elgar, Publishing 2020) 75–76.

[4] B Wagner, 'Governing Internet Expression: How Public and Private Regulation Shape Expression Governance' (2013) 10 *Journal of Information Technology & Politics* 389, 390.

[5] Tambini, Leonardi and Marsden, *Codifying Cyberspace* (2008).

that inspired their implementation). These policies range from Internet shutdowns to mandated filtering and user-targeted criminal responsibility. Beyond the risks to democracy posed by these strategies, they have also postponed debates about innovative regulatory strategies that could apply to digital platforms. In turn, judicial review is both the constitutional prescription for isolated rights conflicts and also notoriously limited to adjudication on broader policy issues. The institutional characteristics that shape the judiciary's competences in the democratic separation of powers (such as its lack of sectorial expertise, selectivity and intra-party effects) often result in decisions that do not adhere to digital governance systems such as those operating in social media.[6]

In the face of both unchecked self-regulation and a 'distinct redistribution of governance capacity away from states',[7] claims for co-regulation as an institutional solution for different fields of Internet regulation have grown. In the case of social media, the summoning of co-regulation relates to the idea of constitutionalisation in two different ways. First, co-regulation is presented as an answer to private power. As an Internet-related activity, social media platforms are inherently governed by a combination of actors and their practices,[8] but one can say that the companies that operate these services have long played a determinant role regarding the implementation of potentially rights-restrictive standards. In this perspective, co-regulation allows for more state participation in such a market. Secondly, co-regulation would answer the claims for constitutionalisation that call for what is actually law enforcement. Although the protection of fundamental rights has long stood among the justifications for regulation, social media platforms remain an environment where state policies struggle to deter or account infringement.

In view of this scenario, co-regulation has been deemed by some authors as a paradigm of efficient intervention for the services rendered through the Internet. This is because, while co-regulation allows for the decentralised operational regulatory actions of private agents, such arrangements also guarantee some entailment to a governmental institution, be it either underpinning legislation, oversight, or the sharing of enforcement actions. In his 2011 work, Chris Marsden referred to co-regulation as a paradigm of 'constitutionally responsive'[9] Internet regulation, referring to its potential to promote 'a general adherence to principles of administrative justice' and addressing 'the types of fundamental rights that may be affected by Internet regulation … notably the rights to privacy and to freedom of expression'.[10] According to Marsden, co-regulation is not only a solution, but

[6] I have further elaborated on these institutional characteristics in my previous work, 'Policy by Judicialisation: The Institutional Framework for Intermediary Liability in Brazil' (2020) *International Review of Law, Computers & Technology* 1.

[7] Wagner, 'Governing Internet Expression' (2013) 390.

[8] J Hofmann, C Katzenbach and K Gollatz, 'Between Coordination and Regulation: Finding the Governance in Internet Governance' (2017) 19 *New Media & Society* 1406, 1409.

[9] CT Marsden, *Internet Co-Regulation: European Law, Regulatory Governance and Legitimacy in Cyberspace*. (Cambridge University Press, 2011).

[10] ibid 3.

also a natural product of the Internet being 'a testing ground' for new forms of regulation. The expansion of co-regulation to address the needs of online content regulation was also identified by Frydman et al for whom co-regulation is a way for governments 'to outsource the implementation of their national law, at least within their own territory'.[11]

While these works reflect a take on co-regulation that is anchored on feasibility (ie, it is the only way to insert states into an environment inherently defined by private power), co-regulation has also recently been presented as a certain type of regulatory technique that is more efficient in addressing social media, ie, as an external alternative. This reasoning has been applied to different digital fields, such as data governance[12] (as a promising strategy to address 'complex, dynamic and innovative environments'),[13] sharing economy platforms[14] and digital disinformation.[15]

While reinforcing the potential of hybrid arrangements to address regulatory failures in the social media environment, this chapter argues that the current claims for co-regulation are insufficiently nuanced to provide effective solutions to the problems that inspired them. In fact, co-regulation in itself is too shallow a theoretical concept to address the complex regulatory matrix of social media services. The current debates bring a series of distinct institutional arrangements under the label 'co-regulation', and despite maintaining a mix of public and private participation at the centre of the concept, these arrangements produce very different regulatory mechanisms and power (im)balances. Additionally, calls for co-regulation of social media often overlook the theoretical basis of co-regulation, notably its well-known limitations (eg their poor enforcement of standards, and in particular, of third parties' rights),[16] in favour of assuring feasibility.

In view of this, this chapter discusses how recent references to co-regulation encompass a myriad of different institutional arrangements, with very distinct

[11] B Frydman, L Hennebel and G Lewkowicz, 'Co-Regulation and the Rule of Law' in E Brousseau, M Marzouki and C Méadel, *Regulation, Governance and Powers on the Internet* (Cambridge University Press, 2012) 148.

[12] M Grafenstein, 'Co-Regulation and the Competitive Advantage in the GDPR: Data Protection Certification Mechanisms, Codes of Conduct and the "State of the Art" of Data Protection-by-Design' in G González Fuster, R van Brakel and P de Hert, *Research Handbook on Privacy and Data Protection Law: Values, Norms and Global Politics* (Edward Elgar Publishing, 2022), see papers.ssrn.com/sol3/papers.cfm?abstract_id=3336990; I Kamara, 'Co Regulation in EU Personal Data Protection: The Case of Technical Standards and the Privacy by Design Standardisation "Mandate"' (2017) 8 *European Journal of Law and Technology*.

[13] Grafenstein (ibid).

[14] S Ranchordás and C Goanta, 'The New City Regulators: Platform and Public Values in Smart and Sharing Cities' (2020) 36 *Computer Law & Security Review* 105375; M Finck, 'Digital Regulation: Designing a Supranational Legal Framework for the Platform Economy' [2017] LSE Law, Society and Economy Working Papers.

[15] C Marsden, T Meyer and I Brown, 'Platform Values and Democratic Elections: How Can the Law Regulate Digital Disinformation?' (2020) 36 *Computer Law & Security Review* 105373; F Durach, A Bârgăoanu and C Nastasiu, 'Tackling Disinformation: EU Regulation of the Digital Space' (2020) 20 *Romanian Journal of European Affairs*, available at rjea.ier.gov.ro/wp-content/uploads/2020/05/RJEA_vol.-20_no.1_June-2020_Full-issue.pdf#page=6.

[16] A Ogus, 'Rethinking Self-Regulation' (1995) 15 *Oxford Journal of Legal Studies* 97.

degrees of binding legislation, power balances and implications; the fact that, even though co-regulation has been claimed as a way to improve state oversight over markets that have long been privately ordered, it is originally a variant of self-regulation; and how, for this reason, its implementation is subject to some limitations that are rarely voiced in these debates – namely its shortcomings with regard to fundamental rights enforcement. The last argument builds on the previous ones, to show that co-regulation is a limited concept to address structural solutions for the dilemmas of constitutionalising social media. Hence, the chapter concludes with the insufficiency of co-regulation as a theoretical concept to address social media regulation, as it does not capture the complexity of power dynamics in this environment and thus does not provide much clarity. The goal is to offer a more nuanced perspective of co-regulation as a solution to social media regulation and fostering more specific discussions on the means and structures to implement co-regulation.

II. Theoretical Framework

Regulation can be implemented through state regulation, self-regulation or co-regulation, the latter encompassing diverse models of 'multi-actor arrangements'.[17] Although these concepts approach rule-making and enforcement in different ways, they share an overarching agent-centred meaning. State regulation is performed by governments, either through formal legislation or secondary norms; and self-regulation consists of regulatory 'operations and initiatives in which the government is not involved in any level regarding the formulation or implementation of the regulation'.[18] With self-regulation, literature and policy guidelines often differentiate typologies according to the type of rule-making and enforcement mechanisms they tend to promote. In these approaches, self-regulation refers, in general terms, to the self-organisation of private agents, internally or among various actors of a specific sector (in which case self-regulation is founded either on the enforcement support of contractual law or on social consensus).[19] With reference to enforcement means, self-regulation is associated with the adoption of codes of conduct, technical standards, guidelines and other non-legal and soft law means.[20] While these concepts might presume bilateral or multilateral agreement to a set of rules, self-regulation models of different kinds of organisations[21] may well include 'unilateral adoption of neo-corporatist

[17] Hofmann, Katzenbach and Gollatz, 'Between Coordination and Regulation' (2017).

[18] J Black, 'Decentring Regulation: Understanding the Role of Regulation and Self-Regulation in a "Post-Regulatory" World' (2001) 54 *Current Legal Problems* 103.

[19] B Morgan and K Yeung, *An Introduction to Law and Regulation: Text and Materials* (Cambridge University Press, 2007) 92.

[20] Black, 'Decentring Regulation' (2001) 116.

[21] R Baldwin, M Cave and M Lodge, *Understanding Regulation: Theory, Strategy, and Practice*, 2nd edn (Oxford University Press, 2012) 138.

arrangements and standards',[22] 'intra-firm regulation'[23] or groups of firms or individuals exerting control over their membership's behaviour.[24]

The space between the state and the self- and co-regulation is essentially characterised by hybrid arrangements, as it takes place through the combination of different non-state actors (such as companies, business groups and not-for-profit organisations) with a certain level of state involvement. This involvement can vary according to the manner, moment and intensity of state control,[25] but outlining effective (and useful) distinctions between different taxonomies can be challenging. Within the co-regulation spectrum, one can find references to regulated self-regulation, enforced self-regulation, meta-regulation[26] and quasi-regulation,[27] for example. Whilst plural, these approaches are not exactly diverse. Except for quasi- and meta-regulation,[28] most of them focus to some degree on underpinning legislation. This includes any state involvement that 'lasts through monitoring of compliance'[29] or even overarching legislation (such as tort and civil law compliance) that would be applicable to 'violations of the privately written and publicly ratified rules'.[30]

As with self-regulation, co-regulation can be equated to soft law enforcement,[31] an interpretation generally depicted as an alternative to command and control strategies – which is arguable, given that co- and self-regulatory bodies can also operate by pairing legal typology with sanctioning.[32] But most importantly, this presentation of co-regulation as an alternative to state regulation has fuelled its popularity as a movement towards regulatory flexibility.

In this sense, co-regulation has been associated with regulatory improvement theories and public policies that aimed to divert the state's bureaucracies

[22] Black (n 18) 120.

[23] ibid.

[24] Baldwin, Cave and Lodge, *Understanding Regulation* (2012) 137.

[25] G Binenbojm, *Poder de Polícia, Ordenação, Regulação: Transformações Político-Jurídicas, Econômicas e Institucionais Do Direito Administrativo Ordenador* (Editora Fórum, 2016) 302.

[26] C Coglianese and E Mendelson, 'Meta-Regulation and Self-Regulation' in R Baldwin, M Cave and M Lodge (eds), *The Oxford Handbook of Regulation* (Oxford University Press, 2010) 147, available at oxfordhandbooks.com/view/10.1093/oxfordhb/9780199560219.001.0001/oxfordhb-9780199560219-e-8.

[27] Black (n 18) 111.

[28] Quasi-regulation, as defined by the Australian Better Regulation Guide, would be 'statutory delegation of power to the industry to regulate and impose codes, by prescribing voluntary or mandatory industry codes of conduct, by establishing minimum standards that the industry can improve, or by imposing to the companies [*sic*] compliance with a code'. In turn, 'meta-regulation' adopts a reflexive view where 'the regulation process becomes subject to regulation'. However, when a supervising entity interact with 'regulators or co-regulatory levels', its meaning would be re-approached to the co-regulation spectrum. Both concepts extracted from Black (n 18) 111.

[29] Including, for instance, legal provision for constitution of self-regulatory bodies; obligations assigned to private parties to develop or materialise a body of basic principles issued by the state, possibly under the supervision of a state regulator; mere delegation of any enforcement-related activities; mandated monitoring or oversight by public authority.

[30] Morgan and Yeung, *An Introduction to Law and Regulation* (2007).

[31] Finck, 'Digital Regulation' [2017]; Grafenstein, 'Co-Regulation and the Competitive Advantage in the GDPR' (2022).

[32] Black (n 18).

by transcending 'the regulation-deregulation dichotomy and … providing a much broader perspective of what regulation can involve'.[33] Some of these movements, known as 'responsive regulation',[34] 'smart regulation'[35] or 'better regulation',[36] originated in the UK and influenced policy frameworks in the UK itself, Australia and New Zealand. They included the search for innovative incentive-based enforcement strategies, such as lowering regulatory burdens (particularly on small businesses) and fostering greater private participation. The underlying assumption has been that such participation will improve the regulatory process once its result reflects the attempts, dialogue and collaboration between the different actors involved in a certain activity. These debates already prescribed co-regulation, in its different guises, as a solution to deal with dynamic regulatory environments. In some legal traditions, co-regulation has driven initiatives in the fields of corporate governance, environmental law, and media and communications regulation. Regarding the latter, co-regulation provides not only flexibility, but also an alternative to the dilemma between the need to assure compliance with fundamental rights and the democratic threats that can be posed by state intervention in the media sector.[37]

The same claims that underpinned these implementations were raised to a different degree with the constant expansion of complex, uncertain and dynamic regulatory fields,[38] especially technology regulation and Internet governance. They further fostered the idea that regulation cannot be solely 'oriented to the state's capability',[39] but rather includes a variety of norms, control mechanisms, controllers – ie including a range of legitimised governmental, non-governmental and supra-governmental organisations and controlees – in the sense that businesses are no longer the sole addressees of regulation, as a series of actors have a significant impact on the social economic order.[40] Here, co-regulation bears 'the promise of better norms created through compromise that facilitate innovation and experimentation while safeguarding public policy concerns'[41] and thus ensure that regulation is 'reflexive' (as in, formulated in a way that is understood and

[33] N Gunningham, PN Grabosky and D Sinclair, *Smart Regulation: Designing Environmental Policy* (Clarendon Press/Oxford University Press, 1998).

[34] I Ayres and J Braithwaite, *Responsive Regulation: Transcending the Deregulation Debate* (Oxford University Press, 1992).

[35] Gunningham, Grabosky and Sinclair, *Smart Regulation* (1998).

[36] R Baldwin, 'Better Regulation: The Search and the Struggle' in R Baldwin, M Cave and M Lodge (eds), *The Oxford Handbook of Regulation* (Oxford University Press, 2010), available at oxfordhandbooks.com/view/10.1093/oxfordhb/9780199560219.001.0001/oxfordhb-9780199560219-e-12.

[37] W Schulz and T Held, *Regulated Self-Regulation as a Form of Modern Government: An Analysis of Case Studies from Media and Telecommunications Law* (John Libbey Pub for University of Luton Press, 2004).

[38] Kamara, 'Co Regulation in EU Personal Data Protection' (2017).

[39] C Scott, 'Regulation in the Age of Governance: The Rise of the Post Regulatory State' in J Jordana and D Levi-Faur, *The Politics of Regulation* (Edward Elgar Publishing, 2004) 147, available at www.elgaronline.com/view/1843764644.xml.

[40] ibid 148–49; A Murray, 'Conceptualising the Post-Regulatory (Cyber) State' in R Brownsword and K Yeung, *Regulating technologies: legal futures, regulatory frames and technological fixes* (Hart. 2008).

[41] Finck (n 14) 17.

influenced by the autonomous social systems it regulates). The alleged reason for this is that in innovative and dynamic environments, the regulator is hardly able to centralise the knowledge about context-specific risks and thus the necessary protection instruments. Legal principles and broad legal terms would therefore be more appropriate regulatory instruments because they leave the regulation addressees enough room to explore, in accordance to their specific context, the risks and thus the best solution to mitigate these risks.[42]

III. Co-Regulation and Fundamental Rights in Social Media

Specialised literature often points at co-regulation as an ideal institutional arrangement to enforce fundamental rights in digital platforms,[43] including social media (as I will describe in detail in the next section). While in harmony with the concept's hybridity and the theoretical prescriptions approached in the last section, these works usually overlook a series of conceptual implications that can compromise results. In this section, I will explore them through the lenses of four arguments: (A) co-regulation is being used to refer to different institutional arrangements, with distinct degrees of binding legislation, power balances, and implications; (B) rather than a means to improve state oversight, co-regulation was originally a variant of self-regulation; (C) its implementation is subject to some limitations that are rarely brought along to these debates; and finally (D) co-regulation is conceptually insufficient to address social media regulation.

A. Various Problems and Various Solutions under the Same Label

To 'constitutionalise social media' – in the sense of assuring the rightful enforcement of fundamental rights across its activities – is a multidimensional task. As for most activities, social media practices will generate risks in various degrees for different sets of rights. Literature has already identified the threats that algorithmic

[42] Grafenstein (n 12). Also, for an approach of the limitations of such strategies, see AP Heldt, 'Upload-Filters: Bypassing Classical Concepts of Censorship?' (2019) 56 *Journal of Intellectual Property, Information Technology and E-Commerce Law*, available at www.jipitec.eu/issues/jipitec-10-1-2019/4877.

[43] A Heldt and S Dreyer, 'Competent Third Parties and Content Moderation on Platforms: Potentials of Independent Decision-Making Bodies From A Governance Structure Perspective' (2021) 11 *Journal of Information Policy* 266; N Helberger, J Pierson and T Poell, 'Governing Online Platforms: From Contested to Cooperative Responsibility' (2018) 34 *The Information Society* 1.

curation can pose to equality and anti-discrimination rights,[44] how data collection for microtargeting purposes can affect privacy[45] and how content moderation shapes and potentially jeopardises freedom of speech.[46] In fact, content moderation also poses threats to labour-related guarantees[47] and carries different risks related to the abuse of free expression, eg child protection, copyright or even national security. Thus, exploring the potential of co-regulatory arrangements for effective fundamental rights enforcement[48] needs to consider the different guarantees at stake (and, as I will shortly address, the very nature of these guarantees).

However, it is also important to consider that the label 'co-regulation' encompasses a variety of institutional arrangements, and this inclusiveness is reflected in its application to digital platforms and social media. Here, co-regulation presents itself as a feasible goal for fields where private intermediation is at the heart of how collective behaviour is influenced. Given that self-regulation has proven insufficient to guarantee the public interest,[49] giving ground to claims for more state involvement, 'The notion of co-regulation has been used with some success in this context for representing "a move to the middle"'.[50] Even though co-regulation emerged as a way out of the state's presumed exclusivity over social ordering and its bureaucracy – perhaps a reflection of it being considered the answer for the demand for decentralisation of regulation[51] – here it has more often been associated with increasing public oversight in markets long subject to self-regulation.

While the search for 'more state' can be clearly identified as a trend,[52] the same cannot be said of the content of co-regulation. This is to be expected: as stated, the theoretical content of the term 'co-regulation' refers to a spectrum of institutional forms, and not to any specific arrangement. Nevertheless, in the field of digital platforms, this nomenclature is applied to mechanisms that promote various degrees of power imbalances between actors, which can limit their potential to meet their declared ends. Below, I will briefly describe some of these approaches in order to highlight the different legal solutions that they encompass.

For instance, Finck has made the case for co-regulation arrangements in sharing economy platforms, as this would enable governments to 're-enter' the policy

[44] J Blass, 'Algorithmic Advertising Discrimination' (2019) 114 *Northwestern University Law Review* 415; M Lim, 'Freedom to Hate: Social Media, Algorithmic Enclaves, and the Rise of Tribal Nationalism in Indonesia' (2017) 49 *Critical Asian Studies* 411.

[45] FJ Zuiderveen Borgesius et al, 'Online Political Microtargeting: Promises and Threats for Democracy' (2018) 14 *Utrecht Law Review* 82.

[46] T Gillespie, *Custodians of the Internet: Platforms, Content Moderation, and the Hidden Decisions That Shape Social Media* (Yale University Press, 2018); K Langvardt, 'Regulating Online Content Moderation' 106 *The Georgetown Law Journal* 1353.

[47] ST Roberts, *Behind the Screen: Content Moderation in the Shadows of Social Media* (Yale University Press, 2019).

[48] Heldt and Dreyer, 'Competent Third Parties' (2021).

[49] Tambini, Leonardi and Marsden (n 1).

[50] Frydman, Hennebel and Lewkowicz, 'Co-Regulation' (2012).

[51] Black (n 18).

[52] With some exceptions, like F Di Porto and M Zuppetta, 'Co-Regulating Algorithmic Disclosure for Digital Platforms' (2021) 40 *Policy and Society* 272.

debate and ensure that privately made policy decisions are 'backed by robust government involvement through the definition of the corresponding legislative framework and review processes'.[53] Similarly, Ranchordás and Goanta suggest the adoption of 'a co-regulatory or negotiated system that seeks to balance platform and public values' as a standard for smart city regulations.[54] This would demand an elaboration on new models of 'negotiated regulation' and co-regulation 'that can bring together platforms and local authorities in the basis of their shared values and guarantee a closer alignment of platform and public values'.[55] While the cry for co-regulation clearly means more state involvement, the question remains regarding what exactly some of these models would eventually look like.

Co-regulation's popularity is also high on the agenda in data governance debates, a relevant aspect of social media activities, where legislation is already deemed insufficient to address privacy challenges.[56] According to Kamara, hybrid co-regulation models grant private companies greater flexibility to adopt technology-specific measures and address the challenge at scale. Given that the sheer number of 'organisations processing personal data and their processing capabilities'[57] has clearly outgrown the capacity of government authorities to enforce command and control mechanisms, decentralisation through co-regulation would enhance feasibility. The association of data protection with co-regulation has grown stronger with the approval of the European GDPR, notably due to the certification processes provided in Articles 42 and 43 (entrusting companies with interpreting legal principles and broad legal terms to develop standards against which compliance with data protection can be certified). Even though the empirical merits of these provisions are not unanimously recognised,[58] the choice of such an institutional arrangement has been praised for laying down 'legal principles and broad legal terms that … leave the regulations' addressees enough room to explore, in accordance with their specific context, the risks and best solutions to mitigate these risks.[59]

With regard to content governance, one can find allusions to all kinds of liability regimes being referred to as co-regulation. Frydman et al include in the realm of co-regulation three different liability regimes that complement section 230 of the American Communication Decency Act (which immunises Internet service providers (ISPs) from civil liability in general).[60] The 1998 Protection of Children from Sexual Predators Act requires ISPs to report images of child abuse to authorities; non-compliance subjects them to financial penalties. The Patriot Act

[53] Finck (n 14) 17.
[54] Ranchordás and Goanta, 'The New City Regulators' (2020) 3.
[55] ibid 13.
[56] Kamara (n 12).
[57] ibid 2.
[58] E Lachaud, 'Why the Certification Process Defined in the General Data Protection Regulation Cannot Be Successful' (2016) 32 *Computer Law & Security Review* 814.
[59] Grafenstein (n 12).
[60] Frydman, Hennebel and Lewkowicz (n 11).

amended by the 2002 Cyber Security Enhancement Act 'encourages ISPs to act as law enforcement authorities, by allowing them to enjoy immunity against law suits [*sic*] involving privacy and data protection violations' (specifically when the cause for such lawsuits is the disclosure of information 'relating to an emergency matter'). The third liability regime is the copyright regime in the Digital Millenium Copyright Act (DMCA), according to which an ISP is liable for copyright infringement when failing to take down infringing content within 10 days of the receipt of notice.[61] In these three cases, American legislation provides exceptions to its First Amendment libertarian approach to speech regulation, by creating incentives for ISPs to act as police authorities, restricting access to potentially infringing content[62] and reporting to authorities. These are inherently liability regimes, which delegate some level of law enforcement to private service providers, including the definition of criteria for removal of content, and hence for the exercise of constitutional freedoms. While the authors classify these mechanisms as co-regulatory, their operation does not require any type of hybrid governance mechanism, but rather demands compliance of private platforms with legal obligations and provides for sanctioning in case of infringement. In this sense, instead of examples of co-regulation, they would be closer to state regulation in its less flexible forms.

In Germany, a different liability regime has become a famous benchmark for co-regulatory governance. The 2017 *Netzwerkdurchsetzungsgesetz* – NetzDG Act requires social media platforms to implement procedures that allow users to report illegal content, notably 22 criminal conducts already provided in Germany's Criminal Code. Section 3(2) requires 'manifestly unlawful' content to be removed within 24 hours of notification (or possibly after seven days or more, with terms to be agreed upon with law enforcement authority). Beside removals, section 2 requires platforms to periodically publish transparency reports on the number of complaints received and how they were handled by the platform, entailing fines of up to €50 million in case of non-compliance.[63] On top of this, the NetzDG expressly provides for the possibility for a 'regulated self-regulation' arrangement, in the form of a self-regulatory body that could potentially unify some of the content adjudication and report attributions imposed by the law. According to section 3(6), for a body to be recognised as such, it would have to: ensure independence and expertise of its analysts; capacity to analyse requests within seven days; establish a complaints service, as well as procedures for such complaints and for affiliation of social media companies; and be funded by several different service providers as well as be open for others to join at a later stage. Even though the NetzDG has been in force since 2017, until 2020 no authority had been established

[61] Copyright law of the United States (December 2016, available at www.copyright.gov/title17/title17.pdf.

[62] B Frydman, L Hennebel, L and G Lewkowicz, 'Co-regulation and The Rule of Law' in E Brousseau, M Marzouki and C Méadel, C (eds), *Regulation, Governance and Powers on the Internet* (Cambridge University Press, 2012) 133–50, 138.

[63] *Network Enforcement Act* (Netzwerkdurchsetzungsgesetz, NetzDG) (September 2017), available at germanlawarchive.iuscomp.org/?p=1245.

in this form. In fact, only in January 2020 was the 'Freiwillige Selbstkontrolle Multimedia' (which already acted as a self-regulatory body for online minors' protection) authorised to act in such capacity.[64]

The implementation of models that are based on monitoring, transparency and due process obligations – especially in Europe – is associated with a shift 'from liability to responsibility'.[65] The NetzDG is often cited as an example of this trend.[66] These systems are considered a step beyond mere liability founded on the possibility of financial reparation. They represent 'a new ethics of responsible platforms, which can provide certainty, fairness and accountability of enforcement of speech rules, but ensure that speech control is strictly autonomous from the state'.[67]

The exceptions to the American libertarian approach, as well as the NetzDG, are examples of intermediary liability regimes. Even though both these systems grant private platforms with great power to enforce speech standards, they have different institutional backgrounds. Within its scope, the NetzDG subordinates platform power to institutions that are meant to increase state oversight and scrutiny over the enforcement of its terms. It is revealing that two alternatives with such different implications can still be labelled as co-regulation, which indicates an inflationary use of the term.

Furthermore, it is within European tradition that we can find some significant implementation of co-regulation directed at social media. Article 4a(1)) of the European Audio-Visual Media Services Directive (AVMSD) 'requires member states to encourage the general use of co-regulation',[68] notably through the implementation of codes of conduct (here, once again, an association of co-regulation with means. Article 28b(2)(4) refers to this strategy when it comes to child protection on video-sharing platforms, and Article 28b(3) further states that video platforms shall apply these instruments through the tools they themselves establish and operate. While the latter refers to formal delegation of law enforcement, the overarching AVMSD provisions refer to co-regulation as certain means (codes of conduct).

Co-regulation also pervades the European debate on digital disinformation. For Durach et al, co-regulation is a distinguished trace of the current strategies in this field,[69] which include: drafting of soft-law instruments; the creation of a

[64] 'FSM beginnt Arbeit als Selbstkontrolle nach NetzDG', available at www.fsm.de/de/presse-und-events/fsm-als-netzdg-selbstkontrolle. Accessed on: 24 Sep 2021.

[65] See ch 10 (Frosio) in this volume.

[66] W Schulz, 'Roles and Responsibilities of Information Intermediaries: Fighting Misinformation as a Test Case for Human-Rights Respecting Governance of Social Media Platforms' (Hoover Institution, Stanford University, 2019) 1904, available at www.hoover.org/sites/default/files/research/docs/schulz_webreadypdf.pdf.

[67] D Tambini, 'Rights and Responsibilities of Internet Intermediaries in Europe: The Need for Policy Coordination' (*CIGI – Centre for International Governance Innovation*, 28 October 2019), available at www.cigionline.org/articles/rights-and-responsibilities-internet-intermediaries-europe-need-policy-coordination.

[68] European Union Audiovisual Media Services Directive, available at rm.coe.int/iris-special-2019-2-self-and-co-regulation-in-the-new-avmsd/1680992dc2.

[69] Durach, Bârgăoanu and Nastasiu, 'Tackling Disinformation' (2020).

High Level Expert Group, whose final report 'offered guidelines on a number of interconnected and mutually reinforcing responses'; and the Code of Practice on disinformation signed by platforms. Against this broad marker for what co-regulation means in disinformation policy, Marsden et al[70] explore its potential to improve results of AI tools designed to prevent disinformation from spreading. '[A]utomated techniques in the recognition and moderation of content and accounts' would be developed by companies and later 'approved and further monitored by democratically legitimate state regulators or legislatures, who also monitor their effectiveness'.[71]

These examples are a testimony to the plasticity of co-regulation in the social media field. The label is used to refer to the possibility of reinserting states into a privately ordered market, to different regimes of intermediary liability over user generated content, and decentralisation of enforcement mechanisms (followed or not by governmental oversight). Their real implications depend on more than assuring shared competences of any kinds, ie on the power balance entailed in institutional designs.

B. Co-Regulation versus Self-Regulation

As mentioned above, in digital platform governance debates, co-regulation is discussed as an alternative to consolidated regimes of self-regulation, allowing for more state participation in a sector that has long been under private ordering, and whose powers have rarely been curtailed. It is interesting to noe, however, that co-regulation is more often than not approached via traditional theories of regulation as a form of self-regulation, rather than a particular arrangement in itself (let alone one that would favour governmental law enforcement).

Proponents of these theories commonly acknowledge that every self-regulatory arrangement will have a certain degree of state intervention, and that this does not detract from the primacy of the private organisation. There will always be a certain degree of state regulation in any self-regulatory regime, and that does not necessarily undermine the primacy of private organisation. In this sense, Morgan and Yeung recognise that some self-regulatory regimes may 'enlist the law's coercive power more extensively, and thus reduce the autonomy of the self-regulatory body to operate independently of state control'.[72] State control is also at the core of Ayres and Braithwaite's 'enforced self-regulation', which refers to the cases where private actors are mandated by government to elaborate on a set of rules aiming at specific purposes.[73] The authors distinguish this from co-regulation, in the sense that, while enforced self-regulation is focused on subcontracting regulatory

[70] Marsden, Meyer and Brown, 'Platform Values and Democratic Elections' (2020).
[71] ibid 3.
[72] Morgan and Yeung (n 19) 95.
[73] Ayres and Braithwaite, *Responsive Regulation* (1992) 101.

functions to private agents, co-regulation refers to self-regulatory bodies with some sort of oversight or ratification by government.[74] Similarly, the concept of 'regulated self-regulation' 'implies that the state should abandon its role of hierarchical control, and aim instead to influence the processes at work in society'[75] – a rather broad meaning that might as well encompass any minimal form of governmental participation.

It is therefore not a matter of affinity between co- and self-regulation, but possibly of equivalence. Black approaches both co- and self-regulation in terms of a decentralised understanding of regulation, based on a

> changed understanding of the nature of society, of government, and of the relationship between them,' and founded on 'complexity, fragmentation and construction of knowledge, fragmentation of the exercise of power and control, autonomy, interactions and interdependencies, and the collapse of the public/private distinction.

This interpretation is in tune with others that attempted to move the debate beyond the division between state regulation and self-regulation by considering instead 'a spectrum containing different degrees of legislative constraints, outsider participation in relation to rule formulation or enforcement, and external control and accountability'.[76] In this context, government participation can be seen as an inescapable part of self-regulation, as there might be 'little purity in self-regulation without at least a lurking government threat to intervene where market actors prove unable to agree'.[77]

It would be inaccurate to infer, from this common genesis, that co- and self-regulation are the absolute same, and that social media regulation, whether left exclusively to private ordering, or subject to oversight, would still produce the same results. Fostering incentives for protection and promotion of constitutional rights through co-regulation does bear the potential to enhance democratic oversight (and consequently trust) in this sector.

Nevertheless, co-regulation is only one piece of the puzzle, and not a complete solution, because it only challenges the status quo of the social media market to

[74] Baldwin, Cave and Lodge (n 21) 146.

[75] As per Heldt and Dreyer's interpretation of the concept developed by Wolfgang Hoffmann-Riem; Heldt and Dreyer (n 43) 4.

[76] Ogus, 'Rethinking Self-Regulation' (1995). Baldwin, Cave and Lodge (n 21) 138. The first variable the authors identify among different forms of self-regulation is 'the governmental nature of self-regulation', in the sense that 'An association may self-regulate in a purely private sense … or it may act governmentally in so far as public policy tasks are delegated to private actors or institutions', and 'The process of self-regulation may, moreover, be constrained governmentally in a number of ways – for instance by statutory rules; oversight by a governmental agency; systems in which ministers approve or draft rules; procedures for the public enforcement of self-regulatory rules; or mechanisms of participation or accountability. Self-regulation may appear to lack any state involvement, but in reality it may constitute a response to threats by government that if nothing is done state action will follow'.

[77] ME Price and SG Verhulst, 'The Concept of Self Regulation and the Internet' in J Waltermann and M Machill, *Protecting our children on the Internet. Towards a new culture of responsibility* (Bertelsmann Foundation Publishers, 2000); CT Marsden, *Network Neutrality: From Policy to Law to Regulation* (Manchester University Press, 2017) 163.

a certain degree. In particular, when its prescription is associated with enhancing governmental oversight, its coincidence with self-regulation reminds us that, unless there is further elaboration on mechanisms, it will end up not being much of an alternative. What is currently being presented as an alternative to current models will in fact pose little to no challenge to the power structures in place.

Also, if we are aware that co- and self-regulation have common origins, it is also fitting to acknowledge the limitations of these approaches. Studies often come accompanied by warnings on what self-regulation can and cannot do, and this includes its suitability to address the enforcement of individual rights.

C. The Nature of Guarantees: Fundamental Rights Enforcement and the Limits to Co-Regulation

Voices in social media policy debates that advocate for more co-regulation rarely address the well-known institutional limitations identified by the literature. These limits mostly accrue from its conceptual overlapping with self-regulation. In this section I will highlight: co-regulation's limitations in addressing the enforcement of fundamental rights regulation;[78] possible legitimacy deficits when relevant objectives are drawn by bodies with no democratic legitimacy;[79] and the scepticism with respect to the representativeness of the stakeholders within such arrangements.

The first set of critiques relates to the superficial perception that the implementation of self-regulatory arrangements is 'an indicative that government is not serious about something'.[80] The assumption here is that the private sector would not be effective in enforcing constitutional rights and pursuing the public interest over its own profit purposes; thus 'self-regulation should not be used for matters which are of high public interest or profile, or for regulating activities which pose particularly high risks'.[81] Nonetheless, in view of contexts distinguished by high information asymmetry, co-regulation can allow for regulated companies to distort the implementation mechanisms of mandated legal standards by prioritising their own interests over those of the regulation.[82]

Assessing this possible limitation is significant for the application of co-regulation to social media, where most of the guarantees at stake are fundamental rights. With this is mind, it must first be highlighted that, depending on how co-regulatory arrangements are tailored, there can be accountability mechanisms

[78] Marsden, *Internet Co-Regulation* (2011) 5; Ogus (n 16).

[79] Baldwin, Cave and Lodge (n 21) 141.

[80] Black (n 18) 115.

[81] ibid.

[82] M von Grafenstein, *The Principle of Purpose Limitation in Data Protection Laws: The Risk-Based Approach, Principles, and Private Standards as Elements for Regulating Innovation* (Nomos, 2018) 53; see also the *Wall Street Journal*'s reporting on the 'Facebook files', available at www.wsj.com/articles/the-facebook-files-11631713039.

to improve private implementation of standards. This means that, among the different models that receive this label, the ones that are restricted to a liability rule, or to collective drafting of a code of conduct (without further monitoring or oversight) are more likely to present risks to fundamental rights – unless they are paired with accountability mechanisms that allow for periodical and insightful oversight. These mechanisms will, however, be limited to a certain degree, and by choosing co-regulatory arrangements, legislation will empower private actors to assess the scope of fundamental rights – a role that can ultimately only be performed by courts.[83] It might, however, still be the most suitable solution for social media, where the right to freedom of expression is at the very core of constitutional rights enforcement, and state intervention over content is associated with censorship and paternalism.

The second criticism – private actors' lack of legitimacy to define rules that apply to third parties – will, to some degree, also depend on the governmental accountability mechanisms implemented. And for these specific purposes, the drafting and evaluation of standards, which are developed solely by platforms, can profit from the implementation of participation mechanisms. This paves the way for the last and third criticism, regarding stakeholders' participation, which highlights the necessity of viewing co-regulation not only as a mix of the state and regulated companies, but also as a multi-actor model,[84] which allows for the involvement of other societal sectors in the regulatory process, 'towards a model of polycentric co-regulation'.[85]

D. Co-Regulation as an Insufficient Concept to Address the Complexity of Social Media Dynamics

The arguments in this section demonstrate that co-regulation as a theoretical concept is vague and does not address the complexity of power dynamics and behavioural influence that takes place on social media. Its content cannot be defined further than a hybrid arrangement that involves public and private actors in different degrees, including a spectrum from loose legal delegations (where the definition and enforcement of standards remain solely at the platform's discretion) to procedural mechanisms for government oversight (eg mandated transparency reports). As we have seen, co-regulation alone is not enough to distinguish regulatory solutions from one another, even though they have very different implications in practice. Also, co-regulation in social media is by itself only an alternative to self-regulation to a certain degree, since it still carries some of its legitimacy-related limitations (as described above).

[83] The legitimate role of courts regarding constitutional rights protection in social media is further explored by Amélie Heldt in ch 15 of this volume.
[84] Hofmann, Katzenbach and Gollatz (n 8).
[85] Finck (n 14) 23.

This can be attributed to the fact that social media is a complex regulatory environment. Within Internet governance, it is not restricted to top-to-bottom regulatory arrangements, where the top refers to public, private or hybrid organisation. What users experience on social media is actually the result of 'patchworks of partly complementary, partly competing regulatory elements in the form of legal rules and ordinances, mandatory and voluntary technical standards and protocols, international and national contracts and agreements, and informal codes of conduct and "netiquette"'.[86] As suggested by Hofmann et al, studying Internet governance structures such as social media requires an account of 'emergent orders prevalent in rule-making in digital contexts and to include the practices of Internet users, providers and other stakeholders'.[87] In this sense, approaches that treat social media regulation as 'a regulatory perspective beyond nation-states, public decision making and formal policy instruments'[88] will bring little nuance to the debate, and thus promote contributions to the field that are essentially limited.

These limitations are also clear in the world of DeNardis, who suggests that approaching social media through the lens of Internet governance raises several areas of inquiry: regulation by states and international legal instruments, e-governance and policy through technology approaches, use of social media as platforms of dissent and civil society organisation; and 'how social media platforms policies and technical design choices serve as form of privatized governance'.[89] Most of the co-regulation debates focus on the first element, and do not acknowledge the greater variety of actors, practices and infrastructures that add complexity to social media policy. When co-regulation proposals put emphasis on reinserting states in this debate, they assume that the current concentration of private power can only be settled by more law enforcement – as if the government were the only possible entity that could be assigned this excess of power (away from social media platforms).

Focusing on co-regulation only accounts for 'a limited set of ordering processes'[90] and does not account for behavioural influence that is performed by other actors – or even the ones performed by private platforms outside of the legal bounds of a certain co-regulatory arrangement. This means that the final result does not rest solely on attaching private actors to underpinning legislation, but on a set of means, actors and practices that transcend even the concept of regulation itself.

[86] J Feick and R Werle, 'Regulation of Cyberspace' in R Baldwin, M Cave and M Lodge (eds), *The Oxford Handbook of Regulation* (Oxford University Press, 2010) 525, available at oxfordhandbooks.com/view/10.1093/oxfordhb/9780199560219.001.0001/oxfordhb-9780199560219-e-21. Hofmann, Katzenbach and Gollatz (n 8). For a deeper dive into some of the different normative mechanisms that integrate this universe, see Part IV of this volume.

[87] Hofmann, Katzenbach and Gollatz (n 8) 7.

[88] ibid.

[89] L DeNardis and AM Hackl, 'Internet Governance by Social Media Platforms' (2015) 39 *Telecommunications Policy* 761, 762.

[90] Hofmann, Katzenbach and Gollatz (n 8).

IV. Conclusions

The goal of this chapter was to explore the prescription of co-regulatory arrangements as a constitutionally responsive solution for online rights enforcement. While Internet regulation certainly profits from regulatory solutions that seek hybrid institutional arrangements and innovative regulatory strategies, the recent debates around co-regulation show that it is an insufficient concept to address the complexity of social media dynamics. Proposals in platform governance debates that refer to this concept as a subterfuge to provide more state presence need to go beyond labels and explore institutional mechanisms with the potential to include more stakeholders in decision-making processes and rebalance the current concentration of power of social media companies. Some experiences (as set out in section III.A) have added complexity to co-regulatory arrangements (eg, by mandating transparency reports or establishing state supervision to self-regulatory arrangement). However, these solutions still largely operate within the 'state vs platforms' divide, which does not address the constellation of actors and practices that mark Internet governance fields. This indicates that the co-regulatory solutions currently on the table for social media regulation have little potential to significantly alter the power imbalances that inspired them.

PART 4

Constitutionalising Social Media

14

Changing the Normative Order of Social Media from Within: Supervisory Bodies

WOLFGANG SCHULZ*

I. Introduction

We are currently witnessing a process of reconfiguration in the field of public communication. Institutions that were created for a pre-digital age of public television and established media are being reinvented to fit digital communication dynamics. If many online communication phenomena were, on closer inspection, not really structural changes, as they only accelerated developments that were already underway, communication on social media platforms was fundamentally new and is still not fully understood. This applies to the emergence of new types of publics,[1] but also to new regulatory structures of communication.[2]

The rules that private platforms set for the communication of their users are a special form of private ordering,[3] set within intricated and interlinked normative orders of the Internet.[4] Their significance for the freedom of public communication is constantly under political discussion and has increasingly become the subject of academic research.[5] Indeed, there is no doubt that these rules significantly influence the balancing of freedom of speech with other

* The author wishes to thank PD Dr Matthias C Kettemann and Martin Fertmann, researchers at the Leibniz Institute for Media Research | Hans-Bredow-Institut, for valuable insights and great support.

[1] J-H Schmidt, 'Vernetzte Öffentlichkeiten: Praktiken und Strukturen' in A Richter (ed), *Vernetzte Organisation* (De Gruyter, 2014) 16–25.

[2] R Gorwa, 'The platform governance triangle: conceptualising the informal regulation of online content' (2019) 8 *Internet Policy Review*, available at doi.org/10.14763/2019.2.1407.

[3] MC Kettemann and W Schulz, 'Setting Rules for 2.7 Billion. A (First) Look into Facebook's Norm-Making System: Results of a Pilot Study' (2020) Working Papers of the Hans-Bredow-Institut, available at leibniz-hbi.de/uploads/media/Publikationen/cms/media/5pz9hwo_AP_WiP001Inside Facebook.pdf.

[4] MC Kettemann, *The Normative Order of the Internet* (Oxford University Press, 2020).

[5] Most recently documented by the emergence of dedicated global academic networks such as the Platform Governance Research Network; see www.platgov.net.

rights (like honour or privacy), and also shape individual and public opinion and decision-making.

On the question of who should decide what, there is no simple answer. The 5 May 2021 decision by the Facebook Oversight Board to keep Donald Trump, for now, off Facebook and Instagram, is more of an invitation for further discussion than the last word.[6] Whether, for example, the President of the United States should be barred from using a service for violations of community standards, should, in the view of some, not be in the hands of private companies. But then, who should decide? The state governed by that president? Probably not. So what institution should have that power, if any?

Against that background, this chapter examines the emergence of specific 'supervisory bodies' for social media platforms, like Facebook's Oversight Board. I argue that this development is taking place in an area in which public and private affairs are inextricably intertwined, so that the interplay between state-legislated law and private rules must be fundamentally reconsidered. Experience we have made in other fields within the media sector – such as co-regulatory arrangements – can help, but cannot be implemented in the same way (section II). Current developments respond to this by transforming institutions and creating new ones, at times trying to imitate existing models of constitutional organs. The discussion of this development requires an understanding of the role of supervisory bodies in platform governance (section III). Different development paths and architecture models are conceivable, which are discussed below (section IV). The chapter concludes with reflections including some ideas on the role of academia in this development (section V).

II. Hybridity of Platform Governance

A. Public and Private Affairs

It is not news that private and public affairs overlap. Negative externalities caused by the production, distribution or consumption of products or services often harm the public good. Legislators can address this and set corresponding obligations that companies must comply with in order to reduce or eliminate these harms. This changes the way in which products are produced, distributed or consumed, and all parties involved – especially the company concerned – must comply with the legal regulations.

What can be the subject of political decision-making and state law as a *res publica* depends on the respective political theory and the theory of the state at an

[6] Facebook Oversight Board Decision 2021-001-FB-FBR (2021), available at oversightboard.com/decision/FB-691QAMHJ.

abstract level. In practice, it is controlled by national constitutions, by the functions and principles of the state, and by the limits that the fundamental rights of citizens impose on the actions of the state. Setting rules that determine the cases in which communication violates a citizen's personal rights, for example, and adjudicating them in court are likely to be largely indisputable elements of the function of a state.[7]

What is interesting now is that the private rules about content on platforms cannot simply be understood as an implementation of the corresponding law set by the state. Rather, the platforms shape their offerings through these rules, defining the profile of their services and thus distinguishing themselves from their competitors.[8] Which user communications have their place on the platform and which do not determines the profile of the platform. The communication rules are therefore not an external requirement like, for example, safety standards in the production of goods: they shape the product; one could even say that they constitute the service. If I run a platform about dachshunds, then it is crucial that I can prohibit cat content on the platform and remove it when it is uploaded in violation of that rule. At the same time, I might have to be compliant with general state-set rules governing platforms dealing with animals (eg regarding the sale of protected species).

Recognising that in this area public and private regulation can be equally justified on the same subject matter is critical to resolving the issues involved.

B. Hybrid Governance

Of course, this simultaneousness of public and private rules is not irrevocable. In a given legal system the state-set law could completely overwrite the domain of private ordering and dissolve this constellation in a legal way, thus tilting the platform into a form of state-sanctioned socialisation which might deprive us of the benefits of social media for individuals and the society at large.

This is not the place to discuss the normative setting of 'hybrid governance' in depth.[9] However, this observation has practical implications for the extent to which concepts from other areas can be drawn upon. This applies, for example, to the area of co-regulation in the media sector.[10] This is a valuable source of

[7] In many legal theories guaranteeing civil justice is a key function of states, cf. MA Shapiro, 'Distributing Civil Justice' (2020) 109 *Georgetown Law Journal* 1473, available at dx.doi.org/10.2139/ssrn.3675848.

[8] Kettemann and Schulz, 'Setting Rules for 2.7 Billion' (2020).

[9] On this, see MC Kettemann and W Schulz, 'Hybrid Governance' (forthcoming).

[10] M Latzer, N Just, F Sauerwein, 'Self- and Co-Regulation. Evidence, Legitimacy and Governance Choice' in ME Price and S Verhulst (eds), *Routledge Handbook of Media Law* (Routledge, 2013) 373–98; W Schulz and T Held, *Regulated self-regulation as a form of modern government* (University of Luton Press, 2004).

inspiration, loaded with theorisations and practical experience in the cooperation between state and privately appointed supervisory bodies in order to protect the integrity of societal discourses and individual rights. However, these systems are fundamentally designed with a goal set by the state in mind. Companies or business associations are given leeway to make the system more effective and efficient overall, but not to open up independent regulatory options. Private normative innovation in such systems thus takes place after and under – not simultaneously and next to – state law, limiting the practical value of such institutional references.

That different actors – not just the state – can set norms is widely recognised and represents the basis of thinking in regulatory structures that has advanced the field of governance research.[11] We propose to define this overlay of private and public rules 'on equal footing' as a category of its own and to reflect on appropriate concepts of hybrid governance for this field.[12] The appropriateness of certain concepts can only be determined from a certain normative perspective, such as which conception can be expected to provide the most effective protection of human rights.

C. Fundamental Reconfiguration

What we are observing in the field of social media, including the emergence of new organs such as oversight boards, is a reconfiguration of the field of socially relevant communication filling this 'hybrid space'.[13] These changes of the normative order brought about by new actors' constellations can be studied from various perspectives:

- the structure of norms governing behaviour in the field
- the development path of that structure and the role of various actors in shaping the development
- the evolving social practices
- the legitimisation of actors and their decisions
- the actors themselves, especially their boundaries as organisations and their relationship with other actors.

I would like to take a sideways look from a perspective that is rather rarely addressed: institutionalisation. I am aware that a deeper analysis would have to clarify the

[11] R Mayntz, 'Von der Steuerungstheorie zu Global Governance' in G Folke Schuppert and M Zürn (eds), *Governance in einer sich wandelnden Welt*, Politische Vierteljahresschrift, Sonderheft 41 (2006) 43, 46ff.

[12] Kettemann and Schulz, 'Hybrid Governance' (forthcoming).

[13] O Jarren, 'Fundamentale Institutionalisierung: Social Media als neue globale Kommunikationsinfrastruktur' (2019) 64 *Publizistik* 163, 164–66, available at doi.org/10.1007/s11616-019-00503-4.

theoretical references to concepts of 'normative order' and 'constitutionalisation'. Here, I limit myself to say that through the lens of institutionalisation research we can observe the process of creating and stabilising a specific social entity within an overarching process of constitutionalisation and to fan out relevant research perspectives. This standpoint is relevant because new oversight bodies are established with the expectation that they will change normative attributions in the long run and thus irritate the institutional structure of public communication.

Institutions can be described in a general understanding as a permanent set of norms, rules and routines that are constitutive for certain social roles and social action. They have been regarded as conditions that are removed from the actors' grasp, created by them, but which then control them through structural coercion and thus contribute to the maintenance of social order.[14] Institutionalisation takes place as soon as normalised actions are reciprocally typified by types of agents.[15]

Communicative institutionalism[16] assumes that institutions engage in institutional work in a variety of ways: as communicative necessity, opportunity and risk.[17] Starting the process of establishing an oversight board can be understood as an institutional work by Facebook.[18] From the very beginning, this institutional project included a normative promise, namely that Facebook wanted to create an institution that was independent and to whose decision Facebook would subsequently bind itself.[19] The point here is not to assert that this independence actually exists, nor how to evaluate the binding nature of decisions by the board, which cannot be legally enforced.[20] From an institutional perspective, it is interesting that the idea was communicated from the outset that a new organisation was being created that would then exert external influence on Facebook's content removal practices. The whole process that Facebook started to further develop the concept, holding workshops with different stakeholders all over the world, was in this respect already part of the institutionalisation process. Potential participants had ideas about the future role – from the perspective of Facebook, but also of all other relevant players – and about the legitimacy of the future oversight board.

[14] U Schimank, *Theorien gesellschaftlicher Differenzierung*, 3rd edn (Verlag für Sozialwissenschaften, 2007).

[15] PL Berger and T Luckmann, *The Social Construction of Reality: A Treatise in the Sociology of Knowledge* (Penguin Books 1966) 71.

[16] cf JP Cornelissen et al, 'Putting communication front and center in institutional theory and analysis', Academy of Management Review 40 (2018), 10–27, https://doi.org/10.5465/amr.2014.0381.

[17] cf TB Lawrence et al, 'Institutional Work: Current Research, New Directions and Overlooked Issues' (2013) 34 *Organization Studies*, available at https://doi.org/10.1177%2F0170840613495305.

[18] O Jarren, 'Fundamentale Institutionalisierung' (2019).

[19] E Klein, 'Mark Zuckerberg on Facebook's hardest year, and what comes next' (Vox.com, 2 April 2018), available at www.vox.com/2018/4/2/17185052/mark-zuckerberg-facebook-interview-fake-news-bots-cambridge.

[20] On the concept and the implementation process, see E Douek, 'Facebook's "Oversight Board:" Move Fast with Stable Infrastructure and Humility' (2019) 21 *North Carolina Journal of Law and Technology* 1, available at ssrn.com/abstract=3365358 and K Klonick, 'The Facebook Oversight Board: Creating an Independent Institution to Adjudicate Online Free Expression' (2020) 129 *Yale Law Journal* 2418, available at www.ssrn.com/abstract=3639234.

Whether and how this institutionalisation process works cannot be arranged by a single actor – not even by Facebook. The criticism that its Oversight Board is a fig leaf or a mere attempt of shifting responsibility was not long in coming. Its labelling as 'Facebook's Supreme Court' fed into a narrative that the newly established body would function like a national court. Only practice can prove whether and how institutionalisation succeeds. Will Facebook actually implement the decisions of the board? To whom will the decisions be attributed by other relevant actors? Will the decisions be perceived as an adequate solution to the conflict at hand? The answers to these questions will ultimately determine which new institutional structure will emerge.

The Oversight Board may be the most ambitious attempt, but it is not the first institutional shot at improving content moderation: other companies aspire to internalise civil society input through initiatives that are ostensibly branded as 'councils', such as TikTok's different regional Councils[21] or Twitter's Trust and Safety Council. These initiatives present themselves as informal company mechanisms for background talks with civil society representatives, and thus as significantly 'softer' initiatives compared to an oversight board. They do not seem to aspire to represent independent institutional structures with defined competencies, proceedings for collective decision-making by members or corresponding self-obligations by the company. Based on publicly available information, their members might not provide any sort of *collective* recommendations or decisions (beyond their individual opinions) at all.[22]

This process of institutionalisation may spontaneously give rise to elements of hybrid governance, however, so far with lack of sufficient critical reflection. Lawyers have carried out extensive research on the development of the legal order: to what extent does action on or by platforms fall within the scope of existing law? How could new regulatory concepts to deal with them be designed in a way that is compatible with superior law like human rights? Through this legal lens community standards appear to be simply part of a series of contractual arrangements. (Non-legal) research on the governance of social media seems often to start from a basis that has been built to understand media governance. This path dependence comes at a price: there is so far rarely any conceptional basis to discuss and assess initiatives such as Facebook's standalone development of an oversight board. It makes, however, a huge difference whether a process is accompanied by a level of intellectual reflection, which is in itself institutionalised in a way and, therefore, relatively stable.

[21] Namely the European Safety Advisory Council (see newsroom.tiktok.com/en-be/meet-tiktoks-european-safety-advisory-council); the Asia Pacific Safety Advisory Council (see newsroom.tiktok.com/en-sg/tiktok-apac-safety-advisory-council); and the (US) TikTok Content Advisory Council (see newsroom.tiktok.com/en-us/introducing-the-tiktok-content-advisory-council).

[22] Regarding these and other comparable institutions, see MC Kettemann and M Fertmann, 'Platform-Proofing Democracy: Social Media Councils as Tools to Increase the Public Accountability of Online Platforms' (2021) 13ff, available at shop.freiheit.org/#!/Publikation/1084.

III. Organising Oversight

A. Oversight Boards within the Governance Structure

To understand the importance of these oversight organisations in the regulatory structure of social media, it is necessary to consider their very complex structure. A distinction must first be made between the level of the rules and the level of the application of these rules to individual cases. This distinction is analytically significant, even though, of course, each individual decision applying a norm always also – to some extent – reconstructs the norm itself.

The regulatory systems of companies have become increasingly differentiated in recent years. Whereas in the beginning there were a few general 'house rules', there are now different, mutually interrelated normative texts, which also change frequently.[23] Not only do the standards affect ever more subject matters, but regular hierarchies of standards can also emerge,[24] such as abstract principles or values that are supposed to guide all the company's actions and then specific regulations that implement these principles or values. When it comes to content moderation decisions, norms typically relate to the interests of others, the community, or the platform provider that may be hampered by content. The process of setting up and changing those rules has also become rather comparable in its complexity with lawmaking by states.[25]

Consequences of violating these standards can apply to an individual piece of content or to the user's account as a whole. In each case, graduated reactions are conceivable, ranging from deletion of the content or permanent blocking of the account to more nuanced measures, such as making a particular user's content (or account) less visible on the platform.[26]

The process of individual case decisions is also sophisticated: it is about the selection of cases, subsumption under the rules, the decision itself and possible recourse. Both corporate initiatives – ie, Facebook's establishment of its Oversight Board – and proposals for cross-company oversight bodies[27] are typically about reviewing content decisions taken by the platform provider. The day-to-day decisions over content remain the task of the company.

[23] Klonick, 'The Facebook Oversight Board' (2020) 1631 ff.

[24] For Facebook see E Douek, 'Why Facebooks Value Update Matters' (Lawfare, 16 September 2019), available at www.lawfareblog.com/why-facebooks-values-update-matters.

[25] Kettemann and Schulz (n 3).

[26] T Gillespie, *Custodians of the internet: Platforms, content moderation, and the hidden decisions that shape social media* (Yale University Press, 2018),173 ff. See also ch 16 (Celeste, Palladino, Redeker and Yilma) in this volume; E Celeste, 'Digital Punishment: Social Media Exclusion and the Constitutionalising Role of National Courts' (2021) 35 *International Review of Law, Computers & Technology* 162.

[27] Article 19, 'Self-regulation and "hate speech" on social media platforms' (2018) 20–22, available at www.article19.org/wp-content/uploads/2018/03/Self-regulation-and-'hate-speech'-on-social-media-platforms_March2018.pdf.

There are two clear challenges for the positioning of an oversight board in this governance structure. The first concerns the distinction between rule-making and rule application. If an oversight board decides that holocaust denial infringes the hate speech rules of the platform (even though the rules do not explicitly mention the denial) it likely has the same effect as a new content standard prohibiting holocaust denial on the platform. The separation of policy-making and applying the rule is – as noted above – analytically sound but limited in practice. That Facebook has given its Oversight Board only a consultative role in policymaking under the Charter[28] that constitutes the basis of its work might just be a formal separation of procedures that fails to describe the substance of what is happening. Facebook might have unintentionally opened the door for a partial socialising of the platform. However, it might be a clever move to 'acknowledge hybridity' and evade further dysfunctional (from its own perspective) regulation by multiple states enforcing a form of normative localisation.

The second observation concerns the separation of decisions about content and those on the use of the platform. That Facebook asked the Oversight Board to rule on the use of the platform by Donald Trump[29] demonstrates that there are cases the company does not want to decide on its own, but for which an external body might be more appropriate.

B. Oversight Boards as Organisations of Hybrid Governance

i. Normative Basis for the Decisions

Based on the concept of hybrid governance proposed above, it makes sense to ask whether supervisory bodies should merely serve to enforce the company's rules, enforce state-set regulations, or both simultaneously. From this perspective, one can look descriptively at the processes and ask to what extent the latter is actually the case; here, for example, principal-agent thinking might be helpful. However, one can also influence the development of these organisations with this perspective in mind, ie by building the organisation in a way that fulfils this hybrid function.

The orientation of an oversight board in that respect is characterised by different features, in particular by which rules it is guided – whether that is just corporate standards or also other norms, such as human rights – and to whom the board is accountable. The latter cannot be formally defined, but is the result of normative attributions. This can be codesigned by the board itself, but others can try to influence it. Institutionalisation is a political power struggle. The establishment of a so-called Real Facebook Oversight Board[30] by a group of academics, researchers

[28] Facebook, Oversight Board Charter, Art 5(1) (2020), available at about.fb.com/wp-content/uploads/2019/09/oversight_board_charter.pdf.

[29] Facebook Oversight Board (2021). (Facebook Oversight Board: Decision 2021-001-FB-FBR (2021), available at oversightboard.com/decision/FB-691QAMHJ.

[30] The Citizens, 'The Real Facebook Oversight Board' (2020), available at the-citizens.com/about-us.

and civil rights leaders supported by the philanthropic organisation Luminate on the grounds that Facebook's Oversight Board serves the company rather than the general public, attempted to position the original board in a certain way in terms of expectations, and expectations of expectations, and thus sits as a tactical contribution in the process of institutionalisation.

The argument above shows that it is useful to first describe institutionalisation neutrally as a social process in order to make visible the extent to which it relates to norms such as human rights, and can thus be understood as constitutionalisation in a stricter and more sophisticated sense.

As regards the former – the normative yardstick for the decisions taken by the Oversight Board – the Charter as Facebook's basis for the creation of the board states in its section on 'Jurisdiction': 'The board will review content enforcement decisions and determine whether they were consistent with Facebook's content policies and values'.[31] However, there is also the reference to human rights: 'When reviewing decisions, the board will pay particular attention to the impact of removing content in light of human rights norms protecting free expression', but interestingly just one human right is mentioned: freedom of speech.

The board has the opportunity to evolve and position itself in the governance structure. As an actor with its own agency, it can now work on its positioning in the actors' constellation, can relate to the expectation of others and contribute to self-institutionalisation. The 'Rulebook' for board members already refers more broadly than the Charter to 'freedom of expression and human rights'[32] as standards for its decisions, thus considering all human rights, not just those protecting freedom of expression, which is underscored by the board's decisions thus far, utilising numerous international human rights law standards beyond freedom of expression.[33] However, the Charter states that its wording may only be amended with the approval of a majority of the individual trustees and with the agreement of Facebook and a majority of the board (Article 6(1)).

ii. Accountability

Closely related to the question of which norms a supervisory body's decisions are based on is the question of to whom the adjudicating institution is accountable. Since there is no overarching normative framework that allocates responsibilities, this is also a question of the actual institutionalisation of a supervisory body. So here, too, the question is what expectations exist and to what extent and how the body meets those expectations. One indicator might be the criteria for case

[31] Oversight Board, 'Governance', available at oversightboard.com/governance.

[32] Oversight Board, 'Rulebook' 3, available at oversightboard.com/sr/rulebook-for-case-review-and-policy-guidance.

[33] As a case in point, for instance, Decision 2020-004-IG-UA, available at /oversightboard.com/decision/IG-7THR3SI1/, citing numerous international human rights standards not just relating to freedom of expression, but also to the right to health, effective remedy, privacy and non-discrimination, and the rights of the child. See also ch 16 (Celeste, Palladino, Redeker and Yilma) in this volume.

selection chosen by the board: according to its bylaws, it prioritises cases that have the potential to affect lots of users around the world, are of critical importance to public discourse, or raise important questions about Facebook's policies. In this way, it signals that it wants to serve Facebook users and the public.

iii. Independence

Effective oversight requires a certain degree of independence from the object one supervises, and from other interests that might hamper the objective the oversight is serving. There is a long debate on the independence of oversight in the field of media, be it the state media regulators or the internal bodies which in many countries supervise public service broadcasters.[34]

Consequently, one of the main arguments against a supervisory body like the Oversight Board was that it could never act independently if it was set up by Facebook itself, especially to shift blame for unpopular decisions.[35] If Facebook selects the members and determines the rules according to which work is done, then – according to the criticism – the panel's work cannot be independent. Subsequently, heated discussions took place within academia and civil society about whether someone should follow Facebook's call to this body. A popular argument was that participation in this organisation would enable Facebook to cover up its own shortcomings.

Facebook tried to address this in an elaborate fashion. The very concept of the Oversight Board was put up for discussion in regional workshops around the world. In addition, a trust was set up to enable other companies to participate in the project, but also to ensure that Facebook could not use financial pressure to influence the decisions of the board. The further development of the board is mainly in the hands of the board itself and the trustees of the foundation. Changes of the Charter as the basis of the board's work require a decision by the trustees.

One point that cannot be overridden by design is that Facebook remains only voluntarily bound by the decision. There is no overarching normative framework on the basis of which a decision could be enforced. However, this does not mean, conversely, that it would cost Facebook nothing to ignore a decision taken by the board. This in turn depends on the institutionalisation process, ie to what extent expectations are frustrated when Facebook does not abide by these decisions and what consequences this has.

The concept of the independence of supervisory bodies, especially in the field of communication, is not as simple as one might think at first glance. It is not about the question of their dependent or independent nature, but about the

[34] cf European Audiovisual Observatory, IRIS Special 2019-1, 'The independence of media regulatory authorities in Europe' (2019), available at book.coe.int/en/european-audiovisual-observatory/8133-iris-special-2019-1-the-independence-of-media-regulatory-authorities-in-europe.html.

[35] R McNamee and M Ressa, 'Facebook's "Oversight Board" Is a Sham. The Answer to the Capitol Riot Is Regulating Social Media' (2021), available at time.com/5933989/facebook-oversight-regulating-social-media.

positioning of a supervisory body in a parallelogram of forces. No organisation can be completely independent of any influence, if only because of its dependence on money. We have developed elsewhere a concept of independence that could be applied to this area.[36]

IV. Architectural Design Choices and Development Paths

A. Upfront Decisions when Creating Oversight Boards

The design of oversight bodies is associated with certain design choices. The first, and most fundamental, is whether it is responsible only for a single company, a single platform operated by that company, or for multiple or all platforms of that type.

While the existing bodies serve just one platform there have been suggestions to form multi-stakeholder boards that could review content decisions by more than one platform. David Kaye, former UN Special Rapporteur on the promotion and protection of the right to freedom of opinion and expression, advanced the idea of a Social Media Council[37] and the human rights NGO ARTICLE 19 elaborated the concept and undertook a public consultation.[38] The concept was also taken up by lawmakers within the debate around Europe's new Digital Services Act, although it was not included in the draft legislation.[39]

Beyond that, there are many individual decisions that also help determine how the organisation fits into the regulatory structure. The work of the Internet & Jurisdiction Policy Network (I&JPN) provides valuable guidance here. One of the main mandates of the I&JPN is to create operational documents based on multi-stakeholder dialogues. Table 14.1 is part of the outcome developed by the networks' Content Group to inform the future creation of oversight boards.

[36] W Schulz, P Valcke and K Irion (eds), *The Independence of the Media and Its Regulatory Agencies* (Intellect Ltd, 2014).

[37] UN General Assembly (2018): 'Report of the Special Rapporteur on the promotion and protection of the right to freedom of opinion and expression', UN A/HRC/38/35, paras 58, 59, 63, 72, available at ap.ohchr.org/documents/dpage_e.aspx?si=A/HRC/38/35.

[38] ARTICLE 19, 'Self-regulation and "hate speech" on social media platforms' (2018), available at www.article19.org/resources/self-regulation-hate-speech-social-media-platforms; see also Stanford Global Digital Policy Incubator, 'Social Media Councils: From Concept to Reality' (2019), available at fsi-live.s3.us-west-1.amazonaws.com/s3fs-public/gdpiart_19_smc_conference_report_wip_2019-05-12_final_1.pdf; Ness et al, 'Freedom and Accountability A Transatlantic Framework for Moderating Speech Online', Transatlantic Working Group, 'Freedom and Accountability: A Transatlantic Framework for Moderating Speech', available at cdn.annenbergpublicpolicycenter.org/wp-content/uploads/2020/07/Freedom_and_Accountability_TWG_Final_Report.pdf, 26; most recently, Kettemann and Fertmann, 'Platform-Proofing Democracy' (2021).

[39] See MEP Alexandra Geese, 'Social Media Councils: Power to the people', available at alexandra-geese.eu/der-dsa-teil-05-social-media-councils-power-to-the-people.

Based on that, it is first necessary to clarify the exact scope of the organisation's tasks. Furthermore, procedural questions are to be clarified together with issues that concern the organisation and its members. Finally, there are relevant individual questions which characterise the respective supervisory body.

Table 14.1 Questions and design options for oversight boards

Competence	Due process	Body	Other
Topics covered	Limited steps/duration	Size	Charter
Normative reference	Written/oral procedure	Composition	Name
Initial source (AI/notices)	Adversarial process	Members' profiles	Advisory role(s)
Cases filtering ('cert')	Role of third parties	Designation	Geographic scope
Mandate focus/ limitation	Decision-making	Mandate duration	Thematic chambers
Applicants	Production of rationale	Meeting frequency	Mutualisation
Remedies	Dissenting opinions	Independence	Electronic tools
	Expedited mechanisms	Secretariat support	Liability protection
	Transparency	Funding	Jurisprudence coherence
	Suspensive procedure		

Source: Internet and Jurisdiction Policy Network, 'Operational Approaches' (2019) 40.[40]

For a discussion of the institutionalisation of such organisations and their further development, it may be helpful to refer to these architectural features. As already shown, the orientation towards private interests of the company or interests of the general public can thus be linked to concrete features of the design (like 'normative reference' or 'role of third parties').

An important point listed under 'Other' in Table 14.1 relates to geographical scope. Since many platforms offer their services on a global scale, the question arises as to what extent it seems appropriate to introduce regional supervisory structures or to provide only for a global board. In the case of Facebook's Oversight Board, the company opted for a global approach, as it envisages uniform standards worldwide and therefore also wanted to construct a uniform board, while at the same time integrating different regional perspectives. Also, in the case of the concept of a social media council envisaged by ARTICLE 19, the question was

[40] Transparency disclaimer: the author of this text is also the coordinator of the content group of the Internet and Jurisdiction Policy Network; the report is available at internetjurisdiction.net/uploads/pdfs/Papers/Content-Jurisdiction-Program-Operational-Approaches.pdf.

raised as feedback in the consultation as to the extent to which regional differentiation makes sense or not.

B. Paths of Institutionalisation

Since boards are emerging in a non-formalised area, many stakeholders are potentially in a position to initiate or contribute to shaping this process. For example, in the case of its board, Facebook took the initiative in shaping the process of organisational development, but proposals have also come from other organisations such as Global Partners Digital[41] or ARTICLE 19.[42]

The boards themselves may also reflect different interests. The answer to the question of who should actually decide whether a US president who violates platform rules should be excluded from using the platform can actually only be: an appropriately composed multistakeholder board. But this raises all the old, familiar questions of multistakeholderism, such as how to convey sufficient legitimacy, how to select the relevant stakeholders and define their roles (especially those of the states), and the possibility of further strategic development of the system itself (instead of pure emergence), into the discussion.[43]

V. Reflection and Outlook

In the process of setting up supervisory bodies for social media providers, it has been mainly these providers themselves who have so far driven the development: initially Facebook, but currently also TikTok. From this angle, it is really a matter of 'changing the normative order of social media from *within*', considering that these companies are the very drivers of these institutional developments. However, NGOs have presented their own proposals. Furthermore, the draft of a Digital Services Act for the European Union approaches the issue of oversight with state regulations as an option.[44]

With a few exceptions, the academic community has so far provided little reflective knowledge. This is to be expected, because the emergence of these oversight boards is a visible manifestation of a fundamental change in the field of socially relevant communication. A realm of hybrid state-private governance is emerging,

[41] Global Partners Digital, 'A Rights-Respecting Model of Online Content Regulation by Platforms' 26–28, available at www.gp-digital.org/wp-content/uploads/2018/05/A-rights-respecting-model-of-online-content-regulation-by-platforms.pdf.

[42] ARTICLE 19, 'Self-regulation' (2018) 20–22.

[43] For an overview, see H Gleckmann, *Multistakeholder Governance and Democracy: A Global Challenge* (Routledge, 2018).

[44] MC Kettemann, W Schulz and M Fertmann, 'Anspruch und Wirklichkeit der Plattformregulierung: Zu den Kommissionsentwürfen der Rechtsakte zu digitalen Diensten und Märkten' (Zeitschrift für Rechtspolitik, 5/2021, 138).

and adequate concepts for it have yet to be developed. Without these concepts, it is quite likely that an unproductive tug-of-war will ensue between states seeking to regain control and companies seeking to preserve their economic leeway.

So, there is room for academic reflection. Firstly, one needs theories that help to describe empirically this development in a consistent way. As alluded to above, figuration theories might be useful as they are not burdened with a stringent set of prerequisites, and allow for focus on various aspects, like a change of organisational borders (is a board part of a social media provider as an organisation?), and which actors are involved in producing 'social sense' and norms. Our exploratory study on the internal rule-making within Facebook attempted to address this.[45] Institutional theories can be helpful in understanding the process of positioning new organisations, such as oversight boards.

Secondly, normative reasoning needs to analyse what the overlap of public and private normative structures means for the normative order at large. We need to elaborate who has a say in the interpretation of norms within this hybrid field, ie who is a legitimate member of the community of norm-interpreters. We can ask whether human rights can be the connecting factor since public lawmakers are bound by them, and private rule-makers at least have a responsibility to respect human rights under the Ruggie principles.[46]

Finally, governance research can provide an aerial perspective which allows insight into what we can learn from studying other regulatory settings, eg co-regulatory arrangements or the inclusion of courts as resolvers of conflict within a system, for the field of hybrid governance. Also, old-fashioned models of multistakeholder-based supervisory boards like broadcasting councils might be worth consideration. Existing research can inform how state regulation in the form of high-level principles might be a way forward, so that the companies could build rules that follow those principles, and at the same time the concrete formulation of the rules can reflect the legitimate interest of the company to shape the platform. Research can also provide guidance on to what extent elements of the constitutionalisation of states can inform the hybrid social media order. Governance research can help identify decision points and provide options that can be discussed by all stakeholders, including options for the structure of supervisory bodies.

From a human rights perspective, there is at any rate an interest in maintaining global communication platforms and a human rights-based solution to conflicts on these platforms. Again, since neither states nor private platforms alone can perform this, specific multi-stakeholder organisations must take on part of the task of conflict resolution.

[45] MC Kettemann and W Schulz, 'Setting Rules for 2.7 Billion. A (First) Look into Facebook's Norm-Making System: Results of a Pilot Study' (2020) Working Papers of the Hans-Bredow-Institut, Works in Progress # 1, available at leibniz-hbi.de/uploads/media/Publikationen/cms/media/5pz9hwo_AP_WiP001InsideFacebook.pdf.

[46] See ch 16 (Celeste, Palladino, Redeker and Yilma) in this volume.

15

Content Moderation by Social Media Platforms: The Importance of Judicial Review

AMÉLIE P HELDT*

I. Introduction

In September 2019, a German court sentenced a man who had shared a video by a German news outlet (Deutsche Welle) reporting on ISIS on Facebook. The man was found guilty of sharing the propaganda material of a forbidden terrorist organisation. Later, the Bavarian High Court reversed this decision due to the first court's error with regard to the element of 'propagation' because sharing content that contains a forbidden symbol is not equal to terror propaganda. Without diving deeper into German criminal law, this case is a good example of the complexity of moderating user-generated content online. It illustrates on different levels that a nuanced approach is needed when it comes to both the content itself and to the way platforms are expected to react. Despite the first (perhaps perplexing) impression it might give, this case most notably shows the importance of judicial review.

Platform governance should not be thought of as something external to the judiciary. Instead, it is important that courts supervise platforms in light of fundamental rights and democratic principles when conceiving standards for public communication online. On the basis of the aforementioned case and other relevant examples, this chapter argues that judicial review is highly relevant even though the fields of action are at different scales: platforms act globally whereas jurisprudence is only applicable on a local or regional scale. Nevertheless, courts and their decisions are essential for democracy and cannot be entirely replaced by corporate oversight bodies. Taking into account the difficulties encountered when trying to protect free speech values on the one hand and protecting individuals and society from harmful content on the other, this chapter will stress the

* I would like to thank Julius Böke and Maximilian Piet for proofreading the manuscript and my co-editors for insightful and helpful comments.

important and irreplaceable role of judicial review in the governance of platforms. It will investigate courts' role by approaching the case of adjudication of content moderation decisions and, based on *Rosenfeld's* observation on the 'constitutionalization of politics',[1] it will argue against the transfer of judicial review from the state to private actors.

In principle, laws made and adopted for speech in the analogue world are supposed to be applicable to the digital sphere. The transferability of laws depends on their according applicability. Because the Internet and, specifically, social media platforms are mostly used to communicate (whether the main purpose is to communicate or whether it is a side-effect has no relevance here), the protection and the regulation of speech is a very critical and challenging issue.[2] Research has shown that communicative behaviour online differs from 'real-life encounters', content- and manner-wise.[3] From a legal perspective, it puts into question the principle mentioned above: do we need specific rules for online speech? The underlying question is whether the rationales that form the basis of how we conceive the constitutional protection of freedom of expression and information are still the same on- and offline. For instance, protecting the speaker's right to express opinions and to disseminate them is legitimised by both the protection of the individual and of society. In order to protect the speaker's freedom to build his or her own opinion and to be a potential participant in the marketplace of ideas, his or her communicative freedom can only be restricted in very limited constellations. This protection is at the same time from the state (defensive right) and by the state (which includes access to justice and promotion of access to information). Protecting individuals' freedom of expression goes hand in hand with the protection of the values and institutions that allow the functioning of liberal democracies.

II. Protection of Speech and Platformisation

In the US, free speech theory builds on three arguments: truth, democracy, and autonomy. Each of them is highly relevant to the principles and values enshrined in the US Constitution and the self-conception of US society.[4] The argument of truth relies on the assumption of a functioning marketplace of ideas.[5] The US legal framework is highly relevant here because the largest social media platforms globally come from the US. Moreover, their private rules for content control are very

[1] M Rosenfeld, 'Judicial Politics versus Ordinary Politics: Is the Constitutional Judge Caught in the Middle?' in C Landfried (ed), *Judicial power: how constitutional courts affect political transformations* (Cambridge University Press, 2018).

[2] As highlighted by many others in this volume.

[3] BM Okdie et al, 'Getting to know you: Face-to-face versus online interactions' (2011) 27 *Computers in Human Behavior* 153.

[4] TI Emerson, 'Toward a General Theory of the First Amendment' (1962) 72 *Yale Law Journal* 877.

[5] *Abrams v United States* 250 US 616, 630 (1919) (Holmes J, dissenting).

much influenced by the First Amendment and Section 230,[6] which is why it is crucial to understand the differences to other national regimes. Moreover, platforms become proxies for the values enshrined in First Amendment theory. The latter shows that while the argument of truth has for a long time been dominant in US scholarship and jurisprudence, it might not be as compatible with communication over social media platforms as it perhaps was in the traditional layout of public communication. Instead, the argument of democracy might gain importance and become prevalent because it does not separate an individual's freedom of speech from the relevance of the same protection for all members of society. This, in turn, affects the scope of protection of freedom of speech. In the US, it is very broad and there are only very few exceptions at the level of the quality of speech as well as the content of the opinion.

With social media platforms, it has become easier and more common to share thoughts with a global community regardless of one's social class and the respective sphere of influence. In the early days of the social web, these new communication possibilities were praised as tools for a truly democratic disruption, eventually giving a voice to every citizen with Internet access. The concerns about the power of the main platforms hosting communication in the digital sphere have increased over time,[7] and probably reached their peak in January 2021 when Facebook, Twitter and YouTube chose to indefinitely ban then-US President, Donald J Trump. Their ability to control information flows on a global scale should be recognised as 'a significant source of power'.[8]

Early on, Volokh pointed out the consequences of the very low costs for speaking online: cheap speech makes it difficult for the speaker to be heard, not to speak.[9] If speech is treated equally without differentiating according to the content and its relevance, there is no 'preferential treatment' for truthful and newsworthy content if it not disseminated via the traditional media outlets. This issue has so far not been resolved, and is also related to the case described in the introduction of this chapter. Another important development due to the increasing platformisation – 'defined as the penetration of infrastructures, economic processes and governmental frameworks of digital platforms in different economic sectors and spheres of life, as well as the reorganisation of cultural practices and imaginations around these platforms'[10] – is the factual merging of private and public communication spaces. Platforms with large user numbers convey the image of a public space without being a state actor and therefore not bound to fundamental rights. The question of how to handle the hybrid character of platforms as actors has, so far, not been answered.

[6] A Chander, 'How Law Made Silicon Valley' (2014) 63 *Emory Law Journal* 639.

[7] J York, *Silicon values: the future of free speech under surveillance capitalism* (Verso Books, 2021).

[8] K Nahon, 'Where There Is Social Media There Is Politics' in A Bruns et al (eds), *The Routledge companion to social media and politics* (Routledge, 2016) 46.

[9] E Volokh, 'Cheap Speech and What It Will Do' (1995) 104 *Yale Law Journal* 1805.

[10] T Poell, D Nieborg and J van Dijck, 'Platformisation' (2019) 8 *Internet Policy Review*, available at policyreview.info/concepts/platformisation.

The recent case of a German Facebook user sentenced for sharing content presumed to be terror propaganda serves as an example of the application of speech-restricting rules in the digital sphere, illustrating the advantages of a justice system with several instances (section III below). Section IV will give an overview of the issues arising when platforms moderate unwanted content. The following section will show that the complexity of how to handle and protect speech adequately should be an absolute argument against giving off the judgement over what is protected speech and what is not (section V). While some laws need to be adapted to the digital sphere (after carefully assessing if the situation requires novity in the law), the principles of separation of powers and of access to justice remain as absolute as before.

III. The *Deutsche Welle* Case and its Context

In September 2019, a district court in Germany sentenced a man for sharing a video on his Facebook profile.[11] The video was a short news story about how ISIS had access to guns and arms produced in Western countries and the origin of ISIS's financial resources. It was produced by a German news outlet, Deutsche Welle, which is part of the German public broadcasting network. In the video, ISIS's symbol was twice visible on flags held by members of the terror organisation. The defendant shared a link to the Russian language version of the article on the publicly accessible part of his Facebook profile. According to the district court's opinion, sharing on online platforms is a form of propagating signs of a prohibited association. Six months later, the Bavarian High Court reversed the district court's decision and held that the court of first instance had mistakenly not taken into account that the author of the video was a public broadcaster and not the defendant himself. Sharing this video on a social media platform such as Facebook was not to share propaganda material but rather to express his opinion on the matter and to contribute to the ongoing discussion about the international challenge of terrorism. Hence, by diminishing these aspects, the district court violated the defendant's freedom of expression in its ruling. Moreover, the second decision stresses the importance of courts and their appeal stages, as well as their role in shaping the interpretation of speech-restricting laws to the digital sphere.

This case raises both familiar and new questions in the context of moderating user-generated content; that is, defining the limits of accepted content and applying them. Harmful content such as terror propaganda, hate speech and disinformation (amongst others) is a challenge to the platforms hosting content globally because their own sets of rules for content control are increasingly under scrutiny. So far, there is no one-size-fits-all legal framework they could apply. Additionally, content moderation is highly dependent on who is actually enforcing the private

[11] Amtsgericht Augsburg 11 Cs 101 Js 112076/18 (2).

rules of platforms. Human moderators are, generally speaking, not trained lawyers and will have to make decisions on the legality of content in a short timespan despite the high complexity of some cases.[12] When automated, content moderation is not necessarily better.[13] In fact, the case described here demonstrates that even if systems can be trained to recognise certain symbols like ISIS's sign, it would not be sufficient.

IV. Challenge(s) in Content Moderation

Social media platforms offer a communicative infrastructure with the aim of connecting people worldwide, allowing them to share content with others, regardless of the type of content, and whether it is third-party content or self-produced. Hence, legal issues connected to user-generated content (UGC) arise at different levels, including whether it is permissible to moderate content only on the basis of community standards (or similar), according to which legal order should the legality of content be assessed, how to apply laws online in a coherent interpretation, and, if a knowing violation of law is asserted, who should be held responsible. These matters, generally discussed under the heading of content moderation, demonstrate the importance of judicial review because they always comprise the task of defining the scope of freedom of expression.

A. Defining the Limits of Acceptable Content

Content moderation is 'the organized practice of screening user-generated content posted to Internet sites, social media, and other online outlets, in order to determine the appropriateness of the content for a given site, locality, or jurisdiction'.[14] Content moderation on social media platforms with important user communities is best referred to as 'commercial content moderation' because, as Roberts defines it, in a commercial context it is 'mostly undertaken by individuals or firms who receive remuneration for their services'.[15]

The relevant actors in this configuration are the platforms (hosting UGC), the users (sharing UGC) and the lawmakers (regulating communication spaces). Defining the limits of acceptable content and what should be banned is an issue. There is a discrepancy between constitutions allowing speech-restricting

[12] ST Roberts, 'Content Moderation' in LA Schintler and CL McNeely (eds), '*Encyclopedia of Big Data*' (Springer International Publishing, 2017), available at link.springer.com/10.1007/978-3-319-32001-4_44-1.

[13] R Gorwa, R Binns and C Katzenbach, 'Algorithmic Content Moderation: Technical and Political Challenges in the Automation of Platform Governance' (2020) 7 *Big Data & Society* 1.

[14] Roberts, 'Content Moderation' (2017).

[15] ibid.

laws and others who base their understanding of freedom of expression on the concept of the marketplace of ideas, ie, the argument of truth. What is unlawful differs between national contexts and legal orders. In Germany, for instance, the restriction of speech by law is allowed by constitutional provision if the speech-restricting law meets the requirements of Article 5, para 2 Basic Law, eg, criminal offences such as insults, defamation and sedition. In contrast, under the First Amendment's Free Speech clause of the US Bill of Rights, there can be no regulatory intervention that could potentially restrict the freedoms of speech and assembly. Hence, the broad protection of speech against the coercive power of the state makes content moderation by platforms indispensable because, in the US context, private actors may set the rules as to what cannot be said – unlike the state.

Content-related rules by social media platforms (eg, Facebook's Community Standards) mostly ban hate speech, terror propaganda, child pornography, disinformation, etc from their platform. In order to minimise costs and frictions with single jurisdictions, their rules regarding content are supposed to be as comprehensive as possible on a global scale. This strategy is perceived as a threat to freedom of expression and information because it does not take into account local laws and contexts, but can instead lead to an over-removal of content by platforms.[16] Gillespie rightly pointed out that the governance *of* platforms cannot fully be separated from the governance *by* platforms.[17] As long as platforms are the ones to define the limits of accepted content, regardless of regional differences, they are the factual governors of communication in the digital sphere. The governance of platforms is inherently linked to how platforms govern UGC because, early on, specific legislation was adopted to protect hosting platforms from liability (more below). As platforms become the *de facto* norm-setters of speech restrictions, and because this trend accelerated even during the COVID-19 pandemic,[18] the need for judicial review has not declined.

B. The Duality of Content Moderation Rules and Borderline Content

The general framework described above contributes to the unavoidable truth that content moderation is a moving target. This is also due to the nature of the matter: communication is always embedded in a social context, subject to not only laws

[16] D Keller, 'Who Do You Sue? State and Platform Hybrid Power Over Online Speech' (2019) Hoover Institution Aegis Paper Series, available at www.hoover.org/research/who-do-you-sue.

[17] T Gillespie, 'Governance of and by platforms' in J Burgess, A Marwick and T Poell (eds), *SAGE Handbook of Social Media* (Sage Publications Ltd, 2017).

[18] E Douek, 'Governing Online Speech: From "Posts-As-Trumps" to Proportionality and Probability' (2021) 121 *Columbia Law Review*, available at papers.ssrn.com/abstract=3679607.

but also social norms. Borderline speech is a clear example of the duality of content moderation rules. Several platforms have deployed policies against 'borderline' content.[19] The closer content is to the 'red line' of 'potentially harmful' according to community standards, the higher are the odds to take the content down. This type of policy goes hand in hand with the efforts of social media platforms to counteract allegations their algorithms would favour harmful content to increase user engagement.[20] Instead of waiting for content to cross a certain line, they prefer removing it ahead.

But borderline content is not necessarily unlawful.[21] It might, in fact, not even be forbidden under a platform's community standards but the stronger the probability of content being close to crossing the red line of community standards and, eventually, the law, the higher is the likelihood of taking content down on the grounds of a term that lacks objective elements. Borderline means 'being in an intermediate position or state: not fully classifiable as one thing or its opposite',[22] hence rather alien to legal scholarship. Not only are platforms making the rules of online communication (ie community standards) and enforcing them regardless of local laws in order to provide a global service to their users, but the rules will be subject to modifications whenever deemed necessary and the platform's legal opinion is based on corporate principles instead of existing jurisprudence.[23]

In the above-described *Deutsche Welle* case, there is no doubt that ISIS flags and symbols were clearly visible in the footage. However, the footage was produced by a public broadcaster and protected by media freedom. The question raised in this case is whether a type of media privilege also applies when media content is shared by users and if this would subsequently be an argument for a 'trusted source' privilege on platforms. Some platforms have in the past given a special status to content produced by news outlets. Consequently, it would not be flagged or removed as quickly as UGC. This type of protected status does not define what type of media would benefit from that privilege when everyone can be a journalist in times of social media.[24]

[19] J Constine, 'Instagram Now Demotes Vaguely "Inappropriate" Content' (2019) TechCrunch, available at social.techcrunch.com/2019/04/10/instagram-borderline; M Sands, 'YouTube's "Borderline Content" Is A Hate Speech Quagmire' Forbes (2019), available at www.forbes.com/sites/masonsands/2019/06/09/youtubes-borderline-content-is-a-hate-speech-quagmire.

[20] MJ Crockett, 'Moral Outrage in the Digital Age' (2017) 1 *Nature Human Behaviour* 769; S Zuboff, *The Age of Surveillance Capitalism: The Fight for a Human Future at the New Frontier of Power* (PublicAffairs, 2019); R DiResta, 'Free Speech in the Age of Algorithmic Megaphones' Wired (2018), available at www.wired.com/story/facebook-domestic-disinformation-algorithmic-megaphones.

[21] AP Heldt, 'Borderline Speech: Caught in a Free Speech Limbo?' (2020) *Internet Policy Review*, available at policyreview.info/articles/news/borderline-speech-caught-free-speech-limbo/1510.

[22] Definition by Merriam-Webster, available at www.merriam-webster.com/dictionary/borderline.

[23] eg, YouTube's 'four essential freedoms' statement, available at www.youtube.com/intl/en/about.

[24] Moreover, it does not address the issue of disinformation and how it is handled by the platforms' respective policies. Recently, this issue has become particularly pressing when platforms faced a peak of false information regarding the spread of COVID-19. Indeed, the pandemic crisis has become a crucial test for the platforms' policies against disinformation.

C. Current Rules on Intermediary Liability

A non-negligible aspect with regard to the role of platforms in online communication is how they have replaced previous authorities in information procurement ('new gatekeepers') and how lawmakers in the US and the EU somewhat facilitated this process by adopting laws providing immunity for intermediaries, such as Section 230 CDA and Article 14 E-Commerce-Directive.[25] By treating intermediaries hosting UGC as 'information pipes' rather than editors, regulators have spared them from taking responsibility for their users' content. Prima facie, the regulatory instruments are different in the US and in the EU because Section 230(c)(2)(A) CDA protects intermediaries from being held liable when moderating UGC,[26] whereas Article 14, para 1(a) E-Commerce protects them from liability when they do *not* moderate content.[27] Despite their fundamental differences, these laws have led to similar effects. In both cases, states entrusted the task of governing UGC to private actors and – at least in the EU – relied on soft law instruments to control them. Social media platforms did not become 'new gatekeepers' or 'new governors'[28] overnight – the regulatory framework was propitious to this development.[29]

Similarly, none of these laws included any obligation regarding implementing human rights-related prioritisation rules, procedural standards such as human-made decision, justification, right to appeal, etc. Given the amount of data uploaded every minute, social media platforms increasingly rely on algorithms and AI to control unwanted content. Often, machines enforce community standards although they are not fit for purpose.[30] The priority is to remove unwanted content quickly and avoid spread as much as possible. This goal is not erroneous in itself. In many cases, such as child pornography, incitement to immediate violence, or terror propaganda, fast action is mandatory. At the same time, it bears great risks for freedom of expression and due process because, according to the platforms' rules, protecting fundamental rights and principles of democratic systems will not be prioritised if they cannot be integrated in the business model.

All in all, the issue of content moderation on social media platforms is difficult to handle because of the several levels it contains, that is, the rules for online

[25] Chander, 'Silicon Valley' (2014).

[26] 'No provider or user of an interactive computer service shall be held liable on account of … any action voluntarily taken in good faith to restrict access to or availability of material that the provider or user considers to be obscene, lewd, lascivious, filthy, excessively violent, harassing, or otherwise objectionable, whether or not such material is constitutionally protected.'

[27] 'Member States shall ensure that the service provider is not liable for the information stored at the request of a recipient of the service, on condition that: (a) the provider does not have actual knowledge of illegal activity or information and, as regards claims for damages, is not aware of facts or circumstances from which the illegal activity or information is apparent.'

[28] K Klonick, 'The New Governors: The People, Rules, and Processes Governing Online Speech' (2018) 131 *Harvard Law Review* 1598.

[29] Chander (n 6).

[30] Gorwa, Binns and Katzenbach, 'Algorithmic Content Moderation' (2020).

speech, their enforcement, and the responsibility of the respective actor in this context. If all of this is allocated to social media platforms without the option of interference, there is a severe risk of a power concentration over communication in the digital sphere with a handful of private actors and the state.

V. Why Judicial Review Matters

This concentration of power results, indeed, out of the multi-dimensional challenges connected to social media platforms. In light of the current calls for action vis-à-vis the state, one needs to carefully differentiate between the constitutional bodies to be considered. The constitutionalisation discussion is very much about platforms observing their users' fundamental rights, and while this goal might be reached by non-content-based regulation, it needs judicial review to reach decisions on a case-by-case basis.

In an article on the 'constitutional bounds of database protection', Benkler summarisd the importance of judicial review as follows:

> The reason for the robust judicial review created by these cumulative constraints on congressional power has to do with the importance of information to our society and with the systematic biases of the political economy of enclosure. The capacity to access information, to rework it, and to communicate it to others in society is central both to political self-governance and to personal autonomy.[31]

The emergence of social media platforms as powerful actors in the digital sphere does not make this statement obsolete. In fact, the importance of information to our society has not decreased at all, and the protection of information flows has gained more attention. This development of power relations does not make it less essential to stay vigilant with regard to the coercive power of the state in the digital sphere. However, there is a need for adaptation in two regards: first, constraints should not apply to 'congressional power' only;[32] and, second, the interpretation and application of the law have to remain the role of the judiciary, which is threatened by the features of content moderation highlighted in the above section.

A. The Challenges to Separation of Powers

The principle of separation of powers lays the foundation of democratic systems: power comes from the people ('we the people') and is divided between government bodies. In representative democracies, legislative power is the most immediate

[31] Y Benkler, 'Constitutional Bounds of Database Protection: The Role of Judicial Review in the Creation and Definition of Private Rights in Information' (2000) 15 *Berkeley Technology Law Journal* 535.

[32] Referring to Benkler's citation, cf Benkler (ibid).

form of power by the people; that is, a parliament or, similarly, chambers of elected representatives. In addition, the executive serves the enforcement of the law and the judiciary controls the constitutionality of legislative acts and the exercise of power. While lawmaking serves the most prominent function in democratic states, the executive power holds a 'head start' in the interpretation of legislative acts when enforcing them, compared to the judiciary. Enforcement of laws creates facts and, subsequently, constitutes precedent. Only if a party chooses to file a case in court or to act against a specific measure by means of judicial review will the judiciary be able to exercise power. This makes it less comprehensive: it can only respond to matters brought to court, be it an individual case or the abstract review of a legislative act. This interdependency is one of the characteristics of judicial power.

Another characteristic is its independence in structure and substantively. First, courts are separated from the two other forms of power, and from the political arena in general. Of course, one can argue that the judicial power is a type of political power as well because – at the level of constitutionality – it can shape lawmaking and law enforcement. In principle, however, courts apply the law and shall not interfere with political agenda-setting. Indeed, they ought to counterbalance the influence of political bargaining on legislative acts. Hence, in liberal democracies magistracy is usually organised in such way that the judges' independence is guaranteed regardless of their rulings. Courts are still perceived as a foreign body in platform governance and a negligible factor in setting up rules for the digital sphere. They seem relevant only at a national scale because they review and apply law within a national regulatory framework. This perspective overlooks the relevance of case law for legal theory and the rule of law. A functioning system of courts is both a prerequisite of and a result in deliberative democracies, and therefore highly relevant for the governance of the digital sphere. Moreover, constitutional courts use authoritative and discursive elements when reaching a decision which makes them an integral part of the public debate,[33] eg, about the limits of free speech.

Broadly speaking, digitalisation has brought challenges to the separation-of-powers-principle, not because a 'digital revolution' overturned our democratic system, but because the normative power of the state (ie, the legislative power) has been challenged by private actors who create rules for the digital sphere. The notion of separation of powers remains state-centred but needs to also capture private ordering, since it has become an attribute of cyber-regulation.[34] As described above, this is especially true for norms governing communicative processes. In addition, these new rules by private actors are enforced by themselves, a process

[33] MK Klatt, 'Autoritative und diskursive Instrumente des Bundesverfassungsgerichts' in O Lepsius et al (eds), *Jahrbuch des öffentlichen Rechts der GegenwartI* vol 68 (Mohr Siebeck, 2020).

[34] L Belli and J Venturini, 'Private Ordering and the Rise of Terms of Service as Cyber-Regulation' (2016) 5 *Internet Policy Review*, available at policyreview.info/articles/analysis/private-ordering-and-rise-terms-service-cyber-regulation.

that can be described as a combination of private ordering and new administrative law.[35] Teubner pointed out that digitisation is 'bringing about a kind of nuclear fusion of law-making, application and enforcement', which, according to him, leads to the disappearance of both the 'constitutional separation of powers within the legal process and an important guarantee for individual and institutional autonomy'.[36] Of course, the emergence of private power in communication is not solely due to technological progress: globalisation stimulated digitisation, and vice-versa.[37] With the sophistication of technology, the complexity and the sophistication of communication can generally be increased, not only since the Internet.[38] The latter has led to not only the emergence of users as producers of media content,[39] but also new concepts in journalism as the datafication of society evolves.[40] Either way, digital communicative tools complete and nourish the traditional form of the public sphere.[41]

Assuming that social media platforms have a supplementary effect for the customary communicative infrastructure,[42] and for the rules governing them,[43] two forms of power generally allocated with the state (norm-making and norm-enforcing) are now primarily with private actors. Their rules are particularly relevant in areas where states have refrained from regulating, ie, speech. So-called 'new school speech regulation' aims at controlling speech online via the control of digital networks.[44] It does not make old-school speech regulation obsolete; in fact

[35] AP Heldt, 'Let's Meet Halfway: Sharing New Responsibilities in a Digital Age' (2019) *Journal of Information Policy* 336.

[36] Translated from: G Teubner, 'Globale Zivilverfassungen: Alternativen Zur Staatszentrierten Verfassungstheorie' (2003) 63 *Zeitschrift für ausländisches öffentliches Recht und Völkerrecht* 1.

[37] M Castells, 'The New Public Sphere: Global Civil Society, Communication Networks, and Global Governance' (2008) 616 *The ANNALS of the American Academy of Political and Social Science* 78.

[38] C Neuberger, C Nuernbergk and M Rischke (eds), *Journalismus im Internet: Profession, Partizipation, Technisierung* (Springer VS, 2009) 19; see also RA Dahl, *Democracy and Its Critics* (Yale University Press, 1989) 339.

[39] A Bruns, 'Towards produsage: Futures for user-led content production' in F Sudweeks, H Hrachovec and C Ess (eds), *Proceedings Cultural Attitudes towards Communication and Technology* (School of Information Technology, Murdoch University, 2006).

[40] W Loosen, 'Data-Driven Gold-Standards: What the Field Values as Award-Worthy Data Journalism and How Journalism Co-Evolves with the Datafication of Society' in J Gray and L Bounegru (eds), *The Data Journalism Handbook 2 – Towards a Critical Data Practice.* (European Journalism Centre and Google News Initiative, 2019), available at datajournalism.com/read/handbook/two/situating-data-journalism/data-driven-gold-standards-what-the-field-values-as-award-worthy-data-journalism-and-how-journalism-co-evolves-with-the-datafication-of-society.

[41] Among others: K Kamps, 'Die Agora des Internets – Zur Debatte politischer Öffentlichkeit und Partizipation im Netz' in O Jarren, K Imhof and R Blum (eds), *Zerfall der Öffentlichkeit?* (Westdt Verl, 2000) 233; U Klinger, 'Aufstieg der Semiöffentlichkeit: Eine relationale Perspektive' (2018) 63 *Publizistik* 245.

[42] D Kreiss and SC McGregor, 'Technology Firms Shape Political Communication: The Work of Microsoft, Facebook, Twitter, and Google With Campaigns During the 2016 U.S. Presidential Cycle' (2017) 35 *Political Communication* 1; A Jungherr and R Schroeder, 'Disinformation and the Structural Transformations of the Public Arena: Addressing the Actual Challenges to Democracy' (2021) 7 *Social Media + Society*.

[43] T Gillespie, *Custodians of the Internet: Platforms, Content Moderation, and the Hidden Decisions That Shape Social Media* (Yale University Press, 2018).

[44] JM Balkin, 'Old School/New School Speech Regulation' (2014) 127 *Harvard Law Review* 2296.

they supplement each other. Germany, for instance, allows speech-restricting laws under constitutional proviso by Article 5(2) Basic Law. Since its adoption 2017, the German Network Act (NetzDG) forces social media platforms to ensure that 'obviously unlawful content' is deleted within 24 hours. The NetzDG was meant to enhance the protection of users against hate speech and to provide more clarity on the way platforms handle and moderate unlawful content.[45] It led the way in terms of platform regulation for a while.[46] Now, the EU is catching up, with the Digital Services Package. However, while statutory regulation might address some of the issues related to content moderation, the underlying question regarding the platforms' concentration of power in a constitutional framework remains unaffected.

B. Platforms as Non-State Actors

The separation of state and non-state actors, as well as contractual freedom, gives market participants the freedom to shape their relationship without being bound to fundamental rights such as freedom of expression. This is particularly true for countries where the marketplace of ideas is not or very little limited by regulation, such as the US. According to the state action doctrine, only the state is bound to fundamental rights and the relationship between private parties shall be immune to the application of constitutional rights.[47] This strict distinction allows social media platforms to moderate their users' speech, whereas, as state actors, they would be bound to the First Amendment like governmental actors. Only a few exceptions to the state action doctrine exist. Courts have, so far, been reluctant to apply free speech principles to private actors.[48] In First Amendment theory, an argument closely linked to the one of truth and the one of democracy (perhaps a combination of both), is the one of 'free speech as a check on abuse of authority, especially government authority'.[49] In other words, if power abuses can be prevented by transparency, they need not necessarily be exercised by a government. Such risk can emanate from a private actor and still represent a similar threat to free speech. However, this approach is highly controversial.

The controversy whether social media platforms provide a public forum is at the intersection of the state action and public forum doctrines. In recent decisions,

[45] T Wischmeyer, '"What Is Illegal Offline Is Also Illegal Online" – The German Network Enforcement Act 2017' in B Petkova and T Ojanen (eds), *Fundamental Rights Protection Online: The Future Regulation of Intermediaries* (Edward Elgar, 2019) 7.

[46] Experts agree that it should stay this way because they fear more authoritarian regimes could copy and take advantage of it for censorship purposes. eg, J Mchangama and N Alkiviadou, '*The Digital Berlin Wall: How Germany (Accidentally) Created a Prototype for Global Online Censorship – Act Two*' (Justitia, 2020).

[47] Civil Rights Cases 109 US 3 (1883); E Chemerinsky, *Constitutional Law: Principles and Policies*, 4th edn (Wolters Kluwer Law & Business, 2011) 524.

[48] *Marsh v Alabama* 326 US 501 (1946).

[49] K Greenawalt, 'Free Speech Justifications' (1989) 89 *Columbia Law Review* 119.

the Supreme Court made it clear that social media constitute a very significant platform for speech.[50] In *Packingham v North Carolina*, the Supreme Court found that such 'websites can provide perhaps the most powerful mechanisms available to a private citizen to make his or her voice heard'. It, nonetheless, refrains from treating such platforms as public fora in a doctrinal sense. In the case of *Knight Institute v Trump*, the US Court of Appeals for the Second Circuit considered the Twitter account of then-President Trump a designated public forum.[51] The Knight Institute's lawsuit was based on Trump's blocking seven people from the @realDonaldTrump Twitter account. Again, this decision stresses the relevance of social media, but the court based its decision on the fact that the account was run by a governmental actor. Following the 2020 Presidential elections, the Supreme Court vacated the judgment.[52] Nonetheless, in his concurring opinion, Justice Thomas emphasised the problematic concentration of power with social media platforms, criticising the 'unbridled control … in the hands of a private party'.

While the Court's approach can be criticised as formalism[53] and a doctrinal cul-de-sac,[54] an argument in favour of a clear separation between state actors and private parties is the power distribution.[55] Considering the state's ability to deploy discursive power and to propagate ideas, it needs be to treated differently (legally speaking).[56] The rationale of the First Amendment to protect free speech from the state's coercive power is still valid in many ways.[57] The *Knight Institute* case shows that we do not need to fall back on Internet shutdowns in authoritarian regimes to illustrate this theory.[58] In other words, the distinction between state actors and private entities matters, but there are arguments in favour of social media platforms taking on responsibility for the content they host and the communicative space they provide.

C. Bridging the Gap

While platforms are non-state actors because their hybrid role in today's communicative setting is not yet fully grasped, they could still be bound to their users'

[50] *Reno v ACLU* 521 US 844 (1997).
[51] *Knight First Amendment Institute, et al v Donald J. Trump, et al*, No 18 Civ 1691 (2d Cir 2020).
[52] *Joseph R Biden, Jr, President of the United States, et al v Knight First Amendment Institute at Columbia University, et al*, No 20-197, 593 US ____ (2021).
[53] K Werhan, 'The Supreme Court's Public Forum Doctrine and the Return of Formalism' (1986) 7 *Cardozo Law Review* 335.
[54] AP Heldt, 'Merging the Social and the Public: How Social Media Platforms Could Be a New Public Forum' (2020) 46 *Mitchell Hamline Law Review* 997.
[55] LR Bevier, 'Rehabilitating Public Forum Doctrine: In Defense of Categories' (1992) 1992 *Supreme Court Review* 79.
[56] Greenawalt, 'Free Speech Justifications' (1989) 134–35.
[57] JN Gathegi, 'The Public Library as a Public Forum: The (De)Evolution of a Legal Doctrine' (2005) 75 *The Library Quarterly* 1.
[58] eg G De Gregorio and N Stremlau, 'Internet Shutdowns in Africa | Internet Shutdowns and the Limits of Law' (2020) 14 *International Journal of Communication* 20.

right to freedom of expression according to the horizontal effect doctrine. In First Amendment theory, protecting free speech means protecting the individual from the coercive power of the state. Similarly, freedom of expression in Article 5, para 1 German Basic Law or in Article 10 ECHR is protecting the individual against the state. Their wording does not include relations between private parties and will not unfold unless courts recognise the need to apply the constitutional values via the interpretation of statutory law.[59] Indeed, the indirect horizontal effect of fundamental rights is quite prominent in Germany and currently being revived in the context of content moderation. The horizontal effect of fundamental rights can only emerge *through* jurisprudence – hence the need for judicial review despite its limitations.

When there is neither 'new school' speech regulation nor intermediary liability, and when the scope of protection of freedom of expression technically prevents lawmakers from passing speech-restricting laws, the factual governors of online speech are social media platforms.[60] Should the enforcement of their content rules subsequently be reviewed by a corporate body? On the very contrary: trusting social media platforms with the control of their decisions based on their own rules would lead to an unjustifiable concentration of power of online communication. Judicial review is an irreplaceable component of our democracy. Hence, there can only be additional support from non-state actors, but not as a substitution of courts.

How effective can judicial review be? From a performance-based perspective, judicial review might do poorly. Courts reach decisions on a case-by-case basis, hence their work is considered not scalable for the purposed of mass content moderation on social media platforms.[61] At the same time, guiding principles in verdicts do not address issues at small scale whereas the difficulty of content moderation often lies in small differences and details. Moreover, context plays an important role to adjudicate on speech-related matters but cannot be foreseen in an online environment (as opposed to traditional news outlets). Landmark cases, however, have a game-changing impact on how the law is interpreted and, subsequently, on private actors' behaviour. Therefore, building on constitutional case law can help preserve legal pluralism despite the platforms' global business model. Although the indirect effect is perceived like a vague doctrine,[62] courts in Germany have shown how to develop criteria to balance freedom of expression with other fundamental rights. These criteria still preserve the significance of free expression for democracy while leaving enough room for individual cases to be evaluated and decided.

Additionally, one might caution against too much judicial power and overestimating the positive influence of constitutional legal practice versus the platforms'

[59] Primarly: BVerfGE [FCC] 7, 198 – Lüth.
[60] Klonick, 'The New Governors' (2018) 1603, 1662 f.
[61] Douek, 'Governing Online Speech' (2021).
[62] The state action doctrine likewise.

private ordering. The first argument is a prominent one amongst scholars who diagnose a 'creeping constitutionalism'.[63] They perceive increasing 'juristocracy'[64] as an alleged inevitable institutional response to counterbalance contemporary challenges due to globalisation.[65] Based on Kelsen, Shapiro and Stone-Sweet, for instance, argue that

> in systems in which the supremacy of the constitutional law within the general hierarchy of norms defended by a jurisdictional authority, all separation of powers notions are contingent because they are secondary to, rather than constitutive of, the judicial function.[66]

The political effects of judicialisation on content moderation are still under scrutiny.[67] While acknowledging the rights-preserving impact of courts on legal discourse, one might criticise the lack of democratic legitimacy of constitutional courts as opposed to elected members of parliament. While this Gordian knot cannot be unravelled in this chapter, I would argue in favour of a stronger influence of constitutional courts on the lawmaking process, specifically for the digital sphere. This position must be understood in the current context, ie, one that is significantly influenced by companies and is accordingly in their favour. Not only can court decisions lead to stronger protection of fundamental rights thanks to their discursive authority beyond the individual case, but they can also be the mouthpiece of minorities whose voice is completely left out of platform regulation.

VI. Outlook

Facts can be checked by experts and distributed by journalists. Traditional mass media in particular play a key role in reflecting and conveying what is relevant for the formation of public opinion. The way media frame and distribute a story can completely change its meaning. But when it comes to applying the law, the findings can only be made by courts. Content moderation by social media platforms needs an independent control by courts and the horizontal effect doctrine can contribute to the development of rules that include the development of protection human rights such as freedom of expression.

[63] G Teubner, 'Societal Constitutionalism: Alternatives to State-Centred Constitutional Theory?' in C Joerges, I-J Sand and G Teubner (eds), *Transnational governance and constitutionalism* (Bloomsbury, 2004).

[64] R Hirschl, *Towards Juristocracy: The Origins and Consequences of the New Constitutionalism* (Harvard University Press, 2004).

[65] R Hirschl, 'The Nordic Counternarrative: Democracy, Human Development, and Judicial Review' (2011) 9 *International Journal of Constitutional Law* 449.

[66] MM Shapiro and AS Sweet, *On Law, Politics, and Judicialization* (Oxford University Press, 2002) 364.

[67] CI Keller, 'Policy by Judicialisation: The Institutional Framework for Intermediary Liability in Brazil' (2020) *International Review of Law, Computers & Technology*, available at www.tandfonline.com/doi/full/10.1080/13600869.2020.1792035.

16

Digital Constitutionalism: In Search of a Content Governance Standard

EDOARDO CELESTE, NICOLA PALLADINO, DENNIS REDEKER AND KINFE MICHEAL YILMA*

I. Introduction

One of the main issues of global content governance on social media relates to the definition of the rules governing online content moderation.[1] One could think that it would be sufficient for online platforms to refer to existing human rights standards. However, a more careful analysis shows that international law only provides general principles, which do not specifically address the context of online content moderation, and that a single human rights standard does not exist. Even identical provisions and principles are interpreted by courts in different ways across the world. This is one of the reasons why, since their inception, major social media platforms have set their own rules, adopting their own peculiar language, values and parameters. Yet, this normative autonomy too has raised serious concerns. Why should private companies establish the rules governing the biggest public forum for the exchange of ideas? Is it legitimate to depart from minimal human rights standards and impose more stringent rules?

The current situation exposes a dilemma for online content governance. On the one hand, if social media platforms simply adopted international law standards, they would be compelled to operate a choice on which standard to

* This work is the output of a project funded by Facebook Research. The authors conducted their research independently and their findings were subject to external peer review. No review by Facebook Research or its associates took place. We thank the participants at the Conference 'Constitutionalising Social Media' (Dublin, 20–21 May 2021) for their helpful comments on an earlier draft of this chapter as well as the peer reviewers for their constructive criticism.

[1] For a definition of content moderation, see T Gillespie, *Custodians of the Internet: Platforms, Content Moderation, and the Hidden Decisions That Shape Social Media* (Yale University Press, 2018); S Myers West, 'Censored, Suspended, Shadowbanned: User Interpretations of Content Moderation on Social Media Platforms' (2018) 20 *New Media & Society* 4366; on platform governance, see R Gorwa, 'What Is Platform Governance?' (2019) 22 *Information, Communication & Society* 854.

follow – for example, between the US freedom of expression-dominated approach or the European standard, which balances freedom of expression with other social values. Moreover, they would also need to put in place a mechanism able to translate, or 'operationalise' such general standards in the context of online content moderation. On the other hand, where social media platforms adopt their own values, rules and terminology to regulate content moderation, thus departing from international law standards, they are accused of censorship or laxity, intrusiveness or negligence.

The core issue and key to solving this dilemma lies in the capacity to define principles and values for online content governance, a task which is part of the broader process of constitutionalising the digital society.[2] This chapter aims to contribute to disentangle this Gordian knot. Firstly, we will clarify to what extent international law standards may provide useful guidance in the context of online content moderation and what their limitations are (section II). Secondly, we will examine a source of normative standards that has been so far neglected by the scholarship: civil society impulses. Over the past few years, a series of initiatives have emerged at societal level, and especially among civil society groups, including NGOs, think tanks, academia, trade unions, and grassroot associations, to articulate rights and principles for the digital age. The output of these efforts mostly consists of non-legally binding declarations, often intentionally adopting a constitutional tone and therefore termed 'Internet bills of rights'.

Our chapter aims to understand what social media platforms' online content governance rules can learn from these civil society initiatives. A peculiarity of these documents lies indeed in their surfacing outside traditional institutionalised constitutional processes. They can be considered as expressing the 'voice' of global communities that struggle to propose an innovative constitutional message within traditional institutional channels: one of the layers of the complex process of constitutionalisation that is pushing towards reconceptualising core constitutional principles in light of the challenges of the digital society in a new form of 'digital constitutionalism'.[3] We have collected a dataset of 40 documents and performed an empirical analysis of their content, looking specifically at how these declarations have articulated the rights and principles related to online content governance (section III). The chapter will then conclude with a case study focusing on Facebook's online content moderation rules, examining to what extent they reflect or depart from international and civil society standards (section IV).

[2] See E Celeste, 'Digital Constitutionalism: A New Systematic Theorisation' (2019) 33 *International Review of Law, Computers & Technology* 76.

[3] See D Redeker, L Gill and U Gasser, 'Towards Digital Constitutionalism? Mapping Attempts to Craft an Internet Bill of Rights' (2018) 80 *International Communication Gazette* 302; C Padovani and M Santaniello, 'Digital Constitutionalism: Fundamental Rights and Power Limitation in the Internet Eco-System' (2018) 80 *International Communication Gazette* 295; Celeste (ibid).

II. International Standards

Recent years have seen a growing attention in the potential of international law in offering normative guidance to address human rights concerns in content governance.[4] Partly in response to pressure from civil society groups, including through the launch of Internet bills of rights that advance progressive content governance standards, social media platforms are also increasingly turning attention to international human rights law.[5] This section considers the extent to which international law offers such guidance to the complex world of platform content governance.

A. Generic International Law Standards Applicable to Content Governance

The first set of international law standards applicable to content governance are general in scope and formulation. One such generic standard concerns human rights provisions that define the scope and nature of state human rights obligations.[6] The International Covenant on Civil and Political Rights (ICCPR), a human rights treaty widely ratified by states, provides the general framework for any consideration of content governance in international law. One way it does so is by defining the scope of state obligations vis-à-vis Covenant rights. States generally owe two types of obligations under the Covenant: negative and positive obligations.[7] States' negative obligation imposes a duty to 'respect' the enjoyment of rights. As such, it requires states and their organs to refrain from any conduct that would impair the enjoyment of rights guaranteed in the Covenant. States' positive obligations, on the other hand, impose a duty to 'protect' the exercise of rights. This obligation thus concerns state regulation of third parties including private actors to ensure respect for Covenant rights.

Secondly, one finds little-explored norms that would potentially apply to non-state actors, including social media companies directly. One is the Preamble of the Universal Declaration of Human Rights (UDHR), which – at the highest level – states that 'every organ of society' shall strive to promote respect for rights

[4] See M Lwin, 'Applying International Human Rights Law for Use by Facebook' (2020) 38 *Yale Journal on Regulation Online Bulletin* 53.

[5] See Facebook's Corporate Human Rights Policy (2021), available at about.fb.com/wp-content/uploads/2021/04/Facebooks-Corporate-Human-Rights-Policy.pdf. Note that almost all the decisions handed down thus far by Facebook's Oversight Board have drawn upon international human rights standards. See the decisions of the board at oversightboard.com/decision.

[6] For an analysis of the role of states in social media regulation, see the contributions in Chapter III of this volume.

[7] Art 2(1) ICCPR.

guaranteed in the Declaration.[8] Scholars argue that the reference to 'every organ of society' is said to include the duty of companies to 'respect' human rights.[9] This preambular proviso finds some concrete expression in international human rights law in the form of prohibition of abuse of rights. International law bestows no right upon anyone including 'groups and persons' as well as states to impair or destruct the enjoyment of the rights guaranteed in the Declaration and the Covenant.[10] This abuse of rights prohibition arguably would also apply to social media companies in a sense that their policies and practices, including those relating to content moderation, must not have the effect of impairing or destructing the enjoyment of human rights. In that sense, there is a negative obligation to 'respect' human rights which requires them to refrain from measures that would affect the enjoyment of rights. Indeed, the tendency in these provisions to address private actors directly – albeit generically – appears to be at odds with the state-centred nature of human rights law generally. But the sheer fact that these provisions appear to impose binding duties, regardless of how they would be enforced, would certainly add weight to recent scholarly arguments that international human rights law does, or should, apply to content moderation practices of platforms.[11]

B. Content Governance Standards in Human Rights and Principles

Content governance standards in international law are also to be found in the catalogue of human rights and principles. First, human rights law prohibits certain types of speech: war propaganda,[12] advocacy for racial, religious and national hatred[13] and racist speech.[14] In outlawing certain types of expression, international human rights law sets forth content governance standards that must be implemented by state parties to the relevant treaties, including in social media platforms. Social media companies are not bound by such international standards, but they may ban or restrict such types of speech to comply with national law or volitionally as they now do in practice.[15] Second, human rights law not

[8] Preamble, para 8 UDHR.

[9] See L Henkin, 'The Universal Declaration at 50 and the Challenges of Global Markets' (1999) 25 *Brooklyn Journal of International Law* 17, 25.

[10] Art 30 UDHR; Art 5(1) ICCPR.

[11] See L McGregor et al, 'International Human Rights Law as a Framework for Algorithmic Accountability' (2020) 68 *International Comparative Law Quarterly* 309.

[12] See Art 20(1) ICCPR.

[13] Art 20(2) ICCPR.

[14] Art 4 of the International Convention on the Elimination of All Forms of Racial Discrimination (21 December 1965).

[15] See M Bickert (Facebook), 'Updating the Values That Inform Our Community Standards' (12 September 2019), available at about.fb.com/news/2019/09/updating-the-values-that-inform-our-community-standards.

only guarantees the right to freedom of expression but also provides standards for permissible restrictions, namely, legality, necessity and legitimacy.[16]

Third, in addition to freedom of expression, content governance engages a broad range of human rights guaranteed in international law. Common acts of content moderation would normally limit freedom of expression of users. But other human rights and principles such as the right to equality/non-discrimination, right to effective remedy, right to fair hearing, right to honour and reputation and freedom of religion are also impacted by platform content moderation policies and practices. The right to 'enjoy the arts and to share in scientific advancements and its benefits' is another set of socio-economic rights that relates to content governance.[17] This 'right to science and culture' is aimed at enabling all persons who have not taken part in scientific inventions to participate in enjoying its benefits.[18] This provision has barely been invoked in practice, but it arguably would apply to counter aggressive content moderation practices of platforms vis-à-vis copyrighted material. As shall be highlighted in the next section, 'freedom from censorship', including the right not to be subjected to onerous copyright restrictions, is one of the content moderation-related standards proposed by civil society groups.

The 'right to science' has been interpreted to embody the right of individuals to be protected from the adverse effects of scientific inventions and the right to public participation in decision-making about science and its uses.[19] And this, as we will see, comes closer to civil society content governance standards that envisage duties on social media platforms to prevent harm and safeguard vulnerable social groups on social media platforms as well as the need to ensure meaningful participation in the development of policies.

C. International Soft Law on Content Governance

The UN Guiding Principles on Business and Human Rights (UNGPs, alternatively referred to as the Ruggie Principles) are a potential source of specific international content governance standards. The Ruggie Principles are currently the only international instrument that seeks to address the conduct of businesses and its impact on human rights (with some limits).[20] Not only do they primarily affirm

[16] See Art 19(3) ICCPR.

[17] Art 27(1) UDHR; Art 15(1)(b) of the International Covenant on Economic, Social and Cultural Rights (16 December 1966).

[18] R Adalsteinsson and P Thörhallson, 'Art 27', in G Alfreðsson and A Eide (eds), *The Universal Declaration of Human Rights: A Common Standard of Achievement* (Martinus Nijhoff Publishers, 1999) 575–78.

[19] Report of the Special Rapporteur in the field of Cultural Rights, Farida Shaheed, on the Right to Enjoy the Benefits of Scientific Progress and Its Applications, UN Doc A/HRC/20/26 (14 May 2012) Paras 25, 43–44; see also Committee on Economic, Social and Cultural Rights, General Comment No. 25: On Science and Economic, Social and Cultural Rights, UN Doc E/C.12/GC/25 (30 April 2020) para 74.

[20] OHCHR, Guiding Principles on Business and Human Rights: Implementing the United Nations 'Protect, Respect and Remedy' Framework, HRC Res 17/4 (16 June 2011).

states as the sole and primary duty-bearers in human rights law[21] but they are also couched in general principles. And this makes them less suited to the complex world of content moderation. It is, however, vital to note that the scope of the Ruggie Principles is defined in a manner to apply to businesses of all types and sectors.[22] This means that the principles would, theoretically, apply to social media platforms.

In a series of reports, the UN Special Rapporteur on Freedom of Expression, David Kaye, has sought to adapt the Ruggie Principles to the social media context.[23] While such elaborative reports provide useful intellectual guidance, they are legally non-binding, meaning that compliance by platforms would be entirely voluntary. Yet, this attests to the fact that a process of adaptation of international law standards, including the Ruggie Principles, to the social media context, is in the process of development.[24] Added to frequent exhortations of civil society groups on the normative value of the Ruggie Principles, emerging attempts at translating the UNGPs to the digital context may potentially contribute to this evolution of international standards on content governance.

Relatively progressive content moderation-related international standards are emerging through the work of Kaye. He has been part of a coalition of intergovernmental mandates on freedom of expression which, through Joint Declarations, outlined progressive standards on content moderation.[25] The Joint Declarations constitute international soft law that tend to unpack general free speech standards envisaged in the ICCPR as well as regional human rights treaties. The 2019 Resolution, for instance, states in its Preamble that the primary aim of the Joint Declarations is one of 'interpreting' human rights guarantees thereby 'providing guidance' to, inter alia, governments, civil society organisations and the business sector.[26] It further provides that the Joint Declarations have – over the years – 'contributed to the establishment of authoritative standards' on various aspects of free speech.[27]

Intermediary liability is one of the content governance-related themes addressed with some details in the Joint Declarations.[28] Current international hard law on free speech does not address the role of intermediaries, such as social media platforms, in curating and moderating content online. Intermediaries play a key role in the enjoyment of the right to freedom of expression online which makes appropriate regulation of their conduct an imperative. The objective of fair

[21] ibid Part I.

[22] Ruggie Principles (n 20) Part II, para 14.

[23] See Report of the Special Rapporteur on the Promotion and Protection of the Right to Freedom of Opinion and Expression, UN Doc HRC/38/35 (6 April 2018).

[24] See McGregor et al, 'International Human Rights Law' (2020) 326.

[25] See OSCE, 'Joint Declarations', available at www.osce.org/fom/66176?page=1.

[26] See Twentieth Anniversary Joint Declaration: Challenges to Freedom of Expression in the Next Decade (UN, OSCE, OAS & ACHPR, 10 July 2019) Preamble, para 3.

[27] ibid Preamble, para 4.

[28] See also the Joint Declaration on Freedom of Expression and 'Fake News', Disinformation and Propaganda (UN, OSCE, OAS & ACHPR, 3 March 2017).

intermediary liability, then, is to define the exceptional circumstances where intermediaries would be held liable for problematic content of their users. In filling the normative void in international law, the 2019 Joint Declaration in particular offers some international standards on intermediary liability. On top of the overarching 'responsibility' of intermediaries to 'respect human rights', the Declaration stipulates the principle to put in place clear and predetermined content moderation policies that are adopted after consultation with users, in line with what is called in international human rights law the requirement of legality, the requirement to institute minimum due process guarantees, such as prompt notification to users whose content may be subjected to content action and avenues by which users may challenge impending content actions.

Soft law generally offers authoritative interpretation of high-level principles of international hard law, but the approach in the Joint Declaration raises questions of form and substance in international law. One such question is whether a soft human rights instrument – drawing upon a human rights treaty – can directly address private actors that are not party to the treaty. But this point goes beyond the scope of this chapter.

D. The Role of International Standards

In conclusion, despite the recent turn to international human rights law for content governance standards, it appears to offer little guidance. It is uncertain, for instance, as to how it would apply to platform content governance. As shown above, this is mainly because international human rights law is – by design – state-centred and hence does not go far in attending to human rights concerns in the private sector. This is exacerbated by the characteristically generic formulation of international human rights standards which – in turn – make them less suited to the world of platform content moderation. The complex, voluminous and routine nature of content moderation requires a rather granular and dynamic system of norms. What is more, the generic international content governance standards have not adequately been unpacked by relevant adjudicative bodies, such as the United Nations Human Rights Committee, to make them fit for purpose to the present realities of content moderation. By and large, content governance jurisprudence at the international level remains thin. However, international law's primary value, thus far, has been to provide the overarching normative framework, on which recent progressive civil society content governance standards build, as we will explore in the next section.

III. Civil Society Initiatives

This section analyses a selected sample of 40 Internet bills of rights developed by civil society groups, and articulating rights and principles addressing online content governance.[29] Table 16.1 provides for a synthetic overview of the principles we detected in the corpus, grouped into three major categories. The first one collects all the provisions explicitly concerned with international human rights law compliance. The other two categories distinguish respectively between substantive and procedural standards. 'Substantive standards' refer to people's rights and responsibilities related to the creation and publication of content on the Internet. 'Procedural principles' indicate formal rules and procedures through which substantive rights shall be exercised and enforced, ie the rules through which decisions about users' contents are made, including the rulemaking process itself.

Table 16.1 Civil society initiatives

Categories	No of documents	Principles included
General compliance with human rights standards	19	
Substantive principles	**39**	
Freedom of expression	38	Freedom from censorship, freedom from copyright restriction, freedom of religion
Prevention of harm	16	Harassment, cyberbullying, defamation, incitement to violence, cybercrime, human dignity
Protection of social groups	13	Non-discrimination of marginalised group, discriminating content, hate speech, children rights and protection
Public interest	6	Public health or morality, public order and national security, fake news and disinformation, protection of infrastructure layer
Intermediary liability	9	Full immunity, conditional liability, intermediaries are liable in the case of actual knowledge of infringing content, intermediaries are liable when they fail to comply with adjudicatory order
Procedural principles	**32**	
Rule of law	24	Legality, legal certainty, rule of law, judicial oversight, legal remedy, necessity and proportionality

(continued)

[29] See Annex 1, available at bit.ly/3pPmBmr.

Table 16.1 *(Continued)*

Categories	No of documents	Principles included
Good governance principles	19	Transparency, accountability, fairness, participation, multistakeholderism, democratic governance
Platform-specific principles	21	Notification procedures, human oversight, human rights due diligence, limitations to automated content moderation, informed consent, right to appeal and remedy

A. Substantive Principles

Our analysis shows a high degree of consistency among the documents analysed. A consensus emerges on a shared set of principles to be applied to content governance, which, taken together, outline a coherent normative framework. Civil society declarations draw extensively on human rights law. Half of our sample refers explicitly to one of the international human rights law instruments discussed in the previous section (especially ICCPR, UDHR, Ruggie Principles), or more generally advocates for the respect of human rights standards. Moreover, even when not referred to explicitly, the documents we analysed provide for rights and principles drawn from the international human rights literature.

Within this framework, freedom of expression emerges as the core principle and main concern of civil society when dealing with content moderation in the context of digital constitutionalism initiatives. Not only is it the most quoted principle, but most of the other rights and interests emerge within discussions about free speech and its limitations, and are clearly presented as subordinate to freedom of expression. Three categories of substantive principles, respectively related to the prevention of online and offline harm, the protection of social groups and public interest, set the boundaries of what civil society considers acceptable derogation to the principle of freedom of expression, and which in turn justifies content removal. Sixteen documents refer to the protection of individuals from potential harms including harassment, cyberbullying, incitement to violence, damage to reputation and dignity. Thirteen documents call into question principles aiming at protecting minorities or vulnerable groups from troubling content, or content that constitute incitement to hatred, violence or discrimination. Six documents refer to some articulations of public interest, such as protection of national security, public health, morals, or more recently fake news and disinformation. It is worth noting that these kinds of permissible restrictions reflect those foreseen by international law, and in particular Article 19 of UDHR and ICCPR.

B. Procedural Principles

In relation to substantive principles, civil society initiatives limit themselves to reiterate general international human rights standards in the context of social media platforms. Conversely, as regards procedural principles, Internet bills of rights perform a more articulated 'generalisation and respecification' of international standards in light of the peculiar nature of the social media environment.[30] The procedural principles advanced by civil society can be divided into three subcategories. Firstly, a series of principles address states and online platforms, and can be collected under the label of 'rule of law' principles. Civil society organisations require, on the one hand, governments to establish a legal framework providing certainty and predictability for content moderation, and on the other hand, platforms to execute content removal requests from states only when provided by law. As a minimum, civil society require states to:

(1) define freedom of expression restrictions and what constitutes illegal content through democratic processes and according to international human rights law standards, adopting in particular the tripartite test of legality, necessity and proportionality
(2) clearly establish under which conditions intermediaries are deemed responsible for user-generated content, and which kind of actions they must undertake
(3) guarantee appropriate judicial oversight over content removal and the right to legal remedy.

The main concern here is that constitutional safeguards and rule of law are circumvented by outsourcing online content moderation adjudication and enforcement to private entities. Furthermore, civil society groups in particular claim that states must not impose a 'general monitoring obligation' to intermediaries.[31] Human rights defenders fear that encouraging a 'proactive' content moderation will lead to 'over-removal of content or outright censorship'.[32] In doing so, civil society groups recall the warnings advanced by the UN Special Rapporteur David Kaye in his 2018 report on the promotion and protection of the right to freedom of opinion and expression.[33]

[30] See E Celeste, 'Terms of Service and Bills of Rights: New Mechanisms of Constitutionalisation in the Social Media Environment?' (2019) 33 *International Review of Law, Computers & Technology* 122; see also G Teubner, *Constitutional Fragments: Societal Constitutionalism and Globalization* (Oxford University Press, 2012).

[31] Access Now, '26 Recommendations on Content Governance' (2020). See also The Manila Principles (2015).

[32] Access Now (2020) 13. See also, among others, Association for Progressive Communication, 'Content Regulation in the Digital Age' (2018); Art 19 The Universal Declaration of Digital Rights (2017); EDRI, 'The Charter of Digital Rights' (2014); Declaration on Freedom of Expression In response to the adoption of the Network Enforcement Law (2017).

[33] D Kaye, 'Report of the Special Rapporteur on the Promotion and Protection of the Right to Freedom of Opinion and Expression – A/HRC/38/35' (June 2019), available at documents-dds-ny.un.org/doc/UNDOC/GEN/G18/096/72/PDF/G1809672.pdf?OpenElement.

The second category refers to a series of 'good governance' standards that apply both to states and private companies. They include the principles of transparency, accountability, fairness and participatory decision-making. However, the most interesting group of procedural principles is the third one, which we termed 'platforms-specific principles'. It is indeed here that civil society contextualises and adapts general international human rights standards into more granular norms and rules to be implemented in the platform environment.

This last group includes six procedural principles:

(1) *Certainty and predictability*. As discussed above in relation to transparency, platforms are asked to provide certainty and predictability through accessible terms of service and community standards, including well-defined and transparent decision-making processes. These principles articulate rule of law standards with specific reference to social media platforms.
(2) *Appeal and remedy*. Fourteen civil society documents affirm a right to appeal and remedy. This principle partially overlaps with the right to legal remedy mentioned in the previous category, but in this case specifically focuses on private companies' practices. According to the Santa Clara Principles, 'Companies should provide a meaningful opportunity for timely appeal of any content removal or account suspension', then describing what the 'minimum standards for a meaningful appeal' are.[34] Companies are also requested to provide remedies, such as 'restoring eliminated content in case of an illegitimate or erroneous removal', 'providing a right to reply', 'issuing apologies or corrections' or 'providing economic compensation'.[35]
(3) *Notification procedures*. Social media companies should provide notice to each user whose contents have been subject to content moderation decisions. This notification must include at least all relevant details about the content removed, which provision of the Terms of Service breached, how it was detected and an explanation of the user's possibilities to appeal the decision.[36]
(4) *Limitations to automated content moderation*. Companies should limit the use of automated content moderation systems to well-defined manifestly illegal content. Platforms should provide clear and transparent policies for automated content moderation. Users should be informed about the usage of automated systems. Companies should provide for human oversight or human review of automated decisions and should adopt an approach to minimize human rights risks by design.
(5) *Human rights due diligence or impact assessment*. Social media platforms should scrutinise on an ongoing basis their policies, products, services with the consultation of third-party human rights experts in order to evaluate their

[34] Santa Clara Principles on Transparency and Accountability in Content Moderation (2018).
[35] 'Access Now' (2020) 40.
[36] On notification requirements see also Access Now (n 31); and Association for Progressive Communication, 'Content Regulation' (2018).

impact on human rights. Companies are also called to share information and data with researchers and civil society organisations and to support independent research.

(6) *Independent self-regulation bodies.* Some civil society organizations call for the establishment of independent self-regulatory bodies, following the example of press councils or ethics committees. The most developed attempt in this regard is provided by the NGO Article19, which outlines the model of a Social Media Council.[37]

IV. A Comparison with Facebook's Community Standards

Facebook is a global social media platform, offering its services across jurisdictions. Its transnational nature implies that content moderation on Facebook generates a variety of normative conflicts, among users and between users and state actors. Since, in principle, no single cultural or legal standard can be applied to decide how to reconcile these normative conflicts, Facebook resorted to a solution in its scale 'unique to communication practices in the digital age':[38] it set its own rules for a communication space used by almost 1.8 billion daily users.[39] The norms that guide Facebook's content moderation practices – its Community Standards – are perhaps the most important example of 'platform law' today.[40] The Community Standards are described as a 'living set of guidelines'[41] governing what is allowed and prohibited on the platform. These guidelines are made and remade by the company's Policy Team in a process that brings in academics and other experts in the field, but that failed to be grounded in a 'popular' vote by the platform's users.[42]

Following the articulation of the previous two sections which examined substantive and procedural principles of international law and civil society declarations in the context of online content moderation, this section assesses how

[37] ARTICLE 19, 'Self-Regulation and "Hate Speech" on Social Media Platforms' (2018), available at www.article19.org/wp-content/uploads/2018/03/Self-regulation-and-'hate-speech'-on-social-media-platforms_March2018.pdf; cf also UK Government, 'Online Harms White Paper' (2019) 46, available at assets.publishing.service.gov.uk/government/uploads/system/uploads/attachment_data/file/973939/Online_Harms_White_Paper_V2.pdf.

[38] See MC Kettemann and W Schulz, 'Setting Rules for 2.7 Billion. A (First) Look into Facebook's Norm-Making System: Results of a Pilot Study' (January 2020), available at www.hans-bredow-institut.de/uploads/media/default/cms/media/k0gjxdi_AP_WiP001InsideFacebook.pdf.

[39] See Statista, 'Number of Daily Active Facebook Users Worldwide as of 4th Quarter 2020', available at www.statista.com/statistics/346167/facebook-global-dau.

[40] See LA Bygrave, *Internet Governance by Contract* (Oxford University Press, 2015); Kaye, 'Report of the Special Rapporteur' (2019).

[41] See Facebook, 'Writing Facebook's Rulebook', available at about.fb.com/news/2019/04/insidefeed-community-standards-development-process.

[42] See Kettemann and Schulz, 'Setting Rules for 2.7 Billion' (2020); N Suzor, 'Digital Constitutionalism: Using the Rule of Law to Evaluate the Legitimacy of Governance by Platforms' (2018) 4 *Social Media + Society* 1.

Facebook's content governance standards measure up in these two dimensions, starting with a discussion of substantive principles.

A. Substantive Principles Entailed in the Community Standards

Facebook's Community Standards are informed by the organisation's self-proclaimed 'core values', which emphasise creating 'a place for expression and giving people voice'.[43] What limits free expression are four values – authenticity, safety, privacy and dignity – and the application of copyright rules and national law. The focus on freedom of expression is absolutely consistent with the emphasis on this principle by civil society, as we observed in section III of this chapter.

The Community Standards are structured into six chapters, of which the first four outline restrictions on content based on Facebook's core values; chapter V affirms intellectual property and its protection, whereas chapter VI outlines procedural questions and refers to the Oversight Board. The first four chapters currently entail a total of 23 principles defining content that must not be posted on the platform.[44] These 23 substantive principles align rather well with the principles we found in civil society documents. Specifically, addressing the three categories of 'prevention of harm', 'protection of social groups' and 'public interest' as outlined above, this section considers which of these categories is most often used to justify limitations on the chief principle of freedom of expression. Facebook issues content moderation transparency reports[45] covering 12 of the 23 principles associated with these three categories of limitations of freedom of expression.[46] Two principles – prohibitions on fake accounts and on spam – are not associated with the three most important categories of civil society demands. Table 16.2 indicates each category from the civil society documents and the corresponding Community Standards principles on which transparency reporting occurs.[47] It also shows the number of content takedowns in 2020 and the share of those takedowns appealed by users.[48] Finally, the table shows the shares of content takedowns triggered by

[43] See Facebook, 'Community Standards', available at www.facebook.com/communitystandards.

[44] If content is posted that violates these principles, it is deleted (unless a successful appeal is lodged). Recently, academics have proposed to keep copies of violating content in a 'poison cabinet'. See J Bowers, E Sedenberg and J Zittrain, 'Platform Accountability Through Digital "Poison Cabinets"' (Knight First Amendment Institute at Columbia University, 13 April 2021), available at knightcolumbia.org/content/platform-accountability-through-digital-poison-cabinets.

[45] See Facebook, 'Community Standards Enforcement Report', available at transparency.facebook.com/community-standards-enforcement.

[46] Facebook provides separate transparency reports for its actions concerning content that is covered by copyright rules (although also referenced in the Community Standards), See Facebook, 'Intellectual Property', available at transparency.facebook.com/intellectual-property, and, concerning legal requests by states, see Facebook, 'Content Restrictions Based on Local Law', available at transparency.facebook.com/content-restrictions.

[47] As of early May 2021.

[48] This data is for Facebook only: Instagram has its own, very similar but not identical, transparency reporting based on the same standards ('Facebook and Instagram share content policies. This means

automatic recognition, as opposed to flagging done by humans, in the last quarter of 2020.

Table 16.2 Content moderation by category derived from civil society documents, 2020[49]

Category/principle	Number of content actions	% appealed	% of automation (Q4, 2020)
Prevention of harm	**73.3m**	**0.2%**	–
– Bullying and harassment	14.5m	0.3%	48.8%
– Suicide and self-injury	6.4m	0.8%	92.8%
– Organised hate	19.1m	0.2%	98.3%
– Terrorism	33.3m	0.1%	99.8%
Protection of social groups	**332.3m**	**1.1%**	–
– Child nudity and sexual exploitation of children	35.9m	0.1%	98,8%
– Adult nudity and sexual activity	139.9m	1.7%	98.1%
– Violent and graphic content	75.5m	0.1%	99.5%
– Hate speech	81m	1.5%	97.1%
Public interest	**27.8m**	**1.2%**	–
– Regulated goods: firearms	5.1m	5.5%	92.2%
– Regulated goods: drugs	22.7m	0.2%	97.3%
Not categorised	**12.0bn**	**0,0%**	–
– Fake accounts	5.8bn	–	99.6%
– Spam	6.2m	0.0%	99.8%

The data reveals that, in 2020, most removal actions occurred to safeguard specific groups (around 332 million). More than 40 per cent of these actions relate to adult nudity and sexual activity, ostensibly protecting minors (Facebook generally allows accounts for anyone over 13 years old) and those who 'may be sensitive to this type of content'.[50] The category 'prevention of harm' counted for more than 73 million content removal actions in 2020, of which the removal of terrorist content makes up almost half (45.4 per cent). An association of categories from the previous section with the 12 principles Facebook reports on appears difficult with regard to the category of terrorism, which could also have been coded as public interest issue (specifically referring to the civil society principle of

if content is considered violating on Facebook, it is also considered violating on Instagram'.) See Facebook, 'Community Standards Enforcement Report' (n 45).

[49] See Facebook, 'Community Standards Enforcement Report' (n 45).

[50] See Facebook, 'Adult Nudity and Sexual Activity', available at www.facebook.com/communitystandards/adult_nudity_sexual_activity.

'public order and national security'), rather than a matter of harm prevention. However, such is the case with all illegal activities that bring in the state as an interested person *qua* the nature of criminal law. Content moderation based on the 'public interest' category identified above made up only about 28 million cases in 2020, with a clear concentration on identifying posts designed to 'purchase, sell or trade non-medical drugs, pharmaceutical drugs and marijuana' compared to a lower number of actions against content related to the 'purchase, sale, gifting, exchange and transfer of firearms'[51] (only accounting for about 18 per cent of this category). A great number of content actions are not associated with the demands that we found in civil society declarations to limit free speech (see the category 'not categorised' above): in 2020, 12 billion actions were taken by Facebook to remove fake accounts or spam.[52]

Overall, the substantive standards found in the 40 civil society documents analysed in the previous section appear well captured by the Community Standards. However, on the level of individual principles, ie below the broader categories, some substantial differences can be identified. Freedom of expression, the most-often cited value, is at times extended to the freedom from copyright restrictions when advocated for by civil society. Facebook's Community Standards, being less aspirational – and encompassing binding copyright rules – explicitly emphasise the protection of intellectual property and dedicate a separate chapter to it. The company states that protection of intellectual property is 'important to promoting expression, creativity and innovation in our community'.[53]

With regard to standards in international law, Facebook's Community Standards appear, once again, particularly conducive toward enabling and protecting free expression, based on its relatively limited list of exceptions. Its preamble stresses this focus on the provision of 'voice'. At the same time, considering the billions of content removals that occurred on the platform, one clearly sees that Facebook takes on the role of making and enacting rules to protect other important rights and principles, too. Some of these principles cover norms articulated in the UDHR and the ICCPR: for instance, with regard to prohibitions on advocacy for racial, religious and national hatred, the Community Standards expressly prohibit content that constitutes 'a direct attack against people on the basis of … protected characteristics: race, ethnicity, national origin, disability, religious affiliation, caste, sexual orientation, sex, gender identity and serious disease'.[54] However, while international law includes protections for groups, not merely individuals, Facebook's Community Standards, in practice, focus on protecting individuals

[51] See Facebook, 'Regulated Goods', available at www.facebook.com/communitystandards/regulated_goods.

[52] Here, fake accounts relate to the lack of an authentic person or organisation setting them up, unrelated to whether these accounts are engaged in spreading fake news/misinformation.

[53] See Facebook, 'Respecting Intellectual Property', available at m.facebook.com/communitystandards#!/communitystandards/respecting_intellectual_property; see L Lessig, 'Copyright's First Amendment Melville B. Nimmer Memorial Lecture' (2001) 48 *UCLA Law Review* 1057.

[54] See Facebook, 'Hate Speech', available at www.facebook.com/communitystandards/hate_speech.

with these attributes rather than the respective group. More recently, Facebook's moderation practices shifted toward a stronger emphasis on groups that are particularly vulnerable – in contrast to protecting all groups equally, including, for instance, white male Americans.[55]

In 2021, Facebook created a corporate human rights policy to demonstrate that it is 'committed to respecting human rights in [their] business operations, product development, policies and programming'.[56] In this document the company specifically refers to the UNGPs and vows to regularly report on how it addresses human rights. The company sees its human rights commitment as an extension of its work as part of the Global Network Initiative (GNI), the multistakeholder group behind the GNI Principles on Freedom of Expression and Privacy, included in the dataset of civil society declaration in the previous section. As part of the policy, next to public reporting on its human rights due diligence and the establishment of the independent Oversight Board, Facebook aims to alter 'key content policies, including creating a new policy to remove verified misinformation and unverifiable rumours that may put people at risk for imminent physical harm'.[57] The latter is a reaction to its assessment of human rights impacts in Sri Lanka, based on the framework of the UNGPs.[58]

B. Procedural Principles in the Community Standards

Without a way to enforce the Community Standards, they would be moot. Facebook's content moderation practices entail both automated moderation and human moderation teams, the latter consisting of 15,000 content moderators working in 50 languages.[59] As can be seen from Table 16.2, a large majority of content takedowns are not reviewed by humans at all. These 'proactive' content removals are based on algorithms that automatically (and probabilistically) detect supposed infractions of the Community Standards in audio-visual and textual user content. Reviews against these decisions can be requested by affected users.

[55] E Dwoskin, N Tiku and H Kelly, 'Facebook to start policing anti-Black hate speech more aggressively than anti-White comments, documents show' *Washington Post* (3 December 2020), available at www.washingtonpost.com/technology/2020/12/03/facebook-hate-speech.

[56] See Facebook, 'Our Commitment to Human Rights', available at about.fb.com/news/2021/03/our-commitment-to-human-rights.

[57] See Facebook, 'Our Commitment to Human Rights', available at about.fb.com/news/2021/03/our-commitment-to-human-rights.

[58] In addition to the UNGPs, Facebook's new human rights policy includes specific international law instruments including the International Convention on the Elimination of All Forms of Racial Discrimination, the Convention on the Elimination of All Forms of Discrimination Against Women, the Convention on the Rights of the Child, the Convention on the Rights of Persons with Disabilities, the Charter of Fundamental Rights of the European Union and the American Convention on Human Rights (see Facebook, 'Corporate Human Rights Policy', available at about.fb.com/wp-content/uploads/2021/04/Facebooks-Corporate-Human-Rights-Policy.pdf).

[59] See Facebook, 'Understanding the Community Standards Enforcement Report', available at transparency.facebook.com/community-standards-enforcement/guide.

If a human review remains unsuccessful, an appeal to the newly created Oversight Board can be lodged. The nuts and bolts of the process are indeed what civil society groups are particularly concerned with.

The previous section identified six procedural categories of principles representing civil society demands with regard to the process of content moderation: certainty and predictability; appeal and remedy; procedure; limitations to automated content moderation; rights due diligence and impact assessment; and self-regulatory bodies. The existence of Community Standards makes Facebook's content governance relatively *certain and predictable*. Its policies also state both the consequences of violating posts, ie removal of the content and – depending on repeated infractions – changes to the ability to post or to use the account altogether, and the decision-making procedures (in general terms) and pathways, including regular transparency reporting.

Opportunities to *appeal and remedy* can be readily found by users on the platform itself. While the percentage of content decisions for which a human review was requested is generally low, as shown in Table 16.2, there exists some variance. Content decisions based on the above-defined category of 'prevention of harm' are rather unlikely to be appealed by users (0.2 per cent overall), whereas the rate is significantly higher for the 'protection of social groups' and 'public interest' categories (at 1.1 per cent and 1.2 per cent respectively). Users are most likely to request a review for content that has been deemed to violate the policy to not sell firearms (5.5 per cent). The remedy is usually for Facebook to restore the content and, possibly, account functionality. The outcome of the review procedure is then communicated to users. However, the rate of successful reversal of an initial content removal differs between principles of the Community Standards. For instance, in the last quarter of 2020, concerning the principle on the sale and promotion of drugs, a total of 80,200 reviews were requested and 58,600 decisions reversed (73 per cent).[60] In contrast, concerning the principle on bullying and harassment, 443,000 initial decisions were appealed to, but only 41,000 content restorations upon appeal were reported (9 per cent).[61] At least theoretically, this variance points to a differing ability of Facebook's algorithms to detect content correctly and not to over-censor it. It should be noted that Facebook's appeal procedures provide users with limited opportunities to argue against alleged violation of community standards. Notifications of violations and reviews do not give explanations of the reasoning that informed the decision and, in the case of review, they do not usually refer to users' replies. Usually, they consist of standardised sentences.

The *notification procedure* employed by Facebook appears only partly in line with the demands by civil society. Users do not always receive sufficient notification about the reason for a content or account action as well as information about

[60] See Facebook, 'Community Standards Enforcement Report – Regulated Goods: Drugs and Firearms', available at transparency.fb.com/data/community-standards-enforcement/regulated-goods/facebook.

[61] See Facebook, 'Community Standards Enforcement Report – Bullying and Harassment', available at transparency.fb.com/data/community-standards-enforcement/bullying-and-harassment/facebook.

how to appeal the decision. In cases of copyright content takedowns, contact details about the alleged owner of the intellectual property are provided to allow direct interaction.[62] Users are not informed whether the decision has been made by a human or a machine, a demand entailed in the civil society documents. While the notification process with regard to content takedown and account actions appears to be at least fairly consistent with demands by civil society, there is an important difference between this system and the News Feed ranking process. The downranking of individual posts does not in principle make it impossible to discover a post. However, in practice, a low ranking score in the Feed means that a post will be viewed by others less frequently. Assuming that communication of content to be viewed by others is the primary purpose of posting on Facebook, a low rank represents a severe limitation.[63] While there are reasons to rank a post lower or higher, eg depending on if a post is made up of text, a picture or a video, increasingly, content is in the focus here, too. Specifically, in early 2021, Facebook changed its ranking to downrank website links considered more borderline to appear less often on users' Feeds.[64] Similar mechanisms exist with regard to misinformation and clickbait.[65] The processes concerning borderline content have been criticised for their lack of notification.[66] This process is entirely unrelated to the Community Standards, and yet it creates questions concerning the civil society demand of appropriate notification. The lack of notification about certain posts being 'punished' by the algorithm or the clear statement of the criteria for such down-ranking mean that users are unaware and unable to appeal to the decision or alter their behaviour. Whereas the Community Standards represent a written code with an elaborate appeals procedure, the News Feed ranking is more akin to computer code involved in content decisions without these safeguards.[67]

Relatedly, a relatively high number of civil society documents entail demands for *limitations to automated content moderation*. Limitations on so-called 'proactive' moderation may help to reduce false positives, thereby strengthening freedom of expression. On the other hand, since human moderators would take

[62] See Facebook, 'Content that I posted on Facebook was removed because it was reported for intellectual property infringement. What are my next steps?', available at www.facebook.com/help/365111110185763.

[63] This does not relate to the part of Facebook's ranking algorithm where it is based on people's prior interests, but to criteria that go beyond the individual. See Facebook, 'How machine learning powers Facebook's News Feed ranking algorithm', available at engineering.fb.com/2021/01/26/ml-applications/news-feed-ranking.

[64] See E Dreyfuss and I Lapowsky, 'Facebook is Changing News Feed (Again) to Stop Fake News' (Wired, 4 October 2019), available at www.wired.com/story/facebook-click-gap-news-feed-changes.

[65] See Facebook, 'Working to Stop Misinformation and False News', available at www.facebook.com/formedia/blog/working-to-stop-misinformation-and-false-news.

[66] A Heldt, 'Borderline speech: caught in a free speech limbo?' (15 October 2020) *Internet Policy Review*, available at policyreview.info/articles/news/borderline-speech-caught-free-speech-limbo/1510.

[67] cf L Lessig, *Code: And Other Laws of Cyberspace, Version 2.0* (Basic Books, 2006).

longer to react to (automatically) flagged content, proactive moderation means that less material presumed to infringe the Community Standards will be viewed by users. The degree to which posts that are removed from the platform are either proactively found, mostly through algorithms, or flagged by users depends on which principle is concerned, as shown in Table 16.2. For instance, in the last quarter of 2020, the rate of automation has been high for most infractions such as offering or promoting drugs (97.3 per cent), terrorism (99.8 per cent) and adult nudity and sexual activity (98.1 per cent). An outlier is the principle on bullying and harassment: only 48.8 per cent of posts sanctioned under this provision of the Community Standards were proactive – the remainder had to be flagged by users. This shows how some rules require more contextual knowledge and human understanding of a situation to be applied effectively.[68]

The rate of automation has increased over the last few years, even in those areas that can be considered more difficult to judge compared to others. While the proactive detection of hate speech made up only 23.6 per cent of all content actions in the last quarter of 2017, the rate rose to 60.7 per cent in the same quarter of 2018, on to 80.9 per cent a year later and further increased to 97.1 per cent in the last quarter of 2020.[69] For other principles entailed in the Community Standards, the rate of automation has been consistently above 96–99 per cent over the same period.[70] This clearly shows that there is even a tendency away from the demand by civil society documents that automated content moderation should be limited to 'manifestly illegal content'. In addition, as pointed out above, although demanded by some civil society documents, not all automated content decisions are being reviewed by a human.

The demand by civil society documents that social media platforms conduct *human rights due diligence or impact assessments* has been met through such assessments on the country level, such as recently in Sri Lanka, Indonesia and Cambodia.[71] In order to be a more legitimate judge over what content or accounts can remain on the platform, in 2018 Facebook created an independent Oversight Board tasked to pick, deliberate and decide concerning the decision of the platform's content moderation system.[72] It does so based on the Community Standards, and its governing documents and internal rulebook have also been reviewed from a human rights due diligence perspective by an outside non-profit organisation, ensuring its grounding 'in human rights principles, including the rights

[68] See R Gorwa, R Binns and C Katzenbach, 'Algorithmic Content Moderation: Technical and Political Challenges in the Automation of Platform Governance' (2020) 7 *Big Data & Society* 1.

[69] See Facebook, 'Community Standards Enforcement Report – Hate Speech', available at transparency.fb.com/data/community-standards-enforcement/hate-speech/facebook.

[70] See Facebook, 'Community Standards Enforcement Report' (n 45).

[71] See Facebook, 'An Update on Facebook's Human Rights Work in Asia and Around the World', available at about.fb.com/news/2020/05/human-rights-work-in-asia.

[72] See ch 14 (Schulz) in this volume.

to freedom of expression, privacy and remedy'.[73] The board's power extends to making binding decisions on content removal, based on the appealed cases before it. In addition to these decisions, the Oversight Board issued broader 'policy advisory statements' with its initial seven decisions, in which it asks for policy changes, including substantive clarifications and procedural improvements.[74] However, at present, it remains to be seen how the policy teams at Facebook will implement these recommendations and how sustainable the Oversight Board proves to be.[75]

V. Conclusion

Global online content governance is currently facing a problem which is not novel in its essence. Determining which principles govern global spaces is an issue that characterised all phenomena related to globalisation and has affected the Internet since its origin. In his seminal book, *Code 2.0*, Lessig schematised this dilemma as being the choice between a 'no law', 'one law' and 'many laws' worlds.[76] In the social media environment, the decision of private platforms to adopt their own internal rules to bypass the legal pluralism that characterise national and international law has been accused of arbitrariness and lack of accountability, being even associated with a 'no law' scenario.[77] However, this strong critique is gradually pushing online platforms to rethink their internal content moderation rules and procedures in a way that better reflects the relevance of the virtual space they offer vis-à-vis fundamental rights. A process of constitutionalisation of this environment is currently underway. Core principles of contemporary constitutionalism are rearticulated to address the challenges of the social media environment.

Despite the evocative image that 'constitutionalisation' brings to mind, there are no founding fathers sitting in the same room for days to define the constitution of social media.[78] The process of constitutionalisation of this environment reflects the complex, global and pluralist scenario in which social media operate. It is characterised by a high level of fluidity and informality. Social media online content governance rules are being fertilised by a multistakeholder constitutional input, which may also potentially contribute to enhancing the legitimacy of social media rules from a global perspective. Indeed, an aerial view on this phenomenon

[73] See Facebook, 'An Update on Building a Global Oversight Board', available at about.fb.com/news/2019/12/oversight-board-update.

[74] See Oversight Board, 'Board Decisions', available at oversightboard.com/decision.

[75] For a detailed discussion of the creation and the limits of the Oversight Board, see *K Klonick, 'The Facebook Oversight Board: Creating an Independent Institution to Adjudicate Online Free Expression' (2019) 129 Yale Law Journal* 2418.

[76] See Lessig, *Version 2.0* (2006) ch 15.

[77] See N Suzor, *Lawless. The Secret Rules That Govern Our Digital Lives* (Cambridge University Press, 2019).

[78] Celeste, 'Terms of Service and Bills of Rights' (2019); KM Yilma, 'Digital Privacy and Virtues of Multilateral Digital Constitutionalism – Preliminary Thoughts' (2017) 25 *International Journal of Law and Information Technology* 115.

witnesses multiple, simultaneous processes of 'parallel' or 'collateral' constitutionalisation that are currently ongoing.[79] In this chapter, we mapped the contributions of international law, civil society impulses, and the norms developed by social media platforms themselves. Future research in the field is encouraged to take in account the complexity of this multi-layered constitutional landscape, investigating how these normative sources are mutually complementing each other.

[79] See E Celeste, 'The Constitutionalisation of the Digital Ecosystem: Lessons from International Law' (2021) Max Planck Institute for Comparative Public Law and International Law (MPIL) Research Paper No 2021-16, available at papers.ssrn.com/abstract=3872818.

INDEX

www.ingramcontent.com/pod-product-compliance
Ingram Content Group UK Ltd.
Pitfield, Milton Keynes, MK11 3LW, UK
UKHW021909150926
475560UK00003B/281

9 781509 953707